SMALL BUSINESS
FORMATION HANDBOOK

Robert A. Cook

John Wiley & Sons, Inc.

New York • Chichester • Weinheim • Brisbane • Singapore • Toronto

Published by John Wiley & Sons, Inc.
Published simultaneously in Canada.

This publication is designed to provide accurate and authoritative information in regard to the subject
matter covered. It is sold with the understanding that the publisher is not engaged in rendering
professional services. If professional advice or other expert assistance is required, the services of a
competent professional person should be sought.

Library of Congress Cataloging-in-Publication Data:

Cooke, Robert A., 1931–
     Small business formation handbook / Robert A. Cooke.
          p.   cm.
     Includes index.
     ISBN 0-471-31475-7 (pbk. : alk. paper)
     1. Small business—Law and legislation—United States.   I. Title.
     KF1659.C66   1999
     346.73'0652—dc21   98-48157

Printed in the United States of America.

10 9 8 7 6 5 4 3 2 1

PREFACE

Starting, reorganizing, or purchasing a business is one of life's greatest challenges. With your change from employee to entrepreneur, you no longer will need skills limited to only marketing, only production, or only finance. Now, you have to be expert in all fields.

Among your needed skills will be that of selecting the best form in which to organize your business. Should you be a sole proprietor, a corporation, a limited liability company, or a form of partnership? The answer is in the answers to two more questions:

1. How expert about this do you need to be?
2. How much professional help do you need in selecting and setting up the right form of business?

You could wade through thick volumes devoted to tax and other laws relating to forms of business. You could obtain the relevant statutes and regulations from the state or states in which you will operate, as well as pertinent IRS regulations, and become your own expert. But how much time will that take? Wouldn't you be better off to spend the time on design and development of your product, marketing your product, and/or purchasing the goods you will resell?

If you answer yes to that last question, you might decide to leave the decision and process entirely up to your lawyer, accountant, or other professional. Will the professional thoroughly understand your business plan, your hopes for the future, your family situation, other businesses you own or may acquire, and many other details about your financial life? The answer is yes only if you are willing to pay some hefty fees for the professional's time that will be involved.

Between those two, obviously unsatisfactory, extremes, is a logical course: Gain a basic knowledge of the various business forms, how they are taxed, how they can be set up, how the federal and state governments regulate them, and what the advantages and disadvantages of them are for someone in *your* situation. Then, when you seek professional help, you need to buy only the professional time needed to confirm your logic and make sure your decisions do not run afoul of any new regulations. That will mean a large saving of cash—cash that you will need to pay the rent, buy goods, and compensate employees (including yourself).

It was to meet your needs for this basic information that I wrote this book. You will find concise descriptions of each form of business with the advantages and disadvantages of each. In particular, there is coverage about tax aspects and which form should allow you to keep the most of the money you work so hard to earn. There is also discussion of the liability aspects and how each form can provide you (or not provide you) with limited liability—that's the protection that will mean a business failure does not result in the loss of your home and other personal assets.

Once you have decided on a type of business organization, the federal tax forms and the forms that must be filed with state regulators are here, too. Of course, I couldn't include the 19 volumes of tax information that professionals use, but you will find enough about forms and procedures to enable you to better judge the fairness of your professional's fees.

Because of technical limitations, I couldn't include a lucky charm within the covers of the book, but I do wish you luck and prosperity in your venture.

BOB COOKE

CONTENTS

CONTENTS

CONTENTS

LIST OF FORMS

PART I

THE CHOICES—DESCRIPTIONS OF TYPES OF BUSINESS FORMS

Part I describes the various types of business formations. Under each type are specific headings that make it easy to eliminate the type of formations that you cannot or should not use. (That saves reading time and brain strain.)

In our arrangement, the popular *limited liability companies* appear last. This is not because I deem them to be a poor choice for the opposite is true. They are treated last because they have attributes of both a partnership and a corporation, so it is more logical to cover limited liability companies after covering their relatives.

1

SOLE PROPRIETORSHIP

OWNERSHIP

This is the simplest form of business with almost no barrier to entry. It's safe to say that everyone has been a sole proprietor at some time or other. If, as a teenager, you mowed the neighbor's lawn to earn a few dollars, you were a sole proprietor of a lawn-mowing business. The fact that you didn't jump through some bureaucratic hoops, such as obtaining a city license and registering with the IRS, doesn't negate the fact that you were a sole proprietor.

This form is not available to any business that has more than one owner. Any *individual* can be a sole proprietor. A choice does arise, however, when a married couple starts a business. They could operate as a partnership, or one spouse could operate it as a sole proprietorship and hire the other spouse as an employee. The factors involved in this decision include the stability of the marriage, availability of fringe benefits (such as medical coverage) from other employment, and the probable future value of the business (for estate tax purposes).

Why would a married couple operate as a sole proprietor and an employee? The answer lies in the income tax rules about fringe benefits and is discussed under that heading.

LIABILITY FOR DEBTS OF THE BUSINESS

The business owner is responsible for the business debts, without limit. That is, if the business cannot pay its debts, the owner must use his or her personal funds or other assets to pay them.

While careful cash-flow planning can avoid the owner's having to pay the business bills out of his or her pocket, the unexpected incident can bring on disaster.

EXAMPLE: Donald owns Tear-and-Fade Dry Cleaning, a sole proprietorship. Several months ago, a customer dropped a banana peel on the floor by the counter. The next customer was Joan, a professional ballet dancer. She slipped on the banana peel, landed hard on the tile floor, and broke her back. Because she could no longer engage in her profession, the court awarded her $10 million in damages, which Tear-and-Fade Dry Cleaning must pay. However, the $2,200 in the business bank account fell far short, so Donald had to look in his own checkbook for the money. However, he found only $843.21 there, so he was still short some $9,996,956.79. As a result, he has to file for bankruptcy, so he loses everything he owns, including his business. Both his personal and business assets are sold by the court for funds with which to partially pay Joan. (In some states, Donald would not lose his house. In others, he would.)

In this example, it's easy to say that Donald erred in not purchasing insurance that would protect him when something like this happened. Yet, sometimes it turns out that the damage is not covered by insurance. As a further precaution, Donald could have formed his business as a corporation or limited liability company, which are covered later in this chapter.

AMOUNT OF INVESTMENT

Any amount, even millions or billions, can be invested in a sole proprietorship by the owner. He or she can withdraw funds from the business or invest additional funds in it without incurring any additional income tax or contending with the regulations of any government agency.

EXAMPLE: Betty starts Betty's Better Advice, a consulting business. She invests $5,000 cash plus some personal assets she already owns: desk, chair, calculator, and computers. The value of those items is $2,000, so her total investment is $7,000.

If she later finds that Betty's Better Advice did not need the entire $5,000 investment, she can withdraw part of it ($2,000) without any legal or tax consequences. (She doesn't have to ask anyone for permission to do that, which is the significant advantage of a sole proprietorship. It's flexible and simple.)

However, there are reasons large investments in sole proprietorships may be unwise. The obvious one is the lack of limited liability as already covered. Other reasons will become apparent in the discussions of other types of businesses.

WHAT CAN BE INVESTED IN THE BUSINESS

An individual who starts or expands a sole proprietorship may invest cash or any other asset in the business. A sole proprietor may contribute services to his or her business *without any tax consequences.*

EXAMPLE: In order to conserve her cash, Betty lays the carpet, paints the walls, and hangs the curtains in her office. In her sole proprietorship, she pays no income tax on the value of those services to the business. In other forms of business, her labor for the business might create taxable income for the owner who contributed the labor (probably for a share of the business).

FUTURE SIZE OF THE BUSINESS

There is no legal limit on size, although there may be practical limits, as covered under other business forms.

MANAGEMENT

The sole proprietor is top management, although he or she could hire a manager to oversee day-to-day operations.

EMPLOYEE OWNERSHIP OF PART OF BUSINESS

There is no way to make an employee, or anyone else, a part-owner of a sole proprietorship, even for only a tiny fraction of the business. A valuable employee could be paid a share of profits, but that would not imply any ownership.

SALE OF ALL OR PART OF THE BUSINESS

Inasmuch as a sole proprietorship and the proprietor are inseparable, that is, a sole proprietorship is not a separate entity, such a business owner cannot sell the whole business. (In theory he or she might sell himself or herself complete with the business, but in this country, we have laws against selling oneself into bondage.) So, when one tires of the sole proprietorship business, one sells the assets of the business. The buyer of the business buys the assets. That would include equipment, land, buildings, stock-in-trade, accounts receivable, and a nebulous and intangible item—goodwill. The buyer buys the last item by buying the rights to use the name.

This sounds theoretical, for the customers may see no change in the business other than the changed face of the owner. However, it is significant in what must be reported to the IRS, as covered in Part II.

LOCATION OF BUSINESS

This type of business can be located anywhere in the 50 states. The same concept exists in most countries, but foreign business forms are beyond the scope of this book.

GEOGRAPHIC AREA OF OPERATION

A sole proprietor can operate within his or her own state or in any other state. That is not to say that, if you live in Colorado and start a business there, you can open a branch in New Jersey or France without purchasing the appropriate business license and paying other fees in those jurisdictions.

INCOME TAX STATUS

In essence, the profits from a sole proprietorship are added on to any other income that the owner receives, and the tax on that total is what the owner pays, or should pay, to the IRS. Note that the profit (technically, taxable income) is computed from the bookkeeping records of the business and is basically the total sales minus the cost of merchandise sold and minus the expenses of operating the business. The amount of cash that the owner invests in the business or withdraws from the business has no effect on the computation of income tax.

For some people, particularly those with high income from other sources, this stacking of incomes in one pool can have a chilling tax effect.

EXAMPLE: Hal is a successful stockbroker with an income that puts him in the top tax bracket of 39.6 percent. He marries Wanda, who operates a boutique craft shop that earns about $30,000 per year. After her tax deductions, Wanda has an income that was taxed at 15 percent when she was single. Now, because she is married to Hal, that income will be taxed at 39.6 percent.

What should Hal and Wanda do? Assuming they can live on only Hal's income, they should consider incorporating Wanda's business. The reason is covered under the section on S corporations later in this chapter.

SELF-EMPLOYMENT TAXES (E.G., SOCIAL SECURITY OR FICA AND HI TAX)

Sole proprietors must pay these taxes at a rate that is almost double what would be deducted from their earnings if they were employed by someone else. An employer matches the amount the employee has deducted for these taxes, but the sole proprietor is considered both employer and employee by the IRS. Also, sole proprietors pay these taxes on the total annual income of the business, regardless of whether they draw profits out of it in that calendar year.

EXAMPLE: Continue the last example of Wanda and Hal. If Wanda withdraws only $10,000 of her $30,000 profit, she still pays self-employment tax on the entire $30,000.

OTHER TAXES AND FEES

While sole proprietorships and all other forms of businesses have to pay local and state license fees, sole proprietorships do escape the initial and annual registration fees that corporations, some partnerships, and limited liability companies have to pay.

FRINGE BENEFITS

Employers can provide many benefits to employees that are beyond the salaries and wages an employee receives. Technically, they are all fringe benefits. However, in the parlance of business planning, the fringe benefits that an employer usually offers are those that can be deducted as an expense by the employer while the employee pays no immediate income tax on the value of the benefit.

> EXAMPLE: Gretchen hires Sam to stock shelves in her store, for which she pays him $15,000 per year. In addition, she pays for Sam's medical insurance ($3,000 per year) and deducts that figure from her business income. Sam pays income tax on his $15,000 salary, but not on the $3,000 value of his medical insurance.
>
> Gretchen also sets up a retirement plan for Sam into which she contributes $1,000 per year, and she also deducts that $1,000 from her income. Sam does not pay tax on that $1,000 in his working years. However, when he retires, he will pay tax on the retirement income that he receives from the plan.

When I refer to fringe benefits, you can assume I am referring to those benefits that have an effect on saving tax dollars. There are two categories of these fringe benefits to consider when discussing sole proprietorships. First, the benefits for the people whom the owner of the business hires; and second, the benefits for the owner.

The benefit programs that can be set up for employees, such as retirement plans, savings plans, medical coverage, and group term life insurance (up to $50,000) are almost identical to those that can be offered by large corporations, including the tax deductions the business can take for the cost of these plans. (Whether or not the sole proprietor offers them is up to him or her.) The exception is that there is no way a sole proprietor can offer employees partial ownership of the business, as can a corporation through employee stock-purchase plans.

For the owners of the sole proprietorships, the retirement plans they can set up are quite similar to retirement plans that can be set up by corporations, and the contributions to them can be a tax deduction. The owners of a sole proprietorship can be covered by the same retirement plan (often called Keogh plans) as that for employees of a sole proprietorship, and the contribution can be deducted on the owner's tax return.

Similarly, the owner can be covered by a medical insurance or HMO plan; however, only 60 percent of the cost of the coverage is currently deductible, although that percentage gradually rises to 100 percent in the year 2003.

For some sole proprietors, there is a way around this nondeductible medical coverage, and it is probably the most common reason for structuring a family business as a sole proprietorship rather than a partnership.

> EXAMPLE: Mary and Mike, who are happily married and have no other employment, start a lawn care business. They hire Don and Bert at $10 per hour to help them. As a fringe benefit, the partnership provides for membership in a health maintenance organization (HMO) for Mary, Mike, Don, and Bert.
>
> When Mary and Mike compute their taxes at the end of the year, they can deduct the cost of HMO coverage for Don and Bert, but not for themselves. That's because the tax law does not consider partners to be employees, but as self-employed, like sole proprietors, and medical coverage for self-employed people is not fully deductible. (How much is deductible depends on the year in question.)
>
> However, if the business were set up as Mary's sole proprietorship and she hires her husband, Mike, as an employee, the entire cost of Mike's medical coverage would be deductible, just as is the cost of coverage for Don and Bert. Then, because the coverage can include spouses of employees, Mike's coverage includes HMO membership for Mary. Thus, she is covered as a spouse of an employee, and the effect is to render deductible the entire HMO coverage for both Mike and Mary.

Deductions for the cost of other fringe benefits, such as group term life insurance, dependent care, and education assistance is not available to sole proprietorships. If these fringes are important to the owner, he or she should consider forming a corporation. However, see the section on corporations for the disadvantages of that procedure. Also, with respect to education, the cost of most business-related education is deductible as such and not as a fringe benefit. That is, a sole proprietor who takes courses or attends seminars on subjects related to his or her business can deduct the costs thereof.

ESTATE PLANNING CONSIDERATIONS

This may be one of the more important reasons for a sole proprietor to chose another business form once his or her business is profitable and has value as a continuing business after he or she dies or retires. While passing the business to one heir can be accomplished (and without estate tax if it is to one's spouse), passing a sole proprietorship on to two or more heirs is, by definition of a sole proprietorship, impossible. In effect, the business form then becomes a partnership of the heirs and, in the process, it may operate as an estate or trust for a while. As the controlling probate rules vary with the state(s) in which the owner and the business are located, the details are beyond the scope of this book. What is common to all states are these recommendations:

- Every business owner should have a will, drawn up by a competent attorney, and that will should be reviewed at least every five years. (If your children are 5, 7, and 10, your arrangements will be much different than if they are in their thirties and capable of running your business.)

- Consider forming an S corporation. Transferring an interest in a business that is incorporated is relatively simple. (More on that in Chapter 5.) If an S corporation won't work, a limited liability company (LLC) could be the appropriate choice, although transfer of ownership interest in a LLC is more complex.

COMPLEXITY, IN GENERAL

With the exception of the estate planning area, the sole proprietorship is the simplest business form to set up and administer. Starting this type of business can be accomplished by opening a checking account for the business and purchasing whatever business license your town, city, and/or county requires. If you use something other than your own name for the business, your state may also require you to register your business name as a fictitious name.

2 GENERAL PARTNERSHIPS

Small businesses often start as general partnerships because a few people decide to join forces to start a partnership in which they all work. However, partnerships can be large and complex.

OWNERSHIP

Two or more individuals or other entities (any number) can form a partnership. Individuals, corporations, limited liability companies and other partnerships can all be partners in a partnership. In addition to the common partnership of individuals, partnerships consisting of two or more corporations are not unusual, although many of those will be for a single purpose and of limited duration, which makes them a particular type of partnership which is often called a *joint venture*.

LIABILITY OF OWNERS FOR DEBTS OF THE BUSINESS

Unless it is stated otherwise in one of the partnership documents, a partnership is a *general partnership*. That means that each partner is liable for the debts of the partnership. Note that a partner is not liable for just his or her share of the partnership debts, but for the total debts of the partnership.

EXAMPLE: Danny Dimbulb is in the general contracting business and is over his head in the middle of a $10 million contract. To raise needed cash, he convinces Mary Megabucks to join his business. She advances the needed $500,000 cash in exchange for a 20 percent interest in, and 20 percent of the profits from, the new partnership of Dimbulb and Megabucks.

Due to mismanagement by Danny, the partnership is unable to complete the contract and ends up being liquidated. After selling all of the partnership assets and paying what bills it could, the partnership is left with $1 million of debt. Danny has no personal assets, so he files personal bankruptcy. Mary believes she should have to pay only 20 percent of the debts, or $200,000. However, that is not the case. She has to pay off the entire million dollars, which eats a sizeable hole in her total net worth.

There are ways Mary, and all of us, can avoid this disaster. Among them are making sure that she was a *limited partner*, as explained in the next chapter on limited partnerships, or she could have insisted that the business be organized as a corporation or limited liability company.

AMOUNT OF INVESTMENT

A partner can invest any amount, subject to agreement of the other partners.

WHAT CAN BE INVESTED

Investment can be in the form of cash, tangible assets such as equipment, intangibles such as customer lists and goodwill, or even labor and services. Unlike a sole proprietorship, though, the value of the contributed labor and service is usually taxable income to the partner providing the service. (It may be possible to defer this tax on the value of services if receiving the interest in the partnership is contingent on some future event that may not happen.)

FUTURE SIZE OF THE BUSINESS

If you really have invented the better mousetrap and expect the business to be extremely profitable and expand rapidly; you probably will be in need of public financing early in your meteoric rise. If you might raise this capital by attracting equity investors to your business, that may argue for starting as a corporation right off the bat. The point here: There is far more involved in admitting new partners or saying goodbye to old partners than there is in selling stock in a corporation. The buzz word is *transferability* of ownership interest.

MANAGEMENT OF THE BUSINESS

The partners may manage as a committee, select one partner to be the top manager, or hire someone else to manage the business. Be aware, however, that the IRS will expect the partnership to designate a tax matters person, who should be the partner the IRS contacts. For most of us, this is not an enviable job, so a smart tax matters person will keep a CPA or tax attorney on call.

EMPLOYEE OWNERSHIP OF PART OF THE BUSINESS

By definition, a part owner of a partnership is a partner. Therefore, there is no way to cut an employee into a small ownership in the business without making him or her a partner. That is not to say, however, that a partnership cannot pay bonuses to employees that are based on the business's profits.

SALE OF ALL OR PART OF THE BUSINESS

If the entire business is sold to an individual, another partnership, corporation, limited liability company, or some other entity, the same rules apply as for the sale of a sole proprietorship. That is, the buyer buys the assets (which may include goodwill) of the partnership. Sale of part of the business would amount to admitting another entity into the partnership. Be aware that admitting another partner, particularly if he, she, or it invests other than cash in the partnership, can create some complex bookkeeping required by the IRS.

Also, in the eyes of the IRS, a partnership terminates and a new partnership comes into existence "if within a 12-month period there is a sale or exchange of 50 percent or more of the total interest in partnership capital and profits."

LOCATION

Generally, state laws treat partnerships in similar ways. (That is, most states have adopted most of the American Bar Association's model Uniform Partnership Act.) However, there may be some differences that could affect your operation, so, if you are going to operate in more than one state, check with the secretary of state for each state as to registration, reporting requirements, fees, and rules regarding partnership operation. Either read the statutes regarding partnerships in the states in which you will operate or hire legal counsel to guide you.

GEOGRAPHIC AREA OF OPERATIONS

If the partnership operates in other states, it may need to register as a partnership in those states and pay the license and other fees that those states require.

INCOME TAX CONSIDERATIONS

The income that the partnership earns is split up and assigned to the various partners, and those partners pay income tax on their share of the partnership income. Also, the character of the income and deductions carries through to the partners. If the partnership sells some assets and has long-term gains from the sale, each partner reports his or her share of the gains as long-term gains on his or her individual income tax return. Similarly, if the partnership makes a charitable contribution, the partners report their share of it as an itemized deduction on their returns.

> EXAMPLE: David, Ursula, and Horace start a partnership, called DUH Sales, that sells self-tying shoe laces. They each contribute $10,000 in exchange for a one-third partnership interest. At the end of the year, DUH Sales has earned $60,000 and files a partnership return with the IRS, reporting the taxable income of $60,000 and that it is shared equally by David, Ursula, and Horace. DUH also has to report their social security numbers. So, each of the three partners adds $20,000 to his or her other income and pays the resulting income tax.

Note that, as with a sole proprietorship, it is the taxable income (similar to net income or net profit), as computed by the IRS's accounting rules, that is taxed. The cash that the partners withdraw *does not* affect the figure that is taxed, so long as the partnership is profitable.

If the partnership has losses, the partners may be able to deduct their share of the losses on their individual returns. However, the arcane rules are complex and depend on the involvement of the partner in the operation of the business, on how much the partner invested, how much partnership income the partner has paid tax on, and how much cash the partnership has previously distributed to the partner. (That is, cash distributions can affect income tax in a loss situation.) If you have a partnership with a loss, get some professional help.

The DUH partnership was a simple example of a simple partnership. Now look at the next example.

> EXAMPLE: Danielle, Ernie, and Floyd start a partnership to manufacture self-correcting computers. (The product is fictional, the point is not.) The contributions are as follows:

Danielle	$900,000
Ernie	50,000
Floyd	50,000
Total	$1,000,000

Ernie and Floyd will actively manage the business, Danielle will not be active in the business. For their efforts, Ernie will receive a cash "salary" of $75,000 per year and Floyd will receive $60,000 per year.

Then, the profits that are left after paying the salaries will be divided up as follows:

Danielle will receive the first $50,000 of profits in cash. The remaining profits will be allocated as follows:

Danielle	25%
Ernie	40%
Floyd	35%

This partnership agreement was designed to reflect and compensate the partners for various factors. Ernie and Floyd each receive some cash first, as they are devoting full time to management of the business, and Ernie receives more to reflect his greater marketing experience. Next, Danielle receives cash which is in the nature of payment for the use of her $900,000.

This first allocations of profits are to be in cash, and are usually called "guaranteed payments." But the later percentage allocations are bookkeeping entries. If there is cash available, the partners could decide to pay part or all of these allocations in cash. Or, they could decide to keep the cash in the business for expansion. If they do not pay the allocation in cash, then each partner's investment (the jargon term is capital account) in the business is increased by the amount of the allocated profit that was not paid in cash. This is easier to envision if you think of each partner receiving all of his or her share of the profits in cash and then turning some of that cash back to the partnership as an increase in investment.

If the partnership has a loss, the partnership agreement also spells out how each partner shares in the loss.

This example demonstrates how flexible partnership agreements can be. Guaranteed payments to and division of profits for partners can be structured without regard to how much each invested in the partnership or to other factors. The only rule, for the IRS to accept the partnership agreement as bona fide, is that the allocations must have substantial economic effect. What does that mean? Essentially, it means that the allocations cannot be made just for tax reasons. If a partnership agreement stated that all tax-exempt income and losses, should they occur, will be allocated entirely to the wealthy high-income partner, it probably would not fly.

Without some planning, the tax factors from a partnership can create unfairness and disagreement among the partners. For instance, a partner who does not have enough interest, taxes, and other deductions to qualify for itemized deductions cannot make any use of his or her share of a partnership charitable deduction.

Another aspect of taxation that can wreak havoc on partners' finances is the cash flow with which partners can pay the related income tax. If the partnership earns great profits, but uses the resulting cash to buy equipment, increase inventory, or launch a huge advertising campaign, it may not have cash to distribute to the partners. Yet, the partners have a large tax bill (caused by their share of the partnership income) to pay.

If a partnership operates in several states, state income taxes may be complex. If some of the income of the partnership is taxable in other states, each partner should file a state income tax form in the other states, and more tax forms equal more complication.

OTHER TAXES AND FEES

Your state may require that general partnerships register with a state authority, such as the secretary of state. Local licenses and fictitious name registration apply, as will be covered in the sole proprietorship chapter (Chapter 7).

FRINGE BENEFITS

In the area of fringe benefits, tax and other laws treat a partnership as two or more sole proprietors joining together in an enterprise. In other words, the same rules apply as for sole proprietors. That is, the fringe benefits for employees operate the same for any enterprise. For fringe benefits for the owners (partners), the rules for the self-employed apply.

ESTATE PLANNING CONSIDERATIONS

Unless the partnership agreement specifies otherwise, the death of a partner causes the partnership to be dissolved. That can create many financial and operating problems for the remaining partners. To avoid this, it is imperative that the partners have a written agreement that the partnership continues and specifies what happens to the interest of a deceased partner. One fairly simple method is to determine, annually, what each partner's interest is worth and purchase life insurance for that amount on each partner. That gives the remaining partners the cash with which to satisfy the claims of the deceased partner's heirs on the assets of the partnership.

EASE OF DISSOLUTION

How easy it is to terminate a partnership depends on the complexity of the partnership. In a simple partnership of a few partners, each with equal shares and participating equally in the profits of the partnership, it is relatively simple. After all the bills are paid, the partners divide up the remaining cash and other assets equally. If what they receive amounts to more than their capital accounts, they will have some income tax to pay.

However, if the partnership is complex, with various partners having contributed more than others and some having withdrawn more than others, it can be far more complex.

COMPLEXITY, IN GENERAL

The flexibility of partnerships does not come free. As the example of the self-correcting computer company demonstrates, the flexibility can create complexity, and many partnership agreements are complicated. When partners and their attorney draw up a partnership agreement, all have an understanding of each partner's rights, responsibilities, and share of the profits. However, as time passes, memory dims, and the written agreement is the controlling document. What does each sentence and word really mean? Each partner can develop a different opinion, arguments ensue, and the partnership splits. Another promising business falls apart.

3 LIMITED PARTNERSHIPS

Limited partnerships are a modified form of a general partnership. The major difference is that a limited partnership includes two classes of owners: *general* partners and *limited* partners. It is used where only one or a few partners (the general partners) will operate the business and other partners are simply investors (the limited partners).

The comments for *general partnerships* in Chapter 2 apply to *limited partnerships* with the exceptions and changes that are discussed next.

OWNERSHIP

Any type of entity can be a partner. If a corporation is the only general partner, the IRS imposes rules as to the minimum net worth of that general partner.

LIABILITY FOR DEBTS OF BUSINESS

General partners are subject to the same unlimited liability as are the partners in a general partnership. Limited partners have no liability for the debts of the partnership beyond their investment in the partnership.

MANAGEMENT

Only general partners can be involved in management of the business. In most states, if limited partners become involved in management, they lose their status as *limited* partners and therefore lose their limited liability shield. However, some state laws allow some latitude in this rule.

SECURITIES REGULATIONS

If your plans include sale of limited partnership interests to many people, your partnership interests may be classified as publicly traded by the Securities and Exchange Commission (SEC) and your state securities regulators. For the most part, general partnership interests will not be treated as securities, because general partners are viewed as being part of the management of the partnership. However, as limited partners are passive investors, the limited partnership interests are considered to be investments and therefore subject to securities law.

There are exemptions to the requirements that limited partnership interests be registered with the federal SEC and/or the equivalent state regulatory authorities. If you sell only one limited partnership interest for $500,000, and you sell it to your Uncle Harry who makes his living by buying and selling stocks, you have escaped the need for registrations on several counts: The number of limited partnership interests you sell, the dollar amount, and sales to sophisticated investors. However, if you put an ad in the *Wall Street Journal* offering to sell 1,000,000 limited partnership interests at $1,000 each, without registering the interests as securities, you are in real trouble.

There are several ways to avoid having to register securities with the federal government and there are simple methods of registering small issues from small companies when registration is required. See the contact information for the SEC, which has an explanatory brochure in plain English in the Appendix.

4 │ C CORPORATIONS

Rather than being an extension of their owners, as are sole proprietorships and partnerships, corporations are separate entities that keep their identity regardless of who owns them. They are created by the government—usually a state government—at the request of one or more people who take the necessary action to cause the state to form a corporation.

> EXAMPLE: Herb, Inez, and Joan decide to set up an enterprise to manufacture rubber computers. (They can be dropped on tile floors or have coffee spilled over them without damage.) They file the necessary paperwork with their state government that causes the government to form Rubber Computers, Incorporated. In the eyes of the state and of the public this corporation is a separate person. It is responsible for its actions, owns its assets, owes its debts, and its actions are separate from those of its owners. If Joan sells her interest to Ken, that transfer of interest has no effect on the other owners or on the corporation.
>
> (This is a basic concept. Some of the attributes of a corporation and the relationship among individual owners and between owners and the corporation can be modified by various agreements among those parties. How that is done will become evident as you read further in this book.)

The concept of regular, or C corporations, versus S corporations, creates some confusion about corporations. This chapter is devoted to C corporations. Chapter 5 covers S corporations.

OWNERSHIP

Any number of owners are permitted in this form. The owners can be any individual, partnership, corporation, or any other entity.

LIABILITY FOR DEBTS OF BUSINESS

No owner (stockholder) is liable for the debts of the corporation beyond what the stockholder paid or promised to pay for his or her stock. However, a stockholder can assume additional liability by guaranteeing to pay, from personal funds, certain debts of the corporation. This most often occurs when a small, closely held corporation borrows from a bank. Usually, the bank will not make the loan unless the principal stockholder guarantees the loan.

AMOUNT OF INVESTMENT

Technically, the amount of investment is limited only by how many shares of stock the corporation is authorized to issue. Practically, the corporation can always request the state to amend the corporate charter to authorize additional shares, and that request is almost always granted.

TYPE OF INVESTMENT

The investment can be cash, equipment, securities, or a promise to invest in the business. The latter is called a *stock subscription* and is common at the start-up of a corporation when the prospective owners are forming a corporation. They may agree that each will *subscribe* in an amount such as 1,000 shares at $10 per share. Note that if the stockholder does not pay the entire $10,000 and later the corporation is unable to pay a creditor, that creditor can proceed against the stockholder for the unpaid amount of the subscription.

FUTURE SIZE OF BUSINESS

There is no limit as to the future size of the business. This is an important feature of C corporations.

MANAGEMENT

The conventional corporation is tiered. That is, the stockholders, as such, do not manage the company but act only as investors—with few exceptions, the most important of which is that they elect a board of directors that is responsible for making important management decisions, including the appointing of the managers who will run the operations of the company. Historically, they are the president, maybe a vice president, secretary, and treasurer, although they may often be known by more descriptive titles such as chief executive officer, chief operating officer, and chief financial officer. These people may or may not also be stockholders in the corporation.

Some states allow small, closely held corporations to dispense with the board of directors and the corporate officers and allow the stockholders to manage the company directly. (Compare this concept to the management of limited liability companies covered later.)

EMPLOYEE OWNERSHIP OF PART OF BUSINESS

Employees can be sold or given stock in the corporation, or they can be given options allowing them to buy stock later at a bargain price. This might be done as an incentive to work harder, as a reward for accomplishing some goal, just to be generous, or for any reason. In order to have stock available for incentive programs, a new corporation should request authorization for many more shares of stock than it intends to issue initially.

SALE OF ALL OR PART OF BUSINESS

The simple act of one stockholder selling stock to another individual or other entity accomplishes a change of ownership. Stock in larger corporations is bought and sold every day on various stock exchanges. However, for a small corporation, this may not be desirable. Do you really want your ex-spouse selling his or her stock to your cousin, with whom you have a bad relationship? To avoid this, consider including a *stockholder's agreement* in your corporate documents. (See Part II.)

LOCATION OF BUSINESS

Generally, corporations can be formed in any state, even if the principal operations are in another state. Check your state regulations to see if there are any exceptions to this general rule.

GEOGRAPHIC AREA OF OPERATIONS

This is limited by how willing the management is to comply with all the registration and tax headaches involved in operating in several states. If you're starting small, it's easier to service out-of-state customers through mail order or distributors situated in other states.

INCOME TAX CONSIDERATIONS

C corporations pay their own income taxes. Income is not "passed through" to the owners, as in partnerships, where the owners pay the taxes incurred by the profits of the business. This creates the infamous double taxation of corporate profits, in that the corporation pays corporate income tax on the business profits and then, when it pays part of the profits to the stockholders as *dividends*, the stockholders also pay tax on the dividends, because the dividends are considered to be taxable income on the stockholder's tax returns.

EXAMPLE: Carol owns Carol's Cash & Carry Grocery, a profitable company that is a C corporation whose stock is wholly owned by Carol. Last year the company earned $1,000,000 and kept $300,000 in the corporation with which to buy a freezer and some other equipment she needed. After paying the corporate tax, she had the corporation pay her the balance as a dividend. Here's the tax picture, assuming the profit turned up all in the form of cash:

Corporation earned (taxable income)	$1,000,000
Corporate income tax	340,000
Cash remaining	660,000
Subtract cash retained in corporation	300,000
Cash for dividend paid to Carol	360,000
Carol, who is single, pays individual tax of	$ 118,242
Total taxes paid by corporation and Carol:	
Corporate tax on $1,000,000	$ 340,000
Carol's individual tax on $360,000	118,242
Total income tax	$ 458,242

In other words, Carol hands over 45.8 percent of her hard-earned money to the government. And that is just federal tax. There is probably also state income tax on both the corporation and Carol.

With a little planning, Carol might have avoided this. Suppose, instead of causing her corporation to pay her a dividend of $360,000 at the end of the year, she made the corporation pay her a salary of $30,000 per month. Unlike the dividend, the corporation could deduct her salary as an expense, just as it could deduct the salaries of cashiers and butchers. That would have reduced the corporate income tax to $124,100 and the total tax that both the corporation and Carol paid to $242,342—a significant tax saving.

There is some offset to this: Dividends are not subject to social security taxes, while salaries are. On the salary of $300,000, Carol would pay $12,941 and the corporation would pay $12,941 on her salary.

Life is not as simple as this solution sounds. In the above example, Carol's $300,000 salary would probably be accepted by the IRS. However, if the business continues to grow and she takes a salary of $1,000,000, the IRS might question it. The logic of the IRS examiner would go like this: Other managers of small chains of several grocery stores receive a salary of $300,000. Therefore, that is the salary Carol should receive. The other $700,000 that Carol receives is a "disguised" dividend and therefore taxable. There are more thoughts on this in the discussion of corporate minutes in Part II.

As an alternative, Carol may be better off to elect S corporation status, discussed in the next chapter.

There is an area where a C corporation makes good sense. If you review the example of Hal and Wanda, in Chapter 1, you may recall that Wanda's $30,000 income from her small business of a boutique shop gets hit with a tax at rate of 39.6 percent, because of the high income of her husband. Assuming that Wanda does not need to take any cash out of her business, she could incorporate her business and let it pay the tax on the $30,000 at the low rate of 15 percent. Unfortunately, this can't go on forever. When Wanda's corporation accumulates more than $250,000 (more or less, depending on some complex calculations), the IRS can hit the corporation with an accumulated earnings tax at the 39.6 percent rate. Her defense against this is to expand the business, so that she can demonstrate to the IRS that she needs to keep most of the earnings constantly in the corporation for the needs of the business.

OTHER TAXES AND FEES

The states in which the corporation is formed and the other states in which it operates will require initial registration fees and that annual reports be submitted, along with the payment of annual fees.

SECURITIES REGULATIONS

Small, closely held corporations generally don't fall under these federal and state regulations. However, if you set up a corporation and find investors who will be only investors (stockholders) and take no active part in managing the corporation, you should check out whether your situation meets one of the exclusions from the necessity to register your stock with state or federal security regulators. See the discussion about securities regulations in Chapter 3.

FRINGE BENEFITS

In the area of fringe benefits, the C corporation offers the most advantages to stockholders who are also employees (managers) of the corporation. That's because the rules treat these employees almost as all other employees, eligible for medical coverage, some term life insurance, retirement benefits, reimbursement for certain education expenses, child care, and other benefits that are deductible by the corporation and not income to the employee. Again, this is not all clear sailing. The tax law has various clauses that prohibit benefits favoring highly compensated executives, be they also stockholders or not.

ESTATE PLANNING CONSIDERATIONS

A corporation offers much flexibility in the estate and gift area. For instance, assuming you can arrive at a justified value of business and thereby a value of each share of stock, you can use the annual gift tax exclusion to give your heirs some stock each year. That is, you can give stock of a value up to $10,000 to each heir each year, and your spouse can also make a similar gift. Unlike a partnership, which may cease to exist when a partner dies, a corporation continues on. Only the stock changes hands.

EASE OF DISSOLUTION

Ending the life of a corporation requires some specific steps in the state(s) in which it is incorporated or registered, but they amount to little other than additional forms to file. There are tax complications, though. The corporation may be hit with taxes if it owns "appreciated property" (property that is worth more than the corporation paid for it). When it distributes cash and property to the stockholders, they also pay tax if the cash and value of the property are greater than the basis in their stock. (Basis is generally what they paid for the stock when they purchased it.) However, that tax may be at the lower capital gain rates.

COMPLEXITY, IN GENERAL

Corporations are somewhat easier to envision and understand than complex partnership arrangements. If ease of transferring ownership interests among various parties is a concern, corporations are the simplest entity for that.

5

S CORPORATIONS

This business form is a variation of C corporations. The forms differ only in the income tax treatment and how that treatment affects other attributes such as fringe benefits. This chapter does not repeat all the comments about corporations, but only those areas where there are differences.

OWNERSHIP

An S corporation can have no more than 75 owners, but a husband and wife count as one stockholder, even if they own the stock separately rather than jointly. Stockholders must be individuals, or certain types of trusts. In some cases each beneficiary of a trust counts as a stockholder.

CLASSES OF STOCK

There can be only one class of stock, although some stock can be voting and some nonvoting without violating this rule. Otherwise, all stock must be identical as to sharing in profits, and other attributes.

FUTURE SIZE OF BUSINESS

The 75-stockholder limit may inhibit growth. However, the election of S corporation status may be terminated by a majority vote of the stock (including nonvoting stock).

EMPLOYEE OWNERSHIP OF PART OF BUSINESS

As with C corporations, the corporate form facilitates giving employees a piece of the action. However, if any employee becomes the owner of more than 2 percent of the outstanding stock, he or she may suffer some curtailment in fringe benefits.

GEOGRAPHIC AREA OF OPERATIONS

Many states recognize the S corporation status and tax it as does the federal government, as explained below. However, some states have no provision for an S status and tax S corporations as if they were C corporations. Obviously, this complicates tax return preparation.

INCOME TAX CONSIDERATIONS

Basically, the S corporation tax picture looks much like that of a partnership. You compute the taxable income of an S corporation and then allocate it to the stockholders of the corporation, who each reports his or her share of the income on his or her individual income tax return. Unlike a partnership, the allocation of items to various partners cannot be different. The income or loss has to be allocated to the stockholders in the same ratio as that of the number of shares each owns to the total shares outstanding. Also, there are certain items of income, other than from operation of the business, on which S corporations pay corporate tax rather than allocating the items to the stockholders. These are defined in Part II on the income tax form for S corporations.

   S corporations generally do not pay dividends to stockholders. Instead, the payments to stockholders are called *distributions.*

FRINGE BENEFITS

Fringe benefit rules are the same as for partnerships, except that stockholder-employees who own 2 percent or less of the outstanding stock are treated as are any other nonowner employees.

ESTATE PLANNING CONSIDERATIONS

This parallels the situation for C corporations, but it should be noted that testamentary trusts (trusts set up by the will when the business owner dies) can hold S corporation stock for no more than two years after the date of his or her death.

EASE OF DISSOLUTION

This is similar to a C corporation dissolution with the exception that the basis for the stock, against which a stockholder measures gain or loss on dissolution, is unlikely to be what the stockholder paid for the stock. The basis is likely to change every year, for it is computed generally as follows: Start with cost of stock when purchased, add stockholder's share of income for the year, subtract distributions (usually cash) made to the stockholder during the year, and the result is the new basis in the stock.

$$
\begin{array}{l}
\text{Cost of stock} \\
\quad + \text{Shareholder's income} \\
\underline{\quad - \text{Distributions to shareholder}} \\
\quad = \text{New stock base}
\end{array}
$$

Obviously, the basis won't stay the same unless the share of income exactly equals the distribution made to the stockholder. Also, there are other items that can affect the basis.

COMPLEXITY, IN GENERAL

Like most of our tax code, S corporations are somewhat complex with rules to match. However, if you want to avoid the double taxation of C corporations and still have easy transfer of ownership, this may be your best choice.

6 | LIMITED LIABILITY COMPANY

Anyone in business has many needs. Two of the most important ones are:

- Protecting their personal assets from the creditors of the business, and
- Paying as little income tax as is legal.

For years, these goals were almost completely incompatible. The best protection from creditors was the C corporation, but with the double taxation, that hardly met the second goal. When Congress authorized S corporations decades ago, it provided relief to some business owners. However, some requirements, such as a small maximum number of shareholders and other strict rules, make this form inappropriate in a lot of situations. Limited partnerships provide a liability shield for the limited partners, but not for the general partners, who are the promoters and managers of the business and therefore aware of what possible liabilities (such as suits for damages) might be waiting in the wings of their business stage. It is possible for general partners to gain liability protection by setting up a corporation to be the general partner instead of the individual promoters/managers. However, to meet IRS regulations, such corporations must have substantial net worth, and that corporate net worth is exposed to the liabilities of the general partnership. Also, profits from the limited partnership would flow to the corporation and be subject to corporate taxes.

Florida became the first state to answer the businessperson's prayer by passing statutes in 1982 that allowed limited liability companies (LLCs) to be set up by the state, similar to the method by which corporations are set up or chartered. This business form is essentially a combination of a partnership and a corporation. It looks like a partnership, but it is granted the limited liability of a corporation by the state. There are some differences from a partnership. Those who invest in the LLC are *members,* not partners. Those who manage the LLC are not directors and officers, but, simply, *managers.*

The Florida LLCs worked well for businesses that did all of their business in Florida, but look what happened if a Jacksonville limited liability company did any business in nearby Georgia and its delivery truck seriously wounded a pedestrian in that state. If the court's award of damages to the pedestrian was greater than the insurance policy limit, that pedestrian would seek to collect from the LLC. However, because Georgia did not then have an LLC statute nor recognize LLCs from another state, the court would look at the nature of the company and decide it was a general partnership. Presto! The members have become general partners (in Georgia) and personally liable for the huge award.

Fortunately, the possibilities of this scenario occurring diminished as more states adopted LLC statutes, but it was 1997 before all states had LLC provisions. It's not all straightened out yet. Unlike partnerships and corporations who have been around for centuries, there are significant variations in the LLC statutes in the 50 states, and there is as yet no body of court cases that have determined just how an LLC should operate.

The details of an LLC are discussed next.

OWNERSHIP

Some states require at least two owners, while others permit single-owner LLCs, in which there is only one member. Any individual, corporation, partnership, another LLC, trust, or other entity can be an owner.

LIABILITY FOR DEBTS OF BUSINESS

The liability of all members is limited to their investment in the LLC. However, as with corporations, members may voluntarily extend their liability by guaranteeing certain debts of the LLC. (Read "voluntarily" as "the bank insists on personal guarantees.")

AMOUNT AND TYPE OF INVESTMENT

No technical limit. There may be practical or common sense limits, but there are no *set* limits. As with partnerships, there is no limit on the type of investment.

FUTURE SIZE OF BUSINESS

There is no limit on the future size of the business.

MANAGEMENT

In an LLC with a few members, those members can manage the business directly, just as can a small partnership. There is no requirement for a layer of directors and a layer of officers as in most corporations. LLCs with many members would probably opt for designating only a few members to manage the business, or they could simply hire outside managers who are not members of the LLC.

EMPLOYEE OWNERSHIP OF PART OF BUSINESS

The LLC scores better than a partnership here. An employee can be a member without incurring personal liability for company debts, which is impossible in a general partnership and questionable in a limited partnership.

SALE OF ALL OR PART OF BUSINESS

Partnership rules apply here.

LOCATION OF BUSINESS

Any state, as long as there are two or more members. Not all states permit LLCs to be formed with only one member.

GEOGRAPHIC AREA OF OPERATIONS

An LLC with two or more members can operate in every state, but should register with each state in which it operates. Single-member LLCs need to investigate. Not all states recognize this business form.

INCOME TAX CONSIDERATIONS

The federal government taxes a multimember LLC as a partnership, unless the LLC elects to be taxed as a corporation. Single-member LLCs are not recognized for federal tax purposes. An LLC with one individual as the member is taxed as a sole proprietor unless he or she elects to be taxed as a corporation. In an LLC composed of one corporation, this member is taxed.

Most states follow the federal rules, but often vary in their treatment of single-member LLCs.

OTHER TAXES AND FEES

Most states require annual reports and fees from LLCs, similar to the requirement for a corporation.

SECURITIES REGULATIONS

The rules for a limited partnership apply.

FRINGE BENEFITS

Partnership rules apply.

ESTATE PLANNING CONSIDERATIONS

These are the same as for partnerships.

EASE OF DISSOLUTION

These are the same as for partnerships.

COMPLEXITY, IN GENERAL

The complexity is a little bit less than for limited partnerships, inasmuch as there is no general partner, so all members have the same status.

PART II

SETTING UP YOUR BUSINESS—THE FORMS AND THE DETAILS

Part II is devoted to the forms you will need and the procedures you should follow to make your business come alive and start producing the goods or services you sell. If you are already in business, this chapter can help pinpoint some details you may have missed. It's not too late to take care of these details. Many of these steps you should take are important because they can help protect you from disaster or running into penalties from various government regulations—state, local, and federal (most notably the IRS).

Each chapter in this section is devoted to a specific form of doing business. Read the chapter on your chosen business form, as well as the chapters on related forms. (If you have decided to do business as an LLC, much of the information you need is in the chapter on partnerships, the form on which LLCs are based.)

We use the word *form* in a number of ways, including:

- *Business form:* A business form is one of the types of businesses we have been discussing, such as corporation, LLC, partnership, and so on.

- *Legal form:* Lawyers sometimes use these two words in a confusing manner. Legal form is sometimes a synonym for business form. That is, the legal form is the format, in the eyes of the law, in which you operate your business.

   The same words are often used to describe a legal document, such as a partnership agreement or the form that one submits to a state authority requesting a corporate charter. Legal documents generally start as a copy of a form from a book of agreements and other model documents, into which the lawyer introduces modifications that make the form fit the client's situation.

- *Tax and other government forms:* These are the forms that are full of blank boxes and dotted lines on which you are supposed to write information. For the most part, you find these forms in the accountants' domain. The best examples, of course, are the forms that the IRS wants you to fill out and file.

In this chapter, I try to keep any confusion about forms to a minimum by using the more specific terms: *business forms, legal forms, tax forms, government forms.* In other words, in this book, *legal form* refers to a document, not a *business form.*

7 | SETTING UP YOUR BUSINESS AS A SOLE PROPRIETORSHIP

This is called the simplest form of doing business for a reason—it entails the least amount of paperwork of any business form. Because you, and only you, are the owner and CEO of your business, you don't need any agreements between owners or any means of settling a dispute between owners. But, you don't get away scot-free. Here are some forms with which you should be concerned.

APPLICATION FOR EMPLOYER IDENTIFICATION NUMBER (IRS FORM SS-4)

Every business, except for sole proprietorships, must have one of these nine-digit numbers that the IRS assigns. And sole proprietors must have one if they hire even one employee (including a spouse). Also, banks generally will not open an account for an enterprise unless they have the employer identification number (EIN) of the business. In other words, you may as well go ahead and ask the folks at the IRS to assign you a number with which they will forever be able to keep track of your business.

Do not try to avoid this procedure by not opening a bank account for your business. Commingling your personal funds and business funds is foolish. When an IRS examiner runs into that type of sloppy record keeping, it's an invitation to him or her to disallow most of the business expenses. In other words, you could end up in a nasty and unnecessary fight with the IRS.

Filing this form normally brings a flood of mail from the IRS that covers more than you ever wanted to know about payroll taxes. If you have or soon will have employees, you will need much of that information. However, if hiring and firing are far in your future, be sure to enter all zeros in line 13. That should prevent overburdening your mail delivery person with excess IRS stuff.

An example of an Application for Employer Identification Number is on pages 42–45.

REGISTRATION WITH THE STATE TAX AUTHORITIES

Most states require that any business register if it will be subject to any taxes or will act as a tax collector. Yes, you heard right. When you start in business you most likely become a tax collector. Among the reasons you may need to register with the state are:

- The goods and/or services you sell are subject to state sales tax.
- You sell alcoholic beverages, tobacco, or other controlled substances.
- Your state imposes an income tax on individuals, so you will have to withhold state income tax from your employees' paychecks.

Each state has its own forms and registration requirements. Some states put out one form that enables you to register with several state tax offices on a single form. Others put out separate forms for each type of tax. To find out what your state requires, contact your state tax office. It should be listed in the state government pages of your telephone directory. Or, you may be able to find what you need on the Internet. Start with this site: http://www.taxadmin.org/ita/forms.html.

An example of the registration forms for New York state is on pages 46–51.

LOCAL BUSINESS LICENSE

Almost all counties, towns, and cities have some law that requires businesses to obtain a license. These licenses are touted as permits to conduct a business within some jurisdiction. However, there is no requirement that one meet certain qualifications to be licensed, as there is at the state level for lawyers, accountants, architects, engineers, and so on, so the sole purpose of these licenses seems to be to raise money. Usually, the fees are some small percentage of total revenues of the business. Take the initiative to contact city hall and/or your county administration offices. Otherwise, you may be embarrassed by some unpleasant license inspector calling on you when your office or store is occupied by impressionable clients or customers.

REGISTERING YOUR FICTITIOUS NAME

If you use something other than your legal name (that is, your own personal name, such as Mary Smith), the local bureaucrats will insist that you pay another few dollars to register your fictitious name. They require this in order to avoid having duplicate names in their records. That fictitious-name record usually does not have the affect of a tradename registration that protects you against others using the same name in a neighboring city or county. See the next section on registering trademarks.

REGISTERING YOUR BUSINESS NAME AND TRADEMARK

This may or may not be an area that should cause you concern. If you use your own name, and both your first and last names are multisyllabic ethnic names and your business is local, you might skip this section. If you fit a different category, read on.

Let's say yours is a common name, such as Tom Smith. You start the Tom Smith Auto Repair Shop and find out in a few weeks that six other guys named Tom Smith own similar shops in neighboring towns in your county. Confusion reigns. You seem to share customers, telephone calls, and worse, credit ratings.

You can attempt to avoid this situation by using a fictitious name, such as Patch'n'Go Automobile Repair, and hanging a sign that displays that name over your door. However, six other guys in other towns and counties may decide to call their businesses Patch'n'Go Automobile Repair. (It won't matter what their real names are.) Depending on your local county and city laws, those other six guys *might* not be able to obtain a business license using that name, but that won't prevent your business name being used by people in other cities, counties, or states.

There are ways to protect the *tradename* of your business. No one except General Motors can build Chevrolet automobiles and no one except the Kellogg Company can market Kellogg's Corn Flakes. Why? Those tradenames and trademarks belong to the companies that own the names—usually the first to use them. Try using the name Kellogg on the corn flakes you package. It won't be long until you hear from the legal eagles at Kellogg.

You should consider registering your tradename and/or trademark. That can dissuade others from using them and thereby save you heavy legal fees to protect your right to the name or mark. If you plan to be a national business, you register with the federal government. If your business will be local, registering with your state government may suffice.

The form for trademark or tradename registration with the federal Patent and Trademark Office is on pages 52–53. It is complex and needs to be carefully filled in to obtain the protection you want, so hire a knowledgeable attorney to keep you on the right track. (Use the form to make sure you have assembled all the necessary information before you start the professional clock running.) Also, see the U.S. Patent and Trademark Office Web site at http://www.uspta.gov/web/offices/tac/doc/basic.

Help from the U.S. Patent and Trademark Office

If you call this office, the staff will send you a brochure with more details about trademarks. The following excerpt from the brochure (p. 54) provides self-explanatory contact information, including telephone numbers.

BUYING A GOING BUSINESS

If you buy an existing business, there are other considerations. If the business is a sole proprietorship, you cannot, in fact, buy the business. A sole proprietor is the business, and as you cannot buy a person, in this country, you can't buy the sole proprietorship. What you do buy are the assets, and that term can include: equipment, accounts receivable, customer lists, patents, copyrights, goodwill, and various other assets. You might also be paying the seller for his agreement that he will not re-enter the same line of business and compete with you, or for him or her to act as a consultant. Because there are various time periods over which the cost of various assets can be written off (deducted from income), the IRS wants to know about the sale/purchase agreement and the values allocated to the various items.

If you buy a business that is incorporated by buying the common stock of the corporation, the rules are different. They are discussed later under *corporations*.

If you buy the entire business from a partnership, you purchase the assets, as for a sole proprietorship purchase. If you buy only a partnership interest (you become a partner), the rules are more complex. See the discussion under the partnership heading.

Asset Acquisition Statement

To obtain this information, the IRS requires that every seller and every buyer of assets in a transaction that amounts to a sale of a business report this information on Form 8594, *Asset Acquisition Statement Under Section 1060*, and file it with his, her, or its income tax return.

The IRS will compare both the buyer's and seller's information to make certain they agree. (At least, the IRS wants you to think it compares all of these forms.) That means that you will need a detailed purchase agreement with the seller and some negotiation of allocation of the purchase price will be involved. To do that, you need to determine the tax effects of the write-off of various assets you now hold. Either do some study of the tax rules or hire some professional help.

The IRS form and the instructions for it appear on pages 55–58.

COMPLY WITH THE BULK SALES LAW

In addition to the IRS, you need to keep other souls happy, such as: your state government, creditors of the business you are buying, and especially yourself. Consider what would happen if creditors of the business had lien rights on the inventory, equipment, or buildings of the business you're buying. (In other words, the seller had not paid for all of the stuff you are buying.) You could find yourself paying the seller for all of those business assets and then paying various creditors again for the same assets. That's hardly an auspicious beginning for your business.

What can you do? Comply with your state's bulk transfer law (or whatever your state calls it). If you carefully follow the steps described by the law, which will give creditors notice that you are buying the business, you should avoid this trap. It would be wise to use professional help in this area, but on pages 59 and 60, for information, are sample bulk sales agreements.

Obtaining an affidavit that all creditors are listed by the seller is helpful, but only if the seller is honest. Therefore, insist on an escrow of funds arrangement until you are sure all creditors have been paid.

OTHER INCOME TAX FORMS YOU WILL OR MAY BE FILING

While you won't need to file an income tax form the day you open the doors for business, December 31 will arrive all too soon, at which time you will have to start tallying up your sales and expenses and have it ready to mail off in four-and-a-half months. Knowing what you face after the end of the year can influence your decision as to whether you operate as a sole proprietor or in some other business form.

Profit or Loss from Business

As a sole proprietorship is owned by one individual, all of the business income will end up on his or her individual income tax form (Form 1040). That income is computed on a separate schedule that is then part of the Form 1040 package. If the owner files a joint return with his or her spouse, the schedule C is included in that return, although the schedule is headed by only the name and social security number of the proprietor.

Nearly every sole proprietor has to keep his or her business books on a calendar-year basis. Technically, the IRS expects most of us to report our individual taxes that way, and the sole proprietorship tax form (Schedule C, on pages 61–69) is part of the individual tax return.

Unfortunately, there are other forms that generate numbers that go on the Schedule C, and they also have to be included in the Form 1040 package that the proprietor (and spouse, if filing a joint return) sends to the IRS.

Depreciation and Amortization

This is an extremely complex form. It's that way because the laws about depreciation are extremely complex. This is the form on which a business spreads the cost of equipment and buildings over several years. (If you buy a new powerful computer system for $40,000, you can't deduct all of that cost the first year. You can only deduct some of the cost each year over a period of several years.) You can't avoid this tax form by choosing another business form because every business that owns equipment has to contend with depreciation rules.

The form is on pages 70 and 71. The instructions, which ramble on for 12 pages of small print, aren't here. That's because no one but a depreciation-loving accountant (rare) would read them. Most people either use a computer program that computes depreciation, or find one of those depreciation-loving accountants to fill in this form.

Sales of Business Property

If a business sells real estate or equipment used in the business, it is required to report any gain or loss on this form. (Much of the complexity of this form is due to the tax law that may require you to give back your tax savings from depreciation when you sell the property or equipment.) The net long-term gains and losses are then transferred to Schedule D, Capital Gains and Losses, where, in the case of a sole proprietorship, they are included with gains and losses from other capital assets, such as stocks, bonds, and mutual funds.

Although this is an area that is of more concern to an already established business, the form is reproduced here so you can see what may lie ahead in routine tax form preparation. Moral: Include the expense of professional tax help in your business plan.

Expenses for Business Use of Your Home (IRS Form 8829)

Yes, you can deduct the part of your home you use exclusively for business, if you meet various tests that are in the instructions for this form. However, you can't deduct those expenses immediately if your business shows a loss, but you don't lose those expenses. You can carry them forward and use them in a year in which you have enough profits to absorb them. A sample Form 8829 is on pages 74–77.

Self-Employment Tax

This sounds like an extra tax that every self-employed person has to pay, and it is. As you are aware, almost all employees have social security tax withheld from their paycheck at a basic rate of 7.65 percent on the first $68,400 of wages and at 1.45 percent on wages above that figure (1998 figures). Then, their employers match that tax.

Because self-employed people are their own employers, they get to pay both the employee and the employer portions of the tax. In other words, self-employed people pay social security taxes of 15.3 percent on the first $68,400 of earnings and 2.9 percent on earnings above that figure.

To make the payment of this tax easy (!), the IRS collects this tax for the Social Security Administration right along with the self-employed person's income tax. That is accomplished by this form, which is part of the Form 1040 package. For most people subject to this tax, filling out the "Short Schedule SE" on page one of the form is all they need to do. But, make sure. Follow the flow chart on page one of the form. (See form on pages 78–79.)

Form **SS-4** (Rev. February 1998) Department of the Treasury Internal Revenue Service	**Application for Employer Identification Number** (For use by employers, corporations, partnerships, trusts, estates, churches, government agencies, certain individuals, and others. See instructions.) ▶ **Keep a copy for your records.**	EIN OMB No. 1545-0003

Please type or print clearly.

1 Name of applicant (legal name) (see instructions)

2 Trade name of business (if different from name on line 1)	**3** Executor, trustee, "care of" name
4a Mailing address (street address) (room, apt., or suite no.)	**5a** Business address (if different from address on lines 4a and 4b)
4b City, state, and ZIP code	**5b** City, state, and ZIP code

6 County and state where principal business is located

7 Name of principal officer, general partner, grantor, owner, or trustor—SSN or ITIN may be required (see instructions) ▶ _____

8a Type of entity (Check only one box.) (see instructions)

Caution: *If applicant is a limited liability company, see the instructions for line 8a.*

☐ Sole proprietor (SSN) _____
☐ Partnership   ☐ Personal service corp.
☐ REMIC   ☐ National Guard
☐ State/local government   ☐ Farmers' cooperative
☐ Church or church-controlled organization
☐ Other nonprofit organization (specify) ▶ _____
☐ Other (specify) ▶

☐ Estate (SSN of decedent) _____
☐ Plan administrator (SSN) _____
☐ Other corporation (specify) ▶ _____
☐ Trust
☐ Federal government/military
_____ (enter GEN if applicable) _____

8b If a corporation, name the state or foreign country (if applicable) where incorporated | State _____ | Foreign country _____

9 Reason for applying (Check only one box.) (see instructions)
☐ Started new business (specify type) ▶ _____
☐ Hired employees (Check the box and see line 12.)
☐ Created a pension plan (specify type) ▶
☐ Banking purpose (specify purpose) ▶ _____
☐ Changed type of organization (specify new type) ▶ _____
☐ Purchased going business
☐ Created a trust (specify type) ▶ _____
☐ Other (specify) ▶

10 Date business started or acquired (month, day, year) (see instructions) | **11** Closing month of accounting year (see instructions)

12 First date wages or annuities were paid or will be paid (month, day, year). **Note:** *If applicant is a withholding agent, enter date income will first be paid to nonresident alien. (month, day, year)* . . . . ▶

13 Highest number of employees expected in the next 12 months. **Note:** *If the applicant does not expect to have any employees during the period, enter -0-. (see instructions)* . . . . ▶	Nonagricultural	Agricultural	Household

14 Principal activity (see instructions) ▶

15 Is the principal business activity manufacturing? . . . . ☐ **Yes** ☐ **No**
If "Yes," principal product and raw material used ▶

16 To whom are most of the products or services sold? Please check one box.   ☐ Business (wholesale)
☐ Public (retail)   ☐ Other (specify) ▶   ☐ N/A

17a Has the applicant ever applied for an employer identification number for this or any other business? . . . . ☐ **Yes** ☐ **No**
Note: *If "Yes," please complete lines 17b and 17c.*

17b If you checked "Yes" on line 17a, give applicant's legal name and trade name shown on prior application, if different from line 1 or 2 above.
Legal name ▶   Trade name ▶

17c Approximate date when and city and state where the application was filed. Enter previous employer identification number if known.

Approximate date when filed (mo., day, year)	City and state where filed	Previous EIN

Under penalties of perjury, I declare that I have examined this application, and to the best of my knowledge and belief, it is true, correct, and complete. | Business telephone number (include area code)

Fax telephone number (include area code)

Name and title (Please type or print clearly.) ▶

Signature ▶   Date ▶

Note: *Do not write below this line. For official use only.*

Please leave blank ▶	Geo.	Ind.	Class	Size	Reason for applying

For Paperwork Reduction Act Notice, see page 4.   Cat. No. 16055N   Form **SS-4** (Rev. 2-98)

General Instructions

Section references are to the Internal Revenue Code unless otherwise noted.

Purpose of Form

Use Form SS-4 to apply for an employer identification number (EIN). An EIN is a nine-digit number (for example, 12-3456789) assigned to sole proprietors, corporations, partnerships, estates, trusts, and other entities for tax filing and reporting purposes. The information you provide on this form will establish your business tax account.

Caution: *An EIN is for use in connection with your business activities only. Do **NOT** use your EIN in place of your social security number (SSN).*

Who Must File

You must file this form if you have not been assigned an EIN before and:

● You pay wages to one or more employees including household employees.

● You are required to have an EIN to use on any return, statement, or other document, even if you are not an employer.

● You are a withholding agent required to withhold taxes on income, other than wages, paid to a nonresident alien (individual, corporation, partnership, etc.). A withholding agent may be an agent, broker, fiduciary, manager, tenant, or spouse, and is required to file **Form 1042,** Annual Withholding Tax Return for U.S. Source Income of Foreign Persons.

● You file **Schedule C,** Profit or Loss From Business, **Schedule C-EZ,** Net Profit From Business, or **Schedule F,** Profit or Loss From Farming, of **Form 1040,** U.S. Individual Income Tax Return, **and** have a Keogh plan or are required to file excise, employment, or alcohol, tobacco, or firearms returns.

The following must use EINs even if they do not have any employees:

● State and local agencies who serve as tax reporting agents for public assistance recipients, under Rev. Proc. 80-4, 1980-1 C.B. 581, should obtain a separate EIN for this reporting. See **Household employer** on page 3.

● Trusts, except the following:

   1. Certain grantor-owned trusts. (See the **Instructions for Form 1041.)**

   2. Individual Retirement Arrangement (IRA) trusts, unless the trust has to file **Form 990-T,** Exempt Organization Business Income Tax Return. (See the **Instructions for Form 990-T.)**

● Estates

● Partnerships

● REMICs (real estate mortgage investment conduits) (See the **Instructions for Form 1066,** U.S. Real Estate Mortgage Investment Conduit Income Tax Return.)

● Corporations

● Nonprofit organizations (churches, clubs, etc.)

● Farmers' cooperatives

● Plan administrators (A plan administrator is the person or group of persons specified as the administrator by the instrument under which the plan is operated.)

When To Apply for a New EIN

New Business. If you become the new owner of an existing business, **do not** use the EIN of the former owner. IF YOU ALREADY HAVE AN EIN, USE THAT NUMBER. If you do not have an EIN, apply for one on this form. If you become the "owner" of a corporation by acquiring its stock, use the corporation's EIN.

Changes in Organization or Ownership. If you already have an EIN, you may need to get a new one if either the organization or ownership of your business changes. If you incorporate a sole proprietorship or form a partnership, you must get a new EIN. However, **do not** apply for a new EIN if:

● You change only the name of your business,

● You elected on **Form 8832,** Entity Classification Election, to change the way the entity is taxed, or

● A partnership terminates because at least 50% of the total interests in partnership capital and profits were sold or exchanged within a 12-month period. (See Regulations section 301.6109-1(d)(2)(iii).) The EIN for the terminated partnership should continue to be used. This rule applies to terminations occurring after May 8, 1997. If the termination took place after May 8, 1996, and before May 9, 1997, a new EIN must be obtained for the new partnership unless the partnership and its partners are consistent in using the old EIN.

Note: *If you are electing to be an "S corporation," be sure you file **Form 2553,** Election by a Small Business Corporation.*

File Only One Form SS-4. File only one Form SS-4, regardless of the number of businesses operated or trade names under which a business operates. However, each corporation in an affiliated group must file a separate application.

EIN Applied for, But Not Received. If you do not have an EIN by the time a return is due, write "Applied for" and the date you applied in the space shown for the number. **Do not** show your social security number (SSN) as an EIN on returns.

If you do not have an EIN by the time a tax deposit is due, send your payment to the Internal Revenue Service Center for your filing area. (See **Where To Apply** below.) Make your check or money order payable to Internal Revenue Service and show your name (as shown on Form SS-4), address, type of tax, period covered, and date you applied for an EIN. Send an explanation with the deposit.

For more information about EINs, see **Pub. 583,** Starting a Business and Keeping Records, and **Pub. 1635,** Understanding your EIN.

How To Apply

You can apply for an EIN either by mail or by telephone. You can get an EIN immediately by calling the Tele-TIN number for the service center for your state, or you can send the completed Form SS-4 directly to the service center to receive your EIN by mail.

Application by Tele-TIN. Under the Tele-TIN program, you can receive your EIN by telephone and use it immediately to file a return or make a payment. To receive an EIN by telephone, complete Form SS-4, then call the Tele-TIN number listed for your state under **Where To Apply.** The person making the call must be authorized to sign the form. (See **Signature** on page 4.)

An IRS representative will use the information from the Form SS-4 to establish your account and assign you an EIN. Write the number you are given on the upper right corner of the form and sign and date it.

Mail or fax (facsimile) the signed SS-4 within 24 hours to the Tele-TIN Unit at the service center address for your state. The IRS representative will give you the fax number. The fax numbers are also listed in Pub. 1635.

Taxpayer representatives can receive their client's EIN by telephone if they first send a fax of a completed **Form 2848,** Power of Attorney and Declaration of Representative, or **Form 8821,** Tax Information Authorization, to the Tele-TIN unit. The Form 2848 or Form 8821 will be used solely to release the EIN to the representative authorized on the form.

Application by Mail. Complete Form SS-4 at least 4 to 5 weeks before you will need an EIN. Sign and date the application and mail it to the service center address for your state. You will receive your EIN in the mail in approximately 4 weeks.

Where To Apply

The Tele-TIN numbers listed below will involve a long-distance charge to callers outside of the local calling area and can be used only to apply for an EIN. THE NUMBERS MAY CHANGE WITHOUT NOTICE. Call 1-800-829-1040 to verify a number or to ask about the status of an application by mail.

If your principal business, office or agency, or legal residence in the case of an individual, is located in:	Call the Tele-TIN number shown or file with the Internal Revenue Service Center at:
Florida, Georgia, South Carolina	Attn: Entity Control Atlanta, GA 39901 770-455-2360
New Jersey, New York City and counties of Nassau, Rockland, Suffolk, and Westchester	Attn: Entity Control Holtsville, NY 00501 516-447-4955
New York (all other counties), Connecticut, Maine, Massachusetts, New Hampshire, Rhode Island, Vermont	Attn: Entity Control Andover, MA 05501 978-474-9717
Illinois, Iowa, Minnesota, Missouri, Wisconsin	Attn: Entity Control Stop 6800 2306 E. Bannister Rd. Kansas City, MO 64999 816-926-5999
Delaware, District of Columbia, Maryland, Pennsylvania, Virginia	Attn: Entity Control Philadelphia, PA 19255 215-516-6999
Indiana, Kentucky, Michigan, Ohio, West Virginia	Attn: Entity Control Cincinnati, OH 45999 606-292-5467

Kansas, New Mexico, Oklahoma, Texas	Attn: Entity Control Austin, TX 73301 512-460-7843
Alaska, Arizona, California (counties of Alpine, Amador, Butte, Calaveras, Colusa, Contra Costa, Del Norte, El Dorado, Glenn, Humboldt, Lake, Lassen, Marin, Mendocino, Modoc, Napa, Nevada, Placer, Plumas, Sacramento, San Joaquin, Shasta, Sierra, Siskiyou, Solano, Sonoma, Sutter, Tehama, Trinity, Yolo, and Yuba), Colorado, Idaho, Montana, Nebraska, Nevada, North Dakota, Oregon, South Dakota, Utah, Washington, Wyoming	Attn: Entity Control Mail Stop 6271 P.O. Box 9941 Ogden, UT 84201 801-620-7645
California (all other counties), Hawaii	Attn: Entity Control Fresno, CA 93888 209-452-4010
Alabama, Arkansas, Louisiana, Mississippi, North Carolina, Tennessee	Attn: Entity Control Memphis, TN 37501 901-546-3920
If you have no legal residence, principal place of business, or principal office or agency in any state	Attn: Entity Control Philadelphia, PA 19255 215-516-6999

Specific Instructions

The instructions that follow are for those items that are not self-explanatory. Enter N/A (nonapplicable) on the lines that do not apply.

Line 1. Enter the legal name of the entity applying for the EIN exactly as it appears on the social security card, charter, or other applicable legal document.

Individuals. Enter your first name, middle initial, and last name. If you are a sole proprietor, enter your individual name, not your business name. Enter your business name on line 2. Do not use abbreviations or nicknames on line 1.

Trusts. Enter the name of the trust.

Estate of a decedent. Enter the name of the estate.

Partnerships. Enter the legal name of the partnership as it appears in the partnership agreement. **Do not** list the names of the partners on line 1. See the specific instructions for line 7.

Corporations. Enter the corporate name as it appears in the corporation charter or other legal document creating it.

Plan administrators. Enter the name of the plan administrator. A plan administrator who already has an EIN should use that number.

Line 2. Enter the trade name of the business if different from the legal name. The trade name is the "doing business as" name.

Note: *Use the full legal name on line 1 on all tax returns filed for the entity. However, if you enter a trade name on line 2 and choose to use the trade name instead of the legal name, enter the trade name on all returns you file. To prevent processing delays and errors, **always** use either the legal name only or the trade name only on all tax returns.*

Line 3. Trusts enter the name of the trustee. Estates enter the name of the executor, administrator, or other fiduciary. If the entity applying has a designated person to receive tax information, enter that person's name as the "care of" person. Print or type the first name, middle initial, and last name.

Line 7. Enter the first name, middle initial, last name, and SSN of a principal officer if the business is a corporation; of a general partner if a partnership; of the owner of a single member entity that is disregarded as an entity separate from its owner; or of a grantor, owner, or trustor if a trust. If the person in question is an alien individual with a previously assigned individual taxpayer identification number (ITIN), enter the ITIN in the space provided, instead of an SSN. You are not required to enter an SSN or ITIN if the reason you are applying for an EIN is to make an entity classification election (see Regulations section 301.7701-1 through 301.7701-3), and you are a nonresident alien with no effectively connected income from sources within the United States.

Line 8a. Check the box that best describes the type of entity applying for the EIN. If you are an alien individual with an ITIN previously assigned to you, enter the ITIN in place of a requested SSN.

Caution: *This is not an election for a tax classification of an entity. See "Limited liability company" below.*

If not specifically mentioned, check the "Other" box, enter the type of entity and the type of return that will be filed (for example, common trust fund, Form 1065). Do not enter N/A. If you are an alien individual applying for an EIN, see the **Line 7** instructions above.

Sole proprietor. Check this box if you file Schedule C, C-EZ, or F (Form 1040) and have a Keogh plan, or are required to file excise, employment, or alcohol, tobacco, or firearms returns, or are a payer of gambling

winnings. Enter your SSN (or ITIN) in the space provided. If you are a nonresident alien with no effectively connected income from sources within the United States, you do not need to enter an SSN or ITIN.

REMIC. Check this box if the entity has elected to be treated as a real estate mortgage investment conduit (REMIC). See the **Instructions for Form 1066** for more information.

Other nonprofit organization. Check this box if the nonprofit organization is other than a church or church-controlled organization and specify the type of nonprofit organization (for example, an educational organization).

If the organization also seeks tax-exempt status, you must file either **Package 1023**, Application for Recognition of Exemption, or **Package 1024**, Application for Recognition of Exemption Under Section 501(a). Get **Pub. 557**, Tax Exempt Status for Your Organization, for more information.

Group exemption number (GEN). If the organization is covered by a group exemption letter, enter the four-digit GEN. (Do not confuse the GEN with the nine-digit EIN.) If you do not know the GEN, contact the parent organization. Get Pub. 557 for more information about group exemption numbers.

Withholding agent. If you are a withholding agent required to file Form 1042, check the "Other" box and enter "Withholding agent."

Personal service corporation. Check this box if the entity is a personal service corporation. An entity is a personal service corporation for a tax year only if:

● The principal activity of the entity during the testing period (prior tax year) for the tax year is the performance of personal services substantially by employee-owners, and

● The employee-owners own at least 10% of the fair market value of the outstanding stock in the entity on the last day of the testing period.

Personal services include performance of services in such fields as health, law, accounting, or consulting. For more information about personal service corporations, see the **Instructions for Form 1120**, U.S. Corporation Income Tax Return, and **Pub. 542**, Corporations.

Limited liability company (LLC). See the definition of limited liability company in the **Instructions for Form 1065**. An LLC with two or more members can be a partnership or an association taxable as a corporation. An LLC with a single owner can be an association taxable as a corporation or an entity disregarded as an entity separate from its owner. See Form 8832 for more details.

● If the entity is classified as a partnership for Federal income tax purposes, check the "partnership" box.

● If the entity is classified as a corporation for Federal income tax purposes, mark the "Other corporation" box and write "limited liability co." in the space provided.

● If the entity is disregarded as an entity separate from its owner, check the "Other" box and write in "disregarded entity" in the space provided.

Plan administrator. If the plan administrator is an individual, enter the plan administrator's SSN in the space provided.

Other corporation. This box is for any corporation other than a personal service corporation. If you check this box, enter the type of corporation (such as insurance company) in the space provided.

Household employer. If you are an individual, check the "Other" box and enter "Household employer" and your SSN. If you are a state or local agency serving as a tax reporting agent for public assistance recipients who become household employers, check the "Other" box and enter "Household employer agent." If you are a trust that qualifies as a household employer, you do not need a separate EIN for reporting tax information relating to household employees; use the EIN of the trust.

QSSS. For a qualified subchapter S subsidiary (QSSS) check the "Other" box and specify "QSSS."

Line 9. Check only **one** box. Do not enter N/A.

Started new business. Check this box if you are starting a new business that requires an EIN. If you check this box, enter the type of business being started. **Do not** apply if you already have an EIN and are only adding another place of business.

Hired employees. Check this box if the existing business is requesting an EIN because it has hired or is hiring employees and is therefore required to file employment tax returns. **Do not** apply if you already have an EIN and are only hiring employees. For information on the applicable employment taxes for family members, see **Circular E**, Employer's Tax Guide (Publication 15).

Created a pension plan. Check this box if you have created a pension plan and need this number for reporting purposes. Also, enter the type of plan created.

Note: *Check this box if you are applying for a trust EIN when a new pension plan is established.*

Banking purpose. Check this box if you are requesting an EIN for banking purposes only, and enter the banking purpose (for example, a bowling league for depositing dues or an investment club for dividend and interest reporting).

Changed type of organization. Check this box if the business is changing its type of organization, for example, if the business was a sole proprietorship and has been incorporated or has become a partnership. If you check this box, specify in the space provided the type of change made, for example, "from sole proprietorship to partnership."

Purchased going business. Check this box if you purchased an existing business. **Do not** use the former owner's EIN. **Do not** apply for a new EIN if you already have one. Use your own EIN.

Created a trust. Check this box if you created a trust, and enter the type of trust created. For example, indicate if the trust is a nonexempt charitable trust or a split-interest trust.

Note: *Do not check this box if you are applying for a trust EIN when a new pension plan is established. Check "Created a pension plan."*

Exception. Do **not** file this form for certain grantor-type trusts. The trustee does not need an EIN for the trust if the trustee furnishes the name and TIN of the grantor/owner and the address of the trust to all payors. See the Instructions for Form 1041 for more information.

Other (specify). Check this box if you are requesting an EIN for any reason other than those for which there are checkboxes, and enter the reason.

Line 10. If you are starting a new business, enter the starting date of the business. If the business you acquired is already operating, enter the date you acquired the business. Trusts should enter the date the trust was legally created. Estates should enter the date of death of the decedent whose name appears on line 1 or the date when the estate was legally funded.

Line 11. Enter the last month of your accounting year or tax year. An accounting or tax year is usually 12 consecutive months, either a calendar year or a fiscal year (including a period of 52 or 53 weeks). A calendar year is 12 consecutive months ending on December 31. A fiscal year is either 12 consecutive months ending on the last day of any month other than December or a 52-53 week year. For more information on accounting periods, see **Pub. 538,** Accounting Periods and Methods.

Individuals. Your tax year generally will be a calendar year.

Partnerships. Partnerships generally must adopt one of the following tax years:
● The tax year of the majority of its partners,
● The tax year common to all of its principal partners,
● The tax year that results in the least aggregate deferral of income, or
● In certain cases, some other tax year.
See the **Instructions for Form 1065,** U.S. Partnership Return of Income, for more information.

REMIC. REMICs must have a calendar year as their tax year.

Personal service corporations. A personal service corporation generally must adopt a calendar year unless:
● It can establish a business purpose for having a different tax year, or
● It elects under section 444 to have a tax year other than a calendar year.

Trusts. Generally, a trust must adopt a calendar year except for the following:
● Tax-exempt trusts,
● Charitable trusts, and
● Grantor-owned trusts.

Line 12. If the business has or will have employees, enter the date on which the business began or will begin to pay wages. If the business does not plan to have employees, enter N/A.

Withholding agent. Enter the date you began or will begin to pay income to a nonresident alien. This also applies to individuals who are required to file Form 1042 to report alimony paid to a nonresident alien.

Line 13. For a definition of agricultural labor (farmwork), see **Circular A,** Agricultural Employer's Tax Guide (Publication 51).

Line 14. Generally, enter the exact type of business being operated (for example, advertising agency, farm, food or beverage establishment, labor union, real estate agency, steam laundry, rental of coin-operated vending machine, or investment club). Also state if the business will involve the sale or distribution of alcoholic beverages.

Governmental. Enter the type of organization (state, county, school district, municipality, etc.).

Nonprofit organization (other than governmental). Enter whether organized for religious, educational, or humane purposes, and the principal activity (for example, religious organization—hospital, charitable).

Mining and quarrying. Specify the process and the principal product (for example, mining bituminous coal, contract drilling for oil, or quarrying dimension stone).

Contract construction. Specify whether general contracting or special trade contracting. Also, show the type of work normally performed (for example, general contractor for residential buildings or electrical subcontractor).

Food or beverage establishments. Specify the type of establishment and state whether you employ workers who receive tips (for example, lounge—yes).

Trade. Specify the type of sales and the principal line of goods sold (for example, wholesale dairy products, manufacturer's representative for mining machinery, or retail hardware).

Manufacturing. Specify the type of establishment operated (for example, sawmill or vegetable cannery).

Signature. The application must be signed by (a) the individual, if the applicant is an individual, (b) the president, vice president, or other principal officer, if the applicant is a corporation, (c) a responsible and duly authorized member or officer having knowledge of its affairs, if the applicant is a partnership or other unincorporated organization, or (d) the fiduciary, if the applicant is a trust or an estate.

How To Get Forms and Publications

Phone. You can order forms, instructions, and publications by phone. Just call 1-800-TAX-FORM (1-800-829-3676). You should receive your order or notification of its status within 7 to 15 workdays.

Personal computer. With your personal computer and modem, you can get the forms and information you need using:
● IRS's Internet Web Site at **www.irs.ustreas.gov**
● Telnet at **iris.irs.ustreas.gov**
● File Transfer Protocol at **ftp.irs.ustreas.gov**

You can also dial direct (by modem) to the Internal Revenue Information Services (IRIS) at 703-321-8020. IRIS is an on-line information service on FedWorld.

For small businesses, return preparers, or others who may frequently need tax forms or publications, a CD-ROM containing over 2,000 tax products (including many prior year forms) can be purchased from the Government Printing Office.

CD-ROM. To order the CD-ROM call the Superintendent of Documents at 202-512-1800 or connect to **www.access.gpo.gov/su_docs**

Recordkeeping	7 min.
Learning about the law or the form	19 min.
Preparing the form	45 min.
Copying, assembling, and sending the form to the IRS . .	20 min.

If you have comments concerning the accuracy of these time estimates or suggestions for making this form simpler, we would be happy to hear from you. You can write to the Tax Forms Committee, Western Area Distribution Center, Rancho Cordova, CA 95743-0001. **Do not** send this form to this address. Instead, see **Where To Apply** on page 2.

DTF-17 (11/96)   New York State Department of Taxation and Finance

	Department use only

Application for Registration as a Sales Tax Vendor

Please print or type

1 What type of certificate are you applying for?
(You must check one box - see instructions): ☐ Regular ☐ Temporary ☐ Show ☐ Entertainment

2 Legal name

3 Trade name (if different from item 2)

4 Federal employer identification number

5 Address of principal place of business (show/entertainment or temporary vendors use home address, regular vendors use physical address of business)
Number and street   City   State   ZIP code

6 Telephone number (include area code) ( )

7 County of principal place of business

8 Country, if not U.S.

9 Date you will begin business in New York *(see instructions)*   / /

10 Mailing address, if different from business address on line 5
C/O name   Number and street   City   State   ZIP code

Date you will end business in New York if you are a temporary vendor   / /

11 Type of organization ☐ Individual (sole proprietor) ☐ Partnership ☐ Corporation ☐ Trust ☐ Governmental ☐ Exempt organization
☐ Other *(specify)* ☐ Limited Liability Partnership ☐ Limited Liability Company

12 Reason for applying ☐ Started new business ☐ Purchased existing business ☐ Adding a new location ☐ Change in organization ☐ Other (specify)

13 List all owners/officers. Attach a separate sheet if necessary. This section must be completed by all applicants.

Name	Title	Social security number
Home address		City, State, ZIP code / Telephone number ( )
Name	Title	Social security number
Home address		City, State, ZIP code / Telephone number ( )
Name	Title	Social security number
Home address		City, State, ZIP code / Telephone number ( )

14 Does your business currently have tax accounts with New York State for the following taxes? If yes, enter identification number.
Corporation Tax ☐ Yes ☐ No   ID # _____   Withholding Tax ☐ Yes ☐ No   ID #_____
Other Taxes - enter type of tax and identification number _____

15 If you have ever registered as a sales tax vendor before with New York State enter information shown on the last sales tax retun you filed:
Name   Identification number

Questions 16 and 17 apply to regular vendors only. All other vendors go to question 18.

16 Will you operate more than one place of business? ☐ Yes   ☐ No   If *Yes*, check the appropriate box below and follow the instructions.

   A ☐ Separate return will be filed for each location. Fill out and return a **complete** application for **each** business location.
   B ☐ Consolidated return will be filed to cover all places of business. List your business locations on Form DTF-17-ATT and return with this application.

17 Do you expect to collect any sales or use tax or pay any sales or use tax directly to the Department of Taxation and Finance?   ☐ Yes   ☐ No

18 Fill in the boxes below, describing your major business activities:

	Describe your business activity in detail *(attach a separate sheet if necessary)*	Enter letter of major division from Form DTF-17-I, page 2-3	Enter Standard Industrial Code (SIC) *(see instructions)*	Percent of time spent on activity *(total should = 100%)*
Primary Business Activity				
Secondary Business Activity *(if any)*				

19 Are you a sidewalk vendor?... ☐ Yes ☐ No
     If *Yes*, do you sell food? .... ☐ Yes ☐ No
20 Do you participate solely in flea markets, antique shows or other "shows"? .. ☐ Yes ☐ No
21 Do you intend to make retail sales of cigarettes or other tobacco products?.. ☐ Yes ☐ No
22 Are you liable for paying the New York State beverage container tax?....... ☐ Yes ☐ No
23 Do you sell merchandise from door to door or through party plans?........ ☐ Yes ☐ No

Department use only	
Mail code	Certificate No
Type	Status	Sch. Ind.	Aux. sch.
SIC P	SIC S

DTF-17 (11/96) (back)

24 Business size (anticipated gross annual sales)
☐ under $125,000 ☐ $125,000 to $499,999 ☐ $500,000 to $1,499,999
☐ $1,500,000 to $5,000,000 ☐ over $5,000,000

25 If you withhold or will withhold New York State tax from your employees, do you need withholding tax forms or information? ☐ Yes ☐ No

26 Name and address of banking institutions at which your business maintains or will maintain accounts for your business. Give branch office if applicable _____

27 If you acquired this business from a registered vendor, did you file Form AU-196.10, *Notification of Sale, Transfer or Assignment in Bulk*, with the Tax Department? ☐ Yes ☐ No
Former owner's name _____ Address _____ ID # _____

28 Have you been notified that you owe any New York State tax? ☐ Yes ☐ No

Type of tax	Amount due	Assessment number (if any)	Assessment date	Assessment currently being protested ☐ Yes ☐ No

29 Do any responsible officers, directors, partners or employees owe New York State or local sales and use taxes on your behalf, on behalf of another person or as a vendor of property or services? ☐ Yes ☐ No

Individual's name		Street address		City, State, ZIP code
Social security number	Amount due	Assessment number (if any)	Assessment date	Assessment currently being protested ☐ Yes ☐ No

30 Have you been convicted of a crime under the Tax Law during the past year? ☐ Yes ☐ No

Date of conviction	Court of conviction	Disposition (fine, imprisonment, probation, etc.)

31 During the past year, has any responsible officer, director, partner or employee of the applicant been convicted of a crime under the Tax Law? ☐ Yes ☐ No

Individual's name		Street address		City, State, ZIP code
Social security number	Date of conviction	Court of conviction	Disposition (fine, imprisonment, probation, etc.)	

32 If previously registered as a New York State sales tax vendor, was your Certificate of Authority revoked or suspended during that past year? If *Yes*, please indicate why. _____ ☐ Yes ☐ No

Questions 33 to 35 apply to corporations only.

33 If any shareholder owns more than half of the shares of voting stock of the applicant, has this shareholder ever owned more than half of the shares of voting stock of another corporation? **If Yes, complete questions 34 and 35.** ☐ Yes ☐ No

34 Did this shareholder own these shares of another corporation when the corporation had a tax liability that remains unpaid? ☐ Yes ☐ No

Shareholder's name	Corporation name	Federal identification number
Street address		City, State, ZIP code

Type of tax	Amount due	Assessment number (if any)	Assessment due	Assessment currently being protested ☐ Yes ☐ No

35 Did this shareholder own these shares of another corporation at a time during the past year when the corporation was convicted of a crime under the Tax Law? ☐ Yes ☐ No

Corporation name	Federal identification number
Street addresses	City, State, ZIP code

Date of conviction	Court of conviction	Disposition (fine, imprisonment, probation, etc.)

I certify that the information in this application is true and correct. Willfully filing a false application is a misdemeanor punishable under the Tax Law.

Signature	Title	Date

This application will be returned if it is not signed or if any other information is missing.

New York State Department of Taxation and Finance
Instructions for Form DTF-17

DTF-17-I
(11/96)

Line 1 — There are four types of sales tax vendors, as defined below. Select the definition that best describes your business, then check the appropriate box on line 1.

A **regular vendor** is any individual, partnership, company or organization who makes taxable sales within the state or who accepts or issues exemption certificates. Regular vendors always have permanent business locations. In addition, they may sell at craft fairs, flea markets, etc.

A **temporary** vendor is anyone who expects to make sales of tangible personal property or taxable services in New York State for no more than two consecutive quarterly sales tax periods in any 12-month period. A vendor who attends shows or entertainment events on a continual basis, even for only short periods, should register as a show/entertainment vendor, not a temporary vendor.

A **show vendor** is anyone who displays for sale or sells taxable goods or services at a flea market, a craft fair, a coin show, an antique show or any similar enterprise that occurs on either a regular or temporary basis. A show vendor does not have a permanent business location.

An **entertainment vendor** is anyone who makes taxable sales at a concert, an athletic contest or exhibition (other than amateur sports) or similar form of entertainment in which performers do not appear on a regular, systematic or recurring basis, held in a facility or site with capacity to accommodate more than 1,000 persons. An entertainment vendor does not have a permanent business location.

Line 2 — Enter the exact legal name of the business that you are registering. For a corporation, the legal name will be the name that appears on the Certificate of Incorporation filed with the New York State Department of State. For a business that is not incorporated, the legal name is the name in which the business owns property or acquires debt. If the business is a partnership, use the names of the individual partners, if a sole proprietor, show or entertainment vendor, the legal name is the name of the individual owner of the business.

Line 3 — Enter the trade name, doing-business-as name, or assumed name if different from the legal name. For a corporation, enter the name that appears on the trade name certificate filed with the New York State Department of State. For a business that is not incorporated, enter the name filed with the county clerk's office pursuant to Section 130 of the General Business Law.

Line 4 — Enter your federal employer identification number (EIN). If you are not required by the IRS to have an EIN, or you do not yet have a required EIN, leave line 4 blank.

Line 5 — Regular vendors enter the actual street address of your business. Show/entertainment or temporary vendors use home address. Do not enter a PO box on this line. This address **will** appear on your *Certificate of Authority*. It will also be used for mailing unless you list a different mailing address on line 10. If you have more than one location, see the instructions for line 16.

Line 9 — Enter the date you will begin making taxable sales or providing taxable services within New York State or begin issuing or accepting New York State exemption certificates. Do not mail your application more than 90 days before this date. If you are a temporary vendor, enter the date you will end business in New York.

Line 11 — Indicate how your business is organized by checking the box that best describes it.

Governmental organizations include the federal government, New York State and any of its agencies, instrumentalities, public corporations or political subdivisions (counties, towns, cities, villages, school districts, fire districts, etc.).

An exempt organization is one that qualifies under Section 1116 of the Tax Law and has been issued an *Exempt Organization Certificate.*

Line 12 — Check the appropriate box to indicate why you are applying.

Line 13 — Enter the required information for all owners or officers of the business, those who are responsible for the day-to-day operations of the business. This generally includes anyone who:
— signs checks on the company's bank account
— signs business tax returns
— pays creditors
— hires and fires employees
— determines which bills are to be paid
— attends to the general financial affairs of the business

If a partnership, enter the required information for all general partners and for those limited partners who are active in running the business. Indicate whether the partner is a general partner or limited partner by entering (GP) or (LP) after the partner's name.

Include the social security number of all owners, partners or officers listed. (The Tax Law requires you to disclose your social security number.) Your application will be returned to you for missing social security numbers.

Line 16 — If you will be operating from more than one business location, you must have a separate *Certificate of Authority* for each location. Check the appropriate box to indicate whether you will file a consolidated return or a separate return for each location.

If you will be filing a consolidated return, list all your business locations on Form DTF-17-ATT and attach it to your application.

If you will be filing separate returns for each location, you must file Form DTF-17 for each location.

Line 17 — If you are a manufacturer or wholesalers whose activities are such that you are not required to collect any sales and use tax or pay any sales and use tax directly to the Department of Taxation and Finance, check *No.* Because you are registering only to accept or issue exemption certificates, you need only file an annual information return. There are other instances when you may file an annual return. Refer to Publication 750 for instructions on filing returns and for what constitutes a taxable sale. You will, of course, still have to collect sales or use tax and to pay sales or use tax on any taxable retail sale or purchase.

Page 2 DTF-17-I (11/96)

Line 18 — Business activities - Describe your business activities in the spaces provided. If you have only one business activity, leave the boxes for a secondary business activity blank. If you have more than two business activities, attach additional sheets.

If only one business activity is listed, the percent of time spent on that activity should be 100%. If more than one business activity is listed, the total time spent should be divided among the activities but should add up to 100%.

Major division - From the following list, enter the letter identifying the division that pertains to the business activity:
— show and entertainment vendors enter "G."
— regular vendors and temporary vendors - choose the division that best categorizes the business activity. (If a manufacturing activity derives more than 50% of its receipts from its own retail outlets, enter "G" for that activity.)

A. Agriculture, forestry, fishing
B. Mining
C. Construction
D. Manufacturing
E. Transportation, communications, electric, gas, sanitary service
F. Wholesale trade
G. Retail trade
H. Finance, insurance, real estate
I. Service
J. Public administration

Standard Industrial Code - Enter the four-digit code from pages 3 and 4 of these instructions that best describes your business:
— show vendors enter 5934
— entertainment vendors enter 5965
— regular vendors and temporary vendors. Look for the letter that you entered as the major division. Choose one code from that division that further describes the activity. Enter the code in the appropriate box.

Line 19 — You are a sidewalk vendor if you do **not** have a permanent business location, you do **not** participate **only** in flea markets or other shows, and you make sales from a portable stand, pushcart or other device in New York City.

Line 20 — Check "yes" if you do not have a permanent place of business and you participate exclusively in flea markets or other shows.

Line 21 — If yes, you must file Form ST-134. For forms, call us at the numbers listed in the *Need Help?* section on this page.

Line 22 — If yes, you must file Form MT-102. For forms or information about the beverage container tax, call us at the numbers listed in the *Need Help?* section on this page.

Line 27-35 — Answer *Yes* or *No* to each question. If you answer *Yes* to any question, enter the required information for that line. Attach additional sheets as necessary to fully answer all questions.

Responsible officers, directors, partners and employees are those who act for the business in complying with the Tax Law.

Questions 33 through 35 apply **only** to corporations.

Signature - This application must be signed by a person whose responsibility it is to act for the business in complying with the tax law. This person may be a member of a partnership, an officer or director of a corporation, the owner of a sole proprietorship, or an authorized employee of the business.

If the application is not signed or is incomplete, it will be returned.

Mail your application to NYS Tax Department, Sales Tax Registration Unit, W A Harriman Campus, Albany NY 12227, at least 20 days (but not more than 90 days) before you begin doing business in New York State.

Need Help?

For information, forms or publications, call the Business Tax Information Center at 1 800 972-1233. For information, you can also call toll free 1 800 225-5829. For forms or publications, call toll free 1 800 462-8100.

Telephone assistance is available from 8:30 a.m. to 4:25 p.m., Monday through Friday.

From areas outside the U.S. and Canada, call (518) 485-6800.

Hotline for the Hearing and Speech Impaired - If you have a hearing or speech impairment and have access to a telecommunications device for the deaf (TDD), you can get answers to your New York State tax questions by calling toll free from the U.S. and Canada 1 800 634-2110. Hours of operation are from 8:30 a.m. to 4:15 p.m., Monday through Friday. If you do not own a TDD, check with independent living centers or community action programs to find out where machines are available for public use.

Persons with Disabilities - In compliance with the Americans with Disabilities Act, we will ensure that our lobbies, offices, meeting rooms and other facilities are accessible to persons with disabilities. If you have questions about special accommodations for persons with disabilities, please call the information numbers listed above.

If you need to write, address your letter to: NYS Tax Department, Taxpayer Assistance Bureau, W A Harriman Campus, Albany NY 12227.

Privacy Notification
The right of the Commissioner of Taxation and Finance and the Department of Taxation and Finance to collect and maintain personal information, including mandatory disclosure of social security numbers in the manner required by tax regulations, instructions and forms, is found in Articles 22, 26, 26-A, 26-B, 30, 30-A and 30-B of the Tax Law, Article 2-E of the General City Law and 42 USC 405(c)(2)(C)(i).

The Tax Department will use this information primarily to determine and administer tax liabilities due the state and city of New York and the city of Yonkers. We will also use this information for certain tax offset and exchange of tax information programs authorized by law, and for any other purpose authorized by law.

Information concerning quarterly wages paid to employees and identified by unique random identifying code numbers to preserve the privacy of the employees' names and social security numbers will be provided to certain state agencies for research purposes to evaluate the effectiveness of certain employment and training programs.

Failure to provide the required information may result in civil or criminal penalties, or both, under the Tax Law.

This information will be maintained by the Director of the Data Management Services Bureau, NYS Tax Department, Building 8 Room 905, W A Harriman Campus, Albany NY 12227; telephone 1 800 225-5829; from areas outside the U.S. and Canada, call (518) 485-6800.

Code

A. Agriculture, Forestry, and Fishing

0100	Agricultural production - primarily crops
0200	Agricultural production - primarily livestock
0720	Soil and crop services
0740	Veterinary services
0750	Animal husbandry and specialty services
0780	Landscaping, lawn and garden, and tree service
0800	Forestry and Christmas tree farms
0900	Fishing, hunting and trapping, commercial

B. Mining

1000	Metal mining and services
1200	Coal mining and services
1300	Oil and gas extraction and field services
1400	Non-metallic minerals, stone, sand and gravel, etc.

C. Construction

1521	General building contractors
1531	Operative builders
1600	Heavy construction contractors, except building
1711	Plumbing, heating, air conditioning
1721	Painting and paper hanging
1731	Electrical work
1741	Masonry and other stonework
1742	Plastering, drywall, and insulation
1743	Terrazzo, tile, marble, mosaic work
1751	Carpentry work
1752	Floor laying and floor work, not elsewhere classified
1761	Roofing, siding, and sheet metal work
1771	Concrete work
1781	Water well drilling
1791	Structural steel erection
1793	Glaziers
1794	Excavation and foundation work
1795	Demolition
1796	Building equipment installation
1799	Misc. special trade contractors (describe on line 18)

D. Manufacturing

2010	Meat products
2020	Dairy products
2030	Preserved fruits and vegetables
2040	Grain mill products
2050	Bakery products
2060	Sugar and confectionery products
2070	Fats and oils
2082	Malt beverages
2084	Wine and brandy
2085	Liquors, distilled or blended
2086	Soft drinks
2090	Other food products
2100	Tobacco products
2200	Textile mill products
2300	Apparel and other textile products
2411	Logging camps and contractors
2421	Sawmills and planing mills
2431	Millwork, plywood and veneers
2499	Wood products other than furniture
2500	Furniture and fixtures, all materials
2611	Pulp and paper mills
2650	Paper board containers and boxes
2679	Converted paper and paper board products
2711	Newspapers: publishing or publishing and printing
2721	Periodicals: publishing or publishing and printing
2731	Books: publishing or publishing and printing
2759	Commercial print shops
2790	Printing trade services
2810	Industrial chemicals

Code

2820	Plastic materials
2830	Drugs
2840	Soap, cleaners, and toilet goods
2850	Paints and allied products
2870	Agricultural chemical products
2899	Misc. chemical products (describe on line 18)
2900	Petroleum refining and related industries including asphalt and asphalt construction materials
3000	Rubber and misc. plastic products (except bottles)
3085	Plastic bottles
3100	Leather and leather products
3200	Stone, clay, concrete and glass products (except bottles)
3221	Glass bottles
3300	Primary metal industries, smelting and refining, rolling mills
3400	Fabricated metal products (except machinery, transportation equipment and metal cans)
3411	Metal cans
3500	Industrial and commercial machinery and computer equipment
3600	Electronic and other electrical equipment and components (except computer equipment)
3700	Transportation equipment
3800	Measurement, analysis and control instructions; photographic, medical and optical goods; watches and clocks
3900	Miscellaneous manufacturing industries (describe on line 18)

E. Transportation and Public Utilities

4000	Railroad transportation
4100	Local and interurban passenger transit
4200	Trucking and warehousing
4400	Water transportation
4500	Transportation by air
4600	Pipelines, except natural gas (4920)
4700	Miscellaneous transportation services (describe on line 18)
4800	Telephone, telegraph, and other communication services including paging and beeper services and fax services
4830	Radio and television broadcasting
4899	Misc. communications services (describe on line 18)
4911	Electric services
4920	Gas production and distribution
4930	Combination utility services
4941	Water supply
4950	Other sanitary services such as sewerage, refuse collection, landfills, incineration, etc.

F. Wholesale Trade

5010	Motor vehicles and automotive equipment including tires and parts
5020	Furniture and home furnishings
5030	Lumber and construction materials
5040	Professional and commercial equipment and supplies including computers and hospital equipment
5050	Metals and minerals, except gems, petroleum, precious metals
5060	Electrical goods and applicances
5070	Hardware, plumbing and heating equipment and supplies
5080	Machinery, equipment and supplies, construction, farm and industrial
5093	Scrap, including cars and recycling of used materials
5094	Jewelry, precious metals and gems
5099	Other durable goods not classified elsewhere (describe on line 18)
5110	Paper and paper products
5120	Drugs, drug proprietaries, and drugists' sundries
5130	Apparel, piece goods and notions

Code

5140	Groceries and related products
5150	Farm-product raw materials
5160	Chemicals and allied products
5170	Petroleum and petroleum products
5180	Alcoholic beverages
5190	Misc. nondurable goods (describe on line 18)
5194	Tobacco and tobacco products

G. Retail Trade
Building Materials and Garden Supplies

5211	Lumber and other building materials dealers
5231	Paint, glass and wallpaper stores
5251	Hardware stores
5261	Retail nurseries, lawn and garden supply stores and Christmas trees
5271	Mobile home dealers

General Merchandise Stores

5311	Department stores
5331	Variety stores

Food Stores

5411	Grocery stores
5421	Meat and seafood markets including freezer provisioners
5431	Fruit and vegetable markets
5441	Candy, nut and confectionery stores
5451	Dairy products stores
5461	Retail bakeries
5471	Convenience stores with gasoline
5499	Specialty food stores, including coffee stores, health food stores, etc.

Automotive Dealers and Service Stations

5511	Motor vehicle dealers (new and used)
5521	Motor vehicle dealers (used only)
5531	Automotive supply stores
5541	Gasoline service stations
5551	Boat dealers
5561	Recreational vehicle dealers
5571	Motorcycle dealers
5599	Misc. automotive dealers, including airplanes, snowmobiles, etc.

Apparel and Accessory Stores

5611	Men's and boy's clothing and accessory stores
5621	Women's clothing stores
5632	Women's accessory and specialty stores
5641	Children's and infants' wear stores
5651	Family clothing stores
5661	Shoe stores
5699	Misc. apparel and accessory stores, including uniform, T-shirt, and wig stores

Furniture and Home Furnishings Stores

5712	Furniture stores
5713	Floor covering stores
5714	Drapery, curtain and upholstery stores
5722	Household appliance stores
5731	Radio, television and consumer electronics stores
5734	Computer and computer software stores
5735	Record and prerecorded tap stores, except video rentals (7841)
5736	Musical instrument stores

Eating and Drinking Places

5812	Restaurants
5813	Bars
5814	Cafeterias, buffets
5815	Caterers
5816	Sidewalk vendor - food
5822	Fast food
5823	Night clubs, cabarets

Code

Miscellaneous Retail

5912	Drug stores and proprietary stores
5921	Liquor stores
5932	Used merchandise and antique stores
5934	Flea market vendors
5941	Sporting goods and bicycle stores
5942	Book stores
5943	Stationery stores
5944	Jewelry stores
5945	Hobby, toy and game shops
5946	Camera and photographic supply stores
5947	Gift, novelty, card and souvenir shops
5948	Luggage and leather goods
5949	Sewing, needlework and piece goods stores
5961	Catalog and mail-order houses
5962	Automatic merchandising machine operators
5963	Direct selling establishment operators
5965	Entertainer's concert memorabilia-(records, T-shirts, etc.)
5983	Fuel oil dealers
5984	Liquefied petroleum gas dealers
5991	Nonfood peddlers
5992	Florists
5993	Tobacco stores and stands
5994	Newsdealers and newstands
5995	Optical goods stores
5999	Miscellaneous retail stores - art dealers, pet stores, tombstones, etc. (describe on line 18)

H. Finance, Insurance, Real Estate

6000	Depository institutions
6100	Nondepository credit institutions
6200	Security and commodity brokers, dealers, exchanges and services
6300	Insurance carriers
6400	Insurance agents, brokers, and services
6510	Real estate operators, residential and nonresidential
6531	Real estate agents and managers
6541	Title abstracts and title searchers
6552	Land subdividers and developers
6700	Holding and other investment offices

I. Services

Hotels and Other Lodging Places

7011	Hotels
7021	Rooming and boarding houses
7030	Camps and recreational vehicle parks
7041	Organization hotels and lodging houses, membership basis

Personal Services

7211	Power laundries, family and commercial
7213	Linen supply
7215	Coin-operated laundries and dry cleaning
7216	Dry cleaning plants, except rug cleaning
7217	Carpet and upholstery cleaning
7218	Industrial launderers
7219	Tailer shops
7221	Photographic studios, portrait
7231	Beauty shops
7241	Barber shops
7251	Shoe repair shops and shoe-shine parlors
7261	Funeral service and crematories
7291	Tax return preparation services
7299	Miscellaneous personal services including buying services, diet workshops, tanning salons, clothing rental, etc. (describe on line 18)

Business Services

7310	Advertising agencies and services
7320	Consumer credit reporting and collection agencies
7330	Mailing and Reproduction
7335	Commercial photography
7336	Commercial art and graphic design
7338	Stenographic services

Code

7342	Disinfecting and pest control
7349	Building cleaning and maintenance services including domestic housecleaning
7350	Misc. equipment rental and leasing (except computer)
7361	Employment agencies
7371	Computer programming services
7373	Computer integrated systems designs
7374	Computer processing and data preparation and processing
7377	Computer rental and leasing
7378	Computer maintenance and repair
7379	Computer consultants
7381	Detective, guard and armored car service
7382	Security systems services
7383	News syndicates
7384	Photofinishing laboratories
7388	Telephone answering service
7389	Miscellaneous business services including telemarketing, interior decorators, etc. (describe on line 18)

Auto Repair, Services and Parking

7510	Automotive rentals, and leasing without drivers
7521	Automobile parking
7532	Body repair and paint shops
7533	Exhaust system repair shops
7536	Auto glass installation
7537	Transmission shops
7538	General automotive repair shops
7542	Car washes
7549	Automotive services, except repairs (describe on line 18)

Miscellaneous Repair Services

7622	Radio and Television repair
7623	Refrigerator and air conditioner repair
7629	Electrical and electronic repair
7631	Watch, clock and jewelry repair
7641	Reupholstery and furniture repair
7692	Welding repair
7699	Miscellaneous repair shops and services (describe on line 18)

Motion Pictures

7810	Motion picture and video tape production and allied services
7820	Motion picture and video tape distribution
7830	Motion picture theaters
7841	Video tape rentals

Amusement and Recreation Services

7911	Dance halls, studios and schools
7922	Theatrical producers and theatrical services
7929	Bands, orchestras, and entertainers
7933	Bowling alleys
7940	Commercial sports clubs and promoters
7948	Racetrack operation, all types
7991	Physical fitness facilities
7992	Public golf courses
7993	Coin-operated amusement devices
7996	Amusement parks
7997	Membership sports and recreation clubs
7999	Amusement and recreation services including circus, fair and carnival operation, miniature golf, boat rental, rafting, nonmembership golf and tennis, etc. (describe on line 18)

Health Services

8011	Offices and clinics of doctors of medicine
8021	Offices and clinics of dentists
8041	Offices and clinics of chiropractors
8042	Offices and clinics of optometrists
8043	Offices and clinics of podiatrists
8049	Offices and clinics of other health practitioners

Code

8050	Nursing and personal care facilities
8060	Hospitals
8071	Medical laboratories
8072	Dental laboratories
8082	Home health services
8090	Other health services (describe on line 18)

Legal Services

8111	Legal services

Educational Services

8211	Elementary and secondary schools
8221	Colleges, universities, and professional schools
8222	Junior colleges and technical institutions
8231	Libraries
8240	Vocational schools
8299	Educational services including music schools, flying instruction, etc. (describe on line 18)

Social Services

8322	Individual and family services
8331	Job training and related services
8351	Child day care services
8361	Residential care-rest homes, rehabilitation centers, old-age homes, halfway houses
8399	Miscellaneous social services including United Fund, Community Action, etc. (describe on line 18)

Museums, Botanical, Zoological Gardens

8400	Museums, art galleries (not retail art dealers), botanical, zoological gardens

Membership organizations

8611	Business associations
8621	Professional membership organization
8631	Labor unions and labor organizations
8641	Civic, social and fraternal associations
8651	Political associations
8661	Religious organizations
8699	Miscellaneous member organizations including art councils, farm bureaus, humane societies, etc. (describe on line 18)

Engineering and Management Services

8711	Engineering services
8712	Architectural services
8713	Surveying services
8721	Accounting, auditing and bookkeeping services
8731	Commercial physical and biological research
8732	Commercial economic, sociological and educational research
8733	Noncommercial research organizations
8734	Testing laboratories
8741	Management services
8742	Management consulting services
8743	Public relations services
8744	Facilities support management services
8748	Business consulting services

Private Households

8800	Private households employing others for domestic services (those providing the service generally are in 7349 or 0780)

Miscellaneous Services

8999	Services not classified elsewhere - inventors, artists, authors, lecturers, etc. (describe on line 18)

J. Public Administration

9100	Executive, legislative and general government (describe on line 18)

TRADEMARK/SERVICE MARK APPLICATION, PRINCIPAL REGISTER, WITH DECLARATION	MARK (Word(s) and/or Design)	CLASS NO. (If known)

TO THE ASSISTANT COMMISSIONER FOR TRADEMARKS:

APPLICANT'S NAME: _____

APPLICANT'S MAILING ADDRESS: _____

(Display address exactly as it should appear on registration) _____

APPLICANT'S ENTITY TYPE: (**Check one** and supply requested information)

Individual - Citizen of (Country): _____

Partnership - State where organized (Country, if appropriate): _____
Names and Citizenship (Country) of General Partners: _____

Corporation - State (Country, if appropriate) of Incorporation: _____

Other (Specify Nature of Entity and Domicile): _____

GOODS AND/OR SERVICES:

Applicant requests registration of the trademark/service mark shown in the accompanying drawing in the United States Patent and Trademark Office on the Principal Register established by the Act of July 5, 1946 (15 U.S.C. 1051 et. seq., as amended) for the following goods/services (**SPECIFIC GOODS AND/OR SERVICES MUST BE INSERTED HERE**)

_____
_____
_____
_____
_____

BASIS FOR APPLICATION: (Check boxes which apply, **but never both the first AND second boxes,** and supply requested information related to each box checked.)

[ ] Applicant is using the mark in commerce on or in connection with the above identified goods/services. (15 U.S.C. 1051(a), as amended.) Three specimens showing the mark as used in commerce are submitted with this application.
- Date of first use of the mark in commerce which the U.S. Congress may regulate (for example, interstate or between the U.S. and a foreign country): _____
- Specify the type of commerce: _____
(for example, interstate or between the U.S. and a specified foreign country)
- Date of first use anywhere (the same as or before use in commerce date): _____
- Specify manner or mode of use of mark on or in connection with the goods/services: _____
(for example, trademark is applied to labels, service mark is used in advertisements)

[ ] Applicant has a bona fide intention to use the mark in commerce on or in connection with the above identified goods/services. (15 U.S.C. 1051(b), as amended.)
- Specify intended manner or mode of use of mark on or in connection with the goods/services: _____
(for example, trademark will be applied to labels, service mark will be used in advertisements)

[ ] Applicant has a bona fide intention to use the mark in commerce on or in connection with the above identified goods/services, and asserts a claim of priority based upon a foreign application in accordance with 15 U.S.C. 1126(d), as amended.
- Country of foreign filing: _____ ● Date of foreign filing: _____

[ ] Applicant has a bona fide intention to use the mark in commerce on or in connection with the above identified goods/services and, accompanying this application, submits a certification or certified copy of a foreign registration in accordance with 15 U.S.C 1126(e), as amended.
- Country of registration: _____ ● Registration number: _____

NOTE: Declaration, on Reverse Side, MUST be Signed

PTO Form 1478 (REV 6/96)   U.S. DEPARTMENT OF COMMERCE/Patent and Trademark Office
OMB No. 0651-0009 (Exp. 06/30/98) There is no requirement to respond to this collection of information unless a currently valid OMB Number is displayed.

52

DECLARATION

The undersigned being hereby warned that willful false statements and the like so made are punishable by fine or imprisonment, or both, under 18 U.S.C. 1001, and that such willful false statements may jeopardize the validity of the application or any resulting registration, declares that he/she is properly authorized to execute this application on behalf of the applicant; he/she believes the applicant to be the owner of the trademark/service mark sought to be registered, or if the application is being filed under 15 U.S.C. 1051(b), he/she believes the applicant to be entitled to use such mark in commerce; to the best of his/her knowledge and belief no other person, firm, corporation, or association has the right to use the above identified mark in commerce, either in the identical form thereof or in such near resemblance thereto as to be likely, when used on or in connection with the goods/services of such other person, to cause confusion, or to cause mistake, or to deceive; and that all statements made of his/her own knowledge are true and that all statements made on information and belief are believed to be true.

_____   _____
DATE   SIGNATURE

_____   _____
TELEPHONE NUMBER   PRINT OR TYPE NAME AND POSITION

INSTRUCTIONS AND INFORMATION FOR APPLICANT

TO RECEIVE A FILING DATE, THE APPLICATION MUST BE COMPLETED AND SIGNED BY THE APPLICANT AND SUBMITTED ALONG WITH:

1. The prescribed **FEE ($245.00)** for each class of goods/services listed in the application;
2. A **DRAWING PAGE** displaying the mark in conformance with 37 CFR 2.52;
3. If the application is based on use of the mark in commerce, **THREE (3) SPECIMENS** (evidence) of the mark as used in commerce for each class of goods/services listed in the application. All three specimens may be the same. Examples of good specimens include: (a) labels showing the mark which are placed on the goods; (b) photographs of the mark as it appears on the goods, (c) brochures or advertisements showing the mark as used in connection with the services.
4. An **APPLICATION WITH DECLARATION** (this form) - The application must be signed in order for the application to receive a filing date. Only the following persons may sign the declaration, depending on the applicant's legal entity: (a) the individual applicant; (b) an officer of the corporate applicant; (c) one general partner of a partnership applicant; (d) all joint applicants.

SEND APPLICATION FORM, DRAWING PAGE, FEE, AND SPECIMENS (IF APPROPRIATE) TO:

Assistant Commissioner for Trademarks
Box New App/Fee
2900 Crystal Drive
Arlington, VA 22202-3513

Additional information concerning the requirements for filing an application is available in a booklet entitled **Basic Facts About Registering a Trademark,** which may be obtained by writing to the above address or by calling: (703) 308-HELP.

This form is estimated to take an average of 1 hour to complete, including time required for reading and understanding instructions, gathering necessary information, recordkeeping, and actually providing the information. Any comments on this form, including the amount of time required to complete this form, should be sent to the Office of Management and Organization, U.S. Patent and Trademark Office, U.S. Department of Commerce, Washington, D.C. 20231. Do NOT send completed forms to this address.

**EXCERPT FROM
GOVERNMENT BROCHURE
ABOUT TRADEMARKS**

TRADEMARK ASSISTANCE
CENTER

In order to provide improved service to trademark applicants, registrants, and the general public, the Patent and Trademark Office has implemented a pilot program called the "Trademark Assistance Center." The Center provides general information about the trademark registration process and responds to inquiries pertaining to the status of specific trademark applications and registrations. The location of the Center is 2900 Crystal Drive, Room 4B10, Arlington, Virginia 22202-3513. Assistance may be obtained in person or by dialing (703) 308-9000, Monday through Friday, 8:30 A.M. – 5:00 P.M. eastern time, except holidays. Please note that personal assistance concerning trademark as well as patent matters will continue to be available at (703) 308-HELP and recorded information will continue to be available at (703) 557-INFO. Also, automated information about the status of trademark applications and registrations will continue to be available at (703) 305-8747.

Form **8594**	**Asset Acquisition Statement**	OMB No. 1545-1021
(Rev. July 1998) Department of the Treasury Internal Revenue Service	**Under Section 1060** ▶ **Attach to your Federal income tax return.**	Attachment Sequence No. **61**

Name as shown on return	Identification number as shown on return

Check the box that identifies you: ☐ Buyer   ☐ Seller

Part I General Information—To be completed by all filers.

1 Name of other party to the transaction	Other party's identification number

Address (number, street, and room or suite no.)

City or town, state, and ZIP code

2 Date of sale	3 Total sales price

Part II Assets Transferred—To be completed by all filers of an original statement.

4 Assets	Aggregate Fair Market Value (Actual Amount for Class I)	Allocation of Sales Price
Class I	$	$
Class II	$	$
Class III	$	$
Classes IV and V	$	$
Total	$	$

5 Did the buyer and seller provide for an allocation of the sales price in the sales contract or in another written document signed by both parties? . . . . ☐ Yes ☐ No

If "Yes," are the aggregate fair market values listed for each of asset Classes I, II, III, IV and V the amounts agreed upon in your sales contract or in a separate written document? . . . . ☐ Yes ☐ No

6 In connection with the purchase of the group of assets, did the buyer also purchase a license or a covenant not to compete, or enter into a lease agreement, employment contract, management contract, or similar arrangement with the seller (or managers, directors, owners, or employees of the seller)? . . . . ☐ Yes ☐ No

If "Yes," specify (a) the type of agreement, and (b) the maximum amount of consideration (not including interest) paid or to be paid under the agreement. See the instructions for line 6.

Form 8594 (Rev. 7-98)

Part III			

Part III   **Supplemental Statement**—To be completed only if amending an original statement or previously filed supplemental statement because of an increase or decrease in consideration.

7 Assets	Allocation of Sales Price as Previously Reported	Increase or (Decrease)	Redetermined Allocation of Sales Price
Class I	$	$	$
Class II	$	$	$
Class III	$	$	$
Classes IV and V	$	$	$
Total	$		$

8   Reason(s) for increase or decrease. Attach additional sheets if more space is needed.

_____

_____

_____

_____

_____

_____

_____

_____

_____

_____

9   Tax year and tax return form number with which the original Form 8594 and any supplemental statements were filed.

General Instructions

Section references are to the Internal Revenue Code unless otherwise noted.

A Change To Note

New temporary regulations under sections 1060 and 338 clarified the rules for allocating assets acquired after February 13, 1997. Under the new rules, all section 197 intangibles (other than goodwill and going concern value) are included in Class IV. Goodwill and going concern value are assigned to a new class, Class V. See "Class IV" and "Class V" under **Definitions** below.

Purpose of Form

Both the seller and buyer of a group of assets that makes up a trade or business must use Form 8594 to report such a sale if goodwill or going concern value attaches, or could attach, to such assets and if the buyer's basis in the assets is determined only by the amount paid for the assets ("applicable asset acquisition," defined below). Form 8594 must also be filed if the buyer or seller is amending an original or a previously filed supplemental Form 8594 because of an increase or decrease in the buyer's cost of the assets or the amount realized by the seller.

Who Must File

Subject to the exceptions noted below, both the buyer and the seller of the assets must prepare and attach Form 8594 to their Federal income tax returns (Forms 1040, 1041, 1065, 1120, 1120S, etc.).

Exceptions. You are not required to file Form 8594 if any of the following apply:

1. The acquisition is not an applicable asset acquisition (defined below).

2. A group of assets that makes up a trade or business is exchanged for like-kind property in a transaction to which section 1031 applies. However, if section 1031 does not apply to all the assets transferred, Form 8594 is required for the part of the group of assets to which section 1031 does not apply. For information about such a transaction, see Regulations section 1.1060-1T(b)(4).

3. A partnership interest is transferred. See Regulations section 1.755-2T for special reporting requirements.

When To File

Generally, attach Form 8594 to your Federal income tax return for the year in which the sale date occurred. If the amount allocated to any asset is increased or decreased after Form 8594 is filed, the seller and/or buyer (whoever is affected) must complete Part I and the supplemental statement in Part III of a new Form 8594 and attach the form to the Federal tax return for the year in which the increase or decrease is taken into account.

Penalty

If you fail to file a correct Form 8594 by the due date of your return and you cannot show reasonable cause, you may be subject to a penalty. See sections 6721 through 6724.

Definitions

"Applicable asset acquisition" means a transfer of a group of assets that makes up a trade or business in which the buyer's basis in such assets is determined wholly by the amount paid for the assets. An applicable asset acquisition includes both a direct and indirect transfer of a group of assets, such as a sale of a business.

A group of assets makes up a "trade or business" if goodwill or going concern value could under any circumstances attach to such assets. A group of assets could qualify as a trade or business whether or not they qualify as an active trade or business under section 355 (relating to controlled corporations). Factors to consider in making this determination include (a) any excess of the total paid for the assets over the aggregate book value of the assets (other than goodwill or going concern value) as shown in the buyer's financial accounting books and records, or (b) a license, a lease agreement, a covenant not to compete, a management contract, an employment contract, or other similar agreements between buyer and seller (or managers, directors, owners, or employees of the seller).

The buyer's "consideration" is the cost of the assets. The seller's "consideration" is the amount realized.

"Fair market value" is the gross fair market value unreduced by mortgages, liens, pledges, or other liabilities. However, for determining the seller's gain or loss, generally, the fair market value of any property is not less than any nonrecourse debt to which the property is subject.

The following definitions apply to applicable acquisitions after February 13, 1997. For transitional rules that apply to acquisitions before February 14, 1997, see **Transitional Rules** on page 4.

"Class I assets" are cash, demand deposits, and similar accounts in banks, savings and loan associations, and other depository institutions, and other similar items that may be designated in the Internal Revenue Bulletin.

"Class II assets" are certificates of deposit, U.S. Government securities, readily marketable stock or securities, foreign currency, and other items that may be designated in the Internal Revenue Bulletin.

"Class III assets" are all tangible and intangible assets that are not Class I, II, IV, or V assets. Amortizable section 197 intangibles are Class IV assets. Examples of Class III assets are furniture and fixtures, land, buildings, equipment, and accounts receivable.

"Class IV assets" are all amortizable section 197 intangibles, except for goodwill and going concern value. Amortizable section 197 intangibles include:

● Workforce in place,

● Business books and records, operating systems, or any other information base,

● Any patent, copyright, formula, process, design, pattern, know-how, format, or similar item,

● Any customer-based intangible,

● Any supplier-based intangible,

● Any license, permit, or other right granted by a governmental unit,

● Any covenant not to compete entered into in connection with the acquisition of an interest in a trade or a business, and

● Any franchise (other than a sports franchise), trademark, or trade name.

However, the term "section 197 intangible" **does not** include any of the following:

● An interest in a corporation, partnership, trust, or estate,

● Interests under certain financial contracts,

● Interests in land,

● Certain computer software,

● Certain separately acquired interests in films, sound recordings, video tapes, books, or other similar property,

● Certain separately acquired rights to receive tangible property or services,

● Certain separately acquired interests in patents or copyrights,

● Interests under leases of tangible property,

● Interests under indebtedness,

● Professional sports franchises,

● Certain transaction costs.

See section 197(e) for further information.

"Class V assets" are section 197 intangibles in the nature of goodwill and going concern value.

Allocation of Consideration

An allocation of the purchase price must be made to determine the buyer's basis in each acquired asset and the seller's gain or loss on the transfer of each asset. Use the residual method for the allocation of the sales price among the amortizable section 197 intangibles and other assets transferred. See Regulations section 1.1060-1T(d). The amount allocated to an asset, other than a Class V asset, cannot exceed its fair market value on the purchase date. The amount you can allocate to an asset also is subject to any applicable limits under the Internal Revenue Code or general principles of tax law. For example, see section 1056 for the basis limitation for player contracts transferred in connection with the sale of a franchise.

Consideration should be allocated as follows: **(a)** reduce the consideration by the amount of Class I assets transferred, **(b)** allocate the remaining consideration to Class II assets in proportion to their fair market values on the purchase date, **(c)** allocate to Class III assets in proportion to their fair market values on the purchase date, **(d)** allocate to Class IV assets in proportion to their fair market values on the purchase date, and **(e)** allocate to Class V assets.

Reallocation After an Increase or Decrease in Consideration

If an increase or decrease in consideration that must be taken into account to redetermine the seller's amount realized on the sale, or the buyer's cost basis in the assets, occurs after the purchase date, the seller and/or buyer must allocate the increase or decrease among the assets. If the increase or decrease occurs in the same tax year as the purchase date, consider the increase or decrease to have occurred on the purchase date. If the increase or decrease occurs after the tax year of the purchase date, consider it in the tax year in which it occurs.

For an increase or decrease related to a patent, copyright, etc., see **Specific Allocation** below.

Allocation of Increase

Allocate an increase in consideration as described under **Allocation of Consideration.** If an asset has been disposed of, depreciated, amortized, or depleted by the buyer before the increase occurs, any amount allocated to such asset by the buyer must be properly taken into account under principles of tax law applicable when part of the cost of an asset (not previously reflected in its basis) is paid after the asset has been disposed of, depreciated, amortized, or depleted.

Allocation of Decrease

Allocate a decrease in consideration as follows: **(a)** reduce the amount previously allocated to Class V assets, **(b)** reduce the amount previously allocated to Class IV assets in proportion to their fair market values on the purchase date, **(c)** reduce the amount previously allocated to Class III assets in proportion to their fair market values on the purchase date, and **(d)** reduce the amount previously allocated to Class II assets in proportion to their fair market values on the purchase date.

You cannot decrease the amount allocated to an asset below zero. If an asset has a basis of zero at the time the decrease is taken into account because it has been disposed of, depreciated, amortized, or depleted by the buyer, the decrease in consideration allocable to such asset must be properly taken into account under principles of tax law applicable when the cost of an asset (previously reflected in basis) is reduced after the asset has been disposed of, depreciated, amortized, or depleted. An asset is considered to have been disposed of to the extent the decrease allocated to it would reduce its basis below zero.

Transitional Rules

For acquisitions before February 14, 1997, that do not include section 197 intangibles, you must use the prior rules (the rules in effect before the issuance of new temporary regulations on January 9, 1997). See *Allocation of consideration under prior rules* below.

For acquisitions before February 14, 1997, that include section 197 intangibles, you may consistently:

● Apply the rules and definitions contained in these instructions and in Temporary regulations section 1.1060-1T;

● Apply the prior rules and definitions described below under *Allocation of consideration under prior rules;* or

● Apply the prior rules and definitions, but treat amortizable section 197 intangibles as Class IV assets.

Allocation of consideration under prior rules. Under the prior rules, purchase price is allocated to the following four classes:

"Class I assets," which include cash and demand deposits.

"Class II assets," which include highly liquid assets (e.g., readily marketable securities and certificates of deposit).

"Class III assets," which include all transferred assets that are not in Classes I, II, and IV. This includes tangible and intangible assets, whether or not depreciable, depletable, or amortizable (e.g. furniture, equipment, buildings, accounts receivable, and covenants not to compete).

"Class IV assets," which include assets in the nature of goodwill and going concern value.

Patents, Copyrights, and Similar Property

You must make a specific allocation (defined below) if an increase or decrease in consideration is the result of a contingency that directly relates to income produced by a particular intangible asset, such as a patent, a secret process, or a copyright, and the increase or decrease is related only to such asset and not to other assets. If the specific allocation rule does not apply, make an allocation of any increase or decrease as you would for any other assets as described under **Allocation of Increase** and **Allocation of Decrease.**

Specific Allocation

Limited to the fair market value of the asset, any increase or decrease in consideration is allocated first specifically to the patent, copyright, or similar property to which the increase or decrease relates, and then to the other assets in the order described under **Allocation of Increase** and **Allocation of Decrease.** For purposes of applying the fair market value limit to the patent, copyright, or similar property, the fair market value of such property is redetermined when the increase or decrease is taken into account by considering only the reasons for the increase or decrease. The fair market values of the other assets are not redetermined.

Specific Instructions

For an original statement, complete Parts I and II. For a Supplemental Statement, complete Parts I and III.

Enter your name and taxpayer identification number (TIN) at the top of the form. Then check the box for buyer or seller.

Part I

Line 1. Enter the name, address, and TIN of the other party to the transaction (buyer or seller). You are required to enter the TIN of the other party. If the other party is an individual or sole proprietor, enter the social security number. If the other party is a corporation, partnership, or other entity, enter the employer identification number.

Line 2. Enter the date on which the sale of the assets occurred.

Line 3. Enter the total consideration transferred for the assets.

Part II

Line 4. For a particular class of assets, enter the total fair market value of all the assets in the class and the total allocation of the sales price. For Classes IV and V, enter the total fair market value of Class IV and Class V combined, and the total portion of the sales price allocated to Class IV and Class V combined.

Line 6. This line must be completed by the buyer and the seller. To determine the maximum consideration to be paid, assume that any contingencies specified in the agreement are met and that the consideration paid is the highest amount possible. If you cannot determine the maximum consideration, state how the consideration will be computed and the payment period.

Part III

Complete Part III and file a new Form 8594 for each year that an increase or decrease in consideration occurs. Give the reason(s) for the increase or decrease in allocation. Also, enter the tax year(s) and form number with which the original and any supplemental statements were filed. For example, enter "1997 Form 1040."

Paperwork Reduction Act Notice

We ask for the information on this form to carry out the Internal Revenue laws of the United States. You are required to give us the information. We need it to ensure that you are complying with these laws and to allow us to figure and collect the right amount of tax.

You are not required to provide the information requested on a form that is subject to the Paperwork Reduction Act unless the form displays a valid OMB control number. Books or records relating to a form or its instructions must be retained as long as their contents may become material in the administration of any Internal Revenue law. Generally, tax returns and return information are confidential, as required by section 6103.

The time needed to complete and file this form will vary depending on individual circumstances. The estimated average time is:

Recordkeeping	8 hr., 51 min.
Learning about the law or the form	1 hr., 35 min.
Preparing and sending the form to the IRS . . .	1 hr., 49 min.

If you have comments concerning the accuracy of these time estimates or suggestions for making this form simpler, we would be happy to hear from you. You can write to the IRS at the address listed in the instructions for the tax return with which this form is filed.

BULK SALES AGREEMENT

Reprinted by permission of the 'Lectric Law Library Legal Website at www.lectlaw.com.

1. PARTIES. This contract is made this _____, 19 ____ between _____ of _____ , herein called "Sellers," and _____ herein called "Buyer."

2. AGREEMENT TO SALE. The Sellers shall sell to the Buyer, and the Buyer shall buy from the Sellers, all of that certain stock of goods, wares and merchandise belonging to the Sellers, and now located in the storeroom at _____ , together with all furniture and fixtures therein, belonging to the Sellers.

3. STORE CLOSED FOR INVENTORY. Upon the execution and delivery of this contract, properly signed and executed, and the payment of the earnest money hereinafter mentioned, the store shall be closed temporarily, and an inventory taken immediately, and delivered to the Buyer, at the invoice cost $ _____ , without including transportation charges or expenses, deducting, however, any depreciation on account of damage, wear and tear.

4. INVOICE VALUATION OR ARBITRATION. The goods, wares and merchandise and furniture and fixtures shall be inventoried at _____ .

5. TIME TO COMPLETE INVENTORY. Ten days shall be allowed to complete the inventories, upon which date all of the property shall be thereupon delivered by the Sellers to the Buyer.

6. DEPOSIT IN ESCROW TO SECURE COMPLIANCE WITH BULK SALES LAW. The Buyer, in consideration of the premises, shall, upon the execution of this contract, deposit in escrow in the _____ Bank, the sum of $ _____ as earnest money to bind the trade, the sum to be returned to the Buyer in case the Sellers fail to make good title to the property, and upon the consummation of the deal and the tender of the Sellers to the Buyer of their certain bill of sale to the property, showing that the Sellers have complied with all the requirements and conditions of the Bulk Sales Law of _____ and that they will furnish to Buyer a full and complete list of all creditors of the store, together with the amounts due the creditors, that the creditors shall be immediately paid in full such amounts as may be due them, and that the total amount shown to be due by the Sellers shall be deposited in escrow in _____ Bank, until all creditors of the store shall give a release of their claim against the store, or the individual members thereof, the Buyer shall pay to the Sellers the total amount of the invoice in cash and the payment shall be accepted in full payment for the property.

7. LIQUIDATED DAMAGES. All the stipulations, agreements and conditions contained in this contract are to apply to and to bind the heirs, executors and administrators of the respective parties hereto, and, in case of failure, the parties bind themselves each to the other in the sum of $ _____ Dollars, as fixed and settled damages to be paid by the failing party.

_____   _____
SELLERS   BUYER

BULK SALES AFFIDAVIT

Reprinted by permission of the 'Lectric Law Library Legal Website at www.lectlaw.com.

State of _____

County of _____

_____ ,of lawful age, being first duly sworn, on oath states:

That he the Seller in that certain contract for the sale of the assets dated _____ , 19 _____ between himself, as Seller, and _____ as Buyer:

That this Affidavit is make pursuant to the terms and provisions of the Uniform Commercial Code and is furnished to the above named Buyer in connection with the sale and transfer described and referred to in the above mentioned contract;

That the following is a true, complete and accurate list of all of the creditors of affiant and of all persons who, to the knowledge of affiant, assert of have claimed to assert one or more claims against affiant, together with the correct business addresses or each such creditor or claimant and the amounts due and owing to such creditors and claimants, to wit:

Name and address of Creditor	Business of Claim	Amount Disputed	Admitted or Not
1. _____	_____	_____	_____
2. _____	_____	_____	_____
3. _____	_____	_____	_____

_____
SIGNATURE

SUBSCRIBED and sworn to before me this _____ day of _____ , 19 _____ .

_____
Notary Public

My commission expires: _____

[Notarial Seal]

SCHEDULE C (Form 1040)	**Profit or Loss From Business**	OMB No. 1545-0074
Department of the Treasury Internal Revenue Service (99)	(Sole Proprietorship) ▶ **Partnerships, joint ventures, etc., must file Form 1065 or Form 1065-B.** ▶ **Attach to Form 1040 or Form 1041.** ▶ **See Instructions for Schedule C (Form 1040).**	19**98** Attachment Sequence No. **09**

Name of proprietor | Social security number (SSN)

A Principal business or profession, including product or service (see page C-1) | **B** Enter NEW code from pages C-8 & 9 ▶

C Business name. If no separate business name, leave blank. | **D** Employer ID number (EIN), if any

E Business address (including suite or room no.) ▶ ....
City, town or post office, state, and ZIP code

F Accounting method: **(1)** ☐ Cash **(2)** ☐ Accrual **(3)** ☐ Other (specify) ▶ ....

G Did you "materially participate" in the operation of this business during 1998? If "No," see page C-2 for limit on losses ☐ **Yes** ☐ **No**

H If you started or acquired this business during 1998, check here . . . . ▶ ☐

Part I   Income

1	Gross receipts or sales. **Caution:** *If this income was reported to you on Form W-2 and the "Statutory employee" box on that form was checked, see page C-3 and check here* . . . . . ▶ ☐	**1**	
2	Returns and allowances	**2**	
3	Subtract line 2 from line 1	**3**	
4	Cost of goods sold (from line 42 on page 2)	**4**	
5	**Gross profit.** Subtract line 4 from line 3	**5**	
6	Other income, including Federal and state gasoline or fuel tax credit or refund (see page C-3) . . .	**6**	
7	**Gross income.** Add lines 5 and 6 . . . . ▶	**7**	

Part II   Expenses. Enter expenses for business use of your home **only** on line 30.

8	Advertising	**8**		**19** Pension and profit-sharing plans	**19**	
9	Bad debts from sales or services (see page C-3) . .	**9**		**20** Rent or lease (see page C-5):		
10	Car and truck expenses (see page C-3)	**10**		**a** Vehicles, machinery, and equipment .	**20a**	
				b Other business property . .	**20b**	
11	Commissions and fees . .	**11**		**21** Repairs and maintenance . . .	**21**	
12	Depletion	**12**		**22** Supplies (not included in Part III) .	**22**	
13	Depreciation and section 179 expense deduction (not included in Part III) (see page C-4) . .	**13**		**23** Taxes and licenses	**23**	
				24 Travel, meals, and entertainment:		
14	Employee benefit programs (other than on line 19) . . .	**14**		**a** Travel	**24a**	
15	Insurance (other than health) .	**15**		**b** Meals and entertainment .		
16	Interest:			**c** Enter 50% of line 24b subject to limitations (see page C-6) .		
a	Mortgage (paid to banks, etc.) .	**16a**		**d** Subtract line 24c from line 24b .	**24d**	
b	Other	**16b**		**25** Utilities	**25**	
17	Legal and professional services	**17**		**26** Wages (less employment credits) .	**26**	
18	Office expense	**18**		**27** Other expenses (from line 48 on page 2)	**27**	

28	**Total expenses** before expenses for business use of home. Add lines 8 through 27 in columns ▶	**28**	
29	Tentative profit (loss). Subtract line 28 from line 7	**29**	
30	Expenses for business use of your home. Attach **Form 8829**	**30**	
31	**Net profit or (loss).** Subtract line 30 from line 29. • If a profit, enter on **Form 1040, line 12,** and ALSO on **Schedule SE, line 2** (statutory employees, see page C-6). Estates and trusts, enter on Form 1041, line 3. • If a loss, you MUST go on to line 32.	**31**	
32	If you have a loss, check the box that describes your investment in this activity (see page C-6). • If you checked 32a, enter the loss on **Form 1040, line 12,** and ALSO on **Schedule SE, line 2** (statutory employees, see page C-6). Estates and trusts, enter on Form 1041, line 3. • If you checked 32b, you MUST attach **Form 6198.**	**32a** ☐ All investment is at risk. **32b** ☐ Some investment is not at risk.

For Paperwork Reduction Act Notice, see Form 1040 instructions.   Cat. No. 11334P   **Schedule C (Form 1040) 1998**

Schedule C (Form 1040) 1998   Page **2**

Part III   Cost of Goods Sold (see page C-7)

33   Method(s) used to value closing inventory: **a** ☐ Cost   **b** ☐ Lower of cost or market   **c** ☐ Other (attach explanation)

34   Was there any change in determining quantities, costs, or valuations between opening and closing inventory? If "Yes," attach explanation . . . . ☐ Yes   ☐ No

35	Inventory at beginning of year. If different from last year's closing inventory, attach explanation . .	35
36	Purchases less cost of items withdrawn for personal use	36
37	Cost of labor. Do not include any amounts paid to yourself	37
38	Materials and supplies	38
39	Other costs	39
40	Add lines 35 through 39	40
41	Inventory at end of year	41
42	**Cost of goods sold.** Subtract line 41 from line 40. Enter the result here and on page 1, line 4 . .	42

Part IV   Information on Your Vehicle. Complete this part ONLY if you are claiming car or truck expenses on line 10 and are not required to file Form 4562 for this business. See the instructions for line 13 on page C-4 to find out if you must file.

43   When did you place your vehicle in service for business purposes? (month, day, year) ▶ .... / .... / ....

44   Of the total number of miles you drove your vehicle during 1998, enter the number of miles you used your vehicle for:

a Business ....   **b** Commuting ....   **c** Other ....

45   Do you (or your spouse) have another vehicle available for personal use? . . . . ☐ Yes   ☐ No

46   Was your vehicle available for use during off-duty hours? . . . . ☐ Yes   ☐ No

47a   Do you have evidence to support your deduction? . . . . ☐ Yes   ☐ No

   b   If "Yes," is the evidence written? . . . . ☐ Yes   ☐ No

Part V   Other Expenses. List below business expenses not included on lines 8–26 or line 30.

....		
....		
....		
....		
....		
....		
....		
....		
48 **Total other expenses.** Enter here and on page 1, line 27	48	

1998 Instructions for Schedule C, Profit or Loss From Business

Use Schedule C (Form 1040) to report income or loss from a business you operated or a profession you practiced as a sole proprietor. Also, use Schedule C to report wages and expenses you had as a statutory employee. An activity qualifies as a business if your primary purpose for engaging in the activity is for income or profit and you are involved in the activity with continuity and regularity. For example, a sporadic activity or a hobby does not qualify as a business. To report income from a nonbusiness activity, see the Instructions for Form 1040, line 21.

Small businesses and statutory employees with expenses of $2,500 or less may be able to file Schedule C-EZ instead of Schedule C. See Schedule C-EZ to find out if you qualify to file it.

This activity may subject you to state and local taxes and other requirements such as business licenses and fees. Check with your state and local governments for more information.

General Instructions

A Change To Note

New Activity Codes. The new principal business or professional activity codes on pages C-8 and C-9 are based on the North American Industry Classification System (NAICS), which was developed by the statistical agencies of Canada, Mexico, and the United States in cooperation with the Office of Management and Budget. The NAICS-based codes replace the activity codes previously based on the Standard Industrial Classification (SIC) system.

Other Schedules and Forms You May Have To File

Schedule A to deduct interest, taxes, and casualty losses not related to your business.

Schedule E to report rental real estate and royalty income or (loss) that is **not** subject to self-employment tax.

Schedule F to report profit or (loss) from farming.

Schedule SE to pay self-employment tax on income from any trade or business.

Form 4562 to claim depreciation on assets placed in service in 1998, to claim amortization that began in 1998, or to report information on listed property.

Form 4684 to report a casualty or theft gain or loss involving property used in your trade or business or income-producing property.

Form 4797 to report sales, exchanges, and involuntary conversions (not from a casualty or theft) of trade or business property.

Form 8271 if you are claiming or you are reporting on Schedule C or C-EZ any income, deduction, loss, credit, or other tax benefit from a tax shelter.

Form 8594 to report certain purchases or sales of groups of assets that constitute a trade or business.

Form 8824 to report like-kind exchanges.

Form 8829 to claim expenses for business use of your home.

Heavy Vehicle Use Tax

If you use certain highway trucks, truck-trailers, tractor-trailers, or buses in your trade or business, you may have to pay a Federal highway motor vehicle use tax. See **Form 2290** to find out if you owe this tax.

Information Returns

You may have to file information returns for wages paid to employees, certain payments of fees and other nonemployee compensation, interest, rents, royalties, real estate transactions, annuities, and pensions. You may also have to file an information return if you sold $5,000 or more of consumer products to a person on a buy-sell, deposit-commission, or other similar basis for resale. For more information, see the **Instructions for Forms 1099, 1098, 5498, and W-2G.**

If you received cash of more than $10,000 in one or more related transactions in your trade or business, you may have to file **Form 8300.** For details, see **Pub. 1544.**

Additional Information

See **Pub. 334** for more information for small businesses.

Specific Instructions

Filers of Form 1041

Do not complete the block labeled "Social security number." Instead, enter your employer identification number (EIN) on line D.

Line A

Describe the business or professional activity that provided your principal source of income reported on line 1. If you owned more than one business, you must complete a separate Schedule C for each business. Give the general field or activity and the type of product or service. If your general field or activity is wholesale or retail trade, or services connected with production services (mining, construction, or manufacturing), also give the type of customer or client. For example, "wholesale sale of hardware to retailers" or "appraisal of real estate for lending institutions."

Line D

You need an employer identification number (EIN) only if you had a Keogh plan or were required to file an employment, excise, estate, trust, or alcohol, tobacco, and firearms tax return. If you need an EIN, file **Form SS-4.** If you do not have an EIN, leave line D blank. **Do not** enter your SSN.

Line E

Enter your business address. Show a street address instead of a box number. Include the suite or room number, if any. If you conducted the business from your home located at the address shown on

C-1

Cat. No. 24329W

Form 1040, page 1, you do not have to complete this line.

Line F

You must use the cash method on your return unless you kept account books. If you kept such books, you can use the cash method or the accrual method. However, if inventories are required, you must use the accrual method for sales and purchases. Special rules apply to long-term contracts. See Internal Revenue Code section 460 for details. The method used must clearly reflect your income.

If you use the **cash method,** show all items of taxable income actually or constructively received during the year (in cash, property, or services). Income is constructively received when it is credited to your account or set aside for you to use. Also, show amounts actually paid during the year for deductible expenses.

If you use the **accrual method,** report income when you earn it and deduct expenses when you incur them even if you do not pay them during the tax year.

Accrual-basis taxpayers are put on a cash basis for deducting business expenses owed to a related cash-basis taxpayer. Other rules determine the timing of deductions based on economic performance. See **Pub. 538.**

To change your accounting method (including treatment of inventories), you must usually get permission from the IRS. In general, file **Form 3115** within the first 180 days of the tax year in which you want to make the change.

Line G

Participation, for purposes of the following seven material participation tests, generally includes any work you did in connection with an activity if you owned an interest in the activity at the time you did the work. The capacity in which you did the work does not matter. However, work is not treated as participation if it is work that an owner would not customarily do in the same type of activity and one of your main reasons for doing the work was to avoid the disallowance of losses or credits from the activity under the passive activity rules.

Work you did as an investor in an activity is not treated as participation unless you were directly involved in the day-to-day management or operations of the activity. Work done as an investor includes:

1. Studying and reviewing financial statements or reports on operations of the activity.

2. Preparing or compiling summaries or analyses of the finances or operations of the activity for your own use.

3. Monitoring the finances or operations of the activity in a nonmanagerial capacity.

Participation by your spouse during the tax year in an activity you own can be counted as your participation in the activity. This applies even if your spouse did not own an interest in the activity and whether or not you and your spouse file a joint return for the tax year.

Material Participation. For purposes of the passive activity rules, you materially participated in the operation of this trade or business activity during 1998 if you meet any of the following seven tests:

1. You participated in the activity for more than 500 hours during the tax year.

2. Your participation in the activity for the tax year was substantially all of the participation in the activity of all individuals (including individuals who did not own any interest in the activity) for the tax year.

3. You participated in the activity for more than 100 hours during the tax year, and you participated at least as much as any other person for the tax year. This includes individuals who did not own any interest in the activity.

4. The activity is a significant participation activity for the tax year, and you participated in all significant participation activities for more than 500 hours during the year. An activity is a "significant participation activity" if it involves the conduct of a trade or business, you participated in the activity for more than 100 hours during the tax year, and you did not materially participate under any of the material participation tests (other than this test 4).

5. You materially participated in the activity for any 5 of the prior 10 tax years.

6. The activity is a personal service activity in which you materially participated for any 3 prior tax years. A personal service activity is an activity that involves performing personal services in the fields of health, law, engineering, architecture, accounting, actuarial science, performing arts, consulting, or any other trade or business in which capital is not a material income-producing factor.

7. Based on all the facts and circumstances, you participated in the activity

C-2

on a regular, continuous, and substantial basis during the tax year. But you do not meet this test if you participated in the activity for 100 hours or less during the tax year. Your participation in managing the activity does not count in determining if you meet this test if any person (except you) —

a. Received compensation for performing management services in connection with the activity, or

b. Spent more hours during the tax year than you spent performing management services in connection with the activity (regardless of whether the person was compensated for the services).

If you meet any of the above tests, check the "Yes" box.

If you **do not** meet any of the above tests, check the "No" box. This business is a **passive activity.** If you have a loss from this business, see **Limit on Losses** below. If you have a profit from this business activity but have current year losses from other passive activities or you have prior year unallowed passive activity losses, see the instructions for **Form 8582.**

Exception for Oil and Gas. If you are filing Schedule C to report income and deductions from an oil or gas well in which you own a working interest directly or through an entity that does not limit your liability, check the "Yes" box. The activity of owning the working interest is not a passive activity regardless of your participation in the activity.

Limit on Losses. If you checked the "No" box and you have a loss from this business, you may have to use Form 8582 to figure your allowable loss, if any, to enter on Schedule C, line 31. Generally, you can deduct losses from passive activities only to the extent of income from passive activities.

For more details, see **Pub. 925.**

Line H

If you started or acquired this business in 1998, check the box on line H. Also, check the box if you are reopening or restarting this business after temporarily closing it, and you did not file a 1997 Schedule C or C-EZ for this business.

Part I. Income

Line 1

Enter gross receipts from your trade or business. Include amounts you received in your trade or business that were properly shown on **Forms 1099-MISC.** If the total amounts that were reported in box 7 of Forms 1099-MISC are more than the total you are reporting on line 1, attach a statement explaining the difference.

Statutory Employees. If you received a Form W-2 and the "Statutory employee" box in box 15 of that form was checked, report your income and expenses related to that income on Schedule C or C-EZ. Enter your statutory employee income from box 1 of Form W-2 on line 1 of Schedule C or C-EZ, and **check the box** on that line. Social security and Medicare tax should have been withheld from your earnings; therefore, you do not owe self-employment tax on these earnings.

Statutory employees include full-time life insurance agents, certain agent or commission drivers and traveling salespersons, and certain homeworkers.

If you had both self-employment income and statutory employee income, **do not** combine these amounts on a single Schedule C or C-EZ. In this case, you must file two Schedules C. You cannot use Schedule C-EZ.

Installment Sales. Generally, the installment method may not be used to report income from the sale of **(a)** personal property regularly sold under the installment method or **(b)** real property held for resale to customers. But the installment method may be used to report income from sales of certain residential lots and timeshares if you elect to pay interest on the tax due on that income after the year of sale. See Internal Revenue Code section 453(l)(2)(B) for details. If you make this election, include the interest on Form 1040, line 56. Also, enter "453(l)(3)" and the amount of the interest on the dotted line to the left of line 56.

If you use the installment method, attach a schedule to your return. Show separately for 1998 and the 3 preceding years: gross sales, cost of goods sold, gross profit, percentage of gross profit to gross sales, amounts collected, and gross profit on amounts collected.

Line 2

Enter such items as returned sales, rebates, and allowances from the sales price.

Line 6

Report on line 6 amounts from finance reserve income, scrap sales, bad debts you recovered, interest (such as on notes and accounts receivable), state gasoline or fuel tax refunds you got in 1998, credit for Federal tax paid on gasoline or other fuels claimed on your 1997 Form 1040, prizes and awards related to your trade or business, and other kinds of miscellaneous business income. Include amounts you received in your trade or business as shown on **Form 1099-PATR.** Also, include any recapture of the deduction for clean-fuel vehicles used in your business and clean-fuel vehicle refueling property. For more details, see **Pub. 535.**

If the business use percentage of any listed property (defined in the instructions for line 13) decreased to 50% or less in 1998, report on this line any recapture of excess depreciation, including any section 179 expense deduction. Use **Form 4797** to figure the recapture. Also, if the business use percentage drops to 50% or less on leased listed property (other than a vehicle), include on this line any inclusion amount. See **Pub. 946** to figure the amount.

Part II. Expenses

Capitalizing Costs of Property. If you produced real or tangible personal property or acquired property for resale, certain expenses attributable to the property must be included in inventory costs or capitalized. In addition to direct costs, producers of inventory property must also include part of certain indirect costs in their inventory. Purchasers of personal property acquired for resale must include part of certain indirect costs in inventory only if the average annual gross receipts for the 3 prior tax years exceed $10 million. Also, you must capitalize part of the indirect costs that benefit real or tangible personal property constructed for use in a trade or business, or noninventory property produced for sale to customers. Reduce the amounts on lines 8–26 and Part V by amounts capitalized. For more details, see Pub. 538.

Exception for Creative Property. If you are an artist, author, or photographer,
C-3

you may be exempt from the capitalization rules. However, your personal efforts must have created (or reasonably be expected to create) the property. This exception does not apply to any expense related to printing, photographic plates, motion picture films, video tapes, or similar items. These expenses are subject to the capitalization rules. For more details, see Pub. 538.

Line 9

Include debts and partial debts from sales or services that were included in income and are definitely known to be worthless. If you later collect a debt that you deducted as a bad debt, include it as income in the year collected. For more details, see **Pub. 535.**

Line 10

You can deduct the actual expenses of running your car or truck, or take the **standard mileage rate.** You may use the standard mileage rate even if you lease your vehicle. You **must** use actual expenses if you used more than one vehicle simultaneously in your business (such as in fleet operations).

If you deduct actual expenses:

- Include on line 10 the business portion of expenses for gasoline, oil, repairs, insurance, tires, license plates, etc., and
- Show depreciation on line 13 and rent or lease payments on line 20a.

If you choose to take the standard mileage rate, you **cannot** deduct depreciation, rent or lease payments, or your actual operating expenses. To take the standard mileage rate, multiply the number of business miles by 32.5 cents a mile. Add to this amount your parking fees and tolls, and enter the total.

For more details, see **Pub. 463.**

Information on Your Vehicle. If you claim any car and truck expenses, you must provide certain information on the use of your vehicle by completing one of the following:

- Part IV of Schedule C or Part III of Schedule C-EZ if: **(a)** you are claiming the standard mileage rate, you lease your vehicle, or your vehicle is fully depreciated and **(b)** you are **not** required to file **Form 4562** for any other reason. If you used more than one vehicle during the year, attach your own schedule with the information requested in Part IV of Schedule C, or Part III of Schedule C-EZ, for each additional vehicle.

• Part V of Form 4562 if you are claiming depreciation on your vehicle or you are required to file Form 4562 for any other reason (see the instructions for line 13 below).

Line 12

Enter your deduction for depletion on this line. If you have timber depletion, attach **Form T.** See Pub. 535 for details.

Line 13

Depreciation and Section 179 Expense Deduction. Depreciation is the annual deduction allowed to recover the cost or other basis of business or investment property with a useful life of more than 1 year. You can also depreciate improvements made to leased business property. However, stock in trade, inventories, and land are not depreciable.

Depreciation starts when you first use the property in your business or for the production of income. It ends when you take the property out of service, deduct all your depreciable cost or other basis, or no longer use the property in your business or for the production of income.

See the Instructions for Form 4562 to figure the amount of depreciation to enter on line 13.

You may also choose under Internal Revenue Code section 179 to expense part of the cost of certain property you bought in 1998 for use in your business. See the Instructions for Form 4562 for more details.

When To Attach Form 4562. You must complete and attach Form 4562 **only** if:

• You are claiming depreciation on property placed in service during 1998, or

• You are claiming depreciation on listed property (defined below), regardless of the date it was placed in service, or

• You are claiming a section 179 expense deduction.

If you acquired depreciable property for the first time in 1998, see **Pub. 946.**

Listed property generally includes, but is not limited to:

• Passenger automobiles weighing 6,000 pounds or less.

• Any other property used for transportation if the nature of the property lends itself to personal use, such as motorcycles, pickup trucks, etc.

• Any property used for entertainment or recreational purposes (such as photographic, phonographic, communication, and video recording equipment).

• Cellular telephones or other similar telecommunications equipment.

• Computers or peripheral equipment.

Exceptions. Listed property does not include photographic, phonographic, communication, or video equipment used exclusively in your trade or business or at your regular business establishment. It also does not include any computer or peripheral equipment used exclusively at a regular business establishment and owned or leased by the person operating the establishment. For purposes of these exceptions, a portion of your home is treated as a regular business establishment only if that portion meets the requirements under Internal Revenue Code section 280A(c)(1) for deducting expenses for the business use of your home.

If the business use percentage of any listed property decreased to 50% or less in 1998, see the instructions for line 6 on page C-3.

Line 14

Deduct contributions to employee benefit programs that are not an incidental part of a pension or profit-sharing plan included on line 19. Examples are accident and health plans, group-term life insurance, and dependent care assistance programs.

Do not include on line 14 any contributions you made on your behalf as a self-employed person to an accident and health plan or for group-term life insurance. You may be able to deduct on Form 1040, line 28, part of the amount you paid for health insurance on behalf of yourself, your spouse, and dependents, even if you do not itemize your deductions. See the Form 1040 instructions on page 28 for more details.

Line 15

Deduct premiums paid for business insurance on line 15. Deduct on line 14 amounts paid for employee accident and health insurance. Do not deduct amounts credited to a reserve for self-insurance or premiums paid for a policy that pays for your lost earnings due to sickness or disability. For more details, see Pub. 535.

Lines 16a and 16b

Interest Allocation Rules. The tax treatment of interest expense differs depending on its type. For example, home mortgage interest and investment interest are treated differently. "Interest allocation" rules require you to allocate (classify) your interest expense so it is deducted (or capitalized) on the correct line of your return and gets the right tax treatment. These rules could affect how much interest you are allowed to deduct on Schedule C or C-EZ.

Generally, you allocate interest expense by tracing how the proceeds of the loan were used. See Pub. 535 for details.

If you paid interest in 1998 that applies to future years, deduct only the part that applies to 1998. If you paid interest on a debt secured by your main home and any of the proceeds from that debt were used in connection with your trade or business, see Pub. 535 to figure the amount that is deductible on Schedule C or C-EZ.

If you have a mortgage on real property used in your business (other than your main home), enter on line 16a the interest you paid for 1998 to banks or other financial institutions for which you received a **Form 1098.** If you did not receive a Form 1098, enter the interest on line 16b.

If you paid more mortgage interest than is shown on Form 1098 or similar statement, see Pub. 535 to find out if you can deduct the additional interest. If you can, enter the amount on line 16a. Attach a statement to your return explaining the difference. Enter "See attached" in the left margin next to line 16a.

If you and at least one other person (other than your spouse if you file a joint return) were liable for and paid interest on the mortgage and the other person received the Form 1098, report your share of the interest on line 16b. Attach a statement to your return showing the name and address of the person who received the Form 1098. In the left margin next to line 16b, enter "See attached."

Do not deduct interest you paid or accrued on debts allocable to investment property. This interest is generally deducted on **Schedule A** (Form 1040). For details, see **Pub. 550.**

C-4

Line 17

Include on this line fees for tax advice related to your business and for preparation of the tax forms related to your business.

Line 19

Enter your deduction for contributions to a pension, profit-sharing, or annuity plan, or plans for the benefit of your employees. If the plan includes you as a self-employed person, enter contributions made as an employer on your behalf on Form 1040, line 29, not on Schedule C.

Generally, you must file one of the following forms if you maintain a pension, profit-sharing, or other funded-deferred compensation plan. The filing requirement is not affected by whether or not the plan qualified under the Internal Revenue Code, or whether or not you claim a deduction for the current tax year.

Form 5500. Complete this form for each plan with 100 or more participants.

Form 5500-C/R or 5500-EZ. Complete the applicable form for each plan with fewer than 100 participants.

There is a penalty for failure to timely file these forms.

For more information, see **Pub. 560.**

Lines 20a and 20b

If you rented or leased vehicles, machinery, or equipment, enter on line 20a the business portion of your rental cost. But if you leased a vehicle for a term of 30 days or more, you may have to reduce your deduction by an amount called the **inclusion amount.**

You may have to do this if—

The lease term began:	And the vehicle's fair market value on the first day of the lease exceeded:
During 1997 or 1998 . .	$15,800
During 1995 or 1996 . . .	15,500
During 1994	14,600
During 1993	14,300
During 1992	13,700

If the lease term began before 1992, see Pub. 463 to find out if you have an inclusion amount.

Also see Pub. 463 to figure your inclusion amount.

Enter on line 20b amounts paid to rent or lease other property, such as office space in a building.

Line 21

Deduct the cost of repairs and maintenance. Include labor, supplies, and other items that do not add to the value or increase the life of the property. Do not deduct the value of your own labor. Do not deduct amounts spent to restore or replace property; they must be capitalized.

Line 23

You can deduct the following taxes on this line:

- State and local sales taxes imposed on you as the seller of goods or services. If you collected this tax from the buyer, you must also include the amount collected in gross receipts or sales on line 1.
- Real estate and personal property taxes on business assets.
- Social security and Medicare taxes paid to match required withholding from your employees' wages. Also, Federal unemployment tax paid. Reduce your deduction by the amount of the current year credit shown on line 4 of **Form 8846.**
- Federal highway use tax.

Do not deduct on this line:

- Federal income taxes, including your self-employment tax. However, you may deduct one-half of your self-employment tax on Form 1040, line 27.
- Estate and gift taxes.
- Taxes assessed to pay for improvements, such as paving and sewers.
- Taxes on your home or personal use property.
- State and local sales taxes on property purchased for use in your business. Instead, treat these taxes as part of the cost of the property.
- State and local sales taxes imposed on the buyer that you were required to collect and pay over to the state or local governments. These taxes are not included in gross receipts or sales nor are they a deductible expense. However, if the state or local government allowed you to retain any part of the sales tax you collected, you must include that amount as income on line 6.

- Other taxes not related to your business.

Line 24a

Enter your expenses for lodging and transportation connected with overnight travel for business while away from your tax home. Generally, your tax home is your main place of business regardless of where you maintain your family home. You cannot deduct expenses paid or incurred in connection with employment away from home if that period of employment exceeds 1 year. Also, you cannot deduct travel expenses for your spouse, your dependent, or any other individual unless that person is your employee, the travel is for a bona fide business purpose, and the expenses would otherwise be deductible by that person.

Do not include expenses for meals and entertainment on this line. Instead, see the instructions for lines 24b and 24c below.

You cannot deduct expenses for attending a foreign convention unless it is directly related to your trade or business and it is as reasonable for the meeting to be held outside the North American area as within it. These rules apply to both employers and employees. Other rules apply to luxury water travel.

For more details, see Pub. 463.

Lines 24b and 24c

On line 24b, enter your total business meal and entertainment expenses. Include meals while traveling away from home for business. Instead of the actual cost of your meals while traveling away from home, you may use the standard meal allowance. For more details, see Pub. 463.

Business meal expenses are deductible only if they are **(a)** directly related to or associated with the active conduct of your trade or business, **(b)** not lavish or extravagant, and **(c)** incurred while you or your employee is present at the meal.

You cannot deduct any expense paid or incurred for a facility (such as a yacht or hunting lodge) used for any activity usually considered entertainment, amusement, or recreation.

Also, you cannot deduct membership dues for any club organized for business, pleasure, recreation, or other social purpose. This includes country clubs, golf and athletic clubs, airline and hotel clubs, and clubs operated to provide meals under conditions favorable to business discussion. But it does not

C-5

include civic or public service organizations, professional organizations (such as bar and medical associations), business leagues, trade associations, chambers of commerce, boards of trade, and real estate boards, unless a principal purpose of the organization is to entertain, or provide entertainment facilities for, members or their guests.

There are exceptions to these rules as well as other rules that apply to skybox rentals and tickets to entertainment events. See Pub. 463.

Generally, you may deduct **only** 50% of your business meal and entertainment expenses, including meals incurred while traveling away from home on business. However, you may fully deduct meals and entertainment furnished or reimbursed to an employee if you properly treat the expense as wages subject to withholding. You may also fully deduct meals and entertainment provided to a nonemployee to the extent the expenses are includible in the gross income of that person and reported on Form 1099-MISC.

Figure how much of the amount on line 24b is subject to the 50% limit. Then, enter one-half of that amount on line 24c.

Line 25

Deduct only utility expenses for your trade or business.

Local Telephone Service. If you used your home phone for business, do not deduct the base rate (including taxes) of the first phone line into your residence. But you can deduct expenses for any additional costs you incurred for business that are more than the cost of the base rate for the first phone line. For example, if you had a second line, you can deduct the business percentage of the charges for that line, including the base rate charges.

Line 26

Enter the total salaries and wages for the tax year. Do not include salaries and wages deducted elsewhere on your return or amounts paid to yourself. Reduce your deduction by the current year credits claimed on:

• **Form 5884,** Work Opportunity Credit.

• **Form 8844,** Empowerment Zone Employment Credit.

• **Form 8845,** Indian Employment Credit.

• **Form 8861,** Welfare-to-Work Credit.

Caution: *If you provided taxable fringe benefits to your employees, such as personal use of a car, do not deduct as wages the amount applicable to depreciation and other expenses claimed elsewhere.*

Line 30

Business Use of Your Home. You may be able to deduct certain expenses for business use of your home, subject to limitations. Generally, any amount not allowed as a deduction for 1998 because of the limitations can be carried over to 1999. You must attach **Form 8829** if you claim this deduction.

For details, see the Instructions for Form 8829 and **Pub. 587.**

Line 31

If you have a loss, the amount of loss you can deduct this year may be limited. Go on to line 32 before entering your loss on line 31. If you answered "No" to Question G on Schedule C, also see the Instructions for Form 8582. Enter the net profit or **deductible** loss here. Combine this amount with any profit or loss from other businesses, and enter the total on Form 1040, line 12, and Schedule SE, line 2. Estates and trusts should enter the total on Form 1041, line 3.

If you have a net profit on line 31, this amount is earned income and may qualify you for the earned income credit. See the Instructions for Form 1040, lines 59a and 59b, on page 36 for more details.

Statutory Employees. If you are filing Schedule C to report income and expenses as a statutory employee, include your net profit or deductible loss from line 31 with other Schedule C amounts on Form 1040, line 12. However, **do not** report this amount on Schedule SE, line 2. If you are required to file Schedule SE because of other self-employment income, see the Instructions for Schedule SE.

Line 32

At-Risk Rules. Generally, if you have **(a)** a business loss and **(b)** amounts in the business for which you are **not at risk,** you will have to complete **Form 6198** to figure your allowable loss.

The at-risk rules generally limit the amount of loss (including loss on the

disposition of assets) you can claim to the amount you could actually lose in the business.

Check **box 32b** if you have amounts for which you are not at risk in this business, such as the following.

• Nonrecourse loans used to finance the business, to acquire property used in the business, or to acquire the business that are not secured by your own property (other than property used in the business). However, there is an exception for certain nonrecourse financing borrowed by you in connection with holding real property.

• Cash, property, or borrowed amounts used in the business (or contributed to the business, or used to acquire the business) that are protected against loss by a guarantee, stop-loss agreement, or other similar arrangement (excluding casualty insurance and insurance against tort liability).

• Amounts borrowed for use in the business from a person who has an interest in the business, other than as a creditor, or who is related under Internal Revenue Code section 465(b)(3) to a person (other than you) having such an interest.

If all amounts are at risk in this business, check **box 32a** and enter your loss on line 31. But if you answered "No" to Question G, you may need to complete Form 8582 to figure your allowable loss to enter on line 31. See the Instructions for Form 8582 for more details.

If you checked **box 32b,** get Form 6198 to determine the amount of your deductible loss and enter that amount on line 31. But if you answered "No" to Question G, your loss may be further limited. See the Instructions for Form 8582. If your at-risk amount is zero or less, enter zero on line 31. Be sure to attach Form 6198 to your return. If you checked box 32b and you do not attach Form 6198, the processing of your tax return may be delayed.

Statutory Employees. Include your deductible loss with other Schedule C amounts on Form 1040, line 12. **Do not** include this amount on Schedule SE, line 2.

Any loss from this business not allowed for 1998 because of the at-risk rules is treated as a deduction allocable to the business in 1999. For more details, see the Instructions for Form 6198 and Pub. 925.

C-6

Part III. Cost of Goods Sold

If you engaged in a trade or business in which the production, purchase, or sale of merchandise was an income-producing factor, merchandise inventories must be taken into account at the beginning and end of your tax year.

Note: *Certain direct and indirect expenses must be capitalized or included in inventory. See the instructions for Part II.*

Line 33

Your inventories can be valued at cost; cost or market value, whichever is lower; or any other method approved by the IRS.

Part V. Other Expenses

Include all ordinary and necessary business expenses not deducted elsewhere on Schedule C. List the type and amount of each expense separately in the space provided. Enter the total on lines 48 and 27. Do not include the cost of business equipment or furniture, replacements or permanent improvements to property, or personal, living, and family expenses. Do not include charitable contributions. Also, you may not deduct fines or penalties paid to a government for violating any law. For more details on business expenses, see Pub. 535.

Amortization. Include amortization in this part. For amortization that begins in 1998, you must complete and attach Form 4562.

You may amortize:

● The cost of pollution-control facilities.

● Amounts paid for research and experimentation.

● Certain business startup costs.

● Qualified forestation and reforestation costs.

● Amounts paid to acquire, protect, expand, register, or defend trademarks or trade names.

● Goodwill and certain other intangibles.

In general, you **may not** amortize real property construction period interest and taxes. Special rules apply for allo-cating interest to real or personal property produced in your trade or business.

At-Risk Loss Deduction. Any loss from this activity that was not allowed as a deduction last year because of the at-risk rules is treated as a deduction allocable to this activity in 1998.

Capital Construction Fund. Do not claim on Schedule C or C-EZ the deduction for amounts contributed to a capital construction fund set up under the Merchant Marine Act of 1936. To take the deduction, reduce the amount that would otherwise be entered as taxable income on Form 1040, line 39, by the amount of the deduction. In the margin to the left of line 39, enter "CCF" and the amount of the deduction. For more information, see **Pub. 595.**

Deduction for Clean-Fuel Vehicles and Clean-Fuel Vehicle Refueling Property. You may deduct part of the cost of qualified clean-fuel vehicle property used in your business and qualified clean-fuel vehicle refueling property. See Pub. 535 for more details.

Disabled Access Credit and the Deduction for Removing Barriers to Individuals With Disabilities and the Elderly. You may be able to claim a tax credit of up to $5,000 for eligible expenditures paid or incurred in 1998 to provide access to your business for individuals with disabilities. See **Form 8826** for more details. You can also deduct up to $15,000 of costs paid or incurred in 1998 to remove architectural or transportation barriers to individuals with disabilities and the elderly. However, you cannot take both the credit and the deduction on the same expenditures.

C-7

Form **4562**	**Depreciation and Amortization** (Including Information on Listed Property)	OMB No. 1545-0172
Department of the Treasury Internal Revenue Service (99)	▶ See separate instructions. ▶ Attach this form to your return.	19**98** Attachment Sequence No. **67**

Name(s) shown on return	Business or activity to which this form relates	Identifying number

Part I   **Election To Expense Certain Tangible Property (Section 179)** (Note: *If you have any "listed property," complete Part V before you complete Part I.*)

1	Maximum dollar limitation. If an enterprise zone business, see page 2 of the instructions . .	**1**	$18,500
2	Total cost of section 179 property placed in service. See page 2 of the instructions	**2**	
3	Threshold cost of section 179 property before reduction in limitation	**3**	$200,000
4	Reduction in limitation. Subtract line 3 from line 2. If zero or less, enter -0-	**4**	
5	Dollar limitation for tax year. Subtract line 4 from line 1. If zero or less, enter -0-. If married filing separately, see page 2 of the instructions	**5**	

	(a) Description of property	(b) Cost (business use only)	(c) Elected cost
6			

7	Listed property. Enter amount from line 27.	**7**	
8	Total elected cost of section 179 property. Add amounts in column (c), lines 6 and 7 . . .	**8**	
9	Tentative deduction. Enter the smaller of line 5 or line 8	**9**	
10	Carryover of disallowed deduction from 1997. See page 3 of the instructions	**10**	
11	Business income limitation. Enter the smaller of business income (not less than zero) or line 5 (see instructions)	**11**	
12	Section 179 expense deduction. Add lines 9 and 10, but do not enter more than line 11 . .	**12**	
13	Carryover of disallowed deduction to 1999. Add lines 9 and 10, less line 12 ▶	**13**	

Note: *Do not use Part II or Part III below for listed property (automobiles, certain other vehicles, cellular telephones, certain computers, or property used for entertainment, recreation, or amusement). Instead, use Part V for listed property.*

Part II   **MACRS Depreciation For Assets Placed in Service ONLY During Your 1998 Tax Year (Do Not Include Listed Property.)**

Section A—General Asset Account Election

14	If you are making the election under section 168(i)(4) to group any assets placed in service during the tax year into one or more general asset accounts, check this box. See page 3 of the instructions . . . . ▶ ☐

Section B—General Depreciation System (GDS) (See page 3 of the instructions.)

(a) Classification of property	(b) Month and year placed in service	(c) Basis for depreciation (business/investment use only—see instructions)	(d) Recovery period	(e) Convention	(f) Method	(g) Depreciation deduction
15a 3-year property						
b 5-year property						
c 7-year property						
d 10-year property						
e 15-year property						
f 20-year property						
g 25-year property			25 yrs.		S/L	
h Residential rental property			27.5 yrs.	MM	S/L	
			27.5 yrs.	MM	S/L	
i Nonresidential real property			39 yrs.	MM	S/L	
				MM	S/L	

Section C—Alternative Depreciation System (ADS) (See page 5 of the instructions.)

(a)		(b)	(d)	(e)	(f)	
16a Class life					S/L	
b 12-year			12 yrs.		S/L	
c 40-year			40 yrs.	MM	S/L	

Part III   **Other Depreciation (Do Not Include Listed Property.)** (See page 6 of the instructions.)

17	GDS and ADS deductions for assets placed in service in tax years beginning before 1998	**17**	
18	Property subject to section 168(f)(1) election	**18**	
19	ACRS and other depreciation	**19**	

Part IV   **Summary** (See page 6 of the instructions.)

20	Listed property. Enter amount from line 26.	**20**	
21	**Total.** Add deductions on line 12, lines 15 and 16 in column (g), and lines 17 through 20. Enter here and on the appropriate lines of your return. Partnerships and S corporations—see instructions . .	**21**	
22	For assets shown above and placed in service during the current year, enter the portion of the basis attributable to section 263A costs	**22**	

For Paperwork Reduction Act Notice, see the separate instructions.   Cat. No. 12906N   Form **4562** (1998)

Form 4562 (1998)   Page **2**

Part V — Listed Property—Automobiles, Certain Other Vehicles, Cellular Telephones, Certain Computers, and Property Used for Entertainment, Recreation, or Amusement

Note: *For any vehicle for which you are using the standard mileage rate or deducting lease expense, complete **only** 23a, 23b, columns (a) through (c) of Section A, all of Section B, and Section C if applicable.*

Section A—Depreciation and Other Information (Caution: *See page 8 of the instructions for limits for passenger automobiles.*)

23a Do you have evidence to support the business/investment use claimed? ☐ **Yes** ☐ **No**   23b If "Yes," is the evidence written? ☐ **Yes** ☐ **No**

(a) Type of property (list vehicles first)	(b) Date placed in service	(c) Business/ investment use percentage	(d) Cost or other basis	(e) Basis for depreciation (business/investment use only)	(f) Recovery period	(g) Method/ Convention	(h) Depreciation deduction	(i) Elected section 179 cost
24 Property used more than 50% in a qualified business use (See page 7 of the instructions.):								
		%						
		%						
		%						
25 Property used 50% or less in a qualified business use (See page 7 of the instructions.):								
		%				S/L –		
		%				S/L –		
		%				S/L –		

26 Add amounts in column (h). Enter the total here and on line 20, page 1 . . . . . **26**

27 Add amounts in column (i). Enter the total here and on line 7, page 1 . . . . **27**

Section B—Information on Use of Vehicles
Complete this section for vehicles used by a sole proprietor, partner, or other "more than 5% owner," or related person.
If you provided vehicles to your employees, first answer the questions in Section C to see if you meet an exception to completing this section for those vehicles.

	(a) Vehicle 1	(b) Vehicle 2	(c) Vehicle 3	(d) Vehicle 4	(e) Vehicle 5	(f) Vehicle 6
28 Total business/investment miles driven during the year (DO NOT include commuting miles)						
29 Total commuting miles driven during the year						
30 Total other personal (noncommuting) miles driven .						
31 Total miles driven during the year. Add lines 28 through 30						

	Yes	No	Yes	No	Yes	No	Yes	No	Yes	No	Yes	No
32 Was the vehicle available for personal use during off-duty hours?												
33 Was the vehicle used primarily by a more than 5% owner or related person?												
34 Is another vehicle available for personal use?												

Section C—Questions for Employers Who Provide Vehicles for Use by Their Employees
*Answer these questions to determine if you meet an exception to completing Section B for vehicles used by employees who **are not** more than 5% owners or related persons.*

	Yes	No
35 Do you maintain a written policy statement that prohibits all personal use of vehicles, including commuting, by your employees?		
36 Do you maintain a written policy statement that prohibits personal use of vehicles, except commuting, by your employees? See page 9 of the instructions for vehicles used by corporate officers, directors, or 1% or more owners		
37 Do you treat all use of vehicles by employees as personal use?		
38 Do you provide more than five vehicles to your employees, obtain information from your employees about the use of the vehicles, and retain the information received?		
39 Do you meet the requirements concerning qualified automobile demonstration use? See page 9 of the instructions . .		

Note: *If your answer to 35, 36, 37, 38, or 39 is "Yes," you need not complete Section B for the covered vehicles.*

Part VI Amortization

(a) Description of costs	(b) Date amortization begins	(c) Amortizable amount	(d) Code section	(e) Amortization period or percentage	(f) Amortization for this year
40 Amortization of costs that begins during your 1998 tax year:					

41 Amortization of costs that began before 1998 . . . . **41**

42 **Total.** Enter here and on "Other Deductions" or "Other Expenses" line of your return . . . **42**

Form **4797**

Department of the Treasury
Internal Revenue Service   (99)

Sales of Business Property
(Also Involuntary Conversions and Recapture Amounts
Under Sections 179 and 280F(b)(2))
▶ Attach to your tax return.   ▶ See separate instructions.

OMB No. 1545-0184

19**98**

Attachment
Sequence No. **27**

Name(s) shown on return

Identifying number

1 Enter here the gross proceeds from the sale or exchange of real estate reported to you for 1998 on Form(s) 1099-S
(or a substitute statement) that you will be including on line 2, 10, or 20 . . . . | **1**

Part I **Sales or Exchanges of Property Used in a Trade or Business and Involuntary Conversions From Other Than Casualty or Theft—Property Held More Than 1 Year**

(a) Description of property	(b) Date acquired (mo., day, yr.)	(c) Date sold (mo., day, yr.)	(d) Gross sales price	(e) Depreciation allowed or allowable since acquisition	(f) Cost or other basis, plus improvements and expense of sale	(g) GAIN or (LOSS) Subtract (f) from the sum of (d) and (e)	(h) 28% RATE GAIN or (LOSS) * (see instr. below)
2							

3 Gain, if any, from Form 4684, line 39 . . . . | **3**

4 Section 1231 gain from installment sales from Form 6252, line 26 or 37 . . . . . | **4**

5 Section 1231 gain or (loss) from like-kind exchanges from Form 8824 . . . . . . | **5**

6 Gain, if any, from line 32, from other than casualty or theft . . . . | **6**

7 Combine lines 2 through 6 in columns (g) and (h). Enter gain or (loss) here, and on the appropriate line as follows: | **7**

Partnerships—Report the gain or (loss) following the instructions for Form 1065, Schedule K, line 6. Skip lines 8, 9, 11, and 12 below.

S corporations—Report the gain or (loss) following the instructions for Form 1120S, Schedule K, lines 5 and 6. Skip lines 8, 9, 11, and 12 below, unless line 7, column (g) is a gain and the S corporation is subject to the capital gains tax.

All others—If line 7, column (g) is zero or a loss, enter that amount on line 11 below and skip lines 8 and 9. If line 7, column (g) is a gain and you did not have any prior year section 1231 losses, or they were recaptured in an earlier year, enter the gain or (loss) in each column as a long-term capital gain or (loss) on Schedule D and skip lines 8, 9, and 12 below.

8 Nonrecaptured net section 1231 losses from prior years (see instructions) . . . . | **8**

9 Subtract line 8 from line 7. For column (g) **only,** if the result is zero or less, enter -0-. Enter here and on the appropriate line(s) as follows (see instructions): . . . . | **9**

S corporations—Enter only the gain in column (g) on Schedule D (Form 1120S), line 14, and skip lines 11 and 12 below.

All others—If line 9, column (g) is zero, enter the gain from line 7, column (g) on line 12 below. If line 9, column (g) is more than zero, enter the amount from line 8, column (g) on line 12 below, and enter the gain or (loss) in each column of line 9 as a long-term capital gain or (loss) on Schedule D.

* Corporations (other than S corporations) should not complete column (h). Partnerships and S corporations must complete column (h). All others must complete column (h) only if line 7, column (g), is a gain. Use column (h) only to report pre-1998 28% rate gain (or loss) from a 1997-98 fiscal year partnership or S corporation.

Part II **Ordinary Gains and Losses**

10 Ordinary gains and losses not included on lines 11 through 17 (include property held 1 year or less):

11 Loss, if any, from line 7, column (g) . . . . | **11** (   )

12 Gain, if any, from line 7, column (g) or amount from line 8, column (g) if applicable . . . . | **12**

13 Gain, if any, from line 31 . . . . | **13**

14 Net gain or (loss) from Form 4684, lines 31 and 38a . . . . | **14**

15 Ordinary gain from installment sales from Form 6252, line 25 or 36 . . . . | **15**

16 Ordinary gain or (loss) from like-kind exchanges from Form 8824 . . . . | **16**

17 Recapture of section 179 expense deduction for partners and S corporation shareholders from property dispositions by partnerships and S corporations (see instructions) . . . . . . | **17**

18 Combine lines 10 through 17 in column (g). Enter gain or (loss) here, and on the appropriate line as follows: | **18**

a For all except individual returns: Enter the gain or (loss) from line 18 on the return being filed.

b For individual returns:

(1) If the loss on line 11 includes a loss from Form 4684, line 35, column (b)(ii), enter that part of the loss here. Enter the part of the loss from income-producing property on Schedule A (Form 1040), line 27, and the part of the loss from property used as an employee on Schedule A (Form 1040), line 22. Identify as from "Form 4797, line 18b(1)." See instructions . . . | **18b(1)**

(2) Redetermine the gain or (loss) on line 18, excluding the loss, if any, on line 18b(1). Enter here and on Form 1040, line 14 . . . . | **18b(2)**

For Paperwork Reduction Act Notice, see separate instructions.   Cat. No. 13086I   Form **4797** (1998)

Form 4797 (1998)   Page **2**

Part III   Gain From Disposition of Property Under Sections 1245, 1250, 1252, 1254, and 1255

19	(a) Description of section 1245, 1250, 1252, 1254, or 1255 property:	(b) Date acquired (mo., day, yr.)	(c) Date sold (mo., day, yr.)
A			
B			
C			
D			

	These columns relate to the properties on lines 19A through 19D. ▶		Property A	Property B	Property C	Property D
20	Gross sales price (**Note:** See line 1 before completing.)	20				
21	Cost or other basis plus expense of sale	21				
22	Depreciation (or depletion) allowed or allowable	22				
23	Adjusted basis. Subtract line 22 from line 21	23				
24	Total gain. Subtract line 23 from line 20	24				
25	**If section 1245 property:**					
a	Depreciation allowed or allowable from line 22	25a				
b	Enter the **smaller** of line 24 or 25a	25b				
26	**If section 1250 property:** If straight line depreciation was used, enter -0- on line 26g, except for a corporation subject to section 291.					
a	Additional depreciation after 1975 (see instructions)	26a				
b	Applicable percentage multiplied by the **smaller** of line 24 or line 26a (see instructions)	26b				
c	Subtract line 26a from line 24. If residential rental property or line 24 is not more than line 26a, skip lines 26d and 26e	26c				
d	Additional depreciation after 1969 and before 1976	26d				
e	Enter the **smaller** of line 26c or 26d	26e				
f	Section 291 amount (corporations only)	26f				
g	Add lines 26b, 26e, and 26f	26g				
27	**If section 1252 property:** Skip this section if you did not dispose of farmland or if this form is being completed for a partnership (other than an electing large partnership).					
a	Soil, water, and land clearing expenses	27a				
b	Line 27a multiplied by applicable percentage (see instructions)	27b				
c	Enter the **smaller** of line 24 or 27b	27c				
28	**If section 1254 property:**					
a	Intangible drilling and development costs, expenditures for development of mines and other natural deposits, and mining exploration costs (see instructions)	28a				
b	Enter the **smaller** of line 24 or 28a	28b				
29	**If section 1255 property:**					
a	Applicable percentage of payments excluded from income under section 126 (see instructions)	29a				
b	Enter the **smaller** of line 24 or 29a (see instructions)	29b				

Summary of Part III Gains. Complete property columns A through D through line 29b before going to line 30.

30	Total gains for all properties. Add property columns A through D, line 24	30	
31	Add property columns A through D, lines 25b, 26g, 27c, 28b, and 29b. Enter here and on line 13	31	
32	Subtract line 31 from line 30. Enter the portion from casualty or theft on Form 4684, line 33. Enter the portion from other than casualty or theft on Form 4797, line 6	32	

Part IV   Recapture Amounts Under Sections 179 and 280F(b)(2) When Business Use Drops to 50% or Less
       See instructions.

			(a) Section 179	(b) Section 280F(b)(2)
33	Section 179 expense deduction or depreciation allowable in prior years	33		
34	Recomputed depreciation. See instructions	34		
35	Recapture amount. Subtract line 34 from line 33. See the instructions for where to report	35		

✪

Form **8829**	**Expenses for Business Use of Your Home**	OMB No. 1545-1266
Department of the Treasury Internal Revenue Service (99)	▶ File only with Schedule C (Form 1040). Use a separate Form 8829 for each home you used for business during the year. ▶ See separate instructions.	19**98** Attachment Sequence No. **66**

Name(s) of proprietor(s)	Your social security number

Part I   **Part of Your Home Used for Business**

1	Area used regularly and exclusively for business, regularly for day care, or for storage of inventory or product samples. See instructions	1	
2	Total area of home	2	
3	Divide line 1 by line 2. Enter the result as a percentage	3	%

- For day-care facilities not used exclusively for business, also complete lines 4–6.
- All others, skip lines 4–6 and enter the amount from line 3 on line 7.

4	Multiply days used for day care during year by hours used per day .	4		hr.
5	Total hours available for use during the year (365 days × 24 hours). See instructions	5	8,760	hr.
6	Divide line 4 by line 5. Enter the result as a decimal amount . . .	6	.	

7	Business percentage. For day-care facilities not used exclusively for business, multiply line 6 by line 3 (enter the result as a percentage). All others, enter the amount from line 3 . . . . ▶	7	%

Part II   **Figure Your Allowable Deduction**

		(a) Direct expenses	(b) Indirect expenses	
8	Enter the amount from Schedule C, line 29, **plus** any net gain or (loss) derived from the business use of your home and shown on Schedule D or Form 4797. If more than one place of business, see instructions			8
	See instructions for columns (a) and (b) before completing lines 9–20.			
9	Casualty losses. See instructions	9		
10	Deductible mortgage interest. See instructions .	10		
11	Real estate taxes. See instructions	11		
12	Add lines 9, 10, and 11.	12		
13	Multiply line 12, column (b) by line 7		13	
14	Add line 12, column (a) and line 13			14
15	Subtract line 14 from line 8. If zero or less, enter -0- .			15
16	Excess mortgage interest. See instructions . .	16		
17	Insurance	17		
18	Repairs and maintenance	18		
19	Utilities	19		
20	Other expenses. See instructions	20		
21	Add lines 16 through 20	21		
22	Multiply line 21, column (b) by line 7	22		
23	Carryover of operating expenses from 1997 Form 8829, line 41 . .	23		
24	Add line 21 in column (a), line 22, and line 23			24
25	Allowable operating expenses. Enter the **smaller** of line 15 or line 24			25
26	Limit on excess casualty losses and depreciation. Subtract line 25 from line 15			26
27	Excess casualty losses. See instructions	27		
28	Depreciation of your home from Part III below	28		
29	Carryover of excess casualty losses and depreciation from 1997 Form 8829, line 42	29		
30	Add lines 27 through 29			30
31	Allowable excess casualty losses and depreciation. Enter the **smaller** of line 26 or line 30 . .			31
32	Add lines 14, 25, and 31			32
33	Casualty loss portion, if any, from lines 14 and 31. Carry amount to **Form 4684**, Section B .			33
34	Allowable expenses for business use of your home. Subtract line 33 from line 32. Enter here and on Schedule C, line 30. If your home was used for more than one business, see instructions ▶			34

Part III   **Depreciation of Your Home**

35	Enter the **smaller** of your home's adjusted basis or its fair market value. See instructions . .	35	
36	Value of land included on line 35	36	
37	Basis of building. Subtract line 36 from line 35	37	
38	Business basis of building. Multiply line 37 by line 7	38	
39	Depreciation percentage. See instructions	39	%
40	Depreciation allowable. Multiply line 38 by line 39. Enter here and on line 28 above. See instructions	40	

Part IV   **Carryover of Unallowed Expenses to 1999**

41	Operating expenses. Subtract line 25 from line 24. If less than zero, enter -0-	41	
42	Excess casualty losses and depreciation. Subtract line 31 from line 30. If less than zero, enter -0- .	42	

For Paperwork Reduction Act Notice, see page 3 of separate instructions.	Cat. No. 13232M	Form **8829** (1998)

19**98**

Department of the Treasury
Internal Revenue Service

Instructions for Form 8829

Expenses for Business Use of Your Home

Section references are to the Internal Revenue Code.

General Instructions

Purpose of Form

Use Form 8829 to figure the allowable expenses for business use of your home on **Schedule C** (Form 1040) and any carryover to 1999 of amounts not deductible in 1998.

If all of the expenses for business use of your home are properly allocable to inventory costs, do not complete Form 8829. These expenses are figured in Part III of Schedule C and not on Form 8829.

You must meet specific requirements to deduct expenses for the business use of your home. Even if you meet these requirements, your deductible expenses are limited. For details, see **Pub. 587,** Business Use of Your Home (Including Use by Day-Care Providers).

Note: *If you file **Schedule F** (Form 1040) or you are an employee or a partner, **do not** use this form. Instead, use the worksheet in Pub. 587.*

Who May Deduct Expenses for Business Use of a Home

Generally, you may deduct business expenses that apply to a part of your home **only** if that part is exclusively used on a regular basis:

    1. As your principal place of business for any of your trades or businesses; or

    2. As a place of business used by your patients, clients, or customers to meet or deal with you in the normal course of your trade or business; or

    3. In connection with your trade or business if it is a separate structure that is not attached to your home.

Determining Your Principal Place of Business

In determining whether a business location in your home qualifies as your principal place of business, you must consider the following two factors:

    1. The relative importance of the activities performed at each business location; and

    2. The amount of time spent at each location.

First, compare the relative importance of the activities performed at each location. A comparison of the relative importance of the activities performed at each business location depends on the characteristics of each business. If your business requires that you meet or confer with clients or patients, or that you deliver goods or services to a customer, the place where that contact occurs must be given a greater weight in determining where the most important activities are performed. Performance of necessary or essential activities at the business location in your home (such as planning for services or the delivery of goods, or the accounting or billing for those activities or goods) is not controlling.

Then, if you are unable to clearly identify the location of your principal place of business after comparing the relative importance of the activities, you should compare the amount of time spent on business at each location. This may happen when you perform income-producing activities at both your home and some other location.

You may find, after applying both factors, that you have **no** principal place of business.

Exception for Storage of Inventory or Product Samples

You may also deduct expenses that apply to space within your home if it is the **only** fixed location of your trade or business. The space must be used on a regular basis to store inventory or product samples from your trade or business of selling products at retail or wholesale.

Exception for Day-Care Facilities

If you use space in your home on a regular basis in the trade or business of providing day care, you may be able to deduct the business expenses even though you use the same space for nonbusiness purposes. To qualify for this exception, you must have applied for (and not have been rejected), been granted (and still have in effect), or be exempt from having a license, certification, registration, or approval as a day-care center or as a family or group day-care home under state law.

Expenses Related to Tax-Exempt Income

Generally, you cannot deduct expenses that are allocable to tax-exempt income. However, if you receive a tax-exempt parsonage allowance or a tax-exempt military housing allowance, your expenses for mortgage interest and real property taxes are deductible under the normal rules. No deduction is allowed for other expenses allocable to the tax-exempt allowance.

Specific Instructions

Part I

Lines 1 and 2

To determine the area on lines 1 and 2, you may use square feet or any other reasonable method if it accurately figures your business percentage on line 7.

Do not include on line 1 the area of your home you used to figure any expenses allocable to inventory costs. The business percentage of these expenses should have been taken into account in Part III of Schedule C.

Special Computation for Certain Day-Care Facilities

If the part of your home used as a day-care facility included areas used exclusively for business as well as other areas used only partly for business, you **cannot** figure your business percentage using Part I. Instead, follow these three steps:

    1. Figure the business percentage of the part of your home used exclusively for business by dividing the area used exclusively for business by the total area of the home.

    2. Figure the business percentage of the part of your home used only partly for business by following the same method used in Part I of the form, but enter on line 1 of your computation only the area of the home used partly for business.

    3. Add the business percentages you figured in the first two steps and enter the result on line 7. Attach your computation and write "See attached computation" directly above the percentage you entered on line 7.

Cat. No. 15683B

Line 4

Enter the total number of hours the facility was used for day care during the year.

Example. Your home is used Monday through Friday for 12 hours per day for 250 days during the year. It is also used on 50 Saturdays for 8 hours per day. Enter 3,400 hours on line 4 (3,000 hours for weekdays plus 400 hours for Saturdays).

Line 5

If you started or stopped using your home for day care in 1998, you must prorate the number of hours based on the number of days the home was available for day care. Cross out the preprinted entry on line 5. Multiply 24 hours by the number of days available and enter the result.

Part II

Line 8

If all the gross income from your trade or business is from the business use of your home, enter on line 8 the amount from Schedule C, line 29, **plus** any net gain or (loss) derived from the business use of your home and shown on Schedule D or Form 4797. If you file more than one Form 8829, include only the income earned and the deductions attributable to that income during the period you owned the home for which Part I was completed.

If some of the income is from a place of business other than your home, you must first determine the part of your gross income (Schedule C, line 7, and gains from Schedule D and Form 4797) from the business use of your home. In making this determination, consider the amount of time you spend at each location as well as other facts. After determining the part of your gross income from the business use of your home, subtract from that amount the **total expenses** shown on Schedule C, line 28, plus any losses from your business shown on Schedule D or Form 4797. Enter the result on line 8 of Form 8829.

Columns (a) and (b)

Enter as direct or indirect expenses only expenses for the business use of your home (i.e., expenses allowable only because your home is used for business). If you did not operate a business for the entire year, you can only deduct the expenses paid or incurred for the portion of the year you used your home for business. Other expenses not allocable to the business use of your home, such as salaries, supplies, and business telephone expenses, are deductible elsewhere on Schedule C and should not be entered on Form 8829.

Direct expenses benefit only the business part of your home. They include painting or repairs made to the specific area or rooms used for business. Enter 100% of your direct expenses on the appropriate line in column (a).

Indirect expenses are for keeping up and running your entire home. They benefit both the business and personal parts of your home. Generally, enter 100% of your indirect expenses on the appropriate line in column (b).

Exception. If the business percentage of an indirect expense is different from the percentage on line 7, enter only the business part of the expense on the appropriate line in column (a), and leave that line in column (b) blank. For example, your electric bill is $800 for lighting, cooking, laundry, and television. If you reasonably estimate $300 of your electric bill is for lighting and you use 10% of your home for business, enter $30 on line 19 in column (a). **Do not** make an entry on line 19 in column (b) for any part of your electric bill.

Lines 9, 10, and 11

Enter only the amounts that would be deductible whether or not you used your home for business (i.e., amounts allowable as itemized deductions on **Schedule A** (Form 1040)).

Treat **casualty losses** as personal expenses for this step. Figure the amount to enter on line 9 by completing Form 4684, Section A. When figuring line 17 of Form 4684, enter 10% of your adjusted gross income excluding the gross income from business use of your home and the deductions attributable to that income. Include on line 9 of Form 8829 the amount from Form 4684, line 18. See line 27 below to deduct part of the casualty losses not allowed because of the limits on Form 4684.

Do not file or use that Form 4684 to figure the amount of casualty losses to deduct on Schedule A. Instead, complete a separate Form 4684 to deduct the personal portion of your casualty losses.

On line 10, include only **mortgage interest** that would be deductible on Schedule A and that qualifies as a direct or indirect expense. **Do not** include interest on a mortgage loan that did not benefit your home (e.g., a home equity loan used to pay off credit card bills, to buy a car, or to pay tuition costs).

If you itemize your deductions, be sure to claim **only** the personal portion of your deductible mortgage interest and real estate taxes on Schedule A. For example, if your business percentage on line 7 is 30%, you can claim 70% of your deductible mortgage interest and real estate taxes on Schedule A.

Line 16

If the amount of home mortgage interest you deduct on Schedule A is limited, enter the part of the excess mortgage interest that qualifies as a direct or indirect expense. **Do not** include mortgage interest on a loan that did not benefit your home (explained above).

Line 20

Include on this line any 1998 operating expenses not included on lines 9 through 19.

If you rent rather than own your home, include the rent you paid on line 20, column (b). If your housing is provided free of charge and the value of the housing is tax-exempt, you cannot deduct the rental value of any portion of the housing.

Line 27

Multiply your casualty losses in excess of the amount on line 9 by the business percentage of those losses and enter the result.

Line 34

If your home was used in more than one business, allocate the amount shown on line 34 to each business using any method that is reasonable under the circumstances. For each business, enter on Schedule C, line 30, only the amount allocated to that business.

Part III

Lines 35 through 37

Enter on line 35 the cost or other basis of your home, or if less, the fair market value of your home on the date you first used the home for business. **Do not** adjust this amount for depreciation claimed or changes in fair market value after the year you first used your home for business. Allocate this amount between land and building values on lines 36 and 37.

Attach your own schedule showing the cost or other basis of additions and improvements placed in service after you began to use your home for business. **Do not** include any amounts on lines 35 through 38 for these expenditures. Instead, see the instructions for line 40.

Page 2

Line 39

IF you first used your home for business in the following month in 1998 . . .	THEN enter the following percentage on line 39 . . .
January	2.461%
February	2.247%
March	2.033%
April	1.819%
May	1.605%
June	1.391%
July	1.177%
August	0.963%
September	0.749%
October	0.535%
November	0.321%
December	0.107%

Exception. If the business part of your home is qualified Indian reservation property (as defined in section 168(j)(4)), see **Pub. 946,** How To Depreciate Property, to figure the depreciation.

IF you first used your home for business . . .	THEN the percentage to enter on line 39 is . . .
After May 12, 1993, and before 1998	2.564% (except as noted below)
After May 13, 1993, and before 1994, and you either started construction or had a binding contract to buy or build that home before May 13, 1993	3.175% (except as noted below)
After 1991 and before May 13, 1993	3.175% (except as noted below)
After 1991, and you stopped using your home for business before the end of the year	The percentage given in Pub. 946
After 1986 and before 1992	The percentage given in Pub. 946
Before 1987	The percentage given in Pub. 534

Line 40

If no additions and improvements were placed in service after you began using your home for business, multiply line 38 by the percentage on line 39. Enter the result on lines 40 and 28.

IF additions and improvements were placed in service . . .	THEN figure the depreciation allowed on these expenditures by multiplying the business part of their cost or other basis by . . .
During 1998 (but after you began using your home for business)	The percentage in the line 39 instructions for the month placed in service
After May 12, 1993, and before 1998	2.564% (except as noted below)
After May 13, 1993, and before 1994, and you either started construction or had a binding contract to buy or build that home before May 13, 1993	3.175% (except as noted below)
After 1991 and before May 13, 1993	3.175% (except as noted below)
After 1991, and you stopped using your home for business before the end of the year	The percentage given in Pub. 946
After 1986 and before 1992	The percentage given in Pub. 946
Before 1987	The percentage given in Pub. 534

Attach a schedule showing your computation and include the amount you figured in the total for line 40. Write "See attached" below the entry space.

Complete and attach **Form 4562,** Depreciation and Amortization, **only** if:

1. You first used your home for business in 1998, or

2. You are depreciating additions and improvements placed in service in 1998.

If you first used your home for business in 1998, enter on Form 4562, in column (c) of line 15i, the amount from line 38 of Form 8829. Then enter on Form 4562, in column (g) of line 15i, the amount from line 40 of Form 8829. But **do not** include this amount on Schedule C, line 13.

Paperwork Reduction Act Notice. We ask for the information on this form to carry out the Internal Revenue laws of the United States. You are required to give us the information. We need it to ensure that you are complying with these laws and to allow us to figure and collect the right amount of tax.

You are not required to provide the information requested on a form that is subject to the Paperwork Reduction Act unless the form displays a valid OMB control number. Books or records relating to a form or its instructions must be retained as long as their contents may become material in the administration of any Internal Revenue law. Generally, tax returns and return information are confidential, as required by section 6103.

The time needed to complete and file this form will vary depending on individual circumstances. The estimated average time is: **Recordkeeping,** 52 min.; **Learning about the law or the form,** 8 min.; **Preparing the form,** 1 hr., 16 min.; and **Copying, assembling, and sending the form to the IRS,** 20 min.

If you have comments concerning the accuracy of these time estimates or suggestions for making this form simpler, we would be happy to hear from you. See the Instructions for Form 1040.

SCHEDULE SE	Self-Employment Tax	OMB No. 1545-0074
(Form 1040)	▶ See Instructions for Schedule SE (Form 1040).	19**98**
Department of the Treasury Internal Revenue Service	▶ Attach to Form 1040.	Attachment Sequence No. **17**

Name of person with **self-employment** income (as shown on Form 1040)	Social security number of person with **self-employment** income ▶

Who Must File Schedule SE

You must file Schedule SE if:

- You had net earnings from self-employment from **other than** church employee income (line 4 of Short Schedule SE or line 4c of Long Schedule SE) of $400 or more, **OR**
- You had church employee income of $108.28 or more. Income from services you performed as a minister or a member of a religious order **is not** church employee income. See page SE-1.

Note: *Even if you had a loss or a small amount of income from self-employment, it may be to your benefit to file Schedule SE and use either "optional method" in Part II of Long Schedule SE. See page SE-3.*

Exception. If your only self-employment income was from earnings as a minister, member of a religious order, or Christian Science practitioner **and** you filed Form 4361 and received IRS approval not to be taxed on those earnings, **do not** file Schedule SE. Instead, write "Exempt–Form 4361" on Form 1040, line 50.

May I Use Short Schedule SE or MUST I Use Long Schedule SE?

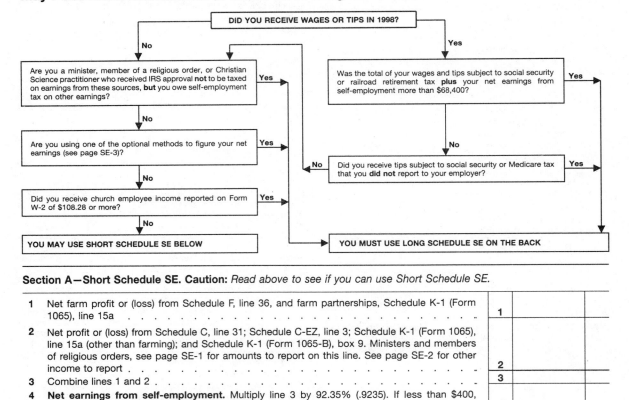

Section A—Short Schedule SE. Caution: *Read above to see if you can use Short Schedule SE.*

1	Net farm profit or (loss) from Schedule F, line 36, and farm partnerships, Schedule K-1 (Form 1065), line 15a	1	
2	Net profit or (loss) from Schedule C, line 31; Schedule C-EZ, line 3; Schedule K-1 (Form 1065), line 15a (other than farming); and Schedule K-1 (Form 1065-B), box 9. Ministers and members of religious orders, see page SE-1 for amounts to report on this line. See page SE-2 for other income to report	2	
3	Combine lines 1 and 2	3	
4	**Net earnings from self-employment.** Multiply line 3 by 92.35% (.9235). If less than $400, **do not** file this schedule; you do not owe self-employment tax . . . . ▶	4	
5	Self-employment tax. If the amount on line 4 is: • $68,400 or less, multiply line 4 by 15.3% (.153). Enter the result here and on **Form 1040, line 50.** • More than $68,400, multiply line 4 by 2.9% (.029). Then, add $8,481.60 to the result. Enter the total here and on **Form 1040, line 50.**	5	
6	**Deduction for one-half of self-employment tax.** Multiply line 5 by 50% (.5). Enter the result here and on **Form 1040, line 27**	6	

For Paperwork Reduction Act Notice, see Form 1040 instructions.   Cat. No. 11358Z   Schedule SE (Form 1040) 1998

Schedule SE (Form 1040) 1998   Attachment Sequence No. **17**   Page **2**

Name of person with **self-employment** income (as shown on Form 1040)	Social security number of person with **self-employment** income ▶		

Section B—Long Schedule SE

Part I   Self-Employment Tax

Note: *If your only income subject to self-employment tax is* **church employee income,** *skip lines 1 through 4b. Enter -0- on line 4c and go to line 5a. Income from services you performed as a minister or a member of a religious order* **is not** *church employee income. See page SE-1.*

A   If you are a minister, member of a religious order, or Christian Science practitioner **and** you filed Form 4361, but you had $400 or more of **other** net earnings from self-employment, check here and continue with Part I . . . . . ▶ ☐

1	Net farm profit or (loss) from Schedule F, line 36, and farm partnerships, Schedule K-1 (Form 1065), line 15a. **Note:** *Skip this line if you use the farm optional method. See page SE-4*	**1**		
2	Net profit or (loss) from Schedule C, line 31; Schedule C-EZ, line 3; Schedule K-1 (Form 1065), line 15a (other than farming); and Schedule K-1 (Form 1065-B), box 9. Ministers and members of religious orders, see page SE-1 for amounts to report on this line. See page SE-2 for other income to report. **Note:** *Skip this line if you use the nonfarm optional method. See page SE-4*	**2**		
3	Combine lines 1 and 2	**3**		
4a	If line 3 is more than zero, multiply line 3 by 92.35% (.9235). Otherwise, enter amount from line 3	**4a**		
b	If you elected one or both of the optional methods, enter the total of lines 15 and 17 here . .	**4b**		
c	Combine lines 4a and 4b. If less than $400, **do not** file this schedule; you do not owe self-employment tax. **Exception.** If less than $400 and you had **church employee income,** enter -0- and continue ▶	**4c**		
5a	Enter your **church employee income** from Form W-2. **Caution:** *See page SE-1 for definition of church employee income* **5a**			
b	Multiply line 5a by 92.35% (.9235). If less than $100, enter -0- . .	**5b**		
6	**Net earnings from self-employment.** Add lines 4c and 5b	**6**		
7	Maximum amount of combined wages and self-employment earnings subject to social security tax or the 6.2% portion of the 7.65% railroad retirement (tier 1) tax for 1998	**7**	68,400	00
8a	Total social security wages and tips (total of boxes 3 and 7 on Form(s) W-2) and railroad retirement (tier 1) compensation **8a**			
b	Unreported tips subject to social security tax (from Form 4137, line 9) **8b**			
c	Add lines 8a and 8b	**8c**		
9	Subtract line 8c from line 7. If zero or less, enter -0- here and on line 10 and go to line 11 . ▶	**9**		
10	Multiply the **smaller** of line 6 or line 9 by 12.4% (.124)	**10**		
11	Multiply line 6 by 2.9% (.029)	**11**		
12	**Self-employment tax.** Add lines 10 and 11. Enter here and on **Form 1040, line 50**	**12**		
13	**Deduction for one-half of self-employment tax.** Multiply line 12 by 50% (.5). Enter the result here and on **Form 1040, line 27** **13**			

Part II   Optional Methods To Figure Net Earnings (See page SE-3.)

Farm Optional Method. You may use this method **only** if:

● Your gross farm income[1] was not more than $2,400, **or**

● Your gross farm income[1] was more than $2,400 and your net farm profits[2] were less than $1,733.

14	Maximum income for optional methods	**14**	1,600	00
15	Enter the **smaller** of: two-thirds (⅔) of gross farm income[1] (not less than zero) **or** $1,600. Also, include this amount on line 4b above	**15**		

Nonfarm Optional Method. You may use this method **only** if:

● Your net nonfarm profits[3] were less than $1,733 and also less than 72.189% of your gross nonfarm income,[4] **and**

● You had net earnings from self-employment of at least $400 in 2 of the prior 3 years.

Caution: *You may use this method no more than five times.*

16	Subtract line 15 from line 14	**16**		
17	Enter the **smaller** of: two-thirds (⅔) of gross nonfarm income[4] (not less than zero) **or** the amount on line 16. Also, include this amount on line 4b above	**17**		

[1] From Sch. F, line 11, and Sch. K-1 (Form 1065), line 15b.   [3] From Sch. C, line 31; Sch. C-EZ, line 3; Sch. K-1 (Form 1065), line 15a; and Sch. K-1 (Form 1065-B), box 9.
[2] From Sch. F, line 36, and Sch. K-1 (Form 1065), line 15a.   [4] From Sch. C, line 7; Sch. C-EZ, line 1; Sch. K-1 (Form 1065), line 15c; and Sch. K-1 (Form 1065-B), box 9.

8 | SETTING UP YOUR BUSINESS AS A PARTNERSHIP

If you are a partner in a simple partnership, where all of the partners participate in managing the business, you are somewhat of a glorified sole proprietor working in conjunction with other sole proprietors. The Internal Revenue Code and other laws don't phrase it that way. Instead the term *self-employed* has come into general use to refer to sole proprietors and partners, as well as members of limited liability companies and, in some respects, stockholders in S corporations.

So, you and your partners, as one entity, will need to complete and file many of the same forms as does a sole proprietor. Specifically, they are as follows. (Refer to the chapter on sole proprietors for details of these forms.)

- Application for Employer Identification Number (SS-4)
- Registration with state tax authorities for collection of sales and other taxes
- Local business license and registration of fictitious name
- Formally registering the business name or trademark (optional)

REGISTERING THE PARTNERSHIP

In addition, most states require that a partnership be registered with the state and there may also be a requirement to register as a partnership with the local city or county government.

PARTNERSHIP AGREEMENT

This is the most important document for this form of business. Unlike a sole proprietorship, no one individual owns all of the business, and, therefore, no one individual should make all of the decisions. Here is a list of the bare minimum questions that should be addressed in a partnership agreement:

Who manages the business?

What decisions require a vote of all of the partners?

How will profits be divided between partners?

How will losses be divided between partners?

Can partners be compelled to make additional investments in the business?

Will any of the partners be passive? That is, do they invest money and then take no active part in the partnership operations?

The partnership agreement on page 83 is an example only and should not be copied and used as is. Every partnership is different, so each partnership agreement should be carefully drawn by an attorney. That doesn't mean you should ask the attorney to make your decisions. Use this agreement and the foregoing list of points to make sure you and your partners have discussed all the points of the agreement before you start the professional clock running.

INCOME TAX FORMS YOU WILL BE FILING

Some of the forms are the same as are filed for a sole proprietorship, but the main partnership form is different and decidedly more complex. To save confusion, we'll list them all but refer to the sole proprietorship section when the comments there are appropriate.

Partnership Return of Income

This is the partnership return that has to be filled annually. In theory, it works like this: The taxable income is computed on the form, similar to the way in which it is computed on a Schedule C for a sole proprietor. The income or loss is recorded on Schedule K, which is a page of Form 1065. Then, the income is split up between the partners, according to the partnership agreement, and each partner's share of the income or loss is stated on a Schedule K-1 that is prepared for each partner. Of course, the total of all of the income or loss on the Schedules K-1 should add up to the figure on Schedule K.

Look at Schedule K or Schedule K-1. Notice the number of items that have to be reported as separate items to each partner. That's because each partner has to report those items separately on his or her Form 1040, Individual Income Tax Return. For example, partners have to report their share of charitable contributions as such, on Schedule A. They don't become merged into the partnership taxable income.

Along with the form, the instructions, which run on for 24 pages, are reprinted on pages 85–115. Why? So you can look through the headings in them to see if any items might apply to the way in which you conduct, or expect to conduct, your business.

Although this form looks like an income tax return and feels like an income tax return, it is actually only an information return. That is, it provides information that goes on someone else's (the partners') tax return.

Note that there is a special Schedule D (p. 116), Capital Gains and Losses, for partnerships.

LIMITED PARTNERSHIPS

There is now little reason to form a limited partnership since recent developments make the formation of a limited liability company (LLC) more desirable. If, for some arcane reason, you should form a limited partnership, the applicable forms are the same as for a general partnership, with two additions: First, the registration with the state may be more complex, and second, because limited partnership interests may be considered to be securities, you will have the worries over compliance with state and federal securities laws. In other words, what applies to sole proprietorships and partnerships applies, generally, to limited partnerships.

The Florida document, Certificate of Limited Partnership, is reproduced on pages 122–125.

EXAMPLE OF GENERAL
PARTNERSHIP AGREEMENT

Reprinted by permission of the 'Lectric Law Library Legal Website at www.lectlaw.com.

PARTNERSHIP AGREEMENT

(NAME), and (NAME), the below signed hereby enter into this Partnership Agreement on behalf of themselves, their heirs, successors and assigns, and set forth following terms and conditions as constituting the Partnership Agreement in its entirety:

1. The partnership shall go by the following name: (NAME).

2. The partnerships' principle place of business shall be (DESCRIBE).

3. The first day that the partnership shall begin business is: (DATE) and it will continue until the partners agree to terminate it or until forced cease its operations by law.

4. The partnerships' operations shall be primarily in the following field or area: (DESCRIBE).

5. The partnership shall be capitalized as follows: For each $ (AMOUNT) (dollars) each partner shall receive (NUMBER) shares with contribution being made as follows:

Partner A contributes $ (AMOUNT), and shall receive (NUMBER) shares, the same being (NUMBER) % of the total shares available.

Partner B contributes $ (AMOUNT), and shall receive (NUMBER) shares, the same being (NUMBER) % of the total shares available.

6. Losses and gains on contributed capital and other property, shall be assigned as follows: (DESCRIBE).

The IRS's general allocation rule shall apply, and gains and losses shall be allocated according to the percentage of total capital contributed by each partner as set out in paragraph 5 above.

7. Profits and losses shall be allocated according to the same percentage allocation set forth in paragraph 6 above.

8. Salary, if any, for the services rendered shall be determined by unanimous approval of the partners.

9. Control and management of the partnership shall be split equally amongst the partners.

10. Each partner shall maintain both an individual drawing account and an individual capital account. Into the capital account shall be placed that partner's initial capitalization and any increases thereto. The drawing accounts shall be used for withdrawal of amounts, the size of which is limited to $ (AMOUNT) on any one day.

11. Adequate accounting records shall be made and maintained. Any partner, of his/her agent, may review any and all accounting or other records at anytime.

12. The partners designate the following as the Partnership's business and checking accounts into which all the funds of the Partnership shall be placed and maintained: (DESCRIBE).

13. Accounting records and books shall be kept on a (select one) 1. cash basis 2. accrual basis and the fiscal year shall begin on the first day of (MONTH) and shall end on the last day of (MONTH).

14. At the close of the fiscal year there shall be an annual audit conducted by the following accounting firm: (DESCRIBE).

15. The partnership shall dissolve upon the retirement, death or incapacity of any partner unless the remaining partner elects the option of buying out that partner's share. If so elected, the partnership shall be valued by submission to arbitration with _____, according to reasonable accounting and valuation principles, and as set forth in paragraph 17 below. The finding of the arbitrator as to the value of the partnership shall be final and binding upon the partners, their heirs, successors, and assigns. Upon the issuance of this finding, the remaining partner shall have (AMOUNT OF TIME) to buy out the previous partner's share. Should more than one remaining partner desire to buy this share, the share shall be split evenly between the same.

16. Upon termination of dissolution of the Partnership, the Partnership will be promptly liquidated, with all debts being paid first, prior to any distribution of the remaining funds. Distribution shall be made according to the percentage of ownership as set out in paragraph 5 above.

17. Any controversy or claim arising out of or relating to this Agreement, or the breach thereof, shall be settled by arbitration in accordance with the Commercial Arbitration Rules of the American Arbitration Association, and judgment upon the award rendered by the arbitrator(s) may be entered in any court having jurisdiction thereof.
So agreed, this (NUMBER) day of (MONTH), 19 _____ .

_____
(NAME)

_____
(NAME)

Form **1065**	**U.S. Partnership Return of Income**	OMB No. 1545-0099
Department of the Treasury Internal Revenue Service	For calendar year 1998, or tax year beginning .... , 1998, and ending .... , 19 .... . ▶ See separate instructions.	**1998**

A Principal business activity	Use the IRS label. Other- wise, please print or type.	Name of partnership	D Employer identification number
B Principal product or service		Number, street, and room or suite no. If a P.O. box, see page 10 of the instructions.	E Date business started
C NEW business code no. (see pages 25–27 of instructions)		City or town, state, and ZIP code	F Total assets (see page 10 of the instructions) $

G Check applicable boxes: **(1)** ☐ Initial return **(2)** ☐ Final return **(3)** ☐ Change in address **(4)** ☐ Amended return

H Check accounting method: **(1)** ☐ Cash **(2)** ☐ Accrual **(3)** ☐ Other (specify) ▶ ....

I Number of Schedules K-1. Attach one for each person who was a partner at any time during the tax year ▶ ....

Caution: *Include **only** trade or business income and expenses on lines 1a through 22 below. See the instructions for more information.*

Income

1a Gross receipts or sales	1a	
b Less returns and allowances	1b	1c
2 Cost of goods sold (Schedule A, line 8)		2
3 Gross profit. Subtract line 2 from line 1c		3
4 Ordinary income (loss) from other partnerships, estates, and trusts *(attach schedule)*		4
5 Net farm profit (loss) *(attach Schedule F (Form 1040))*		5
6 Net gain (loss) from Form 4797, Part II, line 18		6
7 Other income (loss) *(attach schedule)*		7
8 **Total income (loss).** Combine lines 3 through 7		8

Deductions (see page 11 of the instructions for limitations)

9 Salaries and wages (other than to partners) (less employment credits)		9
10 Guaranteed payments to partners		10
11 Repairs and maintenance		11
12 Bad debts		12
13 Rent		13
14 Taxes and licenses		14
15 Interest		15
16a Depreciation (if required, attach Form 4562)	16a	
b Less depreciation reported on Schedule A and elsewhere on return	16b	16c
17 Depletion **(Do not deduct oil and gas depletion.)**		17
18 Retirement plans, etc.		18
19 Employee benefit programs		19
20 Other deductions *(attach schedule)*		20
21 **Total deductions.** Add the amounts shown in the far right column for lines 9 through 20		21

22 **Ordinary income (loss)** from trade or business activities. Subtract line 21 from line 8		22

Please Sign Here

Under penalties of perjury, I declare that I have examined this return, including accompanying schedules and statements, and to the best of my knowledge and belief, it is true, correct, and complete. Declaration of preparer (other than general partner or limited liability company member) is based on all information of which preparer has any knowledge.

▶ Signature of general partner or limited liability company member   ▶ Date

Paid Preparer's Use Only

Preparer's signature ▶	Date	Check if self-employed ▶ ☐	Preparer's social security no.
Firm's name (or yours if self-employed) and address ▶		EIN ▶	
		ZIP code ▶	

For Paperwork Reduction Act Notice, see separate instructions.   Cat. No. 11390Z   Form **1065** (1998)

Form 1065 (1998)   Page **2**

Schedule A	Cost of Goods Sold (see page 14 of the instructions)		

1	Inventory at beginning of year	**1**	
2	Purchases less cost of items withdrawn for personal use	**2**	
3	Cost of labor.	**3**	
4	Additional section 263A costs *(attach schedule)*	**4**	
5	Other costs *(attach schedule)*	**5**	
6	**Total.** Add lines 1 through 5	**6**	
7	Inventory at end of year	**7**	
8	**Cost of goods sold.** Subtract line 7 from line 6. Enter here and on page 1, line 2	**8**	

9a Check all methods used for valuing closing inventory:

    (i) ☐ Cost as described in Regulations section 1.471-3

    (ii) ☐ Lower of cost or market as described in Regulations section 1.471-4

    (iii) ☐ Other (specify method used and attach explanation) ▶ -

  b Check this box if there was a writedown of "subnormal" goods as described in Regulations section 1.471-2(c). . . . ▶ ☐

  c Check this box if the LIFO inventory method was adopted this tax year for any goods *(if checked, attach Form 970)* . . ▶ ☐

  d Do the rules of section 263A (for property produced or acquired for resale) apply to the partnership? . . ☐ **Yes** ☐ **No**

  e Was there any change in determining quantities, cost, or valuations between opening and closing inventory? ☐ **Yes** ☐ **No**

    If "Yes," attach explanation.

Schedule B	Other Information		Yes	No

1 What type of entity is filing this return? Check the applicable box:

  a ☐ General partnership   **b** ☐ Limited partnership   **c** ☐ Limited liability company

  d ☐ Limited liability partnership   **e** ☐ Other ▶ -

2 Are any partners in this partnership also partnerships?. . . . .

3 Is this partnership a partner in another partnership? . . . .

4 Is this partnership subject to the consolidated audit procedures of sections 6221 through 6233? If "Yes," see **Designation of Tax Matters Partner** below . . . .

5 Does this partnership meet **ALL THREE** of the following requirements?

  a The partnership's total receipts for the tax year were less than $250,000;

  b The partnership's total assets at the end of the tax year were less than $600,000; **AND**

  c Schedules K-1 are filed with the return and furnished to the partners on or before the due date (including extensions) for the partnership return.

    If "Yes," the partnership is not required to complete Schedules L, M-1, and M-2; Item F on page 1 of Form 1065; or Item J on Schedule K-1 . . . .

6 Does this partnership have any foreign partners? . . . .

7 Is this partnership a publicly traded partnership as defined in section 469(k)(2)? . . . .

8 Has this partnership filed, or is it required to file, **Form 8264,** Application for Registration of a Tax Shelter? . . .

9 At any time during calendar year 1998, did the partnership have an interest in or a signature or other authority over a financial account in a foreign country (such as a bank account, securities account, or other financial account)? See page 14 of the instructions for exceptions and filing requirements for Form TD F 90-22.1. If "Yes," enter the name of the foreign country. ▶ -

10 During the tax year, did the partnership receive a distribution from, or was it the grantor of, or transferor to, a foreign trust? If "Yes," the partnership may have to file Form 3520. See page 15 of the instructions . . . .

11 Was there a distribution of property or a transfer (e.g., by sale or death) of a partnership interest during the tax year? If "Yes," you may elect to adjust the basis of the partnership's assets under section 754 by attaching the statement described under **Elections Made By the Partnership** on page 6 of the instructions . . . . . .

Designation of Tax Matters Partner (see page 15 of the instructions)

Enter below the general partner designated as the tax matters partner (TMP) for the tax year of this return:

Name of designated TMP ▶		Identifying number of TMP ▶	
Address of designated TMP ▶			

Form 1065 (1998)   Page **3**

Schedule K	**Partners' Shares of Income, Credits, Deductions, etc.**	
	(a) Distributive share items	**(b) Total amount**

Income (Loss)

1 Ordinary income (loss) from trade or business activities (page 1, line 22) — **1**
2 Net income (loss) from rental real estate activities *(attach Form 8825)* — **2**
3a Gross income from other rental activities — **3a**
b Expenses from other rental activities *(attach schedule)* — **3b**
c Net income (loss) from other rental activities. Subtract line 3b from line 3a — **3c**
4 Portfolio income (loss):
a Interest income — **4a**
b Ordinary dividends — **4b**
c Royalty income — **4c**
d Net short-term capital gain (loss) *(attach Schedule D (Form 1065))* — **4d**
e Net long-term capital gain (loss) *(attach Schedule D (Form 1065)):*
(1) 28% rate gain (loss) ► .... (2) Total for year ► **4e(2)**
f Other portfolio income (loss) *(attach schedule)* — **4f**
5 Guaranteed payments to partners — **5**
6 Net section 1231 gain (loss) (other than due to casualty or theft) *(attach Form 4797)* — **6**
7 Other income (loss) *(attach schedule)* — **7**

Deductions

8 Charitable contributions *(attach schedule)* — **8**
9 Section 179 expense deduction *(attach Form 4562)* — **9**
10 Deductions related to portfolio income (itemize) — **10**
11 Other deductions *(attach schedule)* — **11**

Credits

12a Low-income housing credit:
(1) From partnerships to which section 42(j)(5) applies for property placed in service before 1990 — **12a(1)**
(2) Other than on line 12a(1) for property placed in service before 1990 — **12a(2)**
(3) From partnerships to which section 42(j)(5) applies for property placed in service after 1989 — **12a(3)**
(4) Other than on line 12a(3) for property placed in service after 1989 — **12a(4)**
b Qualified rehabilitation expenditures related to rental real estate activities *(attach Form 3468)* — **12b**
c Credits (other than credits shown on lines 12a and 12b) related to rental real estate activities — **12c**
d Credits related to other rental activities — **12d**
13 Other credits — **13**

Investment Interest

14a Interest expense on investment debts — **14a**
b (1) Investment income included on lines 4a, 4b, 4c, and 4f above — **14b(1)**
(2) Investment expenses included on line 10 above — **14b(2)**

Self-Employment

15a Net earnings (loss) from self-employment — **15a**
b Gross farming or fishing income — **15b**
c Gross nonfarm income — **15c**

Adjustments and Tax Preference Items

16a Depreciation adjustment on property placed in service after 1986 — **16a**
b Adjusted gain or loss — **16b**
c Depletion (other than oil and gas) — **16c**
d (1) Gross income from oil, gas, and geothermal properties — **16d(1)**
(2) Deductions allocable to oil, gas, and geothermal properties — **16d(2)**
e Other adjustments and tax preference items *(attach schedule)* — **16e**

Foreign Taxes

17a Type of income ►
b Name of foreign country or U.S. possession ►
c Total gross income from sources outside the United States *(attach schedule)* — **17c**
d Total applicable deductions and losses *(attach schedule)* — **17d**
e Total foreign taxes (check one): ► ☐ Paid ☐ Accrued — **17e**
f Reduction in taxes available for credit *(attach schedule)* — **17f**
g Other foreign tax information *(attach schedule)* — **17g**

Other

18 Section 59(e)(2) expenditures: a Type ► .... b Amount ► **18b**
19 Tax-exempt interest income — **19**
20 Other tax-exempt income — **20**
21 Nondeductible expenses — **21**
22 Distributions of money (cash and marketable securities) — **22**
23 Distributions of property other than money — **23**
24 Other items and amounts required to be reported separately to partners *(attach schedule)*

Form 1065 (1998)   Page **4**

Analysis of Net Income (Loss)

1   Net income (loss). Combine Schedule K, lines 1 through 7 in column (b). From the result, subtract the sum of Schedule K, lines 8 through 11, 14a, 17e, and 18b **1**

2 Analysis by partner type:	(i) Corporate	(ii) Individual (active)	(iii) Individual (passive)	(iv) Partnership	(v) Exempt organization	(vi) Nominee/Other
a General partners						
b Limited partners						

Schedule L   **Balance Sheets per Books** (Not required if Question 5 on Schedule B is answered "Yes.")

Assets	Beginning of tax year (a)	(b)	End of tax year (c)	(d)
1 Cash				
2a Trade notes and accounts receivable				
b Less allowance for bad debts				
3 Inventories				
4 U.S. government obligations				
5 Tax-exempt securities				
6 Other current assets (attach schedule)				
7 Mortgage and real estate loans				
8 Other investments (attach schedule)				
9a Buildings and other depreciable assets				
b Less accumulated depreciation				
10a Depletable assets				
b Less accumulated depletion				
11 Land (net of any amortization)				
12a Intangible assets (amortizable only)				
b Less accumulated amortization				
13 Other assets (attach schedule)				
14 Total assets				
Liabilities and Capital				
15 Accounts payable				
16 Mortgages, notes, bonds payable in less than 1 year				
17 Other current liabilities (attach schedule)				
18 All nonrecourse loans				
19 Mortgages, notes, bonds payable in 1 year or more				
20 Other liabilities (attach schedule)				
21 Partners' capital accounts				
22 Total liabilities and capital				

Schedule M-1   **Reconciliation of Income (Loss) per Books With Income (Loss) per Return**
(Not required if Question 5 on Schedule B is answered "Yes." See page 23 of the instructions.)

1   Net income (loss) per books

2   Income included on Schedule K, lines 1 through 4, 6, and 7, not recorded on books this year (itemize): ....

3   Guaranteed payments (other than health insurance)

4   Expenses recorded on books this year not included on Schedule K, lines 1 through 11, 14a, 17e, and 18b (itemize):
a Depreciation $ ....
b Travel and entertainment $ ....

5   Add lines 1 through 4

6   Income recorded on books this year not included on Schedule K, lines 1 through 7 (itemize):
a Tax-exempt interest $ ....

7   Deductions included on Schedule K, lines 1 through 11, 14a, 17e, and 18b, not charged against book income this year (itemize):
a Depreciation $ ....

8   Add lines 6 and 7

9   Income (loss) (Analysis of Net Income (Loss), line 1). Subtract line 8 from line 5

Schedule M-2   **Analysis of Partners' Capital Accounts** (Not required if Question 5 on Schedule B is answered "Yes.")

1   Balance at beginning of year

2   Capital contributed during year

3   Net income (loss) per books

4   Other increases (itemize): ....

5   Add lines 1 through 4

6   Distributions: a Cash
            b Property

7   Other decreases (itemize): ....

8   Add lines 6 and 7

9   Balance at end of year. Subtract line 8 from line 5

1998

Department of the Treasury
Internal Revenue Service

Instructions for Form 1065

U.S. Partnership Return of Income

Section references are to the Internal Revenue Code unless otherwise noted.

Paperwork Reduction Act Notice. We ask for the information on this form to carry out the Internal Revenue laws of the United States. You are required to give us the information. We need it to ensure that you are complying with these laws and to allow us to figure and collect the right amount of tax.

You are not required to provide the information requested on a form that is subject to the Paperwork Reduction Act unless the form displays a valid OMB control number. Books or records relating to a form or its instructions must be retained as long as their contents may become material in the administration of any Internal Revenue law. Generally, tax returns and return information are confidential, as required by section 6103.

The time needed to complete and file this form and related schedules will vary depending on individual circumstances. The estimated average times are:

Form	Recordkeeping	Learning about the law or the form	Preparing the form	Copying, assembling, and sending the form to the IRS
1065	39 hr., 50 min.	21 hr., 28 min.	37 hr., 11 min.	4 hr., 1 min.
Schedule D (Form 1065)	6 hr., 56 min.	1 hr., 29 min.	1 hr., 40 min.	
Schedule K-1 (Form 1065)	25 hr., 7 min.	9 hr., 20 min.	10 hr., 10 min.	
Schedule L (Form 1065)	15 hr., 32 min.	6 min.	22 min.	
Schedule M-1 (Form 1065)	3 hr., 21 min.	12 min.	16 min.	
Schedule M-2 (Form 1065)	2 hr., 52 min.	6 min.	9 min.	

If you have comments concerning the accuracy of these time estimates or suggestions for making these forms simpler, we would be happy to hear from you. You can write to the Tax Forms Committee, Western Area Distribution Center, Rancho Cordova, CA 95743-0001. **DO NOT** send the tax form to this address. Instead, see **Where To File** on page 3.

Changes To Note

New codes for principal business activity. The new **Codes for Principal Business Activity** beginning on page 25 are based on the North American Industry Classification System (NAICS), which was developed by the statistical agencies of Canada, Mexico, and the United States in cooperation with the Office of Management and Budget. The NAICS-based codes replace industry codes previously based on the Standard Industrial Classification (SIC) system.

Simplified reporting for large partnerships. Generally, nonservice partnerships with 100 or more partners during the preceding tax year may elect a simplified reporting system by filing **Form 1065-B**, U.S. Return of Income for Electing Large Partnerships, instead of Form 1065. See Form 1065-B and its instructions for more information.

Magnetic media filing not required for 1998. Because regulations have not yet been issued under section 6011(e) regarding partnership returns, there is no requirement for partnerships with more than 100 partners to file on magnetic media for 1998. Thus no penalties will be imposed for partnerships that do not file on magnetic media.

Unresolved Tax Problems

Most problems can be solved with one contact either by calling, writing, or visiting an IRS office. But if the partnership has tried unsuccessfully to resolve a problem with the IRS, it should contact the Taxpayer Advocate's Problem Resolution Program (PRP). Someone at PRP will assign the partnership a personal advocate who is in the best position to try to resolve the problem. The Taxpayer Advocate can also offer special help if the partnership has a significant hardship as a result of a tax problem.

Cat. No. 11392V

Contact the Taxpayer Advocate if:
- The partnership has tried unsuccessfully to resolve a problem with the IRS and has not been contacted by the date promised, or
- The partnership is on its second attempt to resolve a problem.

You may contact a Taxpayer Advocate by calling a new toll-free assistance number, **1-877-777-4778**. Persons who have access to TTY/TTD equipment may call 1-800-829-4059 and ask for the Taxpayer Advocate. If the partnership prefers, it may write to the Taxpayer Advocate at the IRS office that last contacted the partnership.

While Taxpayer Advocates cannot change the tax law or make a technical tax decision, they can clear up problems that resulted from previous contacts and ensure that the partnership's case is given a complete and impartial review. Taxpayer Advocates are working to put service first. For more details, see **Pub. 1546**, The Problem Resolution Program of the Internal Revenue Service.

How To Get Forms and Publications

Personal Computer

Access the IRS's Internet web site at **www.irs.ustreas.gov** to do the following:
- Download forms, instructions, and publications.
- See answers to frequently asked tax questions.
- Search publications on-line by topic or keyword.
- Send us coments or request help via e-mail.
- Sign up to receive hot tax issues and news by e-mail from the IRS Digital Dispatch.

You can also reach us using:
- Telnet at **iris.irs.ustreas.gov**
- File transfer protocol at **ftp.irs.ustreas.gov**
- Direct dial (by modem) at **703-321-8020**.

CD-ROM

Order **Pub. 1796**, Federal Tax Products on CD-ROM, and get:
- Current year forms, instructions, and publications.
- Prior year forms and instructions.
- Popular forms that may be filled in electronically, printed out for submission, and saved for recordkeeping.

Buy the CD-ROM on the Internet at **www.irs.ustreas.gov/cdorders** from the National Technical Information Service (NTIS) for $13 (plus a $5 handling fee) and save 35%, or call **1-877-CDFORMS** (1-877-233-6767) toll-free to buy the CD-ROM for $20 (plus a $5 handling fee).

By Phone and In Person

You can order forms and publications 24 hours a day, 7 days a week, by calling **1-800-TAX-FORM** (1-800-829-3676). You can also get most forms and publications at your local IRS office.

General Instructions

Purpose of Form

Form 1065 is an information return used to report the income, deductions, gains, losses, etc., from the operation of a partnership. A partnership does not pay tax on its income but "passes through" any profits or losses to its partners. Partners must include partnership items on their tax returns.

Definitions

Partnership

A partnership is the relationship between two or more persons who join to carry on a trade or business, with each person contributing money, property, labor, or skill and each expecting to share in the profits and losses of the business whether or not a formal partnership agreement is made.

The term "partnership" includes a limited partnership, syndicate, group, pool, joint venture, or other unincorporated organization, through or by which any business, financial operation, or venture is carried on, that is not, within the meaning of the regulations under section 7701, a corporation, trust, estate, or sole proprietorship.

A joint undertaking merely to share expenses is not a partnership. Mere co-ownership of property that is maintained and leased or rented is not a partnership. However, if the co-owners provide services to the tenants, a partnership exists.

General Partner

A general partner is a partner who is personally liable for partnership debts.

General Partnership

A general partnership is composed only of general partners.

Limited Partner

A limited partner is a partner in a partnership formed under a state limited partnership law, whose personal liability for partnership debts is limited to the amount of money or other property that the partner contributed or is required to contribute to the partnership. Some members of other entities, such as domestic or foreign business trusts or limited liability companies that are classified as partnerships, may be treated as limited partners for certain purposes. See, for example, Temporary Regulations section 1.469-5T(e)(3), which treats all members with limited liability as limited partners for purposes of section 469(h)(2).

Limited Partnership

A limited partnership is formed under a state limited partnership law and composed of at least one general partner and one or more limited partners.

Limited Liability Partnership

A limited liability partnership (LLP) is formed under a state limited liability partnership law. Generally, a partner in an LLP is not personally liable for the debts of the LLP or any other partner, nor is a partner liable for the acts or omissions of any other partner, solely by reason of being a partner.

Limited Liability Company

A limited liability company (LLC) is an entity formed under state law by filing articles of organization as an LLC. Unlike a partnership, none of the members of an LLC are personally liable for its debts. An LLC may be classified for Federal income tax purposes either as a partnership, a corporation, or an entity disregarded as an entity separate from its owner by applying the rules in Regulations section 301.7701-3. See **Form 8832**, Entity Classification Election, for more details.

Nonrecourse Loans

Nonrecourse loans are those liabilities of the partnership for which no partner bears the economic risk of loss.

Who Must File

Except as provided below, every domestic partnership must file Form 1065, unless it neither receives income nor incurs any expenditures treated as deductions or credits for Federal income tax purposes.

A foreign partnership that engages in a trade or business within the United States or has gross income derived from sources in the United States must file Form 1065, even if its principal place of business is outside the United States or all its members are nonresident aliens.

Entities formed as limited liability companies and treated as partnerships for Federal income tax purposes must file Form 1065.

A religious or apostolic organization exempt from income tax under section 501(d) must file Form 1065 to report its taxable income, which must be allocated to its members as a dividend, whether distributed or not. Such an organization must figure its taxable income on an attachment to Form 1065 in the same manner as a corporation. **Form 1120**, U.S. Corporation Income Tax Return, may be used for this purpose. Enter the organization's taxable income, if any, on line 4b of Schedule K and each member's pro rata share on line 4b of Schedule K-1. Net operating losses are not deductible by the members but may be carried back or forward by the organization under the rules of section 172.

A qualifying syndicate, pool, joint venture, or similar organization may elect under section 761(a) not to be treated as a partnership for Federal income tax purposes and will not be required to file Form 1065 except for the year of election. See section 761(a) and Regulations section 1.761-2 for more information.

An electing large partnership (as defined in section 775) must file Form 1065-B.

Real estate mortgage investment conduits (REMICs) must file **Form 1066**, U.S. Real Estate Mortgage Investment Conduit (REMIC) Income Tax Return.

Certain publicly traded partnerships treated as corporations under section 7704 must file Form 1120.

Termination of the Partnership

A partnership terminates when:

1. All its operations are discontinued and no part of any business, financial operation, or venture is continued by any of its partners in a partnership, **or**

2. At least 50% of the total interest in partnership capital and profits is sold or exchanged within a 12-month period, including a sale or exchange to another partner. See Regulations section 1.708-1(b)(1) for more details.

The partnership's tax year ends on the date of termination. For purposes of **1** above, the date of termination is the date the partnership completes the winding up of its affairs. For purposes of **2** above, the date of termination is

Page 2

Instructions for Form 1065

the date the partnership interest is sold or exchanged that, of itself or together with other sales or exchanges in the preceding 12 months, transfers an interest of 50% or more in both partnership capital and profits.

Special rules apply in the case of a merger, consolidation, or division of a partnership. See Regulations section 1.708-1(b)(2) for details.

Electronic and Magnetic Media Filing

Qualified partnerships or transmitters can file Form 1065 and related schedules electronically or on magnetic media. Tax return data may be filed electronically using a dial-up MITRON communications device or remote bulletin board system or on magnetic media using magnetic tape or floppy diskette.

If the partnership wishes to do this, **Form 9041,** Application for Electronic/Magnetic Media Filing of Business and Employee Benefit Plan Returns, must be filed. If the partnership return is filed electronically or on magnetic media, **Form 8453-P,** U.S. Partnership Declaration and Signature for Electronic and Magnetic Media Filing, must also be filed. For more details, see **Pub. 1524,** Procedures for Electronic and Magnetic Media Filing of Form 1065, U.S. Partnership Return of Income (Including the "Paper-Parent Option") for Tax Year 1998, and **Pub. 1525,** File Specifications, Validation Criteria, and Record Layouts for Electronic and Magnetic Media Filing of Form 1065, U.S. Partnership Return of Income (Including the "Paper-Parent Option"). To order these forms and publications, or for more information on electronic and magnetic media filing of Form 1065, call the Electronic Filing Section at the Andover Service Center at 978-474-9486 (not a toll-free number), or write to:

Internal Revenue Service Center
Electronic Filing Section, Stop 983
P.O. Box 4050
Woburn, MA 01889-4050

When To File

Generally, a domestic partnership must file Form 1065 by the 15th day of the 4th month following the date its tax year ended as shown at the top of Form 1065. A partnership whose partners are all nonresident aliens must file its return by the 15th day of the 6th month following the date its tax year ended. If the due date falls on a Saturday, Sunday, or legal holiday, file on the next business day.

Private Delivery Services

You can use certain private delivery services designated by the IRS to meet the "timely mailing as timely filing/paying" rule for Form 1065. The IRS publishes a list of the designated private delivery services in September of each year. The list published in September 1998 includes only the following:

● Airborne Express (Airborne): Overnight Air Express Service, Next Afternoon Service, Second Day Service.

● DHL Worldwide Express (DHL): DHL "Same Day" Service, DHL USA Overnight.

● Federal Express (FedEx): FedEx Priority Overnight, FedEx Standard Overnight, FedEx 2Day.

● United Parcel Service (UPS): UPS Next Day Air, UPS Next Day Air Saver, UPS 2nd Day Air, UPS 2nd Day Air A.M.

The private delivery service can tell you how to get written proof of the mailing date.

Extension

If you need more time to file a partnership return, file **Form 8736,** Application for Automatic Extension of Time To File U.S. Return for a Partnership, REMIC, or for Certain Trusts, for an automatic 3-month extension. File Form 8736 by the regular due date of the partnership return.

If, after you have filed Form 8736, you still need more time to file the partnership return, file **Form 8800,** Application for Additional Extension of Time To File U.S. Return for a Partnership, REMIC, or for Certain Trusts, for an additional extension of up to 3 months. The partnership must show reasonable cause to get this additional extension. Form 8800 must be filed by the extended due date of the partnership return.

Period Covered

Form 1065 is an information return for calendar year 1998 and fiscal years beginning in 1998 and ending in 1999. If the return is for a fiscal year or a short tax year, fill in the tax year space at the top of the form.

The 1998 Form 1065 may also be used if:

1. The partnership has a tax year of less than 12 months that begins and ends in 1999; and

2. The 1999 Form 1065 is not available by the time the partnership is required to file its return.

However, the partnership must show its 1999 tax year on the 1998 Form 1065 and incorporate any tax law changes that are effective for tax years beginning after 1998.

Where To File

File Form 1065 at the applicable IRS address listed below.

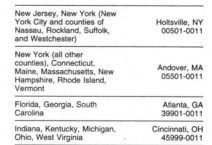

If the partnership's principal business, office, or agency is located in ▼	Use the following Internal Revenue Service Center address ▼
New Jersey, New York (New York City and counties of Nassau, Rockland, Suffolk, and Westchester)	Holtsville, NY 00501-0011
New York (all other counties), Connecticut, Maine, Massachusetts, New Hampshire, Rhode Island, Vermont	Andover, MA 05501-0011
Florida, Georgia, South Carolina	Atlanta, GA 39901-0011
Indiana, Kentucky, Michigan, Ohio, West Virginia	Cincinnati, OH 45999-0011
Kansas, New Mexico, Oklahoma, Texas	Austin, TX 73301-0011
Alaska, Arizona, California (counties of Alpine, Amador, Butte, Calaveras, Colusa, Contra Costa, Del Norte, El Dorado, Glenn, Humboldt, Lake, Lassen, Marin, Mendocino, Modoc, Napa, Nevada, Placer, Plumas, Sacramento, San Joaquin, Shasta, Sierra, Siskiyou, Solano, Sonoma, Sutter, Tehama, Trinity, Yolo, and Yuba), Colorado, Idaho, Montana, Nebraska, Nevada, North Dakota, Oregon, South Dakota, Utah, Washington, Wyoming	Ogden, UT 84201-0011
California (all other counties), Hawaii	Fresno, CA 93888-0011
Illinois, Iowa, Minnesota, Missouri, Wisconsin	Kansas City, MO 64999-0011
Alabama, Arkansas, Louisiana, Mississippi, North Carolina, Tennessee	Memphis, TN 37501-0011
Delaware, District of Columbia, Maryland, Pennsylvania, Virginia	Philadelphia, PA 19255-0011

A partnership without a principal office or agency or principal place of business in the United States must file its return with the Internal Revenue Service Center, Philadelphia, PA 19255-0011.

Who Must Sign

General Partner or Limited Liability Company Member

Form 1065 is not considered to be a return unless it is signed. One general partner or limited liability company member must sign the return. If a receiver, trustee in bankruptcy, or assignee controls the organization's property or business, that person must sign the return.

Paid Preparer's Information

If someone prepares the return and does not charge the partnership, that person should not sign the partnership return.

Generally, anyone who is paid to prepare the partnership return **must:**

● Sign the return, by hand, in the space provided for the preparer's signature. Signature stamps or labels are not acceptable.

● Fill in the other blanks in the **Paid Preparer's Use Only** area of the return.

● Give the partnership a copy of the return in addition to the copy to be filed with the IRS.

Penalties

Late Filing of Return

A penalty is assessed against the partnership if it is required to file a partnership return and it **(a)** fails to file the return by the due date, including extensions, or **(b)** files a return that fails to show all the information required, unless such failure is due to reasonable cause. If the failure is due to reasonable cause, attach an explanation to the partnership return. The penalty is $50 for each month or part of a month (for a maximum of 5 months) the failure continues, multiplied by the total number of persons who were partners in the partnership during any part of the partnership's tax year for which the return is due. This penalty will not be imposed on partnerships for which the answer to Question 4 on Schedule B of Form 1065 is **No,** provided all partners have timely filed income tax returns fully reporting their shares of the income, deductions, and credits of the partnership. See page 14 of the instructions for further information.

Failure To Furnish Information Timely

For each failure to furnish Schedule K-1 to a partner when due and each failure to include on Schedule K-1 all the information required to be shown (or the inclusion of incorrect information), a $50 penalty may be imposed with respect to each Schedule K-1 for which a failure occurs. The maximum penalty is $100,000 for all such failures during a calendar year. If the requirement to report correct information is intentionally disregarded, each $50 penalty is increased to $100 or, if greater, 10% of the aggregate amount of items required to be reported, and the $100,000 maximum does not apply.

Trust Fund Recovery Penalty

This penalty may apply if certain excise, income, social security, and Medicare taxes that must be collected or withheld are not collected or withheld, or these taxes are not paid. These taxes are generally reported on Forms 720, 941, 943, or 945. The trust fund recovery penalty may be imposed on all persons who are determined by the IRS to have been **responsible** for collecting, accounting for, and paying over these taxes, and who acted willfully in not doing so. The penalty is equal to the unpaid trust fund tax. See the instructions for Form 720, **Pub. 15 (Circular E),** Employer's Tax Guide, and **Pub. 51 (Circular A),** Agricultural Employer's Tax Guide, for more details, including the definition of a responsible person.

Accounting Methods

Figure ordinary income using the method of accounting regularly used in keeping the partnership's books and records. Generally, permissible methods include the cash method, the accrual method, or any other method authorized by the Internal Revenue Code. In all cases, the method used must clearly reflect income.

Generally, a partnership may not use the cash method of accounting if **(a)** it has at least one corporate partner, average annual gross receipts of more than $5 million, and it is not a farming business or **(b)** it is a tax shelter (as defined in section 448(d)(3)). See section 448 for details.

Under the accrual method, an amount is includible in income when all the events have occurred that fix the right to receive the income and the amount can be determined with reasonable accuracy.

Generally, an accrual basis taxpayer can deduct accrued expenses in the tax year in which:
• All events that determine liability have occurred,
• The amount of the liability can be figured with reasonable accuracy, and
• Economic performance takes place with respect to the expense. There are exceptions for certain items, including recurring expenses.

Except for certain home construction contracts and other real property small construction contracts, long-term contracts must generally be accounted for using the percentage of completion method described in section 460.

Generally, the partnership may change its method of accounting used to report income (for income as a whole or for any material item) only by getting consent on **Form 3115,** Application for Change in Accounting Method. For more information, see **Pub. 538,** Accounting Periods and Methods.

Accounting Periods

A partnership is generally required to have one of the following tax years:

1. The tax year of a majority of its partners (majority tax year).

2. If there is no majority tax year, then the tax year common to all of the partnership's principal partners (partners with an interest of 5% or more in the partnership profits or capital).

3. If there is neither a majority tax year nor a tax year common to all principal partners, then the tax year that results in the least aggregate deferral of income.

4. Some other tax year, if:
• The partnership can establish that there is a business purpose for the tax year (see Rev. Proc. 87-32, 1987-2 C.B. 396); or
• The tax year is a "grandfathered" year (see Rev. Proc. 87-32); or
• The partnership elects under section 444 to have a tax year other than a required tax year by filing **Form 8716,** Election to Have a Tax Year Other Than a Required Tax Year. For a partnership to have this election in effect, it must make the payments required by section 7519 and file **Form 8752,** Required Payment or Refund Under Section 7519.

A section 444 election ends if a partnership changes its accounting period to its required tax year or some other permitted year or it is penalized for willfully failing to comply with the requirements of section 7519. If the termination results in a short tax year, type or legibly print at the top of the first page of Form 1065 for the short tax year, "SECTION 444 ELECTION TERMINATED."

To change an accounting period, see Pub. 538 and **Form 1128,** Application To Adopt, Change, or Retain a Tax Year, (unless the partnership is making an election under section 444).

Note: *Under the provisions of section 584(h), the tax year of a common trust fund must be the calendar year.*

Rounding Off to Whole Dollars

You may round off cents to whole dollars on your return and accompanying schedules. To do so, drop amounts under 50 cents and increase amounts from 50 to 99 cents to the next higher dollar.

Recordkeeping

The partnership must keep its records as long as they may be needed for the administration of any provision of the Internal Revenue Code. If the consolidated audit procedures of sections 6221 through 6233 apply, the partnership usually must keep records that support an item of income, deduction, or credit on the partnership return for 3 years from the date the return is due or is filed, whichever is later. If the consolidated audit procedures do not apply, these records usually must be kept for 3 years

from the date each partner's return is due or is filed, whichever is later. Keep records that verify the partnership's basis in property for as long as they are needed to figure the basis of the original or replacement property.

The partnership should also keep copies of all returns it has filed. They help in preparing future returns and in making computations when filing an amended return.

Amended Return

To correct an error on a Form 1065 already filed, file an amended Form 1065 and check box G(4) on page 1. If the income, deductions, credits, or other information provided to any partner on Schedule K-1 are incorrect, file an amended Schedule K-1 (Form 1065) for that partner with the amended Form 1065. Also give a copy of the amended Schedule K-1 to that partner. Be sure to check box I(2) on the Schedule K-1 to indicate that it is an amended Schedule K-1.

Exception: *If you are filing an amended partnership return and you answered* **Yes** *to Question 4 in Schedule B, the tax matters partner must file* **Form 8082,** *Notice of Inconsistent Treatment or Administrative Adjustment Request (AAR).*

A change to the partnership's Federal return may affect its state return. This includes changes made as a result of an examination of the partnership return by the IRS. For more information, contact the state tax agency for the state in which the partnership return is filed.

Other Forms That May Be Required

• **Forms W-2** and **W-3,** Wage and Tax Statement; and Transmittal of Wage and Tax Statements.
• **Form 720,** Quarterly Federal Excise Tax Return. Use Form 720 to report environmental excise taxes, communications and air transportation taxes, fuel taxes, luxury tax on passenger vehicles, manufacturers' taxes, ship passenger tax, and certain other excise taxes.
Caution: *See* **Trust Fund Recovery Penalty** *above.*
• **Form 926,** Return by a U.S. Transferor of Property to a Foreign Corporation. Use this form to report certain information required under section 6038B.
• **Form 940** or **Form 940-EZ,** Employer's Annual Federal Unemployment (FUTA) Tax Return. The partnership may be liable for FUTA tax and may have to file Form 940 or 940-EZ if it paid wages of $1,500 or more in any calendar quarter during the calendar year (or the preceding calendar year) or one or more employees worked for the partnership for some part of a day in any 20 different weeks during the calendar year (or the preceding calendar year).
• **Form 941,** Employer's Quarterly Federal Tax Return. Employers must file this form quarterly to report income tax withheld on wages and employer and employee social security and Medicare taxes. Agricultural employers must file **Form 943,** Employer's Annual Tax Return for Agricultural Employees, instead of Form 941, to report income tax withheld and employer and employee social security and Medicare taxes on farmworkers.
Caution: *See* **Trust Fund Recovery Penalty** *above.*

● **Form 945,** Annual Return of Withheld Federal Income Tax. Use this form to report income tax withheld from nonpayroll payments, including pensions, annuities, IRAs, gambling winnings, and backup withholding.

Caution: *See Trust Fund Recovery Penalty on page 4.*

● **Forms 1042** and **1042-S,** Annual Withholding Tax Return for U.S. Source Income of Foreign Persons; and Foreign Person's U.S. Source Income Subject to Withholding. Use these forms to report and send withheld tax on payments or distributions made to nonresident alien individuals, foreign partnerships, or foreign corporations to the extent such payments or distributions constitute gross income from sources within the United States that is not effectively connected with a U.S. trade or business. A domestic partnership must also withhold tax on a foreign partner's distributive share of such income, including amounts that are not actually distributed. Withholding on amounts not previously distributed to a foreign partner must be made and paid over by the earlier of **(a)** the date on which Schedule K-1 is sent to that partner or **(b)** the 15th day of the 3rd month after the end of the partnership's tax year. For more information, see sections 1441 and 1442 and **Pub. 515,** Withholding of Tax on Nonresident Aliens and Foreign Corporations.

● **Form 1096,** Annual Summary and Transmittal of U.S. Information Returns.

● **Form 1098,** Mortgage Interest Statement. Use this form to report the receipt from any individual of $600 or more of mortgage interest and points in the course of the partnership's trade or business for any calendar year.

● **Forms 1099-A, B, INT, LTC, MISC, MSA, OID, R,** and **S.** You may have to file these information returns to report acquisitions or abandonments of secured property; proceeds from broker and barter exchange transactions; interest payments; payments of long-term care and accelerated death benefits; miscellaneous income payments; distributions from a medical savings account; original issue discount; distributions from pensions, annuities, retirement or profit-sharing plans, IRAs, insurance contracts, etc.; and proceeds from real estate transactions. Also, use certain of these returns to report amounts that were received as a nominee on behalf of another person.

For more information, see the Instructions for Forms 1099, 1098, 5498, and W-2G.

Important: *Every partnership must file Forms 1099-MISC if, in the course of its trade or business, it makes payments of rents, commissions, or other fixed or determinable income (see section 6041) totaling $600 or more to any one person during the calendar year.*

● **Form 5471,** Information Return of U.S. Persons With Respect to Certain Foreign Corporations. A partnership may have to file Form 5471 if it **(a)** controls a foreign corporation; or **(b)** acquires, disposes of, or owns 5% or more in value of the outstanding stock of a foreign corporation; or **(c)** owns stock in a corporation that is a controlled foreign corporation for an uninterrupted period of 30 days or more during any tax year of the foreign corporation, and it owned that stock on the last day of that year.

● **Form 5713,** International Boycott Report, is used by persons having operations in, or related to, a "boycotting" country, company, or national of a country, to report those operations and figure the loss of certain tax benefits. The partnership must give each partner a copy of the Form 5713 filed by the partnership if there has been participation in, or cooperation with, an international boycott.

● **Form 8264,** Application for Registration of a Tax Shelter. Tax shelter organizers must file Form 8264 to get a tax shelter registration number from the IRS.

● **Form 8271,** Investor Reporting of Tax Shelter Registration Number. Partnerships that have acquired an interest in a tax shelter that is required to be registered use Form 8271 to report the tax shelter's registration number. Attach Form 8271 to any return on which a deduction, credit, loss, or other tax benefit attributable to a tax shelter is taken or any income attributable to a tax shelter is reported.

● **Form 8275,** Disclosure Statement. File Form 8275 to disclose items or positions, except those contrary to a regulation, that are not otherwise adequately disclosed on a tax return. The disclosure is made to avoid the parts of the accuracy-related penalty imposed for disregard of rules or substantial understatement of tax. Form 8275 is also used for disclosures relating to preparer penalties for understatements due to unrealistic positions or disregard of rules.

● **Form 8275-R,** Regulation Disclosure Statement, is used to disclose any item on a tax return for which a position has been taken that is contrary to Treasury regulations.

● **Forms 8288** and **8288-A,** U.S. Withholding Tax Return for Dispositions by Foreign Persons of U.S. Real Property Interests; and Statement of Withholding on Dispositions by Foreign Persons of U.S. Real Property Interests. Use these forms to report and send withheld tax on the sale of U.S. real property by a foreign person. See section 1445 and the related regulations for additional information.

● **Form 8300,** Report of Cash Payments Over $10,000 Received in a Trade or Business. File this form to report the receipt of more than $10,000 in cash or foreign currency in one transaction or a series of related transactions.

● **Form 8594,** Asset Acquisition Statement. Both the purchaser and seller of a group of assets constituting a trade or business must file this form if section 197 intangibles attach, or could attach, to such assets and if the purchaser's basis in the assets is determined only by the amount paid for the assets.

● **Form 8697,** Interest Computation Under the Look-Back Method for Completed Long-Term Contracts. Partnerships that are not closely held use this form to figure the interest due or to be refunded under the look-back method of section 460(b)(2) on certain long-term contracts that are accounted for under either the percentage of completion-capitalized cost method or the percentage of completion method. Closely held partnerships should see the instructions on page 22 for line 25, item 10, of Schedule K-1 for details on the Form 8697 information they must provide to their partners.

● **Forms 8804, 8805,** and **8813,** Annual Return for Partnership Withholding Tax (Section 1446); Foreign Partner's Information Statement of Section 1446 Withholding Tax; and Partnership Withholding Tax Payment (Section 1446). File Forms 8804 and 8805 if the partnership had effectively connected gross income and foreign partners for the tax year. Use Form 8813 to send installment payments of withheld tax based on effectively connected taxable income allocable to foreign partners.

Exception: *Publicly traded partnerships that do not elect to pay tax based on effectively connected taxable income do not file these forms. They must instead withhold tax on distributions to foreign partners and report and send payments using Forms 1042 and 1042-S. See section 1446 for more information.*

● **Form 8832,** Entity Classification Election. Except for a business entity automatically classified as a corporation, a business entity with at least two members may choose to be classified either as a partnership or an association taxable as a corporation. A domestic eligible entity with at least two members that does not file Form 8832 is classified under the default rules as a partnership. However, a foreign eligible entity with at least two members is classified under the default rules as a partnership only if at least one member does not have limited liability. File Form 8832 **only** if the entity does not want to be classified under these default rules or if it wants to change its classification.

● **Form 8866,** Interest Computation Under the Look-Back Method for Property Depreciated Under the Income Forecast Method. Partnerships that are not closely held use this form to figure the interest due or to be refunded under the look-back method of section 167(g)(2) for certain property placed in service after September 13, 1995, depreciated under the income forecast method. Closely held partnerships should see the instructions on page 23 for line 25, item 20, of Schedule K-1 for details on the Form 8866 information they must provide to their partners.

Attachments

Attach schedules in alphabetical order and other forms in numerical order after Form 1065.

To assist us in processing the return, complete every applicable entry space on Form 1065 and Schedule K-1. **If you attach statements, do not write "See attached" instead of completing the entry spaces on the forms. Penalties may be assessed if the partnership files an incomplete return.**

If you need more space on the forms or schedules, attach separate sheets. Use the same size and format as on the printed forms. **But show your totals on the printed forms.** Be sure to put the partnership's name and employer identification number (EIN) on each sheet.

Separately Stated Items

Partners are required to take into account separately (under section 702(a)) their distributive shares of the following items (whether or not they are actually distributed):

1. Ordinary income or loss from trade or business activities.

2. Net income or loss from rental real estate activities.

3. Net income or loss from other rental activities.

4. Gains and losses from sales or exchanges of capital assets.

5. Gains and losses from sales or exchanges of property described in section 1231.

6. Charitable contributions.

7. Dividends (passed through to corporate partners) that qualify for the dividends-received deduction.

8. Taxes described in section 901 paid or accrued to foreign countries and to possessions of the United States.

9. Other items of income, gain, loss, deduction, or credit, to the extent provided by regulations. Examples of such items include nonbusiness expenses, intangible drilling and development costs, and soil and water conservation expenditures.

Elections Made by the Partnership

Generally, the partnership decides how to figure taxable income from its operations. For example, it chooses the accounting method and depreciation methods it will use. The partnership also makes elections under the following sections:

1. Section 179 (election to expense certain tangible property).

2. Section 614 (definition of property—mines, wells, and other natural deposits). This election must be made before the partners figure their individual depletion allowances under section 613A(c)(7)(D).

3. Section 1033 (involuntary conversions).

4. Section 754 (manner of electing optional adjustment to basis of partnership property).

Under section 754, a partnership may elect to adjust the basis of partnership property when property is distributed or when a partnership interest is transferred. If the election is made with respect to a transfer of a partnership interest (section 743(b)) and the assets of the partnership constitute a trade or business for purposes of section 1060(c), then the value of any goodwill transferred must be determined in the manner provided in Temporary Regulations section 1.1060-1T. Once an election is made under section 754, it applies both to all distributions and to all transfers made during the tax year and in all subsequent tax years unless the election is revoked. See Regulations section 1.754-1(c).

This election must be made in a statement that is filed with the partnership's timely filed return (including any extension) for the tax year during which the distribution or transfer occurs. The statement must include:

• The name and address of the partnership.
• A declaration that the partnership elects under section 754 to apply the provisions of section 734(b) and section 743(b).
• The signature of the general partner authorized to sign the partnership return.

The partnership can get an automatic 12-month extension to make the section 754 election provided corrective action is taken within 12 months of the original deadline for making the election. For details, see Temporary Regulations section 301.9100-2T.

See section 754 and the related regulations for more information.

If there is a distribution of property consisting of an interest in another partnership, see section 734(b).

Elections Made by Each Partner

Elections under the following sections are made by each partner separately on the partner's tax return:

1. Section 59(e) (election to deduct ratably certain qualified expenditures such as intangible drilling costs, mining exploration expenses, or research and experimental expenditures).

2. Section 108 (income from discharge of indebtedness).

3. Section 617 (deduction and recapture of certain mining exploration expenditures paid or incurred).

4. Section 901 (foreign tax credit).

Partner's Dealings With Partnership

If a partner engages in a transaction with his or her partnership, other than in his or her capacity as a partner, the partner is treated as not being a member of the partnership for that transaction. Special rules apply to sales or exchanges of property between partnerships and certain persons, as explained in Pub. 541.

Contributions to the Partnership

Generally, no gain (loss) is recognized to the partnership or any of the partners when property is contributed to the partnership in exchange for an interest in the partnership. This rule does not apply to any gain realized on a transfer of property to a partnership that would be treated as an investment company (within the meaning of section 351) if the partnership were incorporated. If, as a result of a transfer of property to a partnership, there is a direct or indirect transfer of money or other property to the transferring partner, the partner may have to recognize gain on the exchange.

The basis to the partnership of property contributed by a partner is the adjusted basis in the hands of the partner at the time it was contributed, plus any gain recognized (under section 721(b)) by the partner at that time. See section 723 for more information.

Dispositions of Contributed Property

If the partnership disposes of property contributed to the partnership by a partner, income, gain, loss, and deductions from that property must be allocated among the partners to take into account the difference between the property's basis and its fair market value at the time of the contribution.

For property contributed to the partnership, the contributing partner must recognize gain or loss on a distribution of the property to another partner within 5 years of being contributed. For property contributed after June 8, 1997, the 5-year period is generally extended to 7 years. The gain or loss is equal to the amount that the contributing partner should have recognized if the property had been sold for its fair market value when distributed, because of the difference between the property's basis and its fair market value at the time of contribution.

See section 704(c) for details and other rules on dispositions of contributed property. See section 724 for the character of any gain or loss recognized on the disposition of unrealized receivables, inventory items, or capital loss property contributed to the partnership by a partner.

Recognition of Precontribution Gain on Certain Partnership Distributions

A partner who contributes appreciated property to the partnership must include in income any precontribution gain to the extent the fair market value of other property (other than money) distributed to the partner by the partnership exceeds the adjusted basis of his or her partnership interest just before the distribution. Precontribution gain is the net gain, if any, that would have been recognized under section 704(c)(1)(B) if the partnership had distributed to another partner all the property that had been contributed to the partnership by the distributee partner within 5 years of the distribution and that was held by the partnership just before the distribution. For property contributed after June 8, 1997, the 5-year period is generally extended to 7 years.

Appropriate basis adjustments are to be made to the adjusted basis of the distributee partner's interest in the partnership and the partnership's basis in the contributed property to reflect the gain recognized by the partner.

For more details and exceptions, see Pub. 541.

Unrealized Receivables and Inventory Items

Generally, if a partner sells or exchanges a partnership interest where unrealized receivables or inventory items are involved, the transferor partner must notify the partnership, in writing, within 30 days of the exchange. The partnership must then file **Form 8308,** Report of a Sale or Exchange of Certain Partnership Interests.

If a partnership distributes unrealized receivables or substantially appreciated inventory items in exchange for all or part of a partner's interest in other partnership property (including money), treat the transaction as a sale or exchange between the partner and the partnership. Treat the partnership gain (loss) as ordinary income (loss). The income (loss) is specially allocated only to partners other than the distributee partner.

If a partnership gives other property (including money) for all or part of that partner's interest in the partnership's unrealized receivables or substantially appreciated inventory items, treat the transaction as a sale or exchange of the property.

See Rev. Rul. 84-102, 1984-2 C.B. 119, for information on the tax consequences that result when a new partner joins a partnership that has liabilities and unrealized receivables. Also, see Pub. 541 for more information on unrealized receivables and inventory items.

Passive Activity Limitations

In general, section 469 limits the amount of losses, deductions, and credits that partners may claim from "passive activities." The passive activity limitations do not apply to the partnership. Instead, they apply to each partner's share of any income or loss and credit attributable to a passive activity. Because the treatment of each partner's share of partnership income or loss and credit depends on the nature of the activity that generated it, the partnership must report income or loss and credits separately for each activity.

The instructions below (pages 7-10) and the instructions for Schedules K and K-1 (pages 15-23) explain the applicable passive activity limitation rules and specify the type of information the partnership must provide to its partners for each activity. If the partnership has more than one activity, it must report information for each activity on an attachment to Schedules K and K-1.

Generally, passive activities include **(a)** activities that involve the conduct of a trade or business if the partner does not materially participate in the activity; and **(b)** all rental activities (defined below), regardless of the partner's participation. For exceptions, see **Activities That Are Not Passive Activities** below. The level of each partner's participation in an activity must be determined by the partner.

The passive activity rules provide that losses and credits from passive activities can generally be applied only against income and tax from passive activities. Thus, passive losses and credits cannot be applied against income from salaries, wages, professional fees, or a business in which the taxpayer materially participates; against "portfolio income" (defined on page 8); or against the tax related to any of these types of income.

Special provisions apply to certain activities. First, the passive activity limitations must be applied separately with respect to a net loss from passive activities held through a publicly traded partnership. Second, special rules require that net income from certain activities that would otherwise be treated as passive income must be recharacterized as nonpassive income for purposes of the passive activity limitations.

To allow each partner to correctly apply the passive activity limitations, the partnership must report income or loss and credits separately for each of the following types of activities and income: trade or business activities, rental real estate activities, rental activities other than rental real estate, and portfolio income.

Activities That Are Not Passive Activities

Passive activities **do not** include:

1. Trade or business activities in which the partner materially participated for the tax year.

2. Any rental real estate activity in which the partner materially participated and met both of the following conditions for the tax year:

a. More than half of the personal services the partner performed in trades or businesses were performed in real property trades or businesses in which he or she materially participated, and

b. The partner performed more than 750 hours of services in real property trades or businesses in which he or she materially participated.

Note: *For a partner that is a closely held C corporation (defined in section 465(a)(1)(B)), the above conditions are treated as met if more than 50% of the corporation's gross receipts are from real property trades or businesses in which the corporation materially participated.*

For purposes of this rule, each interest in rental real estate is a separate activity, unless the partner elects to treat all interests in rental real estate as one activity.

If the partner is married filing jointly, either the partner or his or her spouse must separately meet both of the above conditions,

without taking into account services performed by the other spouse.

A real property trade or business is any real property development, redevelopment, construction, reconstruction, acquisition, conversion, rental, operation, management, leasing, or brokerage trade or business. Services the partner performed as an employee are not treated as performed in a real property trade or business unless he or she owned more than 5% of the stock (or more than 5% of the capital or profits interest) in the employer.

3. An interest in an oil or gas well drilled or operated under a working interest if at any time during the tax year the partner held the working interest directly or through an entity that did not limit the partner's liability (e.g., an interest as a general partner). This exception applies regardless of whether the partner materially participated for the tax year.

4. The rental of a dwelling unit used by a partner for personal purposes during the year for more than the greater of 14 days or 10% of the number of days that the residence was rented at fair rental value.

5. An activity of trading personal property for the account of owners of interests in the activity. See Temporary Regulations section 1.469-1T(e)(6).

Trade or Business Activities

A trade or business activity is an activity (other than a rental activity or an activity treated as incidental to an activity of holding property for investment) that:

1. Involves the conduct of a trade or business (within the meaning of section 162),

2. Is conducted in anticipation of starting a trade or business, or

3. Involves research or experimental expenditures deductible under section 174 (or that would be if you chose to deduct rather than capitalize them).

If the partner does not materially participate in the activity, a trade or business activity held through a partnership is generally a passive activity of the partner.

Each partner must determine if he or she materially participated in an activity. As a result, while the partnership's overall trade or business income (loss) is reported on page 1 of Form 1065, the specific income and deductions from each separate trade or business activity must be reported on attachments to Form 1065. Similarly, while each partner's allocable share of the partnership's overall trade or business income (loss) is reported on line 1 of Schedule K-1, each partner's allocable share of the income and deductions from each trade or business activity must be reported on attachments to each Schedule K-1. See **Passive Activity Reporting Requirements** on page 9 for more information.

Rental Activities

Generally, except as noted below, if the gross income from an activity consists of amounts paid principally for the use of real or personal tangible property held by the partnership, the activity is a rental activity.

There are several exceptions to this general rule. Under these exceptions, an activity involving the use of real or personal tangible property is not a rental activity if any of the following apply:

● The average period of customer use (defined below) for such property is 7 days or less.

● The average period of customer use for such property is 30 days or less and significant personal services (defined below) are provided by or on behalf of the partnership.

● Extraordinary personal services (defined below) are provided by or on behalf of the partnership.

● The rental of such property is treated as incidental to a nonrental activity of the partnership under Temporary Regulations section 1.469-1T(e)(3)(vi) and Regulations section 1.469-1(e)(3)(vi).

● The partnership customarily makes the property available during defined business hours for nonexclusive use by various customers.

● The partnership provides property for use in a nonrental activity of a partnership or joint venture in its capacity as an owner of an interest in such partnership or joint venture. Whether the partnership provides property used in an activity of another partnership or of a joint venture in the partnership's capacity as an owner of an interest in the partnership or joint venture is determined on the basis of all the facts and circumstances.

In addition, a guaranteed payment described in section 707(c) is not income from a rental activity under any circumstances.

Average period of customer use. Figure the average period of customer use for a class of property by dividing the total number of days in all rental periods by the number of rentals during the tax year. If the activity involves renting more than one class of property, multiply the average period of customer use of each class by the ratio of the gross rental income from that class to the activity's total gross rental income. The activity's average period of customer use equals the sum of these class-by-class average periods weighted by gross income. See Regulations section 1.469-1(e)(3)(iii).

Significant personal services. Personal services include only services performed by individuals. In determining whether personal services are significant personal services, consider all the relevant facts and circumstances. Relevant facts and circumstances include how often the services are provided, the type and amount of labor required to perform the services, and the value of the services in relation to the amount charged for use of the property.

The following services are not considered in determining whether personal services are significant:

● Services necessary to permit the lawful use of the rental property.

● Services performed in connection with improvements or repairs to the rental property that extend the useful life of the property substantially beyond the average rental period.

● Services provided in connection with the use of any improved real property that are similar to those commonly provided in connection with long-term rentals of high-grade commercial or residential property. Examples include cleaning and maintenance of common areas, routine repairs, trash collection, elevator service, and security at entrances.

Extraordinary personal services. Services provided in connection with making rental property available for customer use are extraordinary personal services only if the services are performed by individuals and the

Instructions for Form 1065

Page 7

customers' use of the rental property is incidental to their receipt of the services.

For example, a patient's use of a hospital room generally is incidental to the care received from the hospital's medical staff. Similarly, a student's use of a dormitory room in a boarding school is incidental to the personal services provided by the school's teaching staff.

Rental activity incidental to a nonrental activity. An activity is not a rental activity if the rental of the property is incidental to a nonrental activity, such as the activity of holding property for investment, a trade or business activity, or the activity of dealing in property.

Rental of property is incidental to an activity of holding property for investment if both of the following apply:

• The main purpose for holding the property is to realize a gain from the appreciation of the property.

• The gross rental income from such property for the tax year is less than 2% of the smaller of the property's unadjusted basis or its fair market value.

Rental of property is incidental to a trade or business activity if all of the following apply:

• The partnership owns an interest in the trade or business at all times during the year.

• The rental property was mainly used in the trade or business activity during the tax year or during at least 2 of the 5 preceding tax years.

• The gross rental income from the property for the tax year is less than 2% of the smaller of the property's unadjusted basis or its fair market value.

The sale or exchange of property that is both rented and sold or exchanged during the tax year (where the gain or loss is recognized) is treated as incidental to the activity of dealing in property if, at the time of the sale or exchange, the property was held primarily for sale to customers in the ordinary course of the partnership's trade or business.

See Temporary Regulations section 1.469-1T(e)(3) and Regulations section 1.469-1(e)(3) for more information on the definition of rental activities for purposes of the passive activity limitations.

Reporting of rental activities. In reporting the partnership's income or losses and credits from rental activities, the partnership must separately report rental real estate activities and rental activities other than rental real estate activities.

Partners who actively participate in a rental real estate activity may be able to deduct part or all of their rental real estate losses (and the deduction equivalent of rental real estate credits) against income (or tax) from nonpassive activities. The combined amount of rental real estate losses and the deduction equivalent of rental real estate credits from all sources (including rental real estate activities not held through the partnership) that may be claimed is limited to $25,000. This $25,000 amount is generally reduced for high-income partners.

Report rental real estate activity income (loss) on **Form 8825**, Rental Real Estate Income and Expenses of a Partnership or an S Corporation, and line 2 of Schedules K and K-1 rather than on page 1 of Form 1065. Report credits related to rental real estate activities on lines 12b and 12c and low-income housing credits on line 12a of Schedules K and K-1.

Report income (loss) from rental activities other than rental real estate on line 3 and credits related to rental activities other than rental real estate on line 12d of Schedules K and K-1.

Portfolio Income

Generally, portfolio income includes all gross income, other than income derived in the ordinary course of a trade or business, that is attributable to interest; dividends; royalties; income from a real estate investment trust, a regulated investment company, a real estate mortgage investment conduit, a common trust fund, a controlled foreign corporation, a qualified electing fund, or a cooperative; income from the disposition of property that produces income of a type defined as portfolio income; and income from the disposition of property held for investment.

Solely for purposes of the preceding paragraph, gross income derived in the ordinary course of a trade or business includes (and portfolio income, therefore, does not include) only the following types of income:

• Interest income on loans and investments made in the ordinary course of a trade or business of lending money.

• Interest on accounts receivable arising from the performance of services or the sale of property in the ordinary course of a trade or business of performing such services or selling such property, but only if credit is customarily offered to customers of the business.

• Income from investments made in the ordinary course of a trade or business of furnishing insurance or annuity contracts or reinsuring risks underwritten by insurance companies.

• Income or gain derived in the ordinary course of an activity of trading or dealing in any property if such activity constitutes a trade or business (unless the dealer held the property for investment at any time before such income or gain is recognized).

• Royalties derived by the taxpayer in the ordinary course of a trade or business of licensing intangible property.

• Amounts included in the gross income of a patron of a cooperative by reason of any payment or allocation to the patron based on patronage occurring with respect to a trade or business of the patron.

• Other income identified by the IRS as income derived by the taxpayer in the ordinary course of a trade or business.

See Temporary Regulations section 1.469-2T(c)(3) for more information on portfolio income.

Report portfolio income on line 4 of Schedules K and K-1, rather than on page 1 of Form 1065. Report deductions related to portfolio income on line 10 of Schedules K and K-1.

Grouping Activities

Generally, one or more trade or business activities or rental activities may be treated as a single activity if the activities make up an appropriate economic unit for the measurement of gain or loss under the passive activity rules. Whether activities make up an appropriate economic unit depends on all the relevant facts and circumstances. The factors given the greatest weight in determining whether activities make up an appropriate economic unit are:

• Similarities and differences in types of trades or businesses.

• The extent of common control.

• The extent of common ownership.

• Geographical location.

• Reliance between or among the activities.

Example: The partnership has a significant ownership interest in a bakery and a movie theater in Baltimore and a bakery and a movie theater in Philadelphia. Depending on the relevant facts and circumstances, there may be more than one reasonable method for grouping the partnership's activities. For instance, the following groupings may or may not be permissible: a single activity, a movie theater activity and a bakery activity, a Baltimore activity and a Philadelphia activity, or four separate activities.

Once the partnership chooses a grouping under these rules, it must continue using that grouping in later tax years unless a material change in the facts and circumstances makes it clearly inappropriate.

The IRS may regroup the partnership's activities if the partnership's grouping fails to reflect one or more appropriate economic units and one of the primary purposes of the grouping is to avoid the passive activity limitations.

Limitation on grouping certain activities. The following activities may not be grouped together:

1. A rental activity with a trade or business activity unless the activities being grouped together make up an appropriate economic unit, and

a. The rental activity is insubstantial relative to the trade or business activity or vice versa, or

b. Each owner of the trade or business activity has the same proportionate ownership interest in the rental activity. If so, the portion of the rental activity involving the rental of property to be used in the trade or business activity may be grouped with the trade or business activity.

2. An activity involving the rental of real property with an activity involving the rental of personal property (except for personal property provided in connection with the real property or vice versa).

3. Any activity with another activity in a different type of business and in which the partnership holds an interest as a limited partner or as a limited entrepreneur (as defined in section 464(e)(2)) if that other activity engages in holding, producing, or distributing motion picture films or videotapes; farming; leasing section 1245 property; or exploring for (or exploiting) oil and gas resources or geothermal deposits.

Activities conducted through other partnerships. Once a partnership determines its activities under these rules, the partnership as a partner may use these rules to group those activities with each other, with activities conducted directly by the partnership, and with activities conducted through other partnerships. A partner may not treat as separate activities those activities grouped together by a partnership.

Recharacterization of Passive Income

Under Temporary Regulations section 1.469-2T(f) and Regulations section 1.469-2(f), net passive income from certain passive activities must be treated as nonpassive income. Net passive income is the excess of an activity's passive activity gross income over its passive activity deductions (current year deductions and prior year unallowed losses).

Income from the following six sources is subject to recharacterization. Note that any net passive income recharacterized as nonpassive income is treated as investment income for purposes of figuring investment interest expense limitations if it is from (a) an activity of renting substantially nondepreciable property from an equity-financed lending activity or (b) an activity related to an interest in a pass-through entity that licenses intangible property.

1. Significant participation passive activities. A significant participation passive activity is any trade or business activity in which the partner both participates for more than 100 hours during the tax year and does not materially participate. Because each partner must determine the partner's level of participation, the partnership will not be able to identify significant participation passive activities.

2. Certain nondepreciable rental property activities. Net passive income from a rental activity is nonpassive income if less than 30% of the unadjusted basis of the property used or held for use by customers in the activity is subject to depreciation under section 167.

3. Passive equity-financed lending activities. If the partnership has net income from a passive equity-financed lending activity, the smaller of the net passive income or the equity-financed interest income from the activity is nonpassive income.

Note: *The amount of income from the activities in paragraphs 1 through 3 that any partner will be required to recharacterize as nonpassive income may be limited under Temporary Regulations section 1.469-2T(f)(8). Because the partnership will not have information regarding all of a partner's activities, it must identify all partnership activities meeting the definitions in paragraphs 2 and 3 as activities that may be subject to recharacterization.*

4. Rental of property incidental to a development activity. Net rental activity income is nonpassive income for a partner if all of the following apply: (a) the partnership recognizes gain from the sale, exchange, or other disposition of the rental property during the tax year; (b) the use of the item of property in the rental activity started less than 12 months before the date of disposition (the use of an item of rental property begins on the first day that (i) the partnership owns an interest in the property; (ii) substantially all of the property is either rented or held out for rent and ready to be rented; and (iii) no significant value-enhancing services remain to be performed); and (c) the partner materially participated or significantly participated for any tax year in an activity that involved the performance of services for the purpose of enhancing the value of the property (or any other item of property, if the basis of the property disposed of is determined in whole or in part by reference to the basis of that item of property). "Net rental activity income" means the excess of passive activity gross income from renting or disposing of property over passive activity deductions (current year

deductions and prior year unallowed losses) that are reasonably allocable to the rented property.

Because the partnership cannot determine a partner's level of participation, the partnership must identify net income from property described in items (a) and (b) of paragraph 4 as income that may be subject to recharacterization.

5. Rental of property to a nonpassive activity. If a taxpayer rents property to a trade or business activity in which the taxpayer materially participates, the taxpayer's net rental activity income from the property is nonpassive income.

6. Acquisition of an interest in a pass-through entity that licenses intangible property. Generally, net royalty income from intangible property is nonpassive income if the taxpayer acquired an interest in the pass-through entity after the pass-through entity created the intangible property or performed substantial services, or incurred substantial costs in developing or marketing the intangible property. "Net royalty income" means the excess of passive activity gross income from licensing or transferring any right in intangible property over passive activity deductions (current year deductions and prior year unallowed losses) that are reasonably allocable to the intangible property.

See Temporary Regulations section 1.469-2T(f)(7)(iii) for exceptions to this rule.

Passive Activity Reporting Requirements

To allow partners to correctly apply the passive activity loss and credit rules, any partnership that carries on more than one activity must:

1. Provide an attachment for each activity conducted through the partnership that identifies the type of activity conducted (trade or business, rental real estate, rental activity other than rental real estate, or investment).

2. On the attachment for each activity, provide a schedule, using the same line numbers as shown on Schedule K-1, detailing the net income (loss), credits, and all items required to be separately stated under section 702(a) from each trade or business activity, from each rental real estate activity, from each rental activity other than a rental real estate activity, and from investments.

3. Identify the net income (loss) and credits from each oil or gas well drilled or operated under a working interest that any partner (other than a partner whose only interest in the partnership during the year is as a limited partner) holds through the partnership. Further, if any partner had an interest as a general partner in the partnership during less than the entire year, the partnership must identify both the disqualified deductions from each well that the partner must treat as passive activity deductions, and the ratable portion of the gross income from each well that the partner must treat as passive activity gross income.

4. Identify the net income (loss) and the partner's share of partnership interest expense from each activity of renting a dwelling unit that any partner uses for personal purposes during the year for more than the greater of 14 days or 10% of the number of days that the residence is rented at fair rental value.

5. Identify the net income (loss) and the partner's share of partnership interest expense from each activity of trading personal property conducted through the partnership.

6. For any gain (loss) from the disposition of an interest in an activity or of an interest in property used in an activity (including dispositions before 1987 from which gain is being recognized after 1986):

a. Identify the activity in which the property was used at the time of disposition.

b. If the property was used in more than one activity during the 12 months preceding the disposition, identify the activities in which the property was used and the adjusted basis allocated to each activity.

c. For gains only, if the property was substantially appreciated at the time of the disposition and the applicable holding period specified in Regulations section 1.469-2(c)(2)(iii)(A) was not satisfied, identify the amount of the nonpassive gain and indicate whether the gain is investment income under the provisions of Regulations section 1.469-2(c)(2)(iii)(F).

7. Specify the amount of gross portfolio income, the interest expense properly allocable to portfolio income, and expenses other than interest expense that are clearly and directly allocable to portfolio income.

8. Identify separately any of the following types of payments to partners:

a. Payments to a partner for services other than in the partner's capacity as a partner under section 707(a).

b. Guaranteed payments to a partner for services under section 707(c).

c. Guaranteed payments for use of capital.

d. If section 736(a)(2) payments are made for unrealized receivables or for goodwill, the amount of the payments and the activities to which the payments are attributable.

e. If section 736(b) payments are made, the amount of the payments and the activities to which the payments are attributable.

9. Identify the ratable portion of any section 481 adjustment (whether a net positive or a net negative adjustment) allocable to each partnership activity.

10. Identify the amount of gross income from each oil or gas property of the partnership.

11. Identify any gross income from sources that are specifically excluded from passive activity gross income, including:

a. Income from intangible property if the partner is an individual and the partner's personal efforts significantly contributed to the creation of the property.

b. Income from state, local, or foreign income tax refunds.

c. Income from a covenant not to compete (in the case of a partner who is an individual and who contributed the covenant to the partnership).

12. Identify any deductions that are not passive activity deductions.

13. If the partnership makes a full or partial disposition of its interest in another entity, identify the gain (loss) allocable to each activity conducted through the entity, and the gain allocable to a passive activity that would have been recharacterized as nonpassive gain had the partnership disposed of its interest in property used in the activity (because the property was substantially appreciated at the time of the disposition, and the gain represented more than 10% of the partner's total gain from the disposition).

14. Identify the following items from activities that may be subject to the recharacterization rules under Temporary Regulations section 1.469-2T(f) and Regulations section 1.469-2(f):

a. Net income from an activity of renting substantially nondepreciable property.

b. The smaller of equity-financed interest income or net passive income from an equity-financed lending activity.

c. Net rental activity income from property that was developed (by the partner or the partnership), rented, and sold within 12 months after the rental of the property commenced.

d. Net rental activity income from the rental of property by the partnership to a trade or business activity in which the partner had an interest (either directly or indirectly).

e. Net royalty income from intangible property if the partner acquired the partner's interest in the partnership after the partnership created the intangible property or performed substantial services, or incurred substantial costs in developing or marketing the intangible property.

15. Identify separately the credits from each activity conducted by or through the partnership.

Specific Instructions

These instructions follow the line numbers on the first page of Form 1065 and on the schedules that accompany it. Specific instructions for most of the lines are provided on the following pages. Lines that are not discussed in the instructions are self-explanatory.

Fill in all applicable lines and schedules.

Enter any items specially allocated to the partners on the appropriate line of the applicable partner's Schedule K-1. Enter the total amount on the appropriate line of Schedule K. **Do not** enter separately stated amounts on the numbered lines on Form 1065, page 1, or on Schedule A or D.

Be sure to file all four pages of Form 1065. However, if the answer to Question 5 of Schedule B is **Yes**, the completion of page 4 is optional. Also attach a Schedule K-1 to Form 1065 for each partner.

File only one Form 1065 for each partnership. Mark "duplicate copy" on any copy you give to a partner.

If a syndicate, pool, joint venture, or similar group files Form 1065, it must attach a copy of the agreement and all amendments to the return, unless a copy has previously been filed.

General Information

Name, Address, and Employer Identification Number

Use the label that was mailed to the partnership. Cross out any errors and print the correct information on the label.

Name. If the partnership did not receive a label, print or type the legal name of the partnership as it appears in the partnership agreement.

Address. Include the suite, room, or other unit number after the street address. If a preaddressed label is used, include this information on the label.

If the Post Office does not deliver mail to the street address and the partnership has a P.O.

box, show the box number instead of the street address.

If the partnership's address is outside the United States or its possessions or territories, enter the information on the line for "City or town, state, and ZIP code" in the following order: city, province or state, and the foreign country. Follow the foreign country's practice in placing the postal code in the address. **Do not** abbreviate the country name.

If the partnership has had a change of address, check box G(3).

If the partnership changes its mailing address after filing its return, it can notify the IRS by filing **Form 8822,** Change of Address.

Employer identification number (EIN). Show the correct EIN in item D on page 1 of Form 1065. If the partnership does not have an EIN, it must apply for one on **Form SS-4,** Application for Employer Identification Number. Form SS-4 has information on how to apply for an EIN by mail or by telephone. If the partnership has not received its EIN by the time the return is due, write "Applied for" in the space for the EIN. See **Pub. 583,** Starting a Business and Keeping Records, for more information.

Do not request a new EIN for a partnership that terminated because of a sale or exchange of at least 50% of the total interests in partnership capital and profits.

Items A and C

Enter the applicable activity name and the **NEW** code number from the list beginning on page 25.

For example, if, as its principal business activity, the partnership **(a)** purchases raw materials, **(b)** subcontracts out for labor to make a finished product from the raw materials, and **(c)** retains title to the goods, the partnership is considered to be a manufacturer and must enter "Manufacturer" in item A and enter in item C one of the codes (311110 through 339900) listed under "Manufacturing" on page 25.

Important: *The 6-digit North American Industry Classification System (NAICS) codes are new this year and replace the former 4-digit code. If there is a 4-digit code on the mailing label, cross it out and enter the new 6-digit code.*

Item F—Total Assets

You are not required to complete item F if the answer to Question 5 of Schedule B is **Yes**.

If you are required to complete this item, enter the partnership's total assets at the end of the tax year, as determined by the accounting method regularly used in keeping the partnership's books and records. If there were no assets at the end of the tax year, enter the total assets as of the beginning of the tax year.

Item G

Do not check "Final return" (box G(2)) for a partnership that terminated because of a sale or exchange of at least 50% of the total interests in partnership capital and profits. However, be sure to file a return for the short year ending on the date of termination.

Income

Caution: *Report only trade or business activity income on lines 1a through 8. Do not report*

rental activity income or portfolio income on these lines. See the instructions on Passive Activity Limitations beginning on page 6 for definitions of rental income and portfolio income. Rental activity income and portfolio income are reported on Schedules K and K-1. Rental real estate activities are also reported on Form 8825.

Do not include any tax-exempt income on lines 1a through 8. A partnership that receives any tax-exempt income other than interest, or holds any property or engages in any activity that produces tax-exempt income reports the amount of this income on line 20 of Schedules K and K-1.

Report tax-exempt interest income, including exempt-interest dividends received as a shareholder in a mutual fund or other regulated investment company, on line 19 of Schedules K and K-1.

See **Deductions** on page 11 for information on how to report expenses related to tax-exempt income.

If the partnership has had debt discharged resulting from a title 11 bankruptcy proceeding or while insolvent, see **Form 982,** Reduction of Tax Attributes Due to Discharge of Indebtedness, and **Pub. 908,** Bankruptcy Tax Guide.

Line 1a—Gross Receipts or Sales

Enter the gross receipts or sales from all trade or business operations except those that must be reported on lines 4 through 7. For example, do not include gross receipts from farming on this line. Instead, show the net profit (loss) from farming on line 5. Also, do not include on line 1a rental activity income or portfolio income. See section 460 for special rules that apply to long-term contracts.

Installment sales. Generally, the installment method cannot be used for dealer dispositions of property. A "dealer disposition" is any disposition of personal property by a person who regularly sells or otherwise disposes of personal property of the same type on the installment plan or any disposition of real property held for sale to customers in the ordinary course of the taxpayer's trade or business. The disposition of property used or produced in a farming business is not included as a dealer disposition. See section 453(l) for details and exceptions.

Enter on line 1a the gross profit on collections from installment sales for any of the following:

- Dealer dispositions of property before March 1, 1986.
- Dispositions of property used or produced in the trade or business of farming.
- Certain dispositions of timeshares and residential lots reported under the installment method.

Attach a schedule showing the following information for the current year and the 3 preceding years:
- Gross sales.
- Cost of goods sold.
- Gross profits.
- Percentage of gross profits to gross sales.
- Amount collected.
- Gross profit on amount collected.

Line 2—Cost of Goods Sold

See the instructions for Schedule A on page 14.

Line 4—Ordinary Income (Loss) From Other Partnerships, Estates, and Trusts

Enter the ordinary income (loss) shown on Schedule K-1 (Form 1065) or Schedule K-1 (Form 1041), or other ordinary income (loss) from a foreign partnership, estate, or trust. Be sure to show the partnership's, estate's, or trust's name, address, and EIN on a separate statement attached to this return. If the amount entered is from more than one source, identify the amount from each source.

Do not include portfolio income or rental activity income (loss) from other partnerships, estates, or trusts on this line. Instead, report these amounts on the applicable lines of Schedules K and K-1, or on line 20a of Form 8825 if the amount is from a rental real estate activity.

Ordinary income or loss from another partnership that is a publicly traded partnership is not reported on this line. Instead, report the amount separately on line 7 of Schedules K and K-1.

Treat shares of other items separately reported on Schedule K-1 issued by the other entity as if the items were realized or incurred by this partnership.

If there is a loss from another partnership, the amount of the loss that may be claimed is subject to the at-risk and basis limitations as appropriate.

If the tax year of your partnership does not coincide with the tax year of the other partnership, estate, or trust, include the ordinary income (loss) from the other entity in the tax year in which the other entity's tax year ends.

Line 5—Net Farm Profit (Loss)

Enter the partnership's net farm profit (loss) from **Schedule F (Form 1040)**, Profit or Loss From Farming. Attach Schedule F (Form 1040) to Form 1065. **Do not** include on this line any farm profit (loss) from other partnerships. Report those amounts on line 4. In figuring the partnership's net farm profit (loss), do not include any section 179 expense deduction; this amount must be separately stated.

Also report the partnership's fishing income on this line.

For a special rule concerning the method of accounting for a farming partnership with a corporate partner and for other tax information on farms, see **Pub. 225**, Farmer's Tax Guide.

Note: *Because the election to deduct the expenses of raising any plant with a preproductive period of more than 2 years is made by the partner and not the partnership, farm partnerships that are not required to use an accrual method should not capitalize such expenses. Instead, state them separately on an attachment to Schedule K, line 24, and on Schedule K-1, line 25, Supplemental Information. See Temporary Regulations section 1.263A-4T for more information.*

Line 6—Net Gain (Loss) From Form 4797

Caution: *Include only ordinary gains or losses from the sale, exchange, or involuntary conversion of assets used in a trade or business activity. Ordinary gains or losses from the sale, exchange, or involuntary conversion of rental activity assets are reported separately on line 19 of Form 8825 or line 3 of Schedules*

K and K-1, generally as a part of the net income (loss) from the rental activity.

A partnership that is a partner in another partnership must include on **Form 4797**, Sales of Business Property, its share of ordinary gains (losses) from sales, exchanges, or involuntary conversions (other than casualties or thefts) of the other partnership's trade or business assets.

Do not include any recapture of section 179 expense deduction. See the instructions for line 25, Supplemental Information, item 4, and the Instructions for Form 4797 for more information.

Line 7—Other Income (Loss)

Enter on line 7 trade or business income (loss) that is not included on lines 1a through 6. Examples of such income include:

1. Interest income derived in the ordinary course of the partnership's trade or business, such as interest charged on receivable balances.

2. Recoveries of bad debts deducted in earlier years under the specific charge-off method.

3. Taxable income from insurance proceeds.

4. The amount of credit figured on **Form 6478**, Credit for Alcohol Used as Fuel.

5. All section 481 income adjustments resulting from changes in accounting methods. Show the computation of the section 481 adjustments on an attached schedule.

6. The amount of any deduction previously taken under section 179A that is subject to recapture. See Pub. 535 for details, including how to figure the recapture.

7. The recapture amount for section 280F if the business use of listed property drops to 50% or less. To figure the recapture amount, the partnership must complete Part IV of Form 4797.

Do not include items requiring separate computations that must be reported on Schedules K and K-1. See the instructions for Schedules K and K-1 later in these instructions.

Do not report portfolio or rental activity income (loss) on this line.

Deductions

Caution: *Report only trade or business activity deductions on lines 9 through 21.*

Do not report the following expenses on lines 9 through 21:

• Rental activity expenses. Report these expenses on Form 8825 or line 3b of Schedule K.

• Deductions allocable to portfolio income. Report these deductions on line 10 of Schedules K and K-1.

• Nondeductible expenses (e.g., expenses connected with the production of tax-exempt income). Report nondeductible expenses on line 21 of Schedules K and K-1.

• Qualified expenditures to which an election under section 59(e) may apply. The instructions for lines 18a and 18b of Schedules K and K-1 explain how to report these amounts.

• Items the partnership must state separately that require separate computations by the partners. Examples include expenses incurred for the production of income instead of in a trade or business, charitable contributions, foreign taxes paid, intangible drilling and development costs, soil and water conservation

expenditures, and exploration expenditures. The distributive shares of these expenses are reported separately to each partner on Schedule K-1.

Limitations on Deductions

Section 263A uniform capitalization rules. The uniform capitalization rules of section 263A require partnerships to capitalize or include in inventory certain costs incurred in connection with:

• The production of real and tangible personal property held in inventory or held for sale in the ordinary course of business.

• Personal property (tangible and intangible) acquired for resale.

• The production of property constructed or improved by a partnership for use in its trade or business or in an activity engaged in for profit.

The costs required to be capitalized under section 263A are not deductible until the property to which the costs relate is sold, used, or otherwise disposed of by the partnership.

Exceptions: Section 263A **does not** apply to:

• Personal property acquired for resale if the partnership's average annual gross receipts for the 3 prior tax years were $10 million or less.

• Timber.

• Most property produced under a long-term contract.

• Certain property produced in a farming business. See the note at the end of the instructions for line 5.

The partnership must report the following costs separately to the partners for purposes of determinations under section 59(e):

• Research and experimental costs under section 174.

• Intangible drilling costs for oil, gas, and geothermal property.

• Mining exploration and development costs.

Tangible personal property produced by a partnership includes a film, sound recording, video tape, book, or similar property.

Partnerships subject to the rules are required to capitalize not only direct costs but an allocable part of most indirect costs (including taxes) that benefit the assets produced or acquired for resale.

For inventory, some of the *indirect costs* that must be capitalized are:

• Administration expenses.

• Taxes.

• Depreciation.

• Insurance.

• Compensation paid to officers attributable to services.

• Rework labor.

• Contributions to pension, stock bonus, and certain profit-sharing, annuity, or deferred compensation plans.

Regulations section 1.263A-1(e)(3) specifies other indirect costs that relate to production or resale activities that must be capitalized and those that may be currently deductible.

Interest expense paid or incurred during the production period of certain property must be capitalized and is governed by special rules. For more details, see Regulations sections 1.263A-8 through 1.263A-15.

For more details on the uniform capitalization rules, see Regulations sections 1.236A-1 through 1.263A-3.

Transactions between related taxpayers. Generally, an accrual basis partnership may deduct business expenses and interest owed to a related party (including any partner) only in the tax year of the partnership that includes the day on which the payment is includible in the income of the related party. See section 267 for details.

Business start-up expenses. Business start-up expenses must be capitalized. An election may be made to amortize them over a period of not less than 60 months. See Pub. 535.

Organization costs. Amounts paid or incurred to organize a partnership are capital expenditures. They are not deductible as a current expense.

The partnership may elect to amortize organization expenses over a period of 60 or more months, beginning with the month in which the partnership begins business. Include the amortization expense on line 20. On the balance sheet (Schedule L) show the unamortized balance of organization costs. See the instructions for line 10 for the treatment of organization expenses paid to a partner. See Pub. 535 for more information.

Syndication costs. Costs for issuing and marketing interests in the partnership, such as commissions, professional fees, and printing costs, must be capitalized. They cannot be depreciated or amortized. See the instructions for line 10 for the treatment of syndication fees paid to a partner.

Reducing certain expenses for which credits are allowable. For each of the following credits, the partnership must reduce the otherwise allowable deductions for expenses used to figure the credit by the amount of the current year credit:

1. The work opportunity credit.

2. The welfare-to-work credit.

3. The credit for increasing research activities.

4. The enhanced oil recovery credit.

5. The disabled access credit.

6. The empowerment zone employment credit.

7. The Indian employment credit.

8. The credit for employer social security and Medicare taxes paid on certain employee tips.

9. The orphan drug credit.

If the partnership has any of these credits, be sure to figure each current year credit before figuring the deductions for expenses on which the credit is based.

Line 9—Salaries and Wages

Enter on line 9 the salaries and wages paid or incurred for the tax year, reduced by any applicable employment credits from **Form 5884**, Work Opportunity Credit, **Form 8861**, Welfare-to-Work Credit, **Form 8844**, Empowerment Zone Employment Credit, and **Form 8845**, Indian Employment Credit. See the instructions for these forms for more information.

Do not include salaries and wages reported elsewhere on the return, such as amounts included in cost of goods sold, elective contributions to a section 401(k) cash or deferred arrangement, or amounts contributed under a salary reduction SEP agreement.

Line 10—Guaranteed Payments to Partners

Deduct payments or credits to a partner for services or for the use of capital if the payments or credits are determined without regard to partnership income and are allocable to a trade or business activity. Also include on line 10 amounts paid during the tax year for insurance that constitutes medical care for a partner, a partner's spouse, or a partner's dependents.

Do not include any payments and credits that should be capitalized. For example, although payments or credits to a partner for services rendered in organizing or syndicating a partnership may be guaranteed payments, they are not deductible on line 10. They are capital expenditures. However, they should be separately reported on Schedules K and K-1, line 5.

Do not include distributive shares of partnership profits.

Report the guaranteed payments to the appropriate partners on Schedule K-1, line 5.

Line 11—Repairs and Maintenance

Enter the costs of incidental repairs and maintenance that do not add to the value of the property or appreciably prolong its life, but only to the extent that such costs relate to a trade or business activity and are not claimed elsewhere on the return.

New buildings, machinery, or permanent improvements that increase the value of the property are not deductible. They are chargeable to capital accounts and may be depreciated or amortized.

Line 12—Bad Debts

Enter the total debts that became worthless in whole or in part during the year, but only to the extent such debts relate to a trade or business activity. Report deductible nonbusiness bad debts as a short-term capital loss on Schedule D (Form 1065).

Caution: *Cash method partnerships cannot take a bad debt deduction unless the amount was previously included in income.*

Line 13—Rent

Enter rent paid on business property used in a trade or business activity. Do not deduct rent for a dwelling unit occupied by any partner for personal use.

If the partnership rented or leased a vehicle, enter the total annual rent or lease expense paid or incurred in the trade or business activities of the partnership. Also complete Part V of **Form 4562**, Depreciation and Amortization. If the partnership leased a vehicle for a term of 30 days or more, the deduction for vehicle lease expense may have to be reduced by an amount called the **inclusion amount.** You may have an inclusion amount if:

The lease term began:	And the vehicle's fair market value on the first day of the lease exceeded:
After 12/31/96	$15,800
After 12/31/94 but before 1/1/97	$15,500
After 12/31/93 but before 1/1/95	$14,600
After 12/31/92 but before 1/1/94	$14,300

If the lease term began before January 1, 1993, see **Pub. 463**, Travel, Entertainment, Gift, and Car Expenses, to find out if the partnership has an inclusion amount.

See Pub. 463 for instructions on figuring the inclusion amount.

Line 14—Taxes and Licenses

Enter taxes and licenses paid or incurred in the trade or business activities of the partnership if not reflected in cost of goods sold. Federal import duties and Federal excise and stamp taxes are deductible only if paid or incurred in carrying on the trade or business of the partnership.

Do not deduct the following taxes on line 14:

● State and local sales taxes paid or incurred in connection with the acquisition or disposition of business property. These taxes must be added to the cost of the property, or, in the case of a disposition, subtracted from the amount realized.

● Taxes assessed against local benefits to the extent that they increase the value of the property assessed, such as for paving, etc.

● Federal income taxes or taxes reported elsewhere on the return.

● Section 901 foreign taxes. Report these taxes separately on Schedules K and K-1, line 17e.

● Taxes allocable to a rental activity. Taxes allocable to a rental real estate activity are reported on Form 8825. Taxes allocable to a rental activity other than a rental real estate activity are reported on line 3b of Schedule K.

● Taxes allocable to portfolio income. These taxes are reported on line 10 of Schedules K and K-1.

● Taxes paid or incurred for the production or collection of income, or for the management, conservation, or maintenance of property held to produce income. Report these taxes separately on line 11 of Schedules K and K-1.

See section 263A(a) for rules on capitalization of allocable costs (including taxes) for any property.

Line 15—Interest

Include only interest incurred in the trade or business activities of the partnership that is not claimed elsewhere on the return.

Do not include interest expense on debt required to be allocated to the production of designated property. Designated property includes real property, personal property that has a class life of 20 years or more, and other tangible property requiring more than 2 years (1 year in the case of property with a cost of more than $1 million) to produce or construct. Interest that is allocable to designated property produced by a partnership for its own use or for sale must be capitalized.

In addition, a partnership must also capitalize any interest on debt that is allocable to an asset used to produce designated property. A partner may have to capitalize interest that the partner incurs during the tax year with respect to the production expenditures of the partnership. Similarly, interest incurred by a partnership may have to be capitalized by a partner with respect to the partner's own production expenditures. The information required by the partner to properly capitalize interest for this purpose must be provided by the partnership in an attachment to Schedule K-1. See section 263A(f) and Regulations sections 1.263A-8 through 1.263A-15.

Do not include interest expense on debt used to purchase rental property or debt used in a rental activity. Interest allocable to a rental real estate activity is reported on Form 8825 and is used in arriving at net income (loss) from rental real estate activities on line 2 of Schedules K and K-1. Interest allocable to a rental activity other than a rental real estate activity is included on line 3b of Schedule K and is used in arriving at net income (loss) from a rental activity (other than a rental real estate activity). This net amount is reported on line 3c of Schedule K and line 3 of Schedule K-1.

Do not include interest expense on debt used to buy property held for investment. Do not include interest expense that is clearly and directly allocable to interest, dividend, royalty, or annuity income not derived in the ordinary course of a trade or business. Interest paid or incurred on debt used to purchase or carry investment property is reported on line 14a of Schedules K and K-1. See the instructions for line 14a of Schedules K and K-1 and **Form 4952,** Investment Interest Expense Deduction, for more information on investment property.

Do not include interest on debt proceeds allocated to distributions made to partners during the tax year. Instead, report such interest on line 11 of Schedules K and K-1. To determine the amount to allocate to distributions to partners, see Notice 89-35, 1989-1 C.B. 675.

Temporary Regulations section 1.163-8T gives rules for allocating interest expense among activities so that the limitations on passive activity losses, investment interest, and personal interest can be properly figured. Generally, interest expense is allocated in the same manner that debt is allocated. Debt is allocated by tracing disbursements of the debt proceeds to specific expenditures, as provided in the regulations.

Interest paid by a partnership to a partner for the use of capital should be entered on line 10 as guaranteed payments.

Prepaid interest can only be deducted over the period to which the prepayment applies.

Note: *Additional limitations on interest deductions apply when the partnership is a policyholder or beneficiary with respect to a life insurance, endowment, or annuity contract issued after June 8, 1997. For details, see section 264. Attach a statement showing the computation of the deduction disallowed under section 264.*

Line 16—Depreciation

On line 16a, enter **only** the depreciation claimed on assets used in a trade or business activity. Enter on line 16b the depreciation reported elsewhere on the return (e.g., on Schedule A) that is attributable to assets used in trade or business activities. See the Instructions for Form 4562 or **Pub. 946,** How To Depreciate Property, to figure the amount of depreciation to enter on this line.

For depreciation, you must complete and attach Form 4562 only if the partnership placed property in service during 1998 or claims depreciation on any car or other listed property.

Do not include any section 179 expense deduction on this line. This amount is not deducted by the partnership. Instead, it is passed through to the partners on line 9 of Schedule K-1.

Line 17—Depletion

If the partnership claims a deduction for timber depletion, complete and attach **Form T,** Forest Activities Schedules.

Caution: *Do not deduct depletion for oil and gas properties. Each partner figures depletion on oil and gas properties. See the instructions for Schedule K-1, line 25, item 3, for the information on oil and gas depletion that must be supplied to the partners by the partnership.*

Line 18—Retirement Plans, etc.

Do not deduct payments for partners to retirement or deferred compensation plans including IRAs, Keoghs, and simplified employee pension (SEP) and SIMPLE plans on this line. These amounts are reported on Schedule K-1, line 11, and are deducted by the partners on their own returns.

Enter the deductible contributions not claimed elsewhere on the return made by the partnership for its common-law employees under a qualified pension, profit-sharing, annuity, or SEP or SIMPLE plan, and under any other deferred compensation plan.

If the partnership contributes to an individual retirement arrangement (IRA) for employees, include the contribution in salaries and wages on page 1, line 9, or Schedule A, line 3, and not on line 18.

Employers who maintain a pension, profit-sharing, or other funded deferred compensation plan (other than a SEP), whether or not the plan is qualified under the Internal Revenue Code and whether or not a deduction is claimed for the current year, generally must file one of the following forms:

● **Form 5500,** Annual Return/Report of Employee Benefit Plan, for each plan with 100 or more participants.

● **Form 5500-C/R,** Return/Report of Employee Benefit Plan, for each plan with fewer than 100 participants.

● **Form 5500-EZ,** Annual Return of One-Participant (Owners and Their Spouses) Retirement Plan, for each plan that covers only partners or partners and their spouses.

There are penalties for not filing these forms on time.

Line 19—Employee Benefit Programs

Enter the partnership's contributions to employee benefit programs not claimed elsewhere on the return (e.g., insurance, health, and welfare programs) that are not part of a pension, profit-sharing, etc., plan included on line 18.

Do not include amounts paid during the tax year for insurance that constitutes medical care for a partner, a partner's spouse, or a partner's dependents. Instead, include these amounts on line 10 as guaranteed payments and on Schedule K, line 5, and Schedule K-1, line 5, of each partner on whose behalf the amounts were paid. Also report these amounts on Schedule K, line 11, and Schedule K-1, line 11, of each partner on whose behalf the amounts were paid.

Line 20—Other Deductions

Attach your own schedule, listing by type and amount, all allowable deductions related to a trade or business activity for which there is no separate line on page 1 of Form 1065. Enter the total on this line. Do not include items that must be reported separately on Schedules K and K-1.

A partnership is not allowed the deduction for net operating losses.

Do not include qualified expenditures to which an election under section 59(e) may apply.

Include on line 20 the deduction taken for amortization. You must complete and attach Form 4562 if the partnership is claiming amortization of costs that begins during its 1998 tax year. The instructions for Form 4562 provide code section references for specific amortizable property. See Pub. 535 for more information on amortization.

Do not deduct amounts paid or incurred to participate or intervene in any political campaign on behalf of a candidate for public office, or to influence the general public regarding legislative matters, elections, or referendums. In addition, partnerships generally cannot deduct expenses paid or incurred to influence Federal or state legislation, or to influence the actions or positions of certain Federal executive branch officials. However, certain in-house lobbying expenditures that do not exceed $2,000 are deductible. See section 162(e) for more details.

Do not deduct fines or penalties paid to a government for violating any law.

A deduction is allowed for part of the cost of qualified clean-fuel vehicle property and qualified clean-fuel vehicle refueling property. For more details, see section 179A.

Travel, meals, and entertainment. Subject to limitations and restrictions discussed below, a partnership can deduct ordinary and necessary travel, meals, and entertainment expenses paid or incurred in its trade or business. Special rules apply to deductions for gifts, skybox rentals, luxury water travel, convention expenses, and entertainment tickets. See section 274 and Pub. 463 for more details.

Travel. The partnership cannot deduct travel expenses of any individual accompanying a partner or partnership employee, including a spouse or dependent of the partner or employee, unless:

● That individual is an employee of the partnership, and

● His or her travel is for a bona fide business purpose and would otherwise be deductible by that individual.

Meals and entertainment. Generally, the partnership can deduct only 50% of the amount otherwise allowable for meals and entertainment expenses. In addition (subject to exceptions under section 274(k)(2)):

● Meals must not be lavish or extravagant,

● A bona fide business discussion must occur during, immediately before, or immediately after the meal, and

● A partner or employee of the partnership must be present at the meal.

Membership dues. The partnership may deduct amounts paid or incurred for membership dues in civic or public service organizations, professional organizations (such as bar and medical associations), business leagues, trade associations, chambers of commerce, boards of trade, and real estate boards. However, no deduction is allowed if a principal purpose of the organization is to entertain, or provide entertainment facilities for, members or their guests. In addition, the partnership may not deduct membership dues in any club organized for business, pleasure, recreation, or other social purpose. This includes country clubs, golf and athletic clubs, airline and hotel clubs, and clubs operated to provide meals under conditions favorable to business discussion.

Entertainment facilities. The partnership cannot deduct an expense paid or incurred for a facility (such as a yacht or hunting lodge)

used for an activity usually considered entertainment, amusement, or recreation.

Note: *The partnership may be able to deduct otherwise nondeductible meals, travel, and entertainment expenses if the amounts are treated as compensation and reported on Form W-2 for an employee or on Form 1099-MISC for an independent contractor.*

Schedule A—Cost of Goods Sold

Inventories are required at the beginning and end of each tax year if the production, purchase, or sale of merchandise is an income-producing factor. See Regulations section 1.471-1.

Section 263A Uniform Capitalization Rules

The uniform capitalization rules of section 263A are discussed under **Limitations on Deductions** on page 11. See those instructions before completing Schedule A.

Line 1—Inventory at Beginning of Year

This figure should match the ending inventory reported on the partnership's 1997 Form 1065, Schedule A, line 7. If it is different, attach an explanation.

Line 2—Purchases

Reduce purchases by items withdrawn for personal use. The cost of these items should be shown on line 23 of Schedules K and K-1 as distributions to partners.

Line 4—Additional Section 263A Costs

An entry is required on this line only for partnerships that have elected a simplified method.

For partnerships that have elected the simplified production method, additional section 263A costs are generally those costs, other than interest, that were not capitalized under the partnership's method of accounting immediately prior to the effective date of section 263A that are required to be capitalized under section 263A. Interest is to be accounted for separately. For new partnerships, additional section 263A costs are the costs, other than interest, that must be capitalized under section 263A, but which the partnership would not have been required to capitalize if it had existed before the effective date of section 263A. For more details, see Regulations section 1.263A-2(b).

For partnerships that have elected the simplified resale method, additional section 263A costs are generally those costs incurred with respect to the following categories:

- Off-site storage or warehousing.
- Purchasing.
- Handling, processing, assembly, and repackaging.
- General and administrative costs (mixed service costs).

For more details, see Regulations section 1.263A-3(d).

Enter on line 4 the balance of section 263A costs paid or incurred during the tax year not included on lines 2, 3, and 5. Attach a schedule listing these costs.

Line 5—Other Costs

Enter on line 5 any other inventoriable costs paid or incurred during the tax year not entered on lines 2 through 4. Attach a schedule.

Line 7—Inventory at End of Year

See Regulations sections 1.263A-1 through 1.263A-3 for details on figuring the costs to be included in ending inventory.

Lines 9a through 9c—Inventory Valuation Methods

Inventories can be valued at:

- Cost,
- Cost or market value (whichever is lower), or
- Any other method approved by the IRS that conforms to the requirements of the applicable regulations.

The average cost (rolling average) method of valuing inventories generally does not conform to the requirements of the regulations. See Rev. Rul. 71-234, 1971-1 C.B. 148.

Partnerships that use erroneous valuation methods must change to a method permitted for Federal tax purposes. To make this change, use Form 3115.

On line 9a, check the methods used for valuing inventories. Under lower of cost or market, the term "market" (for normal goods) means the current bid price prevailing on the inventory valuation date for the particular merchandise in the volume usually purchased by the taxpayer. For a manufacturer, market applies to the basic elements of cost—raw materials, labor, and burden. If section 263A applies to the taxpayer, the basic elements of cost must reflect the current bid price of all direct costs and all indirect costs properly allocable to goods on hand at the inventory date.

Inventory may be valued below cost when the merchandise is unsalable at normal prices or unusable in the normal way because the goods are subnormal due to damage, imperfections, shop wear, etc., within the meaning of Regulations section 1.471-2(c). These goods may be valued at the current bona fide selling price minus the direct cost of disposition (but not less than scrap value) if such a price can be established.

If this is the first year the last-in first-out (LIFO) inventory method was either adopted or extended to inventory goods not previously valued under the LIFO method, attach **Form 970,** Application To Use LIFO Inventory Method, or a statement with the information required by Form 970. Also check the box on line 9c.

If the partnership has changed or extended its inventory method to LIFO and has had to write up its opening inventory to cost in the year of election, report the effect of this write-up as income (line 7, page 1, Form 1065) proportionately over a 3-year period that begins in the tax year of the LIFO election.

For more information on inventory valuation methods, see Pub. 538.

Schedule B—Other Information

Question 1

Check box 1(e) for any other type of entity and state the type.

Question 4—Consolidated Audit Procedures

Generally, the tax treatment of partnership items is determined at the partnership level in a consolidated audit proceeding, rather than in separate proceedings with individual partners.

Answer **Yes** to Question 4 if **ANY** of the following apply:

- The partnership had more than 10 partners at any one time during the tax year. For purposes of this question, a husband and wife, and their estates, count as one person.
- Any partner was a nonresident alien or was other than an individual, an estate, or a C corporation.
- The partnership is a "small partnership" that has elected to be subject to the rules for consolidated audit proceedings. "Small partnerships" as defined in section 6231(a)(1)(B)(i) are not subject to the rules for consolidated audit proceedings, but may make an irrevocable election under Temporary Regulations section 301.6231(a)(1)-1T(b)(2) to be covered by them.

Caution: *The partnership does not make this election when it answers* **Yes** *to Question 4. The election must be made separately.*

If a partnership return is filed by an entity for a tax year, but it is determined that the entity is not a partnership for that tax year, the consolidated partnership audit procedures will generally apply to that entity and to persons holding an interest in that entity. See Temporary Regulations section 301.6233-1T for details and exceptions.

Question 6—Foreign Partners

Answer **Yes** to Question 6 if the partnership had any foreign partners (for purposes of section 1446) at any time during the tax year. Otherwise, answer **No.**

If the partnership had gross income effectively connected with a trade or business in the United States **and** foreign partners, it may be required to withhold tax under section 1446 on income allocable to foreign partners (without regard to distributions) and file Forms 8804, 8805, and 8813.

Question 7

Answer **Yes** to Question 7 if interests in the partnership are traded on an established securities market or are readily tradable on a secondary market (or its substantial equivalent).

Question 8

Organizers of certain tax shelters are required to register the tax shelters by filing Form 8264 no later than the day on which an interest in the shelter is first offered for sale. Organizers filing a properly completed Form 8264 will receive a tax shelter registration number that they must furnish to their investors. See the Instructions for Form 8264 for the definition of a tax shelter and the investments exempted from tax shelter registration.

Question 9—Foreign Accounts

Answer **Yes** to Question 9 if either **1** or **2** below applies to the partnership. Otherwise, check the **No** box.

1. At any time during calendar year 1998, the partnership had an interest in or signature or other authority over a bank account, securities account, or other financial account in a foreign country; **AND**

● The combined value of the accounts was more than $10,000 at any time during the calendar year; **AND**

● The accounts were NOT with a U.S. military banking facility operated by a U.S. financial institution.

2. The partnership owns more than 50% of the stock in any corporation that would answer the question **Yes** based on item **1** above.

Get **Form TD F 90-22.1,** Report of Foreign Bank and Financial Accounts, to see if the partnership is considered to have an interest in or signature or other authority over a bank account, securities account, or other financial account in a foreign country.

If you answered **Yes** to Question 9, file Form TD F 90-22.1 by June 30, 1999, with the Department of the Treasury at the address shown on the form. Because Form TD F 90-22.1 is not a tax return, **do not** file it with Form 1065. You may order Form TD F 90-22.1 by calling 1-800-829-3676.

Question 10

The partnership may be required to file **Form 3520,** Annual Return To Report Transactions With Foreign Trusts and Receipt of Certain Foreign Gifts, if:

● It directly or indirectly transferred property or money to a foreign trust. For this purpose, any U.S. person who created a foreign trust is considered a transferor.

● It is treated as the owner of any part of the assets of a foreign trust under the grantor trust rules.

● It received a distribution from a foreign trust.

For more information, see the Instructions for Form 3520.

Note: *An owner of a foreign trust must ensure that the trust files an annual information return on* **Form 3520-A,** *Annual Information Return of Foreign Trust with a U.S. Owner.*

Designation of Tax Matters Partner (TMP)

If the partnership is subject to the rules for consolidated audit proceedings in sections 6221 through 6233, the partnership may designate a partner as the TMP for the tax year for which the return is filed by completing the **Designation of Tax Matters Partner** section on page 2 of Form 1065. See the instructions for Question 4, consolidated audit procedures, to determine if the partnership is subject to these rules. The designated TMP must be a general partner and, in most cases, must also be a U.S. person. For details, see Regulations section 301.6231(a)(7)-1.

For a limited liability company (LLC), only a member-manager of the LLC is treated as a general partner. A member-manager is any owner of an interest in the LLC who, alone or together with others, has the continuing exclusive authority to make the management decisions necessary to conduct the business for which the LLC was formed. If there are no elected or designated member-managers, each owner is treated as a member-manager. For details, see Regulations section 301.6231(a)(7)-2.

General Instructions for Schedules K and K-1— Partners' Shares of Income, Credits, Deductions, etc.

Purpose of Schedules

Although the partnership is not subject to income tax, the partners are liable for tax on their shares of the partnership income, whether or not distributed, and must include their shares on their tax returns.

Schedule K (page 3 of Form 1065) is a summary schedule of all the partners' shares of the partnership's income, credits, deductions, etc. All partnerships must complete Schedule K. Rental activity income (loss) and portfolio income are not reported on page 1 of Form 1065. These amounts are not combined with trade or business activity income (loss). Schedule K is used to report the totals of these and other amounts.

Schedule K-1 (Form 1065) shows each partner's separate share. Attach a copy of each Schedule K-1 to the Form 1065 filed with the IRS; keep a copy with a copy of the partnership return as a part of the partnership's records; and furnish a copy to each partner. If a partnership interest is held by a nominee on behalf of another person, the partnership may be required to furnish Schedule K-1 to the nominee. See Temporary Regulations sections 1.6031(b)-1T and 1.6031(c)-1T for more information.

Be sure to give each partner a copy of either the Partner's Instructions for Schedule K-1 (Form 1065) or specific instructions for each item reported on the partner's Schedule K-1 (Form 1065).

Substitute Forms

The partnership does not need IRS approval to use a substitute Schedule K-1 if it is an exact copy of the IRS schedule, or if it contains only those lines the taxpayer is required to use. The lines must use the same numbers and titles and must be in the same order and format as on the comparable IRS Schedule K-1. The substitute schedule must include the OMB number. The partnership must provide each partner with the Partner's Instructions for Schedule K-1 (Form 1065) or other prepared specific instructions.

The partnership must request IRS approval to use other substitute Schedules K-1. To request approval, write to Internal Revenue Service, Attention: Substitute Forms Program Coordinator, OP:FS:FP:F:CD, 1111 Constitution Avenue, N.W., Washington, DC 20224.

Each partner's information must be on a separate sheet of paper. Therefore, separate all continuously printed substitutes before you file them with the IRS.

The partnership may be subject to a penalty if it files Schedules K-1 that do not conform to the specifications of Rev. Proc. 97-54, 1997-2 C.B. 529.

How Income Is Shared Among Partners

Allocate shares of income, gain, loss, deduction, or credit among the partners according to the partnership agreement for sharing income or loss generally. Partners may agree to allocate specific items in a ratio different from the ratio for sharing income or loss. For instance, if the net income exclusive of specially allocated items is divided evenly among three partners but some special items are allocated 50% to one, 30% to another, and 20% to the third partner, report the specially allocated items on the appropriate line of the applicable partner's Schedule K-1 and the total on the appropriate line of Schedule K, instead of on the numbered lines on page 1 of Form 1065 or Schedules A or D.

If a partner's interest changed during the year, see section 706(d) before determining each partner's distributive share of any item of income, gain, loss, deduction, etc. Income (loss) is allocated to a partner only for the part of the year in which that person is a member of the partnership. The partnership will either allocate on a daily basis or divide the partnership year into segments and allocate income, loss, or special items in each segment among the persons who were partners during that segment. Partnerships that report their income on the cash basis must allocate interest expense, taxes, and any payment for services or for the use of property on a daily basis if there is any change in any partner's interest during the year. See Pub. 541 for more details.

Special rules on the allocation of income, gain, loss, and deductions generally apply if a partner contributes property to the partnership and the fair market value of that property at the time of contribution differs from the contributing partner's adjusted tax basis. Under these rules, the partnership must use a reasonable method of making allocations of income, gain, loss, and deductions from the property so that the contributing partner receives the tax burdens and benefits of any built-in gain or loss (i.e., precontribution appreciation or diminution of value of the contributed property). See Regulations section 1.704-3 for details on how to make these allocations, including a description of specific allocation methods that are generally reasonable.

See **Dispositions of Contributed Property** on page 6 for special rules on the allocation of income, gain, loss, and deductions on the disposition of property contributed to the partnership by a partner.

If the partnership agreement does not provide for the partner's share of income, gain, loss, deduction, or credit, or if the allocation under the agreement does not have substantial economic effect, the partner's share is determined according to the partner's interest in the partnership. See Regulations section 1.704-1 for more information.

Specific Instructions (Schedule K-1 Only)

General Information

Prepare and give a Schedule K-1 to each person who was a partner in the partnership at any time during the year. **Schedule K-1 must be provided to each partner on or before the day on which the partnership return is required to be filed.**

Generally, any person who holds an interest in a partnership as a nominee for another person must furnish to the partnership the name, address, etc., of the other person.

On each Schedule K-1, enter the names, addresses, and identifying numbers of the partner and partnership and the partner's distributive share of each item.

For an individual partner, enter the partner's social security number. For all other partners, enter the partner's EIN. However, if a partner is an individual retirement arrangement (IRA), enter the identifying number of the custodian of the IRA. Do not enter the social security number of the person for whom the IRA is maintained.

If a husband and wife each had an interest in the partnership, prepare a separate Schedule K-1 for each of them. If a husband and wife held an interest together, prepare one Schedule K-1 if the two of them are considered to be one partner.

There is space on line 25 of Schedule K-1 for you to provide information to the partners. This space may be used instead of attachments.

Specific Items and Questions

Question A

Answer Question A on all Schedules K-1. If a partner holds interests as both a general and limited partner, check the first two boxes and attach a schedule for each activity that shows the amounts allocable to the partner's interest as a limited partner.

Question B—What Type of Entity Is This Partner?

State on this line whether the partner is an individual, a corporation, an estate, a trust, a partnership, an exempt organization, or a nominee (custodian). If the partner is a nominee, use one of the following codes to indicate the type of entity the nominee represents: I—Individual; C—Corporation; F—Estate or Trust; P—Partnership; E—Exempt Organization; or IRA—Individual Retirement Arrangement.

Question C—Domestic/Foreign Partner

Check the foreign partner box if the partner is a nonresident alien individual, foreign partnership, foreign corporation, or a foreign estate or trust. Otherwise, check the domestic partner box.

Item D—Partner's Profit, Loss, and Capital Sharing Percentages

Enter in Item D, column (ii), the appropriate percentages as of the end of the year. However, if a partner's interest terminated during the year, enter in column (i) the percentages that existed immediately before the termination. When the profit or loss sharing percentage has changed during the year, show the percentage before the change in column (i) and the end-of-year percentage in column (ii). If there are multiple changes in the profit and loss sharing percentage during the year, attach a statement giving the date and percentage before each change.

"Ownership of capital" means the portion of the capital that the partner would receive if the partnership was liquidated at the end of the year by the distribution of undivided interests in partnership assets and liabilities.

Item F—Partner's Share of Liabilities

Enter each partner's share of nonrecourse liabilities, partnership-level qualified nonrecourse financing, and other liabilities.

"Nonrecourse liabilities" are those liabilities of the partnership for which no partner bears the economic risk of loss. The extent to which a partner bears the economic risk of loss is determined under the rules of Regulations

section 1.752-2. Do not include partnership-level qualified nonrecourse financing (defined below) on the line for nonrecourse liabilities.

If the partner terminated his or her interest in the partnership during the year, enter the share that existed immediately before the total disposition. In all other cases, enter it as of the end of the year.

If the partnership is engaged in two or more different types of at-risk activities, or a combination of at-risk activities and any other activity, attach a statement showing the partner's share of nonrecourse liabilities, partnership-level qualified nonrecourse financing, and other liabilities for **each** activity. See Pub. 925 to determine if the partnership is engaged in more than one at-risk activity.

The at-risk rules of section 465 generally apply to any activity carried on by the partnership as a trade or business or for the production of income. These rules generally limit the amount of loss and other deductions a partner can claim from any partnership activity to the amount for which that partner is considered at risk. However, for partners who acquired their partnership interests before 1987, the at-risk rules do not apply to losses from an activity of holding real property the partnership placed in service before 1987. The activity of holding mineral property does not qualify for this exception. Identify on an attachment to Schedule K-1 the amount of any losses that are not subject to the at-risk rules.

If a partnership is engaged in an activity subject to the limitations of section 465(c)(1) (i.e., films or videotapes, leasing section 1245 property, farming, or oil and gas property), give each partner his or her share of the total pre-1976 losses from that activity for which there existed a corresponding amount of nonrecourse liability at the end of each year in which the losses occurred. See **Form 6198,** At-Risk Limitations, and related instructions for more information.

Qualified nonrecourse financing secured by real property used in an activity of holding real property that is subject to the at-risk rules is treated as an amount at risk. "Qualified nonrecourse financing" generally includes financing for which no one is personally liable for repayment that is borrowed for use in an activity of holding real property and that is loaned or guaranteed by a Federal, state, or local government or that is borrowed from a "qualified" person. Qualified persons include any person actively and regularly engaged in the business of lending money, such as a bank or savings and loan association. Qualified persons generally do not include related parties (unless the nonrecourse financing is commercially reasonable and on substantially the same terms as loans involving unrelated persons), the seller of the property, or a person who receives a fee for the partnership's investment in the real property. See section 465 for more information on qualified nonrecourse financing.

The partner as well as the partnership must meet the qualified nonrecourse rules. Therefore, the partnership must enter on an attached statement any other information the partner needs to determine if the qualified nonrecourse rules are also met at the partner level.

Item G—Tax Shelter Registration Number

If the partnership is a registration-required tax shelter or has invested in a registration-

required tax shelter, it must enter the tax shelter registration number in Item G. Also, a partnership that has invested in a registration-required tax shelter must furnish a copy of its Form 8271 to its partners. See Form 8271 for more details.

Item J—Analysis of Partner's Capital Account

You are not required to complete Item J if the answer to Question 5 of Schedule B is **Yes**. If you are required to complete this item, see the instructions for Schedule M-2 on page 24.

Specific Instructions (Schedules K and K-1, Except as Noted)

Schedules K and K-1 have the same line numbers for lines 1 through 23.

Special Allocations

An item is specially allocated if it is allocated to a partner in a ratio different from the ratio for sharing income or loss generally.

Report specially allocated ordinary gain (loss) on Schedules K and K-1, line 7. Report other specially allocated items on the applicable lines of the partner's Schedule K-1, with the total amount on the applicable line of Schedule K. For example, specially allocated long-term capital gain is entered on line 4e(2) of the partner's Schedule K-1, and the total is entered on line 4e(2) of Schedule K, along with any net long-term capital gain (or loss) from line 12(f) of Schedule D (Form 1065).

Income (Loss)

Line 1—Ordinary Income (Loss) From Trade or Business Activities

Enter the amount from page 1, line 22. Enter the income or loss without reference to (a) the basis of the partners' interests in the partnership, (b) the partners' at-risk limitations, or (c) the passive activity limitations. These limitations, if applicable, are determined at the partner level.

If the partnership has more than one trade or business activity, identify on an attachment to Schedule K-1 the amount from each separate activity. See **Passive Activity Reporting Requirements** on page 9.

Line 1 should not include rental activity income (loss) or portfolio income (loss).

Line 2—Net Income (Loss) From Rental Real Estate Activities

Enter the net income or loss from rental real estate activities of the partnership from Form 8825. Attach this form to Form 1065. If the partnership has more than one rental real estate activity, identify on an attachment to Schedule K-1 the amount attributable to each activity.

Line 3—Net Income (Loss) From Other Rental Activities

On Schedule K, line 3a, enter gross income from rental activities other than rental real estate activities. See page 7 of these instructions and Pub. 925 for the definition of rental activities. Include on line 3a, the gain (loss) from line 18 of Form 4797 that is attributable to the sale, exchange, or involuntary conversion of an asset used in a rental activity other than a rental real estate activity.

On line 3b of Schedule K, enter the deductible expenses of the activity. Attach a schedule of these expenses to Form 1065.

Enter the net income (loss) on line 3c of Schedule K. Enter each partner's share on line 3 of Schedule K-1.

If the partnership has more than one rental activity reported on line 3, identify on an attachment to Schedule K-1 the amount from each activity.

Lines 4a Through 4f—Portfolio Income (Loss)

Enter portfolio income (loss) on lines 4a through 4f.

See page 8 of these instructions for a definition of portfolio income. Do not reduce portfolio income by deductions allocable to it. Report such deductions (other than interest expense) on line 10 of Schedules K and K-1. Interest expense allocable to portfolio income is generally investment interest expense and is reported on line 14a of Schedules K and K-1.

Lines 4a and 4b. Enter only taxable interest and ordinary dividends on these lines. Taxable interest is interest from all sources except interest exempt from tax and interest on tax-free covenant bonds.

Lines 4d, 4e(1), and 4e(2). Enter on line 4d of Schedule K the gain or loss from line 5 of Schedule D (Form 1065) plus any short-term capital gain (loss) that is specially allocated to partners. Report each partner's share on line 4d of Schedule K-1.

Enter on line 4e(1) the gain or loss from line 11 of Schedule D (Form 1065) plus any 28% rate gain (loss) that is specially allocated to partners. Enter on line 4e(2) the gain or loss from line 12 of Schedule D (Form 1065) plus any long-term capital gain (loss) that is specially allocated to partners. Report each partner's share on lines 4e(1) and 4e(2) of Schedule K-1, respectively.

Caution: *If any capital gain or loss is from the disposition of nondepreciable personal property used in a trade or business, it may not be treated as portfolio income. Report such gain or loss on line 7 of Schedules K and K-1.*

Line 4f. Report and identify other portfolio income or loss on an attachment for line 4f.

For example, income reported to the partnership from a real estate mortgage investment conduit (REMIC), in which the partnership is a residual interest holder, would be reported on an attachment for line 4f. If the partnership holds a residual interest in a REMIC, report on the attachment for line 4f the partner's share of the following:

• Taxable income (net loss) from the REMIC (line 1b of Schedules Q (Form 1066)).

• "Excess inclusion" (line 2c of Schedules Q (Form 1066)).

• Section 212 expenses (line 3b of Schedules Q (Form 1066)). Do not report these section 212 expenses on line 10 of Schedules K and K-1.

Because Schedule Q (Form 1066) is a quarterly statement, the partnership must follow the Schedule Q instructions to figure the amounts to report to the partner for the partnership's tax year.

Line 5—Guaranteed Payments to Partners

Guaranteed payments to partners include:
• Payments for salaries, health insurance, and

interest deducted by the partnership and reported on Form 1065, page 1, line 10; Form 8825; or on Schedule K, line 3b; and

• Payments the partnership must capitalize. See the Instructions for Form 1065, line 10.

Generally, amounts reported on line 5 are not considered to be related to a passive activity. For example, guaranteed payments for personal services paid to a partner would not be passive activity income. Likewise, interest paid to any partner is not passive activity income.

Line 6—Net Section 1231 Gain (Loss) (Other Than Due to Casualty or Theft)

Enter on line 6 the net section 1231 gain (loss) from Form 4797, line 7, column (g). Do not include specially allocated ordinary gains and losses or net gains or losses from involuntary conversions due to casualties or thefts on this line. Instead, report them on line 7. If the partnership has more than one activity, attach a statement to Schedule K-1 that identifies the activity to which the section 1231 gain (loss) relates.

Note: *For a partnership that was a partner in a 1997–1998 fiscal year partnership and has a net section 1231 gain (loss) figured using only 28% rate gains and losses shown on Form 4797, line 7, column (h), see the instructions for line 25, item 19.*

Line 7—Other Income (Loss)

Use line 7 to report other items of income, gain, or loss not included on lines 1 through 6. If the partnership has more than one activity, identify on an attachment the amount and the activity to which each amount relates.

Items to report on line 7 include:

• Gains from the disposition of farm recapture property (see Form 4797) and other items to which section 1252 applies.

• Gains from the disposition of an interest in oil, gas, geothermal, or other mineral properties (section 1254).

• Any net gain or loss from section 1256 contracts from **Form 6781,** Gains and Losses From Section 1256 Contracts and Straddles.

• Recoveries of tax benefit items (section 111).

• Gambling gains and losses subject to the limitations in section 165(d).

• Any income, gain, or loss to the partnership under section 751(b).

• Specially allocated ordinary gain (loss).

• Net gain (loss) from involuntary conversions due to casualty or theft. The amount for this line is shown on **Form 4684,** Casualties and Thefts, line 38a, 38b, or 39. Also, separately report the 28% rate gain (loss), if any, from involuntary conversions due to casualty or theft.

Each partner's share must be entered on Schedule K-1. Give each partner a schedule that shows the amounts to be reported on the partner's Form 4684, line 34, columns (b)(i), (b)(ii), and (c).

If there was a gain (loss) from a casualty or theft to property not used in a trade or business or for income-producing purposes, notify the partner. The partnership should not complete Form 4684 for this type of casualty or theft. Instead, each partner will complete his or her own Form 4684.

• Gain from the sale or exchange of qualified small business stock (as defined in the instructions for Schedule D) that is eligible for the 50% section 1202 exclusion. To be eligible

for the section 1202 exclusion, the stock must have been held by the partnership for more than 5 years and sold after August 11, 1998. Corporate partners are not eligible for the section 1202 exclusion. Additional limitations apply at the partner level. Report each partner's share of section 1202 gain on Schedule K-1. Each partner will determine if he or she qualifies for the section 1202 exclusion. Report on an attachment to Schedule K-1 for each sale or exchange the name of the corporation that issued the stock, the partner's share of the partnership's adjusted basis and sales price of the stock, and the dates the stock was bought and sold.

• Gain eligible for section 1045 rollover (replacement stock purchased by the partnership). Include only gain from the sale or exchange of qualified small business stock (as defined in the instructions for Schedule D) that was deferred by the partnership under section 1045 and reported on Schedule D. See the instructions for Schedule D for more details. Corporate partners are not eligible for the section 1045 rollover. Additional limitations apply at the partner level. Report each partner's share of the gain eligible for section 1045 rollover on Schedule K-1. Each partner will determine if he or she qualifies for the rollover. Report on an attachment to Schedule K-1 for each sale or exchange the name of the corporation that issued the stock, the partner's share of the partnership's adjusted basis and sales price of the stock, and the dates the stock was bought and sold.

• Gain eligible for section 1045 rollover (replacement stock not purchased by the partnership). Include only gain from the sale or exchange of qualified small business stock (as defined in the instructions for Schedule D) the partnership held for more than 6 months but that **was not** deferred by the partnership under section 1045. See the instructions for Schedule D for more details. A partner (other than a corporation) may be eligible to defer his or her distributive share of this gain under section 1045 if he or she purchases other qualified small business stock during the 60-day period that began on the date the stock was sold by the partnership. Additional limitations apply at the partner level. Report on an attachment to Schedule K-1 for each sale or exchange the name of the corporation that issued the stock, the partner's share of the partnership's adjusted basis and sales price of the stock, and the dates the stock was bought and sold.

Deductions

Line 8—Charitable Contributions

Enter the total amount of charitable contributions made by the partnership during its tax year on Schedule K. Enter each partner's distributive share on Schedule K-1. On an attachment to Schedules K and K-1, show separately the dollar amount of contributions subject to each of the 50%, 30%, and 20% of adjusted gross income limits. For additional information, see **Pub. 526,** Charitable Contributions.

Generally, no deduction is allowed for any contribution of $250 or more unless the partnership obtains a written acknowledgment from the charitable organization that shows the amount of cash contributed, describes any property contributed, and gives an estimate of the value of any goods or services provided in return for the contribution. The acknowledgment must be obtained by the due date (including extensions) of the partnership return, or if earlier, the date the partnership files its return. Do not attach the acknowledgment to the tax return, but keep it with the partnership's records. These rules apply in addition to the filing requirements for Form 8283 described below.

Certain contributions made to an organization conducting lobbying activities are not deductible. See section 170(f)(9) for more details.

Form 8283, Noncash Charitable Contributions, must be completed and attached to Form 1065 if the deduction claimed for noncash contributions exceeds $500. The partnership must give a copy of its Form 8283 to every partner if the deduction for an item or group of similar items of contributed property exceeds $5,000. Each partner must be furnished a copy even if the amount allocated to any partner is $5,000 or less.

If the deduction for an item or group of similar items of contributed property is $5,000 or less, the partnership should pass through each partner's share of the amount of noncash contributions so the partners will be able to complete their own Forms 8283. See the Instructions for Form 8283 for additional information.

If the partnership made a qualified conservation contribution, include the fair market value of the underlying property before and after the donation and describe the conservation purpose furthered by the donation. Give a copy of this information to each partner.

Line 9—Section 179 Expense Deduction

A partnership may elect to expense part of the cost of certain tangible property the partnership purchased this year for use in its trade or business or certain rental activities. See Pub. 946 for a definition of what kind of property qualifies for the section 179 expense deduction and the Instructions for Form 4562 for limitations on the amount of the section 179 expense deduction.

Complete Part I of Form 4562 to figure the partnership's section 179 expense deduction. The partnership does not claim the deduction itself but instead passes it through to the partners. Attach Form 4562 to Form 1065 and show the total section 179 expense deduction on Schedule K, line 9. Report each partner's allocable share on Schedule K-1, line 9. Do not complete line 9 of Schedule K-1 for any partner that is an estate or trust.

If the partnership is an enterprise zone business, also report on an attachment to Schedules K and K-1 the cost of section 179 property placed in service during the year that is qualified zone property.

See the instructions for line 25 of Schedule K-1, item 4, for any recapture of a section 179 amount.

Line 10—Deductions Related to Portfolio Income

Enter on line 10 and attach an itemized list of the deductions clearly and directly allocable to portfolio income (other than interest expense and section 212 expenses from a REMIC). Interest expense related to portfolio income is investment interest expense and is reported on line 14a of Schedules K and K-1. Section 212 expenses from the partnership's interest in a REMIC are reported on an attachment for line 4f of Schedules K and K-1.

No deduction is allowable under section 212 for expenses allocable to a convention, seminar, or similar meeting.

Line 11—Other Deductions

Use line 11 to report deductions not included on lines 8, 9, 10, 17e, and 18b. On an attachment, identify the deduction and amount, and if the partnership has more than one activity, the activity to which the deduction relates.

Examples of items to be reported on an attachment to line 11 include:

• Amounts paid by the partnership that would be allowed as itemized deductions on any of the partners' income tax returns if they were paid directly by a partner for the same purpose. However, do not enter expenses related to portfolio income or investment interest expense on this line.

If there was a loss from an involuntary conversion due to casualty or theft of income-producing property, include in the total amount for this line the relevant amount from Form 4684, line 32.

• Any penalty on early withdrawal of savings.

• Soil and water conservation expenditures (section 175).

• Expenditures for the removal of architectural and transportation barriers to the elderly and handicapped and which the partnership has elected to treat as a current expense (section 190).

• Contributions to a capital construction fund.

• Any amounts paid during the tax year for health insurance coverage for a partner (including that partner's spouse and dependents). For 1998, a partner may be allowed to deduct up to 45% of such amounts on Form 1040, line 28.

• Payments for a partner to an IRA, Keogh, SEP, or SIMPLE plan. If there is a defined benefit plan (Keogh), attach to the Schedule K-1 for each partner a statement showing the amount of benefit accrued for the tax year.

• Interest expense allocated to debt-financed distributions. See Notice 89-35 for more information.

• Interest paid or accrued on debt properly allocable to each general partner's share of a working interest in any oil or gas property (if the partner's liability is not limited). General partners that did not materially participate in the oil or gas activity treat this interest as investment interest; for other general partners, it is trade or business interest.

Credits

Line 12a—Low-Income Housing Credit

Section 42 provides a credit that may be claimed by owners of low-income residential rental buildings. If the partners are eligible to take the low-income housing credit, complete and attach **Form 8586,** Low-Income Housing Credit; **Form 8609,** Low-Income Housing Credit Allocation Certification; and **Schedule A (Form 8609),** Annual Statement, to Form 1065.

Report on line 12a(1) the total low-income housing credit for property placed in service before 1990 with respect to which a partnership is to be treated under section 42(j)(5) as the taxpayer to which the low-income housing credit was allowed. Report any other low-income housing credit for property placed in service before 1990 on line 12a(2). On lines

12a(3) and (4), report the low-income housing credit for property placed in service after 1989.

Line 12b—Qualified Rehabilitation Expenditures Related to Rental Real Estate Activities

Enter total qualified rehabilitation expenditures related to rental real estate activities of the partnership. Also complete the applicable lines of **Form 3468,** Investment Credit, that apply to qualified rehabilitation expenditures for property related to rental real estate activities of the partnership for which income or loss is reported on line 2 of Schedule K. See Form 3468 for details on qualified rehabilitation expenditures. Attach Form 3468 to Form 1065.

For line 12b of Schedule K-1, enter each partner's distributive share of the expenditures. On the dotted line to the left of the entry space for line 12b, enter the line number of Form 3468 on which the partner should report the expenditures. If there is more than one type of expenditure, or the expenditures are from more than one rental real estate activity, report this information separately for each expenditure or activity on an attachment to Schedules K and K-1.

Caution: *Qualified rehabilitation expenditures for property not related to rental real estate activities must be listed separately on line 25 of Schedule K-1.*

Line 12c—Credits (Other Than Credits Shown on Lines 12a and 12b) Related to Rental Real Estate Activities

Report any information that the partners need to figure credits related to a rental real estate activity, other than the low-income housing credit and qualified rehabilitation expenditures. On the dotted line to the left of the entry space for line 12c (or in the margin), identify the type of credit. If there is more than one type of credit or the credit is from more than one activity, report this information separately for each credit or activity on an attachment to Schedules K and K-1.

Line 12d—Credits Related to Other Rental Activities

Use this line to report information that the partners need to figure credits related to a rental activity other than a rental real estate activity. On the dotted line to the left of the entry space for line 12d, identify the type of credit. If there is more than one type of credit or the credit is from more than one activity, report this information separately for each credit or activity on an attachment to Schedules K and K-1.

Line 13—Other Credits

Enter on line 13 any other credit, except credits or expenditures shown or listed for lines 12a through 12d of Schedules K and K-1. On the dotted line to the left of the entry space for line 13, identify the type of credit. If there is more than one type of credit or the credit is from more than one activity, report this information separately for each credit or activity on an attachment to Schedules K and K-1. The credits to be reported on line 13 and other required attachments are as follows:

• Credit for backup withholding on dividends, interest, or patronage dividends.

• Nonconventional source fuel credit. The credit is figured at the partnership level and then is apportioned to the partners based on their distributive shares of partnership income attributable to sales of qualified fuels. Attach a separate schedule to the return to show the computation of the credit. See section 29 for more information.

- Qualified electric vehicle credit (Form 8834).
- Unused credits from cooperatives. The unused credits are apportioned to persons who were partners in the partnership on the last day of the partnership's tax year.
- Work opportunity credit (Form 5884). This credit is apportioned among the partners according to their interest in the partnership at the time the wages on which the credit is figured were paid or accrued.
- Welfare-to-work credit (Form 8861). This credit is apportioned in the same manner as the work opportunity credit.
- Credit for alcohol used as fuel (Form 6478). This credit is apportioned to persons who were partners on the last day of the partnership's tax year. The credit must be included in income on page 1, line 7, of Form 1065. See section 40(f) for an election the partnership can make to not have the credit apply.

If this credit includes the small ethanol producer credit, identify on a statement attached to each Schedule K-1 **(a)** the amount of the small producer credit included in the total credit allocated to the partner, **(b)** the number of gallons of qualified ethanol fuel production allocated to the partner, and **(c)** the partner's share in gallons of the partnership's productive capacity for alcohol.

- Credit for increasing research activities (Form 6765).
- Enhanced oil recovery credit (Form 8830).
- Disabled access credit (Form 8826).
- Renewable electricity production credit (Form 8835).
- Empowerment zone employment credit (Form 8844).
- Indian employment credit (Form 8845).
- Credit for employer social security and Medicare taxes paid on certain employee tips (Form 8846).
- Orphan drug credit (Form 8820).
- Credit for contributions to selected community development corporations (Form 8847).
- General credits from an electing large partnership.

See the instructions for line 25, item 13 of Schedule K-1 to report expenditures qualifying for the **(a)** rehabilitation credit not related to rental real estate activities, **(b)** energy credit, or **(c)** reforestation credit.

Investment Interest

Lines 14a through 14b(2) must be completed for all partners.

Line 14a—Interest Expense on Investment Debts

Include on this line interest paid or accrued on debt properly allocable to property held for investment. Property held for investment includes property that produces income (unless derived in the ordinary course of a trade or business) from interest, dividends, annuities, or royalties; and gains from the disposition of property that produces those types of income or is held for investment.

Property held for investment also includes each general partner's share of a working interest in any oil or gas property for which the partner's liability is not limited and in which the

partner did not materially participate. However, the level of each partner's participation in an activity is determined by the partner and not by the partnership. As a result, interest allocable to a general partner's share of a working interest in any oil or gas property (if the partner's liability is not limited) should not be reported on line 14a. Instead, report this interest on line 11.

Investment interest does not include interest expense allocable to a passive activity.

The amount on line 14a will be deducted (after applying the investment interest expense limitations of section 163(d)) by individual partners on Schedule A (Form 1040), line 13.

For more information, see **Form 4952,** Investment Interest Expense Deduction.

Lines 14b(1) and 14b(2)—Investment Income and Expenses

Enter on line 14b(1) only the investment income included on lines 4a, 4b, 4c, and 4f of Schedules K and K-1. Do not include other portfolio gains or losses on this line.

Enter on line 14b(2) only the investment expense included on line 10 of Schedules K and K-1.

If there are other items of investment income or expense included in the amounts that are required to be passed through separately to the partner on Schedule K-1, such as net short-term capital gain or loss, net long-term capital gain or loss, and other portfolio gains or losses, give each partner a schedule identifying these amounts.

Investment income includes gross income from property held for investment, the excess of net gain from the disposition of property held for investment over net capital gain from the disposition of property held for investment, and any net capital gain from the disposition of property held for investment that each partner elects to include in investment income under section 163(d)(4)(B)(iii). Generally, investment income and investment expenses do not include any income or expenses from a passive activity.

Property subject to a net lease is not treated as investment property because it is subject to the passive loss rules. Do not reduce investment income by losses from passive activities.

Investment expenses are deductible expenses (other than interest) directly connected with the production of investment income. See the Form 4952 instructions for more information on investment income and expenses.

Self-Employment

Note: If the partnership is an options dealer or a commodities dealer, see section 1402(i) before completing lines 15a, 15b, and 15c, to determine the amount of any adjustment that may have to be made to the amounts shown on the **Worksheet for Figuring Net Earnings (Loss) From Self-Employment** below. If the partnership is engaged solely in the operation of a group investment program, earnings from the operation are not self-employment earnings for either general or limited partners.

General partners. General partners' net earnings (loss) from self-employment do not include:

- Dividends on any shares of stock and interest on any bonds, debentures, notes, etc., unless the dividends or interest are received in

the course of a trade or business, such as a dealer in stocks or securities or interest on notes or accounts receivable.

- Rentals from real estate, except rentals of real estate held for sale to customers in the course of a trade or business as a real estate dealer or payments for rooms or space when significant services are provided.
- Royalty income, except royalty income received in the course of a trade or business.

See the instructions for **Schedule SE (Form 1040),** Self-Employment Tax, for more information.

Limited partners. Generally, a limited partner's share of partnership income (loss) is not included in net earnings (loss) from self-employment. Limited partners treat as self-employment earnings only guaranteed payments for services they actually rendered to, or on behalf of, the partnership to the extent that those payments are payment for those services.

Worksheet Instructions

Line 1b. Include on line 1b any part of the net income (loss) from rental real estate activities from Schedule K, line 2, that is from:

1. Rentals of real estate held for sale to customers in the course of a trade or business as a real estate dealer, or

2. Rentals for which services were rendered to the occupants (other than services usually or customarily rendered for the rental of space for occupancy only). The supplying of maid service is such a service; but the furnishing of heat and light, the cleaning of public entrances, exits, stairways and lobbies, trash collection, etc., are not considered services rendered to the occupants.

Lines 3b and 4b. Allocate the amounts on these lines in the same way Form 1065, page 1, line 22, is allocated to these particular partners.

Line 4a. Include in the amount on line 4a any guaranteed payments to partners reported on Schedules K and K-1, line 5, and derived from a trade or business as defined in section 1402(c). Also include other ordinary income and expense items (other than expense items subject to separate limitations at the partner level, such as the section 179 expense deduction) reported on Schedules K and K-1 that are used to figure self-employment earnings under section 1402.

Line 15a—Net Earnings (Loss) From Self-Employment

Schedule K. Enter on line 15a the amount from line 5 of the worksheet.

Schedule K-1. Do not complete this line for any partner that is an estate, trust, corporation, exempt organization, or individual retirement arrangement (IRA).

Enter on line 15a of Schedule K-1 each individual general partner's share of the amount shown on line 5 of the worksheet and each individual limited partner's share of the amount shown on line 4c of the worksheet.

Line 15b—Gross Farming or Fishing Income

Enter the partnership's gross farming or fishing income from self-employment. Individual partners need this amount to figure net earnings from self-employment under the farm optional method in Section B, Part II of Schedule SE (Form 1040).

Line 15c—Gross Nonfarm Income

Enter the partnership's gross nonfarm income from self-employment. Individual partners need this amount to figure net earnings from self-employment under the nonfarm optional method in Section B, Part II of Schedule SE (Form 1040).

Adjustments and Tax Preference Items

Lines 16a through 16e must be completed for all partners.

Enter items of income and deductions that are adjustments or tax preference items. See **Form 6251,** Alternative Minimum Tax—Individuals; **Form 4626,** Alternative Minimum Tax—Corporations; or Schedule I of **Form 1041,** U.S. Income Tax Return for Estates and Trusts, to determine the amounts to enter and for other information.

Do not include as a tax preference item any qualified expenditures to which an election under section 59(e) may apply. Instead, report these expenditures on lines 18a and 18b. Because these expenditures are subject to an election by each partner, the partnership cannot figure the amount of any tax preference related to them.

Line 16a—Depreciation Adjustment on Property Placed in Service After 1986

Figure the adjustment for line 16a based only on tangible property placed in service after 1986 (and tangible property placed in service after July 31, 1986, and before 1987 for which the partnership elected to use the general depreciation system). **Do not** make an adjustment for motion picture films, videotapes, sound recordings, certain public utility property (as defined in section 168(f)(2)), or property depreciated under the unit-of-production method (or any other method not expressed in a term of years).

Using the same convention you used for regular tax purposes, refigure depreciation as follows:

• For property that is neither real property nor property depreciated using the straight line method, use the 150% declining balance method over the property's class life (instead of the recovery period), switching to straight line for the first tax year that method gives a better result. See Pub. 946 for a table of class lives. For property having no class life, use 12 years.

• For property depreciated using the straight line method (other than real property), use the straight line method over the property's class life (instead of the recovery period). For property having no class life, use 12 years.

• For residential rental and nonresidential real property, use the straight line method over 40 years.

Determine the depreciation adjustment by subtracting the refigured depreciation from the depreciation claimed on Form 4562. If the refigured depreciation exceeds the depreciation claimed on Form 4562, enter the difference as a negative amount. See the instructions for Form 4562 and Form 6251 for more information.

Note to fiscal year 1998–99 filers: *For certain property placed in service after December 31, 1998, the depreciation adjustment is eliminated. This includes residential rental property, nonresidential real property, and other property depreciated using the straight line or 150% declining balance method for regular tax purposes.*

An AMT depreciation adjustment will still have to be computed on MACRS property depreciated using the 200% declining balance method for regular tax purposes. However, the adjustment will equal the difference between the depreciation claimed for regular tax purposes and the depreciation that would have been claimed using the 150% declining balance method. This is because the use of alternative depreciation system (ADS) recovery periods to compute AMT depreciation has been repealed for property placed in service after December 31, 1998.

Line 16b—Adjusted Gain or Loss

If the partnership disposed of any tangible property placed in service after 1986 (or after July 31, 1986, if an election was made to use the general depreciation system), or if it disposed of a certified pollution control facility placed in service after 1986, refigure the gain or loss from the disposition using the adjusted basis for the alternative minimum tax (AMT). The property's adjusted basis for the AMT is its cost or other basis minus all depreciation or amortization deductions allowed or allowable for the AMT during the current tax year and previous tax years. Enter on this line the difference between the regular tax gain (or loss) and the AMT gain (or loss). If the AMT gain is less than the regular tax gain, **or** the AMT loss is more than the regular tax loss, **or** there is an AMT loss and a regular tax gain, enter the difference as a negative amount.

If any part of the adjustment is allocable to net short-term capital gain (loss), net long-term capital gain (loss), or net section 1231 gain (loss), attach a schedule that identifies the amount of the adjustment allocable to each type of gain or loss. For a net long-term capital gain (loss) or net section 1231 gain (loss), also identify the amount of adjustment that is 28% rate gain (loss) and unrecaptured section 1250 gain. No schedule is required if the adjustment is allocable solely to ordinary gain (loss).

Line 16c—Depletion (Other Than Oil and Gas)

Do not include any depletion on oil and gas wells. The partners must figure their depletion deductions and preference items separately.

Refigure the depletion deduction under section 611 for mines, wells (other than oil and gas wells), and other natural deposits for the AMT. Percentage depletion is limited to 50% of the taxable income from the property as figured under section 613(a), using only income and deductions allowed for the AMT. Also, the deduction is limited to the property's adjusted basis at the end of the year, as refigured for the AMT. Figure this limit separately for each property. When refiguring the property's adjusted basis, take into account any AMT adjustments made this year or in previous years that affect basis (other than the current year's depletion).

Enter the difference between the regular tax and AMT deduction. If the AMT deduction is

---

Worksheet for Figuring Net Earnings (Loss) From Self-Employment

1a	Ordinary income (loss) (Schedule K, line 1)	1a	
b	Net income (loss) from **CERTAIN** rental real estate activities (see instructions) . . .	1b	
c	Net income (loss) from other rental activities (Schedule K, line 3c)	1c	
d	Net loss from Form 4797, Part II, line 18, included on line 1a above. Enter as a positive amount	1d	
e	Combine lines 1a through 1d	1e	
2	Net gain from Form 4797, Part II, line 18, included on line 1a above	2	
3a	Subtract line 2 from line 1e. If line 1e is a loss, increase the loss on line 1e by the amount on line 2	3a	
b	Part of line 3a allocated to limited partners, estates, trusts, corporations, exempt organizations, and IRAs	3b	
c	Subtract line 3b from line 3a. If line 3a is a loss, reduce the loss on line 3a by the amount on line 3b. Include each individual general partner's share on line 15a of Schedule K-1	3c	
4a	Guaranteed payments to partners (Schedule K, line 5) derived from a trade or business as defined in section 1402(c) (see instructions)	4a	
b	Part of line 4a allocated to individual limited partners for **other than** services and to estates, trusts, corporations, exempt organizations, and IRAs	4b	
c	Subtract line 4b from line 4a. Include each individual general partner's share and each individual limited partner's share on line 15a of Schedule K-1	4c	
5	Net earnings (loss) from self-employment. Combine lines 3c and 4c. Enter here and on Schedule K, line 15a	5	

greater, enter the difference as a negative amount.

Lines 16d(1) and 16d(2)

Enter only the income and deductions for oil, gas, and geothermal properties that are used to figure the partnership's ordinary income or loss (line 22 of Form 1065). If there are items of income or deduction for oil, gas, and geothermal properties included in the amounts required to be passed through separately to the partners on Schedule K-1 (items not reported on line 1 of Schedule K-1), give each partner a schedule identifying these amounts.

Figure the amount for lines 16d(1) and (2) separately for oil and gas properties that are not geothermal deposits and for all properties that are geothermal deposits.

Give each partner a schedule that shows the separate amounts that are included in the computation of the amounts on lines 16d(1) and (2).

Line 16d(1)—Gross income from oil, gas, and geothermal properties. Enter the aggregate amount of gross income (within the meaning of section 613(a)) from all oil, gas, and geothermal properties that was received or accrued during the tax year and included on page 1, Form 1065.

Line 16d(2)—Deductions allocable to oil, gas, and geothermal properties. Enter the amount of any deductions allowed for the AMT that are allocable to oil, gas, and geothermal properties.

Line 16e—Other Adjustments and Tax Preference Items

Attach a schedule that shows each partner's share of other items not shown on lines 16a through 16d(2) that are adjustments or tax preference items or that the partner needs to complete Form 6251, Form 4626, or Schedule I of Form 1041. See these forms and their instructions to determine the amount to enter.

Other adjustments or tax preference items include the following:

• Accelerated depreciation of real property under pre-1987 rules.

• Accelerated depreciation of leased personal property under pre-1987 rules.

• Long-term contracts entered into after February 28, 1986. Except for certain home construction contracts, the taxable income from these contracts must be figured using the percentage of completion method of accounting for the AMT.

• Losses from tax shelter farm activities. No loss from any tax shelter farm activity is allowed for the AMT.

Foreign Taxes

Lines 17a through 17g must be completed whether or not a partner is eligible for the foreign tax credit if the partnership has foreign income, deductions, or losses or has paid or accrued foreign taxes.

In addition to the instructions below, see the following for more information:

• **Form 1116,** Foreign Tax Credit (Individual, Estate, Trust, or Nonresident Alien Individual), and the related instructions.

• **Form 1118,** Foreign Tax Credit— Corporations, and the related instructions.

• **Pub. 514,** Foreign Tax Credit for Individuals.

Line 17a—Type of Income

Enter the type of income from outside the United States as follows:

• Passive income.

• High withholding tax interest.

• Financial services income.

• Shipping income.

• Dividends from a DISC or former DISC.

• Distributions from a foreign sales corporation (FSC) or former FSC.

• Dividends from each noncontrolled section 902 corporation.

• Taxable income attributable to foreign trade income (within the meaning of section 923(b)).

• General limitation income—all other income from sources outside the United States (including income from sources within U.S. possessions).

If, for the country or U.S. possession shown on line 17b, the partnership had **more than one** type of income, enter **"See attached"** and attach a schedule for each type of income for lines 17c through 17g.

Line 17b—Foreign Country or U.S. Possession

Enter the name of the foreign country or U.S. possession. If, for the type of income shown on line 17a, the partnership had income from, or paid taxes to, **more than one** foreign country or U.S. possession, enter **"See attached"** and attach a schedule for each country for lines 17a and 17c through 17g.

Line 17c—Total Gross Income From Sources Outside the United States

Enter in U.S. dollars the total gross income from sources outside the United States. Attach a schedule that shows each type of income listed in the instructions for line 17a.

Line 17d—Total Applicable Deductions and Losses

Enter in U.S. dollars the total applicable deductions and losses attributable to income on line 17c. Attach a schedule that shows each type of deduction or loss as follows:

• Expenses directly allocable to each type of income listed above.

• Pro rata share of all other deductions not directly allocable to specific items of income.

Do not include interest expense, other than interest expense directly allocated to identified property under Temporary Regulations section 1.861-10T, in the schedule of allocated deductions. Instead, the following two schedules must be attached, if applicable:

1. If any partner's distributive share of interest expense is allocated under Temporary Regulations section 1.861-9T(e)(4), prepare a schedule allocating the partnership's interest expense in accordance with that regulation. The schedule should indicate that this interest allocation is applicable only to a limited partner (whether individual or corporate) or corporate general partner whose direct and indirect interest in the partnership is less than 10%.

2. If any partner's distributive share of interest expense is not allocated under Temporary Regulations section 1.861-9T(e)(4), prepare a schedule stating the gross amount of the partnership's interest expense, other than interest expense directly allocated to identified property under Temporary Regulations section 1.861-10T. The schedule should indicate that an individual general

partner or a partner who is **(a)** a limited partner or a corporate general partner, and **(b)** whose direct and indirect interest in the partnership is 10% or more, must allocate this interest expense based on the partner's method for allocating interest expense.

Line 17e—Total Foreign Taxes

Enter in U.S. dollars the total foreign taxes (described in section 901) that were paid or accrued by the partnership to foreign countries or U.S. possessions. Translate the foreign amounts into U.S. dollars by using the rules in section 986. Attach a schedule that shows the dates the taxes were paid or accrued, the amount in both foreign currency and in U.S. dollars, and the conversion rate for:

• Taxes withheld at source on dividends.

• Taxes withheld at source on rents and royalties.

• Other foreign taxes paid or accrued.

Line 17f—Reduction in Taxes Available for Credit

Enter in U.S. dollars the total reduction in taxes available for credit. Attach a schedule that shows separately the:

• Reduction for foreign mineral income (section 901(e)).

• Reduction for failure to furnish returns required under section 6038.

• Reduction for taxes attributable to boycott operations (section 908).

• Reduction for foreign oil and gas extraction income (section 907(a)).

• Reduction for any other items (specify).

Line 17g—Other Foreign Tax Information

Enter in U.S. dollars any items not covered on lines 17c through 17f. For noncorporate partners, enter gross income from all sources. Noncorporate partners need this information to complete Form 1116. For corporate partners, enter gross income and definitely allocable deductions from sources outside the United States and for foreign branches. Corporations need this information to complete Form 1118, Schedule F.

Other

Lines 18a and 18b

Generally, section 59(e) allows each partner to make an election to deduct the partner's distributive share of the partnership's otherwise deductible qualified expenditures ratably over 10 years (3 years for circulation expenditures), beginning with the tax year in which the expenditures were made (or for intangible drilling and development costs, over the 60-month period beginning with the month in which such costs were paid or incurred). The term "qualified expenditures" includes only the following types of expenditures paid or incurred during the tax year:

• Circulation expenditures.

• Research and experimental expenditures.

• Intangible drilling and development costs.

• Mining exploration and development costs. If a partner makes this election, these items are not treated as tax preference items.

Because the partners are generally allowed to make this election, the partnership cannot deduct these amounts or include them as adjustments or tax preference items on Schedule K-1. Instead, on lines 18a and 18b of Schedule K-1, the partnership passes through the information the partners need to figure their separate deductions.

On line 18a, enter the type of expenditures claimed on line 18b. Enter on line 18b the qualified expenditures paid or incurred during the tax year to which an election under section 59(e) may apply. Enter this amount for all partners whether or not any partner makes an election under section 59(e). If the expenditures are for intangible drilling and development costs, enter the month in which the expenditures were paid or incurred (after the type of expenditure on line 18a). If there is more than one type of expenditure included in the total shown on line 18b (or intangible drilling and development costs were paid or incurred for more than 1 month), report this information separately for each type of expenditure (or month) on an attachment to Schedules K and K-1.

Line 19—Tax-Exempt Interest Income

Enter on line 19 tax-exempt interest income, including any exempt-interest dividends received from a mutual fund or other regulated investment company. This information must be reported by individuals on line 8b of Form 1040. The adjusted basis of the partner's interest is increased by the amount shown on this line under section 705(a)(1)(B).

Line 20—Other Tax-Exempt Income

Enter on line 20 all income of the partnership exempt from tax other than tax-exempt interest (e.g., life insurance proceeds). The adjusted basis of the partner's interest is increased by the amount shown on this line under section 705(a)(1)(B).

Line 21—Nondeductible Expenses

Enter on line 21 nondeductible expenses paid or incurred by the partnership. Do not include separately stated deductions shown elsewhere on Schedules K and K-1, capital expenditures, or items the deduction for which is deferred to a later tax year. The adjusted basis of the partner's interest is decreased by the amount shown on this line under section 705(a)(2)(B).

Line 22—Distributions of Money (Cash and Marketable Securities)

Enter on line 22 the total distributions to each partner of cash and marketable securities that are treated as money under section 731(c)(1). Generally, marketable securities are valued at fair market value on the date of distribution. However, the value of marketable securities does not include the distributee partner's share of the gain on the securities distributed to that partner. See section 731(c)(3)(B) for details.

If the amount on line 22 includes marketable securities treated as money, state separately on an attachment to Schedules K and K-1 (a) the partnership's adjusted basis of those securities immediately before the distribution and (b) the fair market value of those securities on the date of distribution (excluding the distributee partner's share of the gain on the securities distributed to that partner).

Line 23—Distributions of Property Other Than Money

Enter on line 23 the total distributions to each partner of property not included on line 22. In computing the amount of the distribution, use the adjusted basis of the property to the partnership immediately before the distribution. In addition, attach a statement showing the adjusted basis and fair market value of each property distributed.

Line 24 (Schedule K Only)

Attach a statement to report the partnership's total income, expenditures, or other information for the items listed under **Line 25 (Schedule K-1 Only)—Supplemental Information** below.

Lines 24a and 24b (Schedule K-1 Only)—Recapture of Low-Income Housing Credit

If recapture of part or all of the low-income housing credit is required because: (a) prior year qualified basis of a building decreased, or (b) the partnership disposed of a building or part of its interest in a building, see **Form 8611**, Recapture of Low-Income Housing Credit. The instructions for Form 8611 indicate when the form is completed by the partnership and what information is provided to partners when recapture is required.

If a partner's ownership interest in a building decreased because of a transaction at the partner level, the partnership must provide the necessary information to the partner to enable the partner to figure the recapture.

Report on line 24a the total low-income housing credit recapture with respect to a partnership treated under section 42(j)(5) as the taxpayer to which the low-income housing credit was allowed. Report any other low-income housing credit recapture on line 24b.

If the partnership filed **Form 8693**, Low-Income Housing Credit Disposition Bond, to avoid recapture of the low-income housing credit, no entry should be made on line 24 of Schedule K-1.

See Form 8586, Form 8611, and section 42 for more information.

Line 25 (Schedule K-1 Only)—Supplemental Information

Enter in the line 25 Supplemental Information space of Schedule K-1, or on an attached schedule if more space is needed, each partner's share of any information asked for on lines 1 through 24b that must be reported in detail, and items 1 through 22 below. Identify the applicable line number next to the information entered in the Supplemental Information space. Show income or gains as a positive number. Show losses in parentheses.

1. Taxes paid on undistributed capital gains by a regulated investment company or a real estate investment trust (REIT). As a shareholder of a regulated investment company or a REIT, the partnership will receive notice on **Form 2439**, Notice to Shareholder of Undistributed Long-Term Capital Gains, of the amount of tax paid on undistributed capital gains.

2. The number of gallons of each fuel used during the tax year in a use qualifying for the credit for taxes paid on fuels and the applicable credit per gallon. See **Form 4136**, Credit for Federal Tax Paid on Fuels, for details.

3. The partner's share of gross income from each property, share of production for the tax year, etc., needed to figure the partner's depletion deduction for oil and gas wells. The partnership should also allocate to each partner a proportionate share of the adjusted basis of each partnership oil or gas property. The allocation of the basis of each property is made as specified in section 613A(c)(7)(D).

The partnership cannot deduct depletion on oil and gas wells. The partner must determine the allowable amount to report on his or her return. See Pub. 535 for more information.

4. Recapture of section 179 expense deduction. For property placed in service after 1986, the section 179 expense deduction is recaptured at any time the business use of the property drops to 50% or less. Enter the amount that was originally passed through to the partners and the partnership's tax year in which the amount was passed through. Inform the partner if the recapture amount was caused by the disposition of the section 179 property. Do not include this amount in the partnership's income.

5. Recapture of certain mining exploration expenditures (section 617).

6. Any information or statements a partner needs to comply with section 6111 (registration of tax shelters) or section 6662(d)(2)(B)(ii) (regarding adequate disclosure of items that may cause an understatement of income tax).

7. The partner's share of preproductive period farm expenses, if the partnership is not required to use the accrual method of accounting. See Temporary Regulations section 1.263A-4T.

8. Any information needed by a partner to figure the interest due under section 453(l)(3). If the partnership elected to report the disposition of certain timeshares and residential lots on the installment method, each partner's tax liability must be increased by the partner's allocable share of the interest on tax attributable to the installment payments received during the tax year.

9. Any information needed by a partner to figure interest due under section 453A(c). If an obligation arising from the disposition of property to which section 453A applies is outstanding at the close of the year, report each partner's allocable share of the outstanding installment obligation to which section 453A(b) applies.

10. For closely held partnerships (as defined in section 460(b)(4)), provide the information needed by a partner to figure the partner's allocable share of any interest due or to be refunded under the look-back method of section 460(b)(2) on certain long-term contracts that are accounted for under either the percentage of completion-capitalized cost method or the percentage of completion method. Also attach to Form 1065 the information specified in the instructions for Form 8697, Part II, lines 1 and 3, for each tax year in which such a long-term contract is completed.

11. Any information needed by a partner relating to interest expense that the partner is required to capitalize. Under section 263A, a partner may be required to capitalize interest expense incurred by the partner during the tax year with respect to the production expenditures of the partnership. Similarly, interest incurred by a partnership may have to be capitalized by a partner with respect to the partner's own production expenditures. The information required by the partner to properly capitalize interest for this purpose must be provided on an attachment to Schedule K-1. See Regulations sections 1.263A-8 through 1.263A-15 for more information.

12. Any information a partner that is a tax-exempt organization may need to figure that partner's share of unrelated business taxable income under section 512(a)(1) (but excluding any modifications required by paragraphs (8) through (15) of section 512(b)). Partners are required to notify the partnership of their tax-exempt status.

13. Expenditures qualifying for the **(a)** rehabilitation credit not related to rental real estate activities, **(b)** energy credit, or **(c)** reforestation credit. Complete and attach Form 3468 to Form 1065. See Form 3468 and the related instructions for information on eligible property and the lines on Form 3468 to complete. Do not include that part of the cost of the property the partnership has elected to expense under section 179. Attach to each Schedule K-1 a separate schedule in a format similar to that shown on Form 3468 detailing each partner's share of qualified expenditures. Also indicate the lines of Form 3468 on which the partners should report these amounts.

14. Recapture of investment credit. Complete and attach **Form 4255,** Recapture of Investment Credit, when investment credit property is disposed of, or it no longer qualifies for the credit, before the end of the recapture period or the useful life applicable to the property. State the type of property at the top of Form 4255 and complete lines 2, 4, and 5, whether or not any partner is subject to recapture of the credit. Attach to each Schedule K-1 a separate schedule providing the information the partnership is required to show on Form 4255, but list only the partner's distributive share of the cost of the property subject to recapture. Also indicate the lines of Form 4255 on which the partners should report these amounts.

15. Any information a partner may need to figure the recapture of the qualified electric vehicle credit. See Pub. 535 for more information.

16. Any information a partner may need to figure recapture of the Indian employment credit. Generally, if a partnership terminates a qualified employee less than 1 year after the date of initial employment, any Indian employment credit allowed for a prior tax year by reason of wages paid or incurred to that employee must be recaptured. For details, see section 45A(d).

17. Nonqualified withdrawals by the partnership from a capital construction fund.

18. Unrecaptured section 1250 gain. Figure this amount for each section 1250 property in Part III of Form 4797 for which you had an entry in column (g), but not in column (h), of Part I of Form 4797 by subtracting line 26g of Form 4797 from the **smaller** of line 22 or line 24 of Form 4797. Figure the total of these amounts for all section 1250 properties. Report each partner's distributive share of the total amount as "Unrecaptured section 1250 gain."

If the partnership also received a Schedule K-1 or Form 1099-DIV from an estate, a trust, a REIT, or a mutual fund reporting "unrecaptured section 1250 gain," **do not** add it to the partnership's own unrecaptured section 1250 gain. Instead, report it as a separate amount. For example, if the partnership received a Form 1099-DIV from a REIT with unrecaptured section 1250 gain, report it as "Unrecaptured section 1250 gain from a REIT."

19. For a partnership that was a partner in a 1997–98 fiscal year partnership, each partner's share of the net section 1231 gain (loss) figured using only 28% rate gains and losses from Form 4797, line 7, column (h).

20. If the partnership is a closely held partnership (as defined in section 460(b)(4)) and it depreciated certain property placed in service after September 13, 1995, under the income forecast method, it must attach to Form 1065 the information specified in the instructions for Form 8866, line 2, for the 3rd and 10th tax years beginning after the tax year the property was placed in service. It must also report the line 2 amounts to its partners. See the instructions for Form 8866 for more details.

21. Any information a partner that is a publicly traded partnership may need to determine if it meets the 90% qualifying income test of section 7704(c)(2). Partners are required to notify the partnership of their status as a publicly traded partnership.

22. Any other information a partner may need to file his or her return that is not shown anywhere else on Schedule K-1. For example, if one of the partners is a pension plan, that partner may need special information to properly file its tax return.

Specific Instructions

Analysis of Net Income (Loss)

For each type of partner shown, enter the portion of the amount shown on line 1 that was allocated to that type of partner. Report all amounts for limited liability company members on the line for limited partners. The sum of the amounts shown on line 2 must equal the amount shown on line 1. In addition, the amount on line 1 must equal the amount on line 9, Schedule M-1 (if the partnership is required to complete Schedule M-1).

In classifying partners who are individuals as "active" or "passive," the partnership should apply the rules below. In applying these rules, a partnership should classify each partner to the best of its knowledge and belief. It is assumed that in most cases the level of a particular partner's participation in an activity will be apparent.

1. If the partnership's principal activity is a trade or business, classify a general partner as "active" if the partner materially participated in all partnership trade or business activities; otherwise, classify a general partner as "passive."

2. If the partnership's principal activity consists of a working interest in an oil or gas well, classify a general partner as "active."

3. If the partnership's principal activity is a rental real estate activity, classify a general partner as "active" if the partner actively participated in all of the partnership's rental real estate activities; otherwise, classify a general partner as "passive."

4. Classify as "passive" all partners in a partnership whose principal activity is a rental activity other than a rental real estate activity.

5. If the partnership's principal activity is a portfolio activity, classify all partners as "active."

6. Classify as "passive" all limited partners and limited liability company members in a partnership whose principal activity is a trade or business or rental activity.

7. If the partnership cannot make a reasonable determination whether a partner's participation in a trade or business activity is material or whether a partner's participation in a rental real estate activity is active, classify the partner as "passive."

Schedule L—Balance Sheets per Books

Note: *Schedules L, M-1, and M-2 are not required to be completed if the partnership answered* **Yes** *to Question 5 of Schedule B.*

The balance sheets should agree with the partnership's books and records. Attach a statement explaining any differences.

Partnerships reporting to the Interstate Commerce Commission or to any national, state, municipal, or other public officer may send copies of their balance sheets prescribed by the Commission or state or municipal authorities, at the beginning and end of the tax year, instead of completing Schedule L. However, statements filed under this procedure must contain sufficient information to enable the IRS to reconstruct a balance sheet similar to that contained on Form 1065 without contacting the partnership during processing.

All amounts on the balance sheet should be reported in U.S. dollars. If the partnership's books and records are kept in a foreign currency, the balance sheet should be translated in accordance with U.S. generally accepted accounting principles (GAAP).

Exception. *If the partnership or any qualified business unit of the partnership uses the United States dollar approximate separate transactions method, Schedule L should reflect the tax balance sheet prepared and translated into U.S. dollars according to Regulations section 1.985-3(d), and not a U.S. GAAP balance sheet.*

Line 5—Tax-Exempt Securities

Include on this line:

1. State and local government obligations, the interest on which is excludable from gross income under section 103(a), and

2. Stock in a mutual fund or other regulated investment company that distributed exempt-interest dividends during the tax year of the partnership.

Line 18—All Nonrecourse Loans

Nonrecourse loans are those liabilities of the partnership for which no partner bears the economic risk of loss.

Schedule M-1—Reconciliation of Income (Loss) per Books With Income (Loss) per Return

Line 3—Guaranteed Payments

Include on this line guaranteed payments shown on Schedule K, line 5 (other than amounts paid for insurance that constitutes medical care for a partner, a partner's spouse, and a partner's dependents).

Line 4b—Travel and Entertainment

Include on this line:

● 50% of meals and entertainment not allowed under section 274(n).

● Expenses for the use of an entertainment facility.

● The part of business gifts over $25.

● Expenses of an individual allocable to conventions on cruise ships over $2,000.

● Employee achievement awards over $400.

● The part of the cost of entertainment tickets that exceeds face value (also subject to 50% disallowance).

● The part of the cost of skyboxes that exceeds the face value of nonluxury box seat tickets.

- The part of the cost of luxury water travel not allowed under section 274(m).
- Expenses for travel as a form of education.
- Nondeductible club dues.
- Other travel and entertainment expenses not allowed as a deduction.

Schedule M-2—Analysis of Partners' Capital Accounts

Show what caused the changes during the tax year in the partners' capital accounts as reflected on the partnership's books and records. The amounts on Schedule M-2 should equal the total of the amounts reported in Item J of all the partners' Schedules K-1.

The partnership may, but is not required to, use the rules in Regulations section 1.704-1(b)(2)(iv) to determine the partners' capital accounts in Schedule M-2 and Item J of the partners' Schedules K-1. If the beginning and ending capital accounts reported under these rules differ from the amounts reported on Schedule L, attach a statement reconciling any differences.

Line 2—Capital Contributed During Year

Include on line 2 the amount of money and property contributed by each partner to the partnership as reflected on the partnership's books and records.

Line 3—Net Income per Books

Enter on line 3 the net income shown on the partnership books from Schedule M-1, line 1.

Line 6—Distributions

1. On line 6a, enter the amount of money distributed to each partner by the partnership.

2. On line 6b, enter the amount of property distributed to each partner by the partnership as reflected on the partnership's books and records. Include withdrawals from inventory for the personal use of a partner.

Codes for Principal Business Activity and Principal Product or Service

This list of Principal Business Activities and their associated codes is designed to classify an enterprise by the type of activity in which it is engaged to facilitate the administration of the Internal Revenue Code. For tax years beginning after 1997, these Principal Business Activity Codes are based on the North American Industry Classification System.

Using the list of activities and codes below, determine from which activity the business derives the largest percentage of its "total receipts." Total receipts is defined as the sum of gross receipts or sales (page 1, line 1a), all other income (page 1, lines 4 through 7), income (receipts only) reported on Schedule K, lines 3a and 4a through f, and income (receipts only) reported on Form 8825, lines 2, 19, and 20a. If the business purchases raw materials and supplies them to a subcontractor to produce the finished product, but retains title to the product,

the business is considered a manufacturer and must use one of the manufacturing codes (311110–339900).

Once the Principal Business Activity is determined, enter the six-digit code from the list below on page 1, item C. Also enter a brief description of the business activity in item A and the principal product or service of the business in item B.

Agriculture, Forestry, Fishing and Hunting
Code
Crop Production
111100	Oilseed & Grain Farming
111210	Vegetable & Melon Farming (including potatoes & yams)
111300	Fruit & Tree Nut Farming
111400	Greenhouse, Nursery, & Floriculture Production
111900	Other Crop Farming (including tobacco, cotton, sugarcane, hay, peanut, sugar beet & all other crop farming)

Animal Production
112111	Beef Cattle Ranching & Farming
112112	Cattle Feedlots
112120	Dairy Cattle & Milk Production
112210	Hog & Pig Farming
112300	Poultry & Egg Production
112400	Sheep & Goat Farming
112510	Animal Aquaculture (including shellfish & finfish farms & hatcheries)
112900	Other Animal Production

Forestry and Logging
113110	Timber Tract Operations
113210	Forest Nurseries & Gathering of Forest Products
113310	Logging

Fishing, Hunting and Trapping
114110	Fishing
114210	Hunting & Trapping

Support Activities for Agriculture and Forestry
115110	Support Activities for Crop Production (including cotton ginning, soil preparation, planting, & cultivating)
115210	Support Activities for Animal Production
115310	Support Activities For Forestry

Mining
211110	Oil & Gas Extraction
212110	Coal Mining
212200	Metal Ore Mining
212310	Stone Mining & Quarrying
212320	Sand, Gravel, Clay, & Ceramic & Refractory Minerals Mining & Quarrying
212390	Other Nonmetallic Mineral Mining & Quarrying
213110	Support Activities for Mining

Utilities
221100	Electric Power Generation, Transmission & Distribution
221210	Natural Gas Distribution
221300	Water, Sewage & Other Systems

Construction
Building, Developing, and General Contracting
233110	Land Subdivision & Land Development
233200	Residential Building Construction
233300	Nonresidential Building Construction

Code
Heavy Construction
234100	Highway, Street, Bridge, & Tunnel Construction
234900	Other Heavy Construction

Special Trade Contractors
235110	Plumbing, Heating, & Air-Conditioning Contractors
235210	Painting & Wall Covering Contractors
235310	Electrical Contractors
235400	Masonry, Drywall, Insulation, & Tile Contractors
235500	Carpentry & Floor Contractors
235610	Roofing, Siding, & Sheet Metal Contractors
235710	Concrete Contractors
235810	Water Well Drilling Contractors
235900	Other Special Trade Contractors

Manufacturing
Food Manufacturing
311110	Animal Food Mfg
311200	Grain & Oilseed Milling
311300	Sugar & Confectionery Product Mfg
311400	Fruit & Vegetable Preserving & Specialty Food Mfg
311500	Dairy Product Mfg
311610	Animal Slaughtering & Processing
311710	Seafood Product Preparation & Packaging
311800	Bakeries & Tortilla Mfg
311900	Other Food Mfg (including coffee, tea, flavorings & seasonings)

Beverage and Tobacco Product Manufacturing
312110	Soft Drink & Ice Mfg
312120	Breweries
312130	Wineries
312140	Distilleries
312200	Tobacco Manufacturing

Textile Mills and Textile Product Mills
313000	Textile Mills
314000	Textile Product Mills

Apparel Manufacturing
315100	Apparel Knitting Mills
315210	Cut & Sew Apparel Contractors
315220	Men's & Boys' Cut & Sew Apparel Mfg
315230	Women's & Girls' Cut & Sew Apparel Mfg
315290	Other Cut & Sew Apparel Mfg
315990	Apparel Accessories & Other Apparel Mfg

Leather and Allied Product Manufacturing
316110	Leather & Hide Tanning & Finishing
316210	Footwear Mfg (including rubber & plastics)
316990	Other Leather & Allied Product Mfg

Wood Product Manufacturing
321110	Sawmills & Wood Preservation
321210	Veneer, Plywood, & Engineered Wood Product Mfg

Code
321900	Other Wood Product Mfg

Paper Manufacturing
322100	Pulp, Paper, & Paperboard Mills
322200	Converted Paper Product Mfg

Printing and Related Support Activities
323100	Printing & Related Support Activities

Petroleum and Coal Products Manufacturing
324110	Petroleum Refineries (including integrated)
324120	Asphalt Paving, Roofing, & Saturated Materials Mfg
324190	Other Petroleum & Coal Products Mfg

Chemical Manufacturing
325100	Basic Chemical Mfg
325200	Resin, Synthetic Rubber, & Artificial & Synthetic Fibers & Filaments Mfg
325300	Pesticide, Fertilizer, & Other Agricultural Chemical Mfg
325410	Pharmaceutical & Medicine Mfg
325500	Paint, Coating, & Adhesive Mfg
325600	Soap, Cleaning Compound, & Toilet Preparation Mfg
325900	Other Chemical Product & Preparation Mfg

Plastics and Rubber Products Manufacturing
326100	Plastics Product Mfg
326200	Rubber Product Mfg

Nonmetallic Mineral Product Manufacturing
327100	Clay Product & Refractory Mfg
327210	Glass & Glass Product Mfg
327300	Cement & Concrete Product Mfg
327400	Lime & Gypsum Product Mfg
327900	Other Nonmetallic Mineral Product Mfg

Primary Metal Manufacturing
331110	Iron & Steel Mills & Ferroalloy Mfg
331200	Steel Product Mfg from Purchased Steel
331310	Alumina & Aluminum Production & Processing
331400	Nonferrous Metal (except Aluminum) Production & Processing
331500	Foundries

Fabricated Metal Product Manufacturing
332110	Forging & Stamping
332210	Cutlery & Handtool Mfg
332300	Architectural & Structural Metals Mfg
332400	Boiler, Tank, & Shipping Container Mfg
332510	Hardware Mfg
332610	Spring & Wire Product Mfg
332700	Machine Shops; Turned Product; & Screw, Nut, & Bolt Mfg
332810	Coating, Engraving, Heat Treating, & Allied Activities
332900	Other Fabricated Metal Product Mfg

Code
Machinery Manufacturing
333100	Agriculture, Construction, & Mining Machinery Mfg
333200	Industrial Machinery Mfg
333310	Commercial & Service Industry Machinery Mfg
333410	Ventilation, Heating, Air-Conditioning, & Commercial Refrigeration Equipment Mfg
333510	Metalworking Machinery Mfg
333610	Engine, Turbine & Power Transmission Equipment Mfg
333900	Other General Purpose Machinery Mfg

Computer and Electronic Product Manufacturing
334110	Computer & Peripheral Equipment Mfg
334200	Communications Equipment Mfg
334310	Audio & Video Equipment Mfg
334410	Semiconductor & Other Electronic Component Mfg
334500	Navigational, Measuring, Electromedical, & Control Instruments Mfg
334610	Manufacturing & Reproducing Magnetic & Optical Media

Electrical Equipment, Appliance, and Component Manufacturing
335100	Electric Lighting Equipment Mfg
335200	Household Appliance Mfg
335310	Electrical Equipment Mfg
335900	Other Electrical Equipment & Component Mfg

Transportation Equipment Manufacturing
336100	Motor Vehicle Mfg
336210	Motor Vehicle Body & Trailer Mfg
336300	Motor Vehicle Parts Mfg
336410	Aerospace Product & Parts Mfg
336510	Railroad Rolling Stock Mfg
336610	Ship & Boat Building
336990	Other Transportation Equipment Mfg

Furniture and Related Product Manufacturing
337000	Furniture & Related Product Manufacturing

Miscellaneous Manufacturing
339110	Medical Equipment & Supplies Mfg
339900	Other Miscellaneous Manufacturing

Wholesale Trade
Wholesale Trade, Durable Goods
421100	Motor Vehicle & Motor Vehicle Parts & Supplies Wholesalers
421200	Furniture & Home Furnishing Wholesalers
421300	Lumber & Other Construction Materials Wholesalers
421400	Professional & Commercial Equipment & Supplies Wholesalers
421500	Metal & Mineral (except Petroleum) Wholesalers
421600	Electrical Goods Wholesalers

Code

421700	Hardware, & Plumbing & Heating Equipment & Supplies Wholesalers
421800	Machinery, Equipment, & Supplies Wholesalers
421910	Sporting & Recreational Goods & Supplies Wholesalers
421920	Toy & Hobby Goods & Supplies Wholesalers
421930	Recyclable Material Wholesalers
421940	Jewelry, Watch, Precious Stone, & Precious Metal Wholesalers
421990	Other Miscellaneous Durable Goods Wholesalers

Wholesale Trade, Nondurable Goods

422100	Paper & Paper Product Wholesalers
422210	Drugs & Druggists' Sundries Wholesalers
422300	Apparel, Piece Goods, & Notions Wholesalers
422400	Grocery & Related Product Wholesalers
422500	Farm Product Raw Material Wholesalers
422600	Chemical & Allied Products Wholesalers
422700	Petroleum & Petroleum Products Wholesalers
422800	Beer, Wine, & Distilled Alcoholic Beverage Wholesalers
422910	Farm Supplies Wholesalers
422920	Book, Periodical, & Newspaper Wholesalers
422930	Flower, Nursery Stock, & Florists' Supplies Wholesalers
422940	Tobacco & Tobacco Product Wholesalers
422950	Paint, Varnish, & Supplies Wholesalers
422990	Other Miscellaneous Nondurable Goods Wholesalers

Retail Trade

Motor Vehicle and Parts Dealers

441110	New Car Dealers
441120	Used Car Dealers
441210	Recreational Vehicle Dealers
441221	Motorcycle Dealers
441222	Boat Dealers
441229	All Other Motor Vehicle Dealers
441300	Automotive Parts, Accessories, & Tire Stores

Furniture and Home Furnishings Stores

442110	Furniture Stores
442210	Floor Covering Stores
442291	Window Treatment Stores
442299	All Other Home Furnishings Stores

Electronics and Appliance Stores

443111	Household Appliance Stores
443112	Radio, Television, & Other Electronics Stores
443120	Computer & Software Stores
443130	Camera & Photographic Supplies Stores

Building Material and Garden Equipment and Supplies Dealers

444110	Home Centers
444120	Paint & Wallpaper Stores
444130	Hardware Stores
444190	Other Building Material Dealers
444200	Lawn & Garden Equipment & Supplies Stores

Food and Beverage Stores

| 445110 | Supermarkets and Other Grocery (except Convenience) Stores |
| 445120 | Convenience Stores |

Code

445210	Meat Markets
445220	Fish & Seafood Markets
445230	Fruit & Vegetable Markets
445291	Baked Goods Stores
445292	Confectionery & Nut Stores
445299	All Other Specialty Food Stores
445310	Beer, Wine, & Liquor Stores

Health and Personal Care Stores

446110	Pharmacies & Drug Stores
446120	Cosmetics, Beauty Supplies, & Perfume Stores
446130	Optical Goods Stores
446190	Other Health & Personal Care Stores

Gasoline Stations

| 447100 | Gasoline Stations (including convenience stores with gas) |

Clothing and Clothing Accessories Stores

448110	Men's Clothing Stores
448120	Women's Clothing Stores
448130	Children's & Infants' Clothing Stores
448140	Family Clothing Stores
448150	Clothing Accessories Stores
448190	Other Clothing Stores
448210	Shoe Stores
448310	Jewelry Stores
448320	Luggage & Leather Goods Stores

Sporting Goods, Hobby, Book, and Music Stores

451110	Sporting Goods Stores
451120	Hobby, Toy, & Game Stores
451130	Sewing, Needlework, & Piece Goods Stores
451140	Musical Instrument & Supplies Stores
451211	Book Stores
451212	News Dealers & Newsstands
451220	Prerecorded Tape, Compact Disc, & Record Stores

General Merchandise Stores

| 452110 | Department stores |
| 452900 | Other General Merchandise Stores |

Miscellaneous Store Retailers

453110	Florists
453210	Office Supplies & Stationery Stores
453220	Gift, Novelty, & Souvenir Stores
453310	Used Merchandise Stores
453910	Pet & Pet Supplies Stores
453920	Art Dealers
453930	Manufactured (Mobile) Home Dealers
453990	All Other Miscellaneous Store Retailers (including tobacco, candle, & trophy shops)

Nonstore Retailers

454110	Electronic Shopping & Mail-Order Houses
454210	Vending Machine Operators
454311	Heating Oil Dealers
454312	Liquefied Petroleum Gas (Bottled Gas) Dealers
454319	Other Fuel Dealers
454390	Other Direct Selling Establishments (including door-to-door retailing, frozen food plan providers, party plan merchandisers, & coffee-break service providers)

Transportation and Warehousing

Air, Rail, and Water Transportation

481000	Air Transportation
482110	Rail Transportation
483000	Water Transportation

Code

Truck Transportation

484110	General Freight Trucking, Local
484120	General Freight Trucking, Long-distance
484200	Specialized Freight Trucking

Transit and Ground Passenger Transportation

485110	Urban Transit Systems
485210	Interurban & Rural Bus Transportation
485310	Taxi Service
485320	Limousine Service
485410	School & Employee Bus Transportation
485510	Charter Bus Industry
485990	Other Transit & Ground Passenger Transportation

Pipeline Transportation

| 486000 | Pipeline Transportation |

Scenic & Sightseeing Transportation

| 487000 | Scenic & Sightseeing Transportation |

Support Activities for Transportation

488100	Support Activities for Air Transportation
488210	Support Activities for Rail Transportation
488300	Support Activities for Water Transportation
488410	Motor Vehicle Towing
488490	Other Support Activities for Road Transportation
488510	Freight Transportation Arrangement
488990	Other Support Activities for Transportation

Couriers and Messengers

| 492110 | Couriers |
| 492210 | Local Messengers & Local Delivery |

Warehousing and Storage

| 493100 | Warehousing & Storage (except lessors of miniwarehouses & self-storage units) |

Information

Publishing Industries

511110	Newspaper Publishers
511120	Periodical Publishers
511130	Book Publishers
511140	Database & Directory Publishers
511190	Other Publishers
511210	Software Publishers

Motion Picture and Sound Recording Industries

| 512100 | Motion Picture & Video Industries (except video rental) |
| 512200 | Sound Recording Industries |

Broadcasting and Telecommunications

513100	Radio & Television Broadcasting
513200	Cable Networks & Program Distribution
513300	Telecommunications (including paging, cellular, satellite, & other telecommunications)

Information Services and Data Processing Services

| 514100 | Information Services (including news syndicates, libraries, & on-line information services) |
| 514210 | Data Processing Services |

Finance and Insurance

Depository Credit Intermediation

522110	Commercial Banking
522120	Savings Institutions
522130	Credit Unions

Code

| 522190 | Other Depository Credit Intermediation |

Nondepository Credit Intermediation

522210	Credit Card Issuing
522220	Sales Financing
522291	Consumer Lending
522292	Real Estate Credit (including mortgage bankers & originators)
522293	International Trade Financing
522294	Secondary Market Financing
522298	All Other Nondepository Credit Intermediation

Activities Related to Credit Intermediation

| 522300 | Activities Related to Credit Intermediation (including loan brokers) |

Securities, Commodity Contracts, and Other Financial Investments and Related Activities

523110	Investment Banking & Securities Dealing
523120	Securities Brokerage
523130	Commodity Contracts Dealing
523140	Commodity Contracts Brokerage
523210	Securities & Commodity Exchanges
523900	Other Financial Investment Activities (including portfolio management & investment advice)

Insurance Carriers and Related Activities

524140	Direct Life, Health, & Medical Insurance & Reinsurance Carriers
524150	Direct Insurance & Reinsurance (except Life, Health & Medical) Carriers
524210	Insurance Agencies & Brokerages
524290	Other Insurance Related Activities

Funds, Trusts, and Other Financial Vehicles

525100	Insurance & Employee Benefit Funds
525910	Open-End Investment Funds (Form 1120-RIC)
525920	Trusts, Estates, & Agency Accounts
525930	Real Estate Investment Trusts (Form 1120-REIT)
525990	Other Financial Vehicles

Real Estate and Rental and Leasing

Real Estate

531110	Lessors of Residential Buildings & Dwellings
531120	Lessors of Nonresidential Buildings (except Miniwarehouses)
531130	Lessors of Miniwarehouses & Self-Storage Units
531190	Lessors of Other Real Estate Property
531210	Offices of Real Estate Agents & Brokers
531310	Real Estate Property Managers
531320	Offices of Real Estate Appraisers
531390	Other Activities Related to Real Estate

Rental and Leasing Services

532100	Automotive Equipment Rental & Leasing
532210	Consumer Electronics & Appliances Rental
532220	Formal Wear & Costume Rental
532230	Video Tape & Disc Rental

Code

Code	
532290	Other Consumer Goods Rental
532310	General Rental Centers
532400	Commercial & Industrial Machinery & Equipment Rental & Leasing

Lessors of Nonfinancial Intangible Assets (except copyrighted works)

533110	Lessors of Nonfinancial Intangible Assets (except copyrighted works)

Professional, Scientific, and Technical Services

Legal Services

541110	Offices of Lawyers
541190	Other Legal Services

Accounting, Tax Preparation, Bookkeeping, and Payroll Services

541211	Offices of Certified Public Accountants
541213	Tax Preparation Services
541214	Payroll Services
541219	Other Accounting Services

Architectural, Engineering, and Related Services

541310	Architectural Services
541320	Landscape Architecture Services
541330	Engineering Services
541340	Drafting Services
541350	Building Inspection Services
541360	Geophysical Surveying & Mapping Services
541370	Surveying & Mapping (except Geophysical) Services
541380	Testing Laboratories

Specialized Design Services

541400	Specialized Design Services (including interior, industrial, graphic, & fashion design)

Computer Systems Design and Related Services

541511	Custom Computer Programming Services
541512	Computer Systems Design Services
541513	Computer Facilities Management Services
541519	Other Computer Related Services

Other Professional, Scientific, and Technical Services

541600	Management, Scientific, & Technical Consulting Services
541700	Scientific Research & Development Services
541800	Advertising & Related Services
541910	Marketing Research & Public Opinion Polling
541920	Photographic Services
541930	Translation & Interpretation Services
541940	Veterinary Services
541990	All Other Professional, Scientific, & Technical Services

Code

Management of Companies (Holding Companies)

551111	Offices of Bank Holding Companies
551112	Offices of Other Holding Companies

Administrative and Support and Waste Management and Remediation Services

Administrative and Support Services

561110	Office Administrative Services
561210	Facilities Support Services
561300	Employment Services
561410	Document Preparation Services
561420	Telephone Call Centers
561430	Business Service Centers (including private mail centers & copy shops)
561440	Collection Agencies
561450	Credit Bureaus
561490	Other Business Support Services (including repossession services, court reporting, & stenotype services)
561500	Travel Arrangement & Reservation Services
561600	Investigation & Security Services
561710	Exterminating & Pest Control Services
561720	Janitorial Services
561730	Landscaping Services
561740	Carpet & Upholstery Cleaning Services
561790	Other Services to Buildings & Dwellings
561900	Other Support Services (including packaging & labeling services, & convention & trade show organizers)

Waste Management and Remediation Services

562000	Waste Management & Remediation Services

Educational Services

611000	Educational Services (including schools, colleges, & universities)

Health Care and Social Assistance

Offices of Physicians and Dentists

621111	Offices of Physicians (except mental health specialists)
621112	Offices of Physicians, Mental Health Specialists
621210	Offices of Dentists

Offices of Other Health Practitioners

621310	Offices of Chiropractors
621320	Offices of Optometrists
621330	Offices of Mental Health Practitioners (except Physicians)

Code

621340	Offices of Physical, Occupational & Speech Therapists, & Audiologists
621391	Offices of Podiatrists
621399	Offices of All Other Miscellaneous Health Practitioners

Outpatient Care Centers

621410	Family Planning Centers
621420	Outpatient Mental Health & Substance Abuse Centers
621491	HMO Medical Centers
621492	Kidney Dialysis Centers
621493	Freestanding Ambulatory Surgical & Emergency Centers
621498	All Other Outpatient Care Centers

Medical and Diagnostic Laboratories

621510	Medical & Diagnostic Laboratories

Home Health Care Services

621610	Home Health Care Services

Other Ambulatory Health Care Services

621900	Other Ambulatory Health Care Services (including ambulance services & blood & organ banks)

Hospitals

622000	Hospitals

Nursing and Residential Care Facilities

623000	Nursing & Residential Care Facilities

Social Assistance

624100	Individual & Family Services
624200	Community Food & Housing, & Emergency & Other Relief Services
624310	Vocational Rehabilitation Services
624410	Child Day Care Services

Arts, Entertainment, and Recreation

Performing Arts, Spectator Sports, and Related Industries

711100	Performing Arts Companies
711210	Spectator Sports (including sports clubs & racetracks)
711300	Promoters of Performing Arts, Sports, & Similar Events
711410	Agents & Managers for Artists, Athletes, Entertainers, & Other Public Figures
711510	Independent Artists, Writers, & Performers

Museums, Historical Sites, and Similar Institutions

712100	Museums, Historical Sites, & Similar Institutions

Amusement, Gambling, and Recreation Industries

713100	Amusement Parks & Arcades
713200	Gambling Industries
713900	Other Amusement & Recreation Industries (including golf courses, skiing facilities, marinas, fitness centers, & bowling centers)

Code

Accommodation and Food Services

Accommodation

721110	Hotels (except casino hotels) & Motels
721120	Casino Hotels
721191	Bed & Breakfast Inns
721199	All Other Traveler Accommodation
721210	RV (Recreational Vehicle) Parks & Recreational Camps
721310	Rooming & Boarding Houses

Food Services and Drinking Places

722110	Full-Service Restaurants
722210	Limited-Service Eating Places
722300	Special Food Services (including food service contractors & caterers)
722410	Drinking Places (Alcoholic Beverages)

Other Services

Repair and Maintenance

811110	Automotive Mechanical & Electrical Repair & Maintenance
811120	Automotive Body, Paint, Interior, & Glass Repair
811190	Other Automotive Repair & Maintenance (including oil change & lubrication shops & car washes)
811210	Electronic & Precision Equipment Repair & Maintenance
811310	Commercial & Industrial Machinery & Equipment (except Automotive & Electronic) Repair & Maintenance
811410	Home & Garden Equipment & Appliance Repair & Maintenance
811420	Reupholstery & Furniture Repair
811430	Footwear & Leather Goods Repair
811490	Other Personal & Household Goods Repair & Maintenance

Personal and Laundry Services

812111	Barber Shops
812112	Beauty Salons
812113	Nail Salons
812190	Other Personal Care Services (including diet & weight reducing centers)
812210	Funeral Homes & Funeral Services
812220	Cemeteries & Crematories
812310	Coin-Operated Laundries & Drycleaners
812320	Drycleaning & Laundry Services (except Coin-Operated)
812330	Linen & Uniform Supply
812910	Pet Care (except Veterinary) Services
812920	Photofinishing
812930	Parking Lots & Garages
812990	All Other Personal Services

Religious, Grantmaking, Civic, Professional, and Similar Organizations

813000	Religious, Grantmaking, Civic, Professional, & Similar Organizations

SCHEDULE D (Form 1065) Department of the Treasury Internal Revenue Service	Capital Gains and Losses ► Attach to Form 1065.	OMB No. 1545-0099 1998

Name of partnership	Employer identification number

Part I   **Short-Term Capital Gains and Losses—Assets Held 1 Year or Less**

(a) Description of property (e.g., 100 shares of "Z" Co.)	(b) Date acquired (month, day, year)	(c) Date sold (month, day, year)	(d) Sales price (see instructions)	(e) Cost or other basis (see instructions)	(f) Gain or (loss) ((d) minus (e))	
1						

2 Short-term capital gain from installment sales from Form 6252, line 26 or 37 . .	**2**	
3 Short-term capital gain (loss) from like-kind exchanges from Form 8824 . . .	**3**	
4 Partnership's share of net short-term capital gain (loss), including specially allocated short-term capital gains (losses), from other partnerships, estates, and trusts . . .	**4**	
5 **Net short-term capital gain or (loss).** Combine lines 1 through 4 in column (f). Enter here and on Form 1065, Schedule K, line 4d or 7	**5**	

Part II   **Long-Term Capital Gains and Losses—Assets Held More Than 1 Year**

(a) Description of property (e.g., 100 shares of "Z" Co.)	(b) Date acquired (month, day, year)	(c) Date sold (month, day, year)	(d) Sales price (see instructions)	(e) Cost or other basis (see instructions)	(f) Gain or (loss) ((d) minus (e))	(g) 28% rate gain or (loss) *(see instr. below)
6						

7 Long-term capital gain from installment sales from Form 6252, line 26 or 37 . .	**7**	
8 Long-term capital gain (loss) from like-kind exchanges from Form 8824. . . .	**8**	
9 Partnership's share of net long-term capital gain (loss), including specially allocated long-term capital gains (losses), from other partnerships, estates, and trusts . .	**9**	
10 Capital gain distributions	**10**	
11 Combine lines 6 through 10 in column (g). Enter here and on Form 1065, Schedule K, line 4e(1) or 7	**11**	
12 **Net long-term capital gain or (loss).** Combine lines 6 through 10 in column (f). Enter here and on Form 1065, Schedule K, line 4e(2) or 7	**12**	

*28% rate gain or (loss) includes all "collectibles gains and losses" as defined in the instructions.

For Paperwork Reduction Act Notice, see the Instructions for Form 1065.   Cat. No. 11393G   Schedule D (Form 1065) 1998

General Instructions

Section references are to the Internal Revenue Code.

Changes To Note

● For sales, exchanges, and conversions after 1997, property held more than 1 year (instead of more than 18 months) generally is eligible for the 10%, 20%, and 25% maximum capital gains rates at the partner level (for individuals, estates, and trusts). This rule also applies to installment payments received after 1997. Therefore, the partnership should include in column (g) of Schedule D **only** collectibles gains and losses and certain pre-1998 gains from fiscal year pass-through entities.

● The partnership may be able to postpone gain on the sale of qualified small business stock. For details, see **Rollover of gain from qualified stock** on page 3.

Purpose of Schedule

Use Schedule D (Form 1065) to report sales or exchanges of capital assets, capital gain distributions, and nonbusiness bad debts. Do not report on Schedule D capital gains (losses) specially allocated to any partners.

Enter capital gains (losses) specially allocated to the partnership as a partner in other partnerships and from estates and trusts on Schedule D, line 4 or 9, whichever applies. Enter capital gains (losses) of the partnership that are specially allocated to partners directly on line 4d, 4e(1), 4e(2), or 7 of Schedules K and K-1, whichever applies. See **How Income Is Shared Among Partners** in the Instructions for Form 1065 for more information.

To report sales or exchanges of property other than capital assets, including the sale or exchange of property used in a trade or business and involuntary conversions (other than casualties and thefts), see **Form 4797,** Sales of Business Property, and related instructions. If property is involuntarily converted because of a casualty or theft, use **Form 4684,** Casualties and Thefts.

Gains and losses from section 1256 contracts and straddles are reported on **Form 6781,** Gains and Losses From Section 1256 Contracts and Straddles. If there are limited partners, see section 1256(e)(4) for the limitation on losses from hedging transactions.

An exchange of business or investment property for property of a like kind is reported on **Form 8824,** Like-Kind Exchanges.

For more information, see **Pub. 544,** Sales and Other Dispositions of Assets.

What Are Capital Assets?

Each item of property the partnership held (whether or not connected with its trade or business) is a capital asset **except:**

1. Assets that can be inventoried or property held mainly for sale to customers.

2. Depreciable or real property used in the trade or business.

3. Certain copyrights; literary, musical, or artistic compositions; letters or memoranda; or similar property.

4. Accounts or notes receivable acquired in the ordinary course of trade or business for services rendered or from the sale of property described in **1** above.

5. U.S. Government publications, including the Congressional Record, that the partnership received from the government, other than by purchase at the normal sales price, or that the partnership got from another taxpayer who had received it in a similar way, if the partnership's basis is determined by reference to the previous owner.

Items for Special Treatment

● Bonds and other debt instruments. See **Pub. 550,** Investment Income and Expenses.

● Certain real estate subdivided for sale that may be considered a capital asset. See section 1237.

● Gain on the sale of depreciable property to a more than 50%-owned entity, or to a trust in which the partnership is a beneficiary, is treated as ordinary gain.

● Liquidating distributions from a corporation. See Pub. 550 for details.

● Gain on the sale or exchange of stock in certain foreign corporations. See section 1248.

● Gain or loss on options to buy or sell, including closing transactions. See Pub. 550 for details.

● Gain or loss from a short sale of property. See Pub. 550 for details.

● Transfer of property to a political organization if the fair market value of the property exceeds the partnership's adjusted basis in such property. See section 84.

● Any loss on the disposition of converted wetland or highly erodible cropland that is first used for farming after March 1, 1986, is reported as a long-term capital loss on Schedule D, but any gain on such a disposition is reported as ordinary income on Form 4797. See section 1257 for details.

● Transfer of partnership assets and liabilities to a newly formed corporation in exchange for all of its stock. See Rev. Rul. 84-111, 1984-2 C.B. 88.

● Disposition of foreign investment in a U.S. real property interest. See section 897.

● Any loss from a sale or exchange of property between the partnership and certain related persons is not allowed, except for distributions in complete liquidation of a corporation. See sections 267 and 707(b) for details.

● Any loss from securities that are capital assets that become worthless during the year is treated as a loss from the sale or exchange of a capital asset on the last day of the tax year.

● Gain from the sale or exchange of stock in a collapsible corporation is not a capital gain. See section 341.

● Nonrecognition of gain on sale of stock to an employee stock ownership plan (ESOP) or an eligible cooperative. See section 1042 and Temporary Regulations section 1.1042-1T for rules under which the partnership may elect not to recognize gain from the sale of certain stock to an ESOP or an eligible cooperative.

● A nonbusiness bad debt must be treated as a short-term capital loss and can be deducted only in the year the debt becomes totally worthless. For each bad debt, enter the name of the debtor and "schedule attached" in column (a) of line 1 and the amount of the bad debt as a loss in column (f). Also attach a statement of facts to support each bad debt deduction.

● Any loss from a wash sale of stock or securities (including contracts or options to acquire or sell stock or securities) cannot be deducted unless the partnership is a dealer in stock or securities and the loss was sustained in a transaction made in the ordinary course of the partnership's trade or business. A wash sale occurs if the partnership acquires (by purchase or exchange), or has a contract or option to acquire, substantially identical stock or securities within 30 days before or after the date of the sale or exchange. See section 1091 for more information.

● Gains from the sale of property (other than publicly traded stock or securities) for which any payment is to be received in a tax year after the year of sale must be reported using the installment method on **Form 6252,** Installment Sale Income, unless the partnership elects to report the entire gain in the year of sale. The partnership should also use Form 6252 if it received a payment this year from a sale made in an earlier year on the installment method.

If the partnership wants to elect out of the installment method for installment gain that **is not** specially allocated among the partners, it must report the full amount of the gain on a timely filed return (including extensions).

If the partnership wants to elect out of the installment method for installment gain that **is** specially allocated among the partners, it must do the following on a timely filed return (including extensions):

1. For a **short-term capital gain,** report the full amount of the gain on Schedule K, line 4d or 7.

For a **long-term capital gain,** report the full amount of the gain on Schedule K, line 4e(2) or 7. Report the 28% rate gain (defined below) on line 4e(1).

2. Enter each partner's share of the full amount of the gain on Schedule K-1, line 4d, 4e(2), or 7, whichever applies. Report the 28% rate gain, if any, on line 4e(1).

Constructive sales treatment for certain appreciated positions. Generally, the partnership must recognize gain (but not loss) on the date it enters into a constructive sale of any appreciated position in stock, a partnership interest, or certain debt instruments as if the position were disposed of at fair market value on that date.

The partnership is treated as making a constructive sale of an appreciated position when it (or a related person, in some cases) does **one** of the following:

● Enters into a short sale of the same or substantially identical property (i.e., a "short sale against the box").

● Enters into an offsetting notional principal contract relating to the same or substantially identical property.

● Enters into a futures or forward contract to deliver the same or substantially identical property.

● Acquires the same or substantially identical property (if the appreciated position is a short sale, offsetting notional principal contract, or a futures or forward contract).

Exception. Generally, constructive sales treatment **does not** apply if:

● The partnership closed the transaction before the end of the 30th day after the end of the year in which it was entered into,

● The partnership held the appreciated position to which the transaction relates throughout the 60-day period starting on the date the transaction was closed, **and**

● At no time during that 60-day period was the partnership's risk of loss reduced by holding certain other positions.

For details and other exceptions to these rules, see Pub. 550.

Rollover of gain from qualified stock. If the partnership sold qualified small business stock (defined below) it held for more than 6 months, it may postpone gain if it purchased other qualified small business stock during the 60-day period that began on the date of the sale. The partnership must recognize gain to the extent the sale proceeds exceed the cost of the replacement stock. Reduce the basis of the replacement stock by any postponed gain.

If the partnership chooses to postpone gain, report the entire gain realized on the sale on line 1 or 6. Directly below the line on which the partnership reported the gain, enter in column (a) "Section 1045 Rollover" and enter as a (loss) in column (f) the amount of the postponed gain.

Caution: *The partnership also must separately state the amount of the gain rolled over on qualified stock under section 1045 on Form 1065, Schedule K, line 7, because each partner must determine if he or she qualifies for the rollover at the partner level. Also, the partnership must separately state on that line (and not on Schedule D) any gain that would qualify for the section 1045 rollover at the partner level instead of the partnership level (because a partner was entitled to purchase replacement stock) and any gain on qualified stock that could qualify for the 50% exclusion under section 1202.*

To be **qualified small business stock,** the stock must meet **all** of the following tests:

● It must be stock in a C corporation (i.e., not S corporation stock).

● It must have been originally issued after August 10, 1993.

● As of the date the stock was issued, the corporation was a qualified small business. A qualified small business is a domestic C corporation with total gross assets of $50 million or less **(a)** at all times after August 9, 1993, and before the stock was issued, and **(b)** immediately after the stock was issued. Gross assets include those of any predecessor of the corporation. All corporations that are members of the same parent-subsidiary controlled group are treated as one corporation.

● The partnership must have acquired the stock at its original issue (either directly or through an underwriter), either in exchange for money or other property or as pay for services (other than as an underwriter) to the corporation. In certain cases, the partnership may meet the test if it acquired the stock from another person who met this test (such

as by gift or at death) or through a conversion or exchange of qualified business stock by the holder.

● During substantially all the time the partnership held the stock:

1. The corporation was a C corporation,

2. At least 80% of the value of the corporation's assets were used in the active conduct of one or more qualified businesses (defined below), and

3. The corporation **was not** a foreign corporation, DISC, former DISC, corporation that has made (or that has a subsidiary that has made) a section 936 election, regulated investment company, real estate investment trust, REMIC, FASIT, or cooperative.

Note: *A specialized small business investment company (SSBIC) is treated as having met tests **2** and **3** above.*

A **qualified business** is any business **other than** the following:

● One involving services performed in the fields of health, law, engineering, architecture, accounting, actuarial science, performing arts, consulting, athletics, financial services, or brokerage services.

● One whose principal asset is the reputation or skill of one or more employees.

● Any banking, insurance, financing, leasing, investing, or similar business.

● Any farming business (including the raising or harvesting of trees).

● Any business involving the production of products for which percentage depletion can be claimed.

● Any business of operating a hotel, motel, restaurant, or similar business.

Specific Instructions

Columns (b) and (c)—Date Acquired and Date Sold

Use the trade dates for date acquired and date sold for stocks and bonds traded on an exchange or over-the-counter market.

Column (d)—Sales Price

Enter in this column either the gross sales price or the net sales price from the sale. On sales of stocks and bonds, report the gross amount as reported to the partnership by the partnership's broker on **Form 1099-B,** Proceeds From Broker and Barter Exchange Transactions, or similar statement. However, if the broker advised the partnership that gross proceeds (gross sales price) less commissions and option premiums were reported to the IRS, enter that net amount in column (d).

Column (e)—Cost or Other Basis

In general, the cost or other basis is the cost of the property plus purchase commissions and improvements and minus depreciation, amortization, and depletion. If the partnership got the property in a tax-free exchange, involuntary conversion, or wash sale of stock, it may not be able to use the actual cash cost as the basis. If the partnership does not use cash cost, attach an explanation of the basis.

When selling stock, adjust the basis by subtracting all the stock-related nontaxable distributions received before the sale. This includes nontaxable distributions from utility company stock and mutual funds. Also adjust the basis for any stock splits or stock dividends.

If a charitable contribution deduction is passed through to a partner because of a sale of property to a charitable organization, the adjusted basis for determining gain from the sale is an amount that has the same ratio to the adjusted basis as the amount realized has to the fair market value.

See section 852(f) for the treatment of certain load charges incurred in acquiring stock in a mutual fund with a reinvestment right.

If the gross sales price is reported in column (d), increase the cost or other basis by any expense of sale, such as broker's fees, commissions, or option premiums, before making an entry in column (e).

For more information, see **Pub. 551,** Basis of Assets.

Column (f)—Gain or (Loss)

Make a separate entry in this column for each transaction reported on lines 1 and 6 and any other line(s) that applies to the partnership. For lines 1 and 6, subtract the amount in column (e) from the amount in column (d). Enter negative amounts in parentheses.

Column (g)—28% Rate Gain or (Loss)

Enter in column (g) **only** the amount, if any, from Part II, column (f), that is from collectibles gains and losses. A **collectibles gain or loss** is any long-term gain or loss from the sale or exchange of a collectible that is a capital asset.

Collectibles include works of art, rugs, antiques, metals (such as gold, silver, and platinum bullion), gems, stamps, coins, alcoholic beverages, and certain other tangible property.

Also include gain from the sale of an interest in a partnership or trust attributable to unrealized appreciation of collectibles.

Lines 4 and 9—Capital Gains and Losses From Other Partnerships, Estates, and Trusts

See the Schedule K-1 or other information supplied to you by the other partnership, estate, or trust.

Line 10—Capital Gain Distributions

On line 10, column (f), report as capital gain distributions **(a)** capital gain dividends and **(b)** the partnership's share of undistributed capital gains from a regulated investment company or real estate investment trust (REIT). On line 10, column (g), report the 28% rate gain portion of these amounts. Report the partnership's share of taxes paid on undistributed capital gains by a regulated investment company or REIT on Schedule K, line 24, and Schedule K-1, line 25.

| SCHEDULE K-1
(Form 1065)
Department of the Treasury
Internal Revenue Service | Partner's Share of Income, Credits, Deductions, etc.
▶ See separate instructions.
For calendar year 1998 or tax year beginning , 1998, and ending , 19 | OMB No. 1545-0099
1998 |

Partner's identifying number ▶ .... | **Partnership's identifying number** ▶ ....

Partner's name, address, and ZIP code | Partnership's name, address, and ZIP code

A This partner is a ☐ general partner ☐ limited partner
  ☐ limited liability company member
B What type of entity is this partner? ▶ ....
C Is this partner a ☐ domestic or a ☐ foreign partner?
D Enter partner's percentage of:

	(i) Before change or termination	(ii) End of year
Profit sharing	.... %	.... %
Loss sharing	.... %	.... %
Ownership of capital	.... %	.... %

E IRS Center where partnership filed return: ....

F Partner's share of liabilities (see instructions):
  Nonrecourse . . . . $ ....
  Qualified nonrecourse financing . $ ....
  Other . . . . $ ....
G Tax shelter registration number . ▶ ....
H Check here if this partnership is a publicly traded partnership as defined in section 469(k)(2) . . . . ☐
I Check applicable boxes: **(1)** ☐ Final K-1 **(2)** ☐ Amended K-1

J Analysis of partner's capital account:

(a) Capital account at beginning of year	(b) Capital contributed during year	(c) Partner's share of lines 3, 4, and 7, Form 1065, Schedule M-2	(d) Withdrawals and distributions	(e) Capital account at end of year (combine columns (a) through (d))
			( )	

	(a) Distributive share item		(b) Amount	(c) 1040 filers enter the amount in column (b) on:
Income (Loss)	**1** Ordinary income (loss) from trade or business activities . . .	**1**		See page 6 of Partner's Instructions for Schedule K-1 (Form 1065).
	2 Net income (loss) from rental real estate activities	**2**		
	3 Net income (loss) from other rental activities	**3**		
	4 Portfolio income (loss):			
	a Interest	**4a**		Sch. B, Part I, line 1
	b Ordinary dividends	**4b**		Sch. B, Part II, line 5
	c Royalties	**4c**		Sch. E, Part I, line 4
	d Net short-term capital gain (loss)	**4d**		Sch. D, line 5, col. (f)
	e Net long-term capital gain (loss):			
	(1) 28% rate gain (loss)	**e(1)**		Sch. D, line 12, col. (g)
	(2) Total for year.	**e(2)**		Sch. D, line 12, col. (f)
	f Other portfolio income (loss) *(attach schedule)*	**4f**		Enter on applicable line of your return.
	5 Guaranteed payments to partner	**5**		See page 6 of Partner's Instructions for Schedule K-1 (Form 1065).
	6 Net section 1231 gain (loss) (other than due to casualty or theft) .	**6**		
	7 Other income (loss) *(attach schedule)*	**7**		Enter on applicable line of your return.
Deductions	**8** Charitable contributions (see instructions) *(attach schedule)* . .	**8**		Sch. A, line 15 or 16
	9 Section 179 expense deduction.	**9**	.	See pages 7 and 8 of Partner's Instructions for Schedule K-1 (Form 1065).
	10 Deductions related to portfolio income *(attach schedule)* . . .	**10**		
	11 Other deductions *(attach schedule)*.	**11**		
Credits	**12a** Low-income housing credit:			
	(1) From section 42(j)(5) partnerships for property placed in service before 1990	**a(1)**		Form 8586, line 5
	(2) Other than on line 12a(1) for property placed in service before 1990	**a(2)**		
	(3) From section 42(j)(5) partnerships for property placed in service after 1989	**a(3)**		
	(4) Other than on line 12a(3) for property placed in service after 1989	**a(4)**		
	b Qualified rehabilitation expenditures related to rental real estate activities	**12b**		See page 8 of Partner's Instructions for Schedule K-1 (Form 1065).
	c Credits (other than credits shown on lines 12a and 12b) related to rental real estate activities.	**12c**		
	d Credits related to other rental activities	**12d**		
	13 Other credits	**13**		

For Paperwork Reduction Act Notice, see Instructions for Form 1065.   Cat. No. 11394R   **Schedule K-1 (Form 1065) 1998**

Schedule K-1 (Form 1065) 1998   Page **2**

	(a) Distributive share item		(b) Amount	(c) 1040 filers enter the amount in column (b) on:
Investment Interest	**14a** Interest expense on investment debts	**14a**		Form 4952, line 1
	b (1) Investment income included on lines 4a, 4b, 4c, and 4f . .	**b(1)**		See page 9 of Partner's Instructions for Schedule K-1 (Form 1065).
	(2) Investment expenses included on line 10	**b(2)**		
Self-employment	**15a** Net earnings (loss) from self-employment	**15a**		Sch. SE, Section A or B
	b Gross farming or fishing income.	**15b**		See page 9 of Partner's Instructions for Schedule K-1 (Form 1065).
	c Gross nonfarm income.	**15c**		
Adjustments and Tax Preference Items	**16a** Depreciation adjustment on property placed in service after 1986	**16a**		
	b Adjusted gain or loss	**16b**		See page 9 of Partner's Instructions for Schedule K-1 (Form 1065) and Instructions for Form 6251.
	c Depletion (other than oil and gas)	**16c**		
	d (1) Gross income from oil, gas, and geothermal properties . .	**d(1)**		
	(2) Deductions allocable to oil, gas, and geothermal properties	**d(2)**		
	e Other adjustments and tax preference items *(attach schedule)*	**16e**		
Foreign Taxes	**17a** Type of income ▶			Form 1116, check boxes
	b Name of foreign country or possession ▶			
	c Total gross income from sources outside the United States *(attach schedule)*	**17c**		Form 1116, Part I
	d Total applicable deductions and losses *(attach schedule)* . . .	**17d**		
	e Total foreign taxes (check one): ▶ ☐ Paid ☐ Accrued . .	**17e**		Form 1116, Part II
	f Reduction in taxes available for credit *(attach schedule)* . . .	**17f**		Form 1116, Part III
	g Other foreign tax information *(attach schedule)*	**17g**		See Instructions for Form 1116.
Other	**18** Section 59(e)(2) expenditures: **a** Type ▶			See page 9 of Partner's Instructions for Schedule K-1 (Form 1065).
	b Amount	**18b**		
	19 Tax-exempt interest income	**19**		Form 1040, line 8b
	20 Other tax-exempt income.	**20**		See pages 9 and 10 of Partner's Instructions for Schedule K-1 (Form 1065).
	21 Nondeductible expenses	**21**		
	22 Distributions of money (cash and marketable securities) . . .	**22**		
	23 Distributions of property other than money	**23**		
	24 Recapture of low-income housing credit:			
	a From section 42(j)(5) partnerships	**24a**		Form 8611, line 8
	b Other than on line 24a.	**24b**		

Supplemental Information

25 Supplemental information required to be reported separately to each partner *(attach additional schedules if more space is needed)*:

....

....

....

....

....

....

....

....

....

....

....

....

CERTIFICATE OF LIMITED PARTNERSHIP

1. _____
   (Name of Limited Partnership; must contain a suffix such as "Limited", "Ltd.", or "Limited Partnership")

2. _____
   (Business address of Limited Partnership)

3. _____
   (Name of Registered Agent for Service of Process)

4. _____
   (Florida street address for Registered Agent)

5. _____
   (Registered Agent must sign here to accept designation as Registered Agent for Service of Process)

6. _____
   (Mailing Address of the Limited Partnership)

7. The latest date upon which the Limited Partnership is to be dissolved is: _____

8. Name(s) of general partner(s):   Street address:

   _____   _____

   _____   _____

   _____   _____

   _____   _____

Under penalties of perjury I (we) declare that I (we) have read the foregoing and know the contents thereof and that the facts stated herein are true and correct.

Signed this _____ day of _____ , 19 _____ .

Signature of all general partners:

_____   _____
General Partner   General Partner

_____   _____
General Partner   General Partner

_____   _____
General Partner   General Partner

AFFIDAVIT OF CAPITAL CONTRIBUTIONS
FOR FLORIDA LIMITED PARTNERSHIP

The undersigned constituting all of the general partners of _____

_____ ,

a Florida Limited Partnership, certify:

The amount of capital contributions to date of the limited partners is $ _____ .

The total amount contributed and anticipated to be contributed by the limited partners at this time

totals $_____ .

Signed this _____ day of _____ , 19 _____ .

FURTHER AFFIANT SAYETH NOT.

Under the penalties of perjury I (we) declare that I (we) have read the foregoing and know the contents thereof and that the facts stated herein are true and correct.

_____   _____
General Partner   General Partner

_____   _____
General Partner   General Partner

_____   _____
General Partner   General Partner

This will acknowledge receipt of your recent request for information concerning the formation of a Florida limited partnership. Printed on the reverse side of this letter is a copy of Section 620.108, Florida Statutes, which provides information regarding the filing of the certificate of limited partnership and affidavit of capital contributions.

➤ Pursuant to Chapter 620, Florida Statutes, every legal or commercial business entity listed as a general partner on the attached certificate of limited partnership must have an active registration or filing on file with the Florida Department of State before the enclosed documents can be processed by this office. Should you need the forms and instructions to properly register a non-individual general partner, please call
(850) 487-6051.

➤ Section 620.114, Florida Statutes, requires the certificate and the affidavit be signed by all general partners.

➤ The fee to file both the certificate and affidavit is based on the total of the amount contributed and the anticipated amount to be contributed by the limited partners at a rate of $7 per $1000, with the fee no less than $52.50 and no more than $1750. An additional $35 is due for the designation of a registered agent. A certified copy or a certificate under seal may be requested at the time of filing. An additional $52.50 is due for each certified copy requested and an additional $8.75 is due for each certificate requested. Please send one check for the total amount due made payable to the Department of State.

(IMPORTANT: Because Chapter 620, Florida Statutes, requires a Florida limited partnership to file a supplemental affidavit any time the actual contributions of the limited partners exceed the anticipated amount listed on the attached affidavit and to pay an additional filing fee based on the increase at a rate of $7 per $1,000, with a minimum filing fee of $52.50 and maximum filing fee of $1750, it is imperative that the limited partnership review the affidavit for accuracy before submitting it to the Florida Department of State for processing.)

➤ Please be sure to include a cover letter with your documents and check. The cover letter should include the name of the contact person and his/her telephone number during the day and the name and address to which the acknowledgment should be addressed.

Any further inquiries on this matter should be directed to the Bureau of Commercial Recording by telephoning (850) 487-6051, the Registration Section, or by writing: Division of Corporations, P.O. Box 6327, Tallahassee, FL 32314.

NOTE: This form for filing a certificate of limited partnership is basic. Each limited partnership is a separate entity and as such has specific goals, needs and requirements. Additional information may be inserted as required. The Division of Corporations recommends that limited partnership documents be reviewed by your legal counsel. This division is a filing agency and as such does not render any legal, accounting or tax advice. The professional advice of your legal counsel to ascertain exact compliance with all statutory requirements is strongly recommended.

CR2E030(7/97)

620.108   Formation; certificate of limited partnership.--

(1) In order to form a limited partnership, a certificate of limited partnership must be executed and

filed with the Department of State. The certificate must set forth:

    (a) The name of the limited partnership.

    (b) The address of the office and the name and address of the agent for service of process required to be maintain by s. 620.105.

    (c) The name and the business address of each general partner. Each general partner that is a legal or commercial entity and not an individual must be organized or otherwise registered with the Department of State as required by law, must maintain an active status, and must not be dissolved, revoked, or withdrawn.

    (d) A mailing address for the limited partnership;

    (e) The latest date upon which the limited partnership is to dissolve; and

    (f) Any other matters the general partners determine to include therein.

An affidavit declaring the amount of the capital contributions of the limited partners and the amount anticipated to be contributed by the limited partners must accompany the certificate of limited partnership.

(2) A limited partnership is formed at the time of the filing of the certificate of limited partnership with the department or at any later time specified in the certificate of limited partnership if, in either case, there has been a substantial compliance with the requirements of this section.

HISTORY.--S.8,CH.86.263
NOTE.-- EFFECTIVE JANUARY 1, 1987

9 CORPORATIONS

While sole proprietorships and partnerships are created by the individuals who form the business, corporations are created as separate entities by the state, at the request or petition of the individuals involved. Therefore, as you might expect, the procedure to form a corporation is more involved. Yet, there is some logic to it, and it is not onerous if you follow directions accurately.

Before covering the state-required forms and procedures, let's review the differences and similarities between regular or C corporations, and S corporations.

SETTING UP THE CORPORATION AND MAKING IT LEGAL

In the eyes of each state's secretary of state or other agency that oversees formation of corporations, there is no difference between a C corporation and an S corporation. (That is not to say that the state *tax* authority won't see a difference.) In other words, you form either type of corporation in exactly the same way. Once formed, you then elect a *tax status* of either C or S.

So, we start with *forming a corporation*. We'll consider the tax status later.

Pre-Incorporation Agreement

If you, or you and your spouse (in a stable marriage) are forming a corporation of which you will be the only stockholders, there is no need for this document. However, if several people are to be stockholders, it's a good idea to draw up an agreement. This can avoid the disappointment of spending money for state fees and legal advice only to find, after the corporation has been formed, that there are irreconcilable differences between the memories, expectations, and commitments of the would-be stockholders.

You could use a formal agreement, as in the following example. (Because of the great variation in business plans of nascent corporations, you won't find this form in a forms package from your local secretary of state.) Or, if prospects of disagreement seem slim, a simple memo, signed by all, may suffice. In either case, the document should address at least these points:

- The proposed name of the corporation
- How many shares of stock will be authorized
- How many shares of stock will be issued to each stockholder and at what price
- How payment for the stock will be made (Simple, if it's all cash. More complex if certain stockholders are to transfer equipment or other assets to the corporation in exchange for stock.)
- Who is to be elected to the board of directors
- Who will fill each corporate officer slot and at what salary rate
- Who will actually manage the corporation and at what salary, bonus, etc.
- Anything else on which the stockholders-to-be agree (Check the stockholders' preincorporation agreement on page 140 for other items to include in this preliminary agreement.)

Application for Reservation of Corporate Name

Like the pre-incorporation agreement, this form and procedure is not required. However, two corporations with the same name cannot be chartered or operate within the same state. If you and your initial stockholders have agreed on a name but still have details to work out before sending the articles of incorporation (see next section) to the state, you can reserve the corporate name for a specific period (often 90 days). For instance, you may still be looking for additional capital from more stockholders, or a commitment for financing from a bank, before proceeding with the incorporation.

You can save time and possibly fees if you call the appropriate state office and determine if there already is a corporation with your intended name. (You may also be able to find this information on the Internet.) Also, check for similar names. While the state might allow you to use your selected name, you could find the corporation with a similar name hauling you into an argument in court, perhaps seeking an injunction against your use of your corporate name.

We've used the New York state form Application for Reservation of Corporate Name on page 141 as an example.

Articles of Incorporation

This is the document that gets the corporation started on its road to existence. The individual who signs it and submits it to the state (usually to the secretary of state) is the *incorporator.* Although there can be more than one incorporator, there is usually no reason to have more than one. The people who will end up owning the corporation are those who buy the stock, and the incorporator may or may not be included in that group. Indeed, if you engage a lawyer or incorporation service to take care of these details for you, he or she may act as the incorporator to avoid the shuffling of paper to someone else for signature.

Each state has its own rules regarding the drawing and submission of articles of incorporation, and in some states the document goes by a different name. Here are two of them: The first is Nevada's *Articles of Incorporation* (p. 142), which is more or less a fill-in and check-the-box form. The second is Delaware's (p. 144), which is a *Certificate of Incorporation.* Both of these states solicit incorporation by businesses in other states, so, for your information, I have included their advertising literature with the instructions for the forms.

Before you leap to incorporate in a state other than your own, remember that you will still have to register your "foreign" (from another state) corporation in your own state. You will end up paying fees in both states, so check it out before you leap to Nevada or Delaware. To demonstrate, I have included a Texas Application for Certificate of Authority (p. 147). If you do business in Texas, but decide to incorporate in another state, you will have to do the additional paperwork of filing this certificate of authority in Texas. Note that this also incurs an additional $750 fee.

Acceptance of Appointment by Resident Agent

In the articles of incorporation (or the certificate of incorporation), the incorporator must specify who or what firm is the resident agent. That is some individual, or some firm (must be lawyers in some states), on whom the local process server can serve legal papers. (It's difficult to hand papers to a corporation, which is an intangible entity created by the state.) Quite logically, the incorporators cannot designate an individual for this job unless he or she agrees to perform it. Therefore, every filing of articles of incorporation must be accompanied by an acceptance of the job on a form similar to this Nevada form (p. 152). This need not be a permanent arrangement, as the designation of resident agent can be changed at any time by filing an additional form (not shown here) with the state. Usually, a corporate officer can act as registered agent, or the corporation can engage an attorney (or qualified resident-agent firms in some states) to perform this function.

Keeping the Corporation Alive

After you have filed the articles of incorporation (or similar document) and the acceptance of appointment by resident or registered agent, you should receive a response from the state. If you filled out the forms correctly, the reply will be in the form of acceptance of the articles of incorporation and possibly a corporate charter document that you can frame, if you so desire.

You now have your corporation set up—it exists, but you're not finished. There is still much to do, now and in the future. You have to treat your corporation as a corporation if it is to be recognized as such by the Internal Revenue Service and if it is to provide limited liability to the stockholders. Here are the more important tasks.

Annual Reports to the State

Annually, your state will expect the corporation to file a report with the secretary of state (or its equivalent) and pay an annual fee. In most states, this report consists of a list of corporate officers, directors, and confirmation of the current registered agent. You should receive notice from the state on a preprinted form with the direction to make necessary changes. However, if you don't receive it, call the secretary of state's office and ask for your form. (Call your resident agent if you use an outside person to perform that function.) The bottom line is that the corporate officers are responsible for filing the annual report and paying the fee. If they fail, the corporation will soon cease to exist.

Some states expect the first annual report from a new corporation the same date that applies to all existing corporations. Others want the annual report shortly (often 60 days) after incorporation.

Apply to the IRS for the Corporation's Employer Identification Number (EIN)

This is required for every corporation, whether or not it will hire employees. The form was discussed and reproduced in the sole proprietorship section. The comments there apply to corporations, but three items should be clarified.

1. The "name of the applicant" is the name of the corporation, not that of any individual.
2. Line 17a reads: "Has the applicant ever applied for an employer identification number for this or any other. . . . " The applicant is the corporation. Even if the incorporator or any stockholder has had 100 EINs for 100 sole proprietorships, the answer for a new corporation is no.
3. If your corporation is engaging in the personal-service fields of law, medicine, accounting, or consulting, you should check Personal Service

Corporation in box 8a. Note that you are not electing C or S status on this form.

MORE TASKS TO KEEP YOUR CORPORATION ALIVE

All the tasks that we covered for sole proprietors apply here, so review the sole proprietorship section for:

- Registration with state tax authorities
- Local business license application
- Registering a fictitious name (if the corporation uses a trade name that is other than the corporate name)
- Registering business name and mark as trademarks. (Issuance of a corporate charter by the secretary of state or similar office only prevents someone from using the name as a corporate name. A sole proprietor or a general partnership could use the same name. You would have some basis for legal action against that entity, but you would be on stronger ground if you had registered your name and mark.)
- All the earlier comments about buying a business apply to a corporation that purchases the assets of a business.

Corporate Bylaws

None of the documents we have looked at so far addresses the details of how the corporation will operate. For instance, like any organization, a corporation needs rules as to how it will be governed or directed, who will elect the directors, who determines who will be paid how much, and so on. At this stage, or even earlier, such as when the future stockholders are drafting a pre-incorporation agreement, the individuals involved should draft the corporate bylaws. State law, in its variances from state to state, generally specifies defaults in how a corporation is operated. That is, if the bylaws do not cover a certain point, then the state law will control how it is operated. For instance, the state code may specify that, unless the corporate bylaws state otherwise, all stockholders, of every class of stock, have one vote. However, you may have two classes of stock, and one class does not have a vote. (You might specify nonvoting stock in your corporation for your children to own.) Unless you specify that in your bylaws, all of your stockholders will have a vote.

A sample set of corporate bylaws is on pages 153–161. Use it to help determine what should be in yours. Do not copy them blindly, for some clauses inevitably will be unsuitable for your situation.

Yes, good bylaws go on and on for pages, and most of the words seem to be unimportant boilerplate. Yet, those words do serve a purpose. They can resolve various arguments over the management of the corporation and which stockholders have the clout to determine the final decisions, including the election of directors or officers.

Minority Stockholders

Will you be a minority stockholder? That is, will the stock you own represent less than 50 percent of the votes in a stockholder's meeting? (You may or may not want to include stock that your spouse, children, or other relatives own in making this determination.) While, at the formation of your corporation, everyone is amiable and in agreement as to future operations, opinions can diversify in the future and result in strong disagreements. It things become nasty, you, as a minority stockholder, could be frozen out of the board of directors and the decision-making process.

While you cannot overcome all of the disadvantages of being a minority stockholder, you can take some precautions:

- Engage your personal attorney (not the corporate attorney) to review the articles of incorporation and the bylaws from a standpoint of protecting your interests. (Remember, the corporate attorney represents the corporation, not the individual stockholders.)
- Insist the amendment of the bylaws can be accomplished only by a stockholder majority large enough to require your support for passage. For example, if you own 30 percent of the stock, insist that a majority of 71 percent is necessary to amend the bylaws.
- Insist on cumulative voting for directors, if it is legal in your state. This is a process where each share of stock has one vote times the number of directors to be elected. A stockholder who owns 100 shares of stock in a corporation with three directors would have 300 votes. He or she could spread those votes among the three directors or vote all 300 for one director.

EXAMPLE: Archie, Betty, and Charlie each own 100 shares of Crabgrass Corporation. The bylaws specify three directors, and Archie and Betty would like to throw Charlie off of the board and elect Betty's sister, Dawn. (Charlie has strange ideas, they think.)

With cumulative voting, Charlie could cast all of his 300 votes for himself, making sure he is a director, as he has received one-third of the total votes. Without cumulative voting, Archie, Betty, and Dawn, in separate elections, would each receive two votes to Charlie's single vote. Charlie would be a non-director.

This can be accomplished by a clause similar to this one:

At election of directors, each stockholder will have as many votes as he or she has shares times the number of directors to be elected. Each stockholder may cast all of his or her votes for one person or may distribute his or her votes for two or more persons.

Stockholders' Agreement

While the bylaws bind the corporation to do certain things, they extract no agreement from the shareholders. If you and some of your friends decide to start a business, you probably are thinking in terms of a partnership. However, for various reasons, you decide you should operate as a corporation. If you operate as a partnership, either your partnership agreement or state law will probably require that none of the partners can sell his or her partnership interest to another party without the consent of the other partners. However, if you incorporate the business, you have fellow stockholders rather than partners. Unless you take measures as covered in the next paragraph, any of your fellow stockholders can sell their stock to anyone they choose, regardless of your wishes or the wishes of any other stockholder.

> EXAMPLE: Nancy, Oscar, and Patricia each own one-third of the outstanding stock of the Spongy Bottom Boat Corporation. Nancy and Patricia sell all of their stock to Horace, whom Oscar detests. But as Horace now owns two-thirds of the stock, he controls the corporation, and Oscar ends up working for Horace.

That scene is preventable by a shareholders' (or stockholders') agreement. However, the courts usually look askance on shareholders' agreements that make it impossible ever to transfer the stock to someone else. Certainly, estates have to be able to sell the stock that was owned by the deceased. Therefore, to keep it legal, shareholders' agreements make provisions enabling a shareholder to sell his or her stock after first offering it to the other shareholders and/or the corporation. It can get fairly complex, but that's corporate life at the millennium, even for small corporations. That's why this sample document goes on for several pages.

There are even more complex agreements, and the complexity is justified. For instance, a shareholders' agreement can include requirements that the corporation purchase life insurance on each shareholder. That can ensure that there is sufficient cash in the corporate till to buy the stock of the deceased shareholder.

The sample agreement on pages 162–172 uses the term "shareholder," while we have generally used "stockholder" in this book. The terms are essentially synonymous, so don't let "shareholder" throw you off balance.

MORE I'S TO DOT

The theory of corporate governance is that the shareholders elect the members of the board of directors who, as a board, make major decisions about corporate management. The most important of these is who will manage the corporation on a day-to-day basis. Historically, this has been the president, perhaps a vice president or so, the secretary, and the treasurer. Also, there were logical rules that the president and the secretary offices could not be filled by the same person.

This required that, immediately upon issuance of a corporate charter, there would have to be immediate meetings of the stockholders to elect directors followed by an immediate meeting of directors to elect officers. For a small corporation to be owned by only one, two, or three people, this amounted to superfluous paperwork, so the states have simplified it in a variety of ways. Some states allow the stockholders to manage the corporation directly without a management layer of a board of directors. (In small corporations, the directors are usually the stockholders, anyway.) Other states allow the board of directors to be one person, who can also be the president, secretary, and treasurer. Another streamlining is that most states provide that the incorporator(s) can appoint a board of directors, often listing them in the articles of incorporation, and these directors serve as such until the first annual meeting of stockholders. Again, in a corporation with one or a few stockholders, the directors are almost automatically reelected.

To keep your corporation legitimate, you should do the following, unless your state allows direct management by the board of directors or stockholders:

- Formally notify all directors of the time and place for the initial director's meeting, making sure the notice complies with the bylaws, or prepare a waiver of notice for each director to sign. As the waiver of notice route is simpler, that is the sample form included here.
- Hold the director's meeting, and record the discussion and decisions in minutes of the meeting.

Sample forms for these events are on pages 173–176.

Minutes of Organizational Meeting of Incorporators, with Waiver of Notice

In some states, this meeting should be held preceding the first meeting of the board of directors. Sample forms are on pages 177–179.

Section 1244 Clauses

Section 1244 of the Internal Revenue Code (p. 181) allows a stockholder of a small corporation, who sells his stock at a loss (or whose stock becomes worthless), to deduct up to $50,000 of the loss as ordinary loss, rather than capital gain. For most taxpayers, that will result in substantial tax savings. In order to qualify, the stock must have been issued in exchange for money or property that is not securities, and the stock cannot be issued in exchange for services. Also, the initial capital of the corporation cannot exceed one million dollars, and 50 percent of the gross receipts of the corporation must come from business operations.

If a corporation fits this mold, loss on sale of the stock should qualify for this ordinary loss treatment (up to $50,000). However, before 1978, the corporate minutes had to specify that the stock would qualify for section 1244 treatment, and some attorneys and accountants still believe it strengthens an argument with the IRS over qualification of the stock if there is a "section 1244" clause in the minutes. It does no harm to include it, and it may help, so the paragraphs on page 180 can be inserted and substituted at the initial meeting of the board of directors.

YOUR FUTURE CORPORATE LIFE (LEGALITIES AND TAX FILING)

There are ongoing details that, if performed, should keep your corporation alive and well.

Annual Stockholders' Meeting

Don't neglect to hold these annual meetings on the date specified in the corporate bylaws and record the minutes of the meeting. Again, it is simpler to include a waiver of notice than to go through the formality of notifying the stockholders. Be certain that all stockholders sign the waiver.

Routine annual stockholders' meetings usually contain little more than reelection of the same directors. In small corporations, of course, they are the same people as are stockholders of the corporation. However, if there is contemplated action that could alter the percentage of outstanding stock that each stockholder owns, such as a merger or issuance of additional stock to other individuals or other entities, the stockholders must approve.

Annual Board of Directors' Meetings

You may have reason to have several board of directors' meetings during a year—for purposes such as opening new bank accounts, borrowing money, bestowing a vice-presidency on a valued employee, and so on. Nevertheless, be sure you hold and record minutes for an annual board of directors' meeting. As usual, have a waiver of notice signed and in the minute book.

Watch for this: Many lawyers and, in states where they can legally operate, companies that specialize in acting as registered (or resident) agents, will take care of the annual report to the secretary of state and draft the minutes of the annual meetings. Unless you notify these people to the contrary, they will use pure boilerplate. That is, the minutes of the stockholders' meeting will include only the annual election of directors, which may not be all you need. For instance, if the corporation borrows money, the bank will want a resolution by the board of directors. That means a special meeting prior to signing the loan papers.

And this is extremely important: The IRS likes to classify payments to individuals who are both stockholders and officers and other employees as dividends. That means that the payment cannot be deducted as an expense by the corporation, but the stockholder/employee gets to pay tax on it, so it's the infamous double taxation. To avoid this, be sure that annual directors' minutes include the amount of salaries for each stockholder/employee and a formula for any bonuses. Also, lay some groundwork for the future. Assume your corporation becomes hugely successful and pays you a salary of five million dollars. You can expect the IRS will try to classify $4,900,000 as dividends. Solution: Prepare for that possibility from day one. Insert a clause in the directors' minutes to the effect that you are accepting a minimal salary because the corporation cannot afford more with the expectation that the shortfall will be made up in future years. This may not always work, but it's worth a try. Remember, if you use a corporate service, that sort of clause won't appear in your minutes unless you specify that it must. Suggestion: Write the minutes yourself and let your attorney review them. Sample form is on p. 181.

ANNUAL INCOME TAX RETURNS (CORPORATIONS)

If you do not elect S status, you have a C corporation and therefore file annual tax returns on IRS Form 1120, U.S. Corporation Income Tax Return (pp. 182–185), or on Form 1120-A, Corporation Short-Form Income Tax Return (pp. 186–187). The short form is shorter—two pages versus four pages in the long form. However, the difference in ease of completing the form is marginal, for one set of nineteen pages of instructions covers both forms. Should you file the short form? Yes, if you meet the test for doing so in the instructions for Form 1120 and Form 1120-A.

If your corporation had gains and losses from owning stock in other corporations, bonds or other capital assets, you will also need to complete a special Schedule D, Capital Gains and Losses, for corporations (pp. 188–189). If the corporation sold equipment or other property that was used in the business, you would also have to include Form 4797, Sales of Business Property. That form is discussed and reproduced in the section on sole proprietorships.

Because a C corporation pays its own taxes, it will also have to pay estimated taxes during the year. (It cannot wait and pay it all at the end of the year without incurring penalties.) That means you will have to compute the estimated tax on Form 1120-W (pp. 190–195) and make estimated payments as in the instructions. Believe it or not, the IRS does not want checks from you for this estimated tax, but it still wants the money. You get it there by making deposits to the IRS's account at your bank. (The IRS will send you machine-readable cards with which you make those deposits at the bank. You'll receive them automatically when you file the SS-4, Application for Employer Identification Number.)

So, you, or your accountant, will have to close the corporation's accounting records for the year, determine the taxable income, fill in the Form 1120 (or 1120-A), and mail it to the IRS, which expects you to do that in 2½ months. But fear not. As long as you pay the tax that is due on time, the IRS will let you have another six months in which to file the return. Use Form 7004, Application for Automatic Extension of Time to File Corporation Income Tax Return (pp. 196–197), and be sure to mail it (return receipt requested) by the due date of the return, which is March 15 for calendar-year corporations.

S CORPORATION

If you have decided that the corporation should request S corporation status from the IRS, there are several more things that should or must be done. The appropriate forms follow this discussion of them.

Until your embryo corporation gets to this election-of-tax-status stage, the procedures are identical to those covered above. That is, the incorporators draw up a pre-incorporation agreement or memorandum, file the articles of incorporation and designation of registered (or resident) agent, draw up corporate bylaws and a stockholders' agreement, file a Form SS-4 (Application for Employer Identification Number) with the IRS, and hold an initial meeting of the board of directors.

Remember, up to this point there is no difference between the procedure for setting up a C corporation and setting up an S corporation, with the exception of minor changes in the minutes of the directors' meeting and the shareholders' agreement. Now, to elect S corporation status, these additional tasks must be attended to:

Meet the Qualifications for S Corporation Status

The corporation must:

- Have no more than 75 stockholders
- Have no nonresident alien stockholders
- Have only one class of stock, but some stock can be nonvoting
- Keep its books on a January 1 to December 31 tax year (with some exceptions)
- Have agreement from all stockholders that they will consent to the S election
- Not be a bank, insurance company, possession corporation, or domestic international sales corporation. (If you are one of these animals,

you most undoubtedly have legal and accounting expertise already on retainer.)

Action by the Board of Directors

The board of directors should include, in the initial or a special meeting, a resolution (p. 138) reflecting this decision. Also, a fiscal (taxable) year of January 1 to December 31 should be stated in the bylaws. While it is possible to obtain IRS permission to operate an S corporation on other than a calendar-year basis, there are many hoops to jump through if you do that. In most situations, it's not worth the trouble.

Action by the Stockholders

The stockholders have to assent unanimously to the S corporation election. It is wise, therefore, to have their agreement to sign the assent before the corporation is formed. Paragraph 17 (p. 170) of the example of a Shareholders' Agreement provides for this. If it is a separate agreement, it might also require agreement by shareholders' spouses.

Make a Timely Application to the IRS

The corporation must file Form 2553 (pp. 199–202) with the IRS by the 15th of the third month of its fiscal year. Note that this is not 75 days after the start of the corporation, but the 15th day of the third month. Also, note question H on the Form 2553 that follows. The IRS is nit-picky over counting the months and days and from what date it counts them. Moral: File the form right away. If you fail to qualify for S corporation status for your first year, you will operate as a C corporation. This can complicate your tax records and returns in later years when you are an S corporation. Also, do the following:

- *Important:* Be certain that all of the shareholders sign their consent in section J of Form 2553. (To save time, you can obtain their consent on separate documents—just copy the consent in box K word-for-word.)
- Read the instructions to Form 2553 for more details.
- For your own protection, when you send the form to the IRS, send it via certified mail, return receipt requested.
- When you receive a letter from the IRS that grants S corporation status (p. 203), put the letter in your safe or safe deposit box.

After you have elected S corporation status, you can terminate that status in any future year. Thereafter, the rules for a C corporation would apply. There is no specific form for the termination, but it must be approved by the holders of a majority of the stock and filed with the IRS by the 15th day of the third month to be effective for the year. Once the S status is terminated, it generally cannot be elected again for five years.

Minority Stockholder Protection

Like partnerships and limited liability companies, the earnings of an S corporation have to be reported on the stockholders' individual income tax returns. For cash-strapped stockholders, the source of cash to pay those additional taxes should come from the corporation. For a majority stockholder, that is little problem. He or she can easily cause the corporation to make a cash distribution in early April or whenever the additional taxes are due. However, envision this:

> *You are an owner of less than 51 percent of the stock in an S corporation and the other stockholders are well-heeled individuals. They want to keep all of the cash in the corporation for expansion and pay the additional taxes on their individual returns from other sources. But you have no other easy sources of cash. You ask the other stockholders/directors to declare a cash distribution, but they say "tough." And that word describes your situation.*

To avoid this scene, include a clause in the stockholders' agreement to this effect: (Remember, the corporation is also a party to the stockholders' agreement and is bound by it.) (See p. 204.)

ANNUAL INCOME TAX RETURNS (S CORPORATIONS)

This return is something of a hybrid of partnership and C corporation returns.

Ordinary income or loss from trade or business activities is treated pretty much as is ordinary business income or loss on a partnership return. That is, the net income or loss from these activities is computed on page 1 of Form 1120S, U.S. Income Tax Return of an S Corporation. That figure is then entered on line 1, Schedule K, on page 3 of Form 1120S. Income from certain other activities and other items are entered on the appropriate line on Schedule K. Then the numbers on Schedule K are allocated to each stockholder in proportion to the percentage of outstanding stock he or she owns. (Unlike a partnership that can vary from this formula, S corporations must allocate or distribute earnings according to percentage of stock owned.) The figures for each stockholder are then entered on Schedule K-1, Shareholder's Share of Income, Credits, Deductions, etc. (One Form K-1 should be prepared for each stockholder.)

In some other areas of income and loss, the S corporation is not treated as a partnership, but almost as if it were a C corporation. See the lower part of page 1 of Form 1120S. The S corporation has to pay its own tax bill on items such as excess net passive income (income such as more interest and dividend income than an S corporation is allowed), tax on built-in gains (applies only to C corporations that later became S corporations), certain gains from sale of business equipment, and other items.

Sound confusing? It is. Why do CPAs die young? The answer is here. Does that mean you should forget about electing S corporation status? Not necessarily. For a new, relatively small and simple business in such areas as construction, retailing, food service, and similar industries, it can work well. The biggest advantage is that transfer of ownership, such as giving partial ownership to family members or loyal employees, is far simpler with a corporation than with a partnership or a limited liability company. If you are a professional in such fields as law, medicine, accounting, architecture, and so on, this advantage tends to disappear. That's because most states limit ownership to only those qualified to practice that profession, so you couldn't give the stock to children or clerical employees. (A *limited liability partnership,* covered later, may be a better choice for a professional.)

Here are the specific forms for an S corporation are on pages 206–211. The form for automatic six-month extension to file is not included, because it is the same as for a C corporation. (If you file for an extension for the S corporation, each stockholder also will have to apply for an automatic extension of time for his or her individual income tax return.)

SAMPLE PREINCORPORATION
AGREEMENT

Reprinted, with permission, from Michael R. Diamond and Julie L. Williams, *How to Incorporate*, copyright by Michael L. Diamond and Julie L. Williams, 1993, published by John Wiley & Sons.

AGREEMENT made this _____ day of _____ , 19 _____ between _____ , _____ , and _____ .

WHEREAS the parties hereto wish to organize a corporation upon the terms and conditions hereinafter set forth; and

WHEREAS the parties wish to establish their mutual rights and responsibilities in relation to their organizational activities;

NOW, THEREFORE in consideration of the premises and mutual covenants contained herein, it is agreed by and between the parties as follows:

FIRST: The parties will forthwith cause a corporation to be formed and organized under the laws of _____ .

SECOND: The proposed Articles of Incorporation shall be attached hereto as Exhibit A.

THIRD: Within 7 days after the issuance of the corporation's certificate of incorporation, the parties agree that the corporation's authorized stock shall be distributed, and consideration paid, as follows:

1. _____ shares of _____ (insert either common or preferred) stock shall be issued to _____ in consideration of his payment to the corporation of $ _____ cash.

2. _____ shares of _____ stock shall be issued to _____ in consideration of her transfer to the corporation of (list property, real or personal, to be transferred).

FOURTH: The corporation shall employ _____ as its manager for a term of _____ years and at a salary of $ _____ per annum, such employment not to be terminated without cause and such salary not to be increased or decreased without the approval of _____ % of the directors.

FIFTH: The parties agree not to transfer, sell, assign, pledge, or otherwise dispose of their shares until they have first offered them for sale to the corporation, and then, should the corporation refuse such offer, to the other shareholders on a pro rata basis. The shares shall be offered at their book value and, in the event the corporation refuses, the other shareholders shall have thirty (30) days to purchase the shares. If the corporation or other shareholders do not purchase all the offered shares, the remaining shares may be freely transferred by their owner without price restrictions.

SIXTH: The parties to this agreement promise to use their best efforts to incorporate the organization and to commence its business.

OPTIONAL PROVISION (if applicable): The parties agree that the Corporation will elect S Corporation status under Section 1362 of the Internal Revenue Code and they agree to sign consent to this election in the format prescribed by the Internal Revenue Service.

_____

_____

Application for Reservation of Name
Under §303 of the Business Corporation Law

NYS Department of State
DIVISION OF CORPORATIONS, STATE RECORDS and UCC
41 State Street
Albany, NY 12231-0001

PLEASE TYPE OR PRINT

APPLICANT'S NAME AND ADDRESS

NAME TO BE RESERVED

RESERVATION IS INTENDED FOR (CHECK ONE)

☐ New domestic corporation

☐ Foreign corporation intending to apply for authority to do business in New York State*

☐ Proposed foreign corporation, not yet incorporated, intending to apply for authority to conduct business in New York State

☐ Change of name of an existing domestic or an authorized foreign corporation*

☐ Foreign corporation intending to apply for authority to do business in New York State whose corporate name is not available for use in New York State*

☐ Authorized foreign corporation intending to change its fictitious name under which it does business in this state*

☐ Authorized foreign corporation which has changed its corporate name in its jurisdiction, such new corporate name not being available for use in New York State*

X_____   _____

Signature of applicant, applicant's attorney or agent   *Typed/printed name of signer*

(If attorney or agent, so specify)

INSTRUCTIONS:
1. Upon filing this application, the name will be reserved for 60 days and a certificate of reservation will be issued.
2. The certificate of reservation must be returned with and attached to the certificate of incorporation or application for authority, amendment or with a cancellation of the reservation.
3. The name used must be the same as appears in the reservation.
4. A $20 fee payable to the Department of State must accompany this application.
5. Only names for business, transportation, cooperative and railroad corporations may be reserved under §303 of the Business Corporation Law.

*If the reservation is for an existing corporation, domestic or foreign, the corporation must be the applicant.

DOS-234 (Rev. 10/97)

Filing Fee:
Receipt #:

Articles of Incorporation
(PURSUANT TO NRS 78)
STATE OF NEVADA
Secretary of State

(For filing office use) _____ (For filing office use) _____

IMPORTANT: Read instructions on reverse side before completing this form.
TYPE OR PRINT (BLACK INK ONLY)

1. **NAME OF CORPORATION:** _____

2. **RESIDENT AGENT:** (designated resident agent and his STREET ADDRESS in Nevada where process may be served)

   Name of Resident Agent: _____

   Street Address: _____
           Street No.   Street Name   City   Zip

3. **SHARES:** (number of shares the corporation is authorized to issue)
   Number of shares with par value: _____ Par value: _____ Number of shares without par value: _____

4. **GOVERNING BOARD:** shall be styled as (check one): _____ Directors _____ Trustees
   The FIRST BOARD OF DIRECTORS shall consist of _____ members and the names and addresses are as follows (attach additional pages if necessary)

Name	Address	City/State/Zip

   Name _____ Address _____ City/State/Zip

5. **PURPOSE** (optional-- see reverse side): **The purpose of the corporation shall be:**

6. **OTHER MATTERS:** This form includes the minimal statutory requirements to incorporate under NRS 78. You may attach additional information pursuant to NRS 78.037 or any other information you deem appropriate. If any of the additional information is contradictory to this form it cannot be filed and will be returned to you for correction. **Number of pages attached** _____

7. **SIGNATURES OF INCORPORATORS:** The names and addresses of each of the incorporators signing the articles: (Signatures must be notarized) (Attach additional pages if there are more than two incorporators.)

   Name (print) _____ Name (print) _____

   Address _____ City/State/Zip   Address _____ City/State/Zip

   Signature _____ Signature _____

   State of _____ County of _____   State of _____ County of _____

   This instrument was acknowledged before me on   This instrument was acknowledged before me on

   _____ _____, 19_____, by   _____ _____, 19_____, by

   Name of Person _____   Name of Person _____
   as incorporator   as incorporator
   of _____   of _____
   (name of party on behalf of whom instrument was executed)   (name of party on behalf of whom instrument was executed)

   _____   _____
   Notary Public Signature   Notary Public Signature

   (affix notary stamp or seal)   (affix notary stamp or seal)

8. **CERTIFICATE OF ACCEPTANCE OF APPOINTMENT OF RESIDENT AGENT**

   I, _____ hereby accept appointment as Resident Agent for the above named corporation.

   _____   _____
   Signature of Resident Agent   Date

Dean Heller
Nevada Secretary of State
Corporate Information

Why Incorporate in Nevada?

No Corporate Income Tax

No Taxes on Corporate Shares

No Franchise Tax

No Personal Income Tax

No I.R.S. Information Sharing Agreement

Nominal Annual Fees

Minimal Reporting and Disclosure Requirements

Stockholders are not Public Record

Additional Advantages

- Stockholders, directors and officers need not live or hold meetings in Nevada, or even be U.S. Citizens.
- Directors need not be Stockholders.
- Officers and directors of a Nevada corporation can be protected from personal liability for lawful acts of the corporation.
- Nevada corporations may purchase, hold, sell or transfer shares of its own stock.
- Nevada corporations may issue stock for capital, services, personal property, or real estate, including leases and options. The directors may determine the value of any of these transactions and their decision is final.

STATE *of* DELAWARE
CERTIFICATE *of* INCORPORATION
A STOCK CORPORATION

First: The name of this Corporation is _____

_____ .

Second: Its registered office in the State of Delaware is to be located at _____ _____ Street, in the City of _____ County of _____ Zip Code _____ . The registered agent in charge thereof is _____

_____

_____

Third: The purpose of the corporation is to engage in any lawful act or activity for which corporations may be organized under the General Corporation Law of Delaware.

Fourth: The amount of the total authorized capital stock of this corporation is _____ Dollars ($_____) divided into _____ shares of _____ _____ Dollars ($_____) each.

Fifth: The name and mailing address of the incorporator are as follows:

Name _____

Mailing Address_____

_____ Zip Code _____

I, The Undersigned, for the purpose of forming a corporation under the laws of the State of Delaware, do make, file and record this Certificate, and do certify that the facts herein stated are true, and I have accordingly hereunto set my hand this _____ day of _____, A.D. 19 _____ .

BY: _____

(Incorporator)

NAME: _____

(type or print)

Delaware Division of Corporations FAQs

Delaware Division of Corporations

Frequently Asked Questions

Why do so many companies incorporate in Delaware?

Do I have to live in Delaware?

Must I use an attorney to incorporate?

If I am incorporated in another state or jurisdiction, do I need to qualify to do business in the State of Delaware?

How quickly can I incorporate?

How do I reserve a corporate name?

How do I amend my certificate of incorporation?

How do I change my registered office and registered agent?

Where can I obtain a copy of The General Corporation Law of the State of Delaware?

Q: Why do so many companies incorporate in Delaware?

A: The reason is not just one but several. They include the Delaware General Corporation Law that is one of the most advanced and flexible corporation statutes in the nation. Secondly, Delaware courts and, in particular, the Court of Chancery, have over 200 years of legal precedent as a maker of corporation law. Thirdly, the state legislature seriously takes its role in keeping the corporation statute and other business laws current. Lastly, the office of the Secretary of State operates much like a business rather than a government bureaucracy with its modern imaging system and customer service oriented staff.

Q: Do I have to live in Delaware?

A: No. Delaware law requires every corporation to have and maintain a **registered agent in the State** who may be either an individual resident, a domestic corporation, or a foreign corporation authorized to transact business in the State whose business office is identical with the corporation's registered office. (See List of Registered Agents)

Q: Must I use an attorney to incorporate?

A: No, but you should contact an attorney concerning legal matters. The Division of Corporations acts in an administrative capacity only.

Q: If I am incorporated in another state or jurisdiction, do I need to qualify to do business in the State of

http://www.state.de.us/corp/q&a.htm   1/27/1999

Delaware Division of Corporations FAQs   Page 2 of 2

Delaware?

A: Yes, Delaware law requires every corporation to submit a completed "Foreign Corporation" form with the Division of Corporations along with a certificate of existence issued by your state or jurisdiction.

Q: How quickly can I incorporate?

A: The Division of Corporations offers a variety of services including "2-Hour", "Same Day" and "24-hour" processing of documents which are designed to meet your business needs. (See Expedited Services)

Q: How do I reserve a corporate name?

A: You can reserve a name for up to 30 days by calling 900/420-8042. A $10 fee will be charged to your phone bill. The name you choose must be distinguishable from corporations or other entities reserved or registered under the laws of Delaware.

Q: How do I amend my certificate of incorporation?

A: File a Certificate of Amendment. The corporation's president or vice president, attested to by the secretary or assistant secretary must sign this certificate.

Q: How do I change my registered office and registered agent?

A: File a Certificate of Change of Agent form. See Fee Schedule for the amount of the filing fee of this document.

Q: Where can I obtain a copy of The General Corporation Law of the State of Delaware?

A: Contact LEXIS Law Publishing, P.O. Box 7587, Charlottesville, Virginia 22906.
Phone (800) 562-1197.
Fax (804) 972-7666.
Web site:

- Softcover http://www.lexislawpublishing.com/bookstore/Product.cfm?item5=22138
- Diskette http://www.lexislawpublishing.com/Bookstore/Product.cfm?item5=22137

Home * F.A.Q. * Guidelines * Schedule of Fees * Expedited Services
Forms and Certificates * Franchise Tax * UCC * Contacts * Newsletter

Maintained by the Secretary of State's Office
Webmaster
Last Updated October 28, 1998

http://www.state.de.us/corp/q&a.htm   1/27/1999

**Office of the
Secretary of State**

Corporations Section

P.O. Box 13697
Austin, Texas 78711-3697

INSTRUCTIONS FOR MAKING APPLICATION FOR A CERTIFICATE OF AUTHORITY BY A BUSINESS CORPORATION

The following documents are necessary to complete the application of a foreign business corporation for a certificate of authority to transact business in Texas. All documents are to be submitted to: Secretary of State, Statutory Filings Division, Corporations Section, P.O. Box 13697, Austin, Texas 78711-3697. The delivery address is James Earl Rudder Building, 1019 Brazos, Austin, Texas 78701. We will place one document on record and return a file stamped copy. The telephone number is (512) 463-5555, TDD: (800) 735-2989, FAX: (512) 463-5709.

The attached copy of the form promulgated by the secretary of state is for your convenience; the format is mandatory. It is recommended that the services of an attorney be obtained before preparation of the application for the certificate of authority.

Franchise tax information may be obtained from the Comptroller of Public Accounts, Tax Assistance Section, Austin, Texas, 78774-0100, (512) 463-4600 OR (800) 252-1381.

CONTENTS OF COMPLETED APPLICATION ARE LISTED BELOW:

1.	Submit two copies of the application for a certificate of authority. We will place one document on record and return a file stamped copy to you for your files. The document must be signed by an officer of the corporation. <u>Prior to signing, please read the statements on this form carefully. A person commits an offense under the Texas Business Corporation Act, the Texas Limited Liability Company Act or the Texas Non-Profit Corporation Act if the person signs a document the person knows is false in any material respect with the intent that the document be delivered to the secretary of state for filing. The offense is Class A misdemeanor.</u>

2.	A certificate issued by the secretary of state or other authorized officer of the jurisdiction of its incorporation evidencing the corporate existence. The certificate must be dated within 90 days of the receipt of the application. If the certificate is in a language other than English, a translation of the certificate, under oath of the translator, must accompany the certificate.

3.	The statutory fee of $750 must be submitted. (Tex. Bus. Corp. Act Ann. art. 10.01) Please submit a check or money order made payable to the secretary of state. The check or money order must be payable through a U.S. bank or financial institution.

IMPORTANT INFORMATION

CORPORATE NAME (items 1 & 2): Article 8.03 of the Texas Business Corporation Act (TBCA) and the secretary of state's name availability rules provide that a corporate name cannot be the same as, or deceptively similar to, that of any domestic or foreign corporation, limited partnership, limited liability company, or any name reservation or registration filed with the secretary of state. Therefore, the foreign corporation's name will be checked for availability upon submission of the application.

Name availability may be checked prior to submission of the documents by calling (512) 463-5555. <u>This is only a preliminary clearance</u>. The final decision on the name will be made when the document is submitted for filing. If the corporation's name is not available for use in this state, the corporation must obtain its certificate of authority under an assumed name. The assumed name under which a corporation qualifies must meet the same requirements applied to corporate names.

In addition, the corporate name must contain one of the following words of incorporation or an abbreviation thereof: Company, Corporation, Incorporated, or Limited. If the corporate name does not contain one of the words of incorporation, the application should state the name of the corporation with one of the words of incorporation added for purposes of doing business in Texas.

STATED CAPITAL (item 13): The amount of the corporation's stated capital should be specified in the application. Stated capital must always be expressed in U.S. dollars. TBCA, article 1.01 A(17) defines "stated capital": as the sum of:

    (a)   par value of all shares of the corporation having a par value that have been issued;

    (b)   the consideration fixed by the corporation in the manner provided by law for all shares of the corporation without par value that have been issued, except such part of the consideration actually received therefor as may have been allocated to the capital surplus in a manner permitted by law; and

    (c)   such amounts not included in paragraphs (a) and (b) of this subsection as have been transferred to stated capital of the corporation, whether upon the issue of shares as a share dividend or otherwise, minus all reductions from such sum as may have been effected in a manner permitted by law.

CONSIDERATION (item 14): The corporation must have received consideration of the value of at least $1,000 for the issuance of shares prior to obtaining a certificate of authority and the statement of such fact must be included in the application. This $1,000 figure cannot be altered, even if the corporation is permitted by its home state to commence business with a lesser amount of consideration.

DELAYED EFFECTIVE DATE

Under article 10.03 of the Texas Business Corporation Act, a corporation may choose to make the filing of certain documents effective as of a date within 90 days of the date of submission. This can be accomplished by stating either a future date or describing a future event within the document submitted for filing. Please refer to article 10.03 of the Texas Business Corporation Act for the specific requirements necessary for filing documents with a future effective date.

**Office of the
Secretary of State**

Corporations Section

P.O. Box 13697
Austin, Texas 78711-3697

APPLICATION FOR CERTIFICATE OF AUTHORITY

Pursuant to the provisions of article 8.05 of the Texas Business Corporation Act, the undersigned corporation hereby applies for a certificate of authority to transact business in Texas:

1.   The name of the corporation is _____

2.   A. If the name of the corporation in its jurisdiction of incorporation does not contain the word "corporation," "company," "incorporated," or "limited" (or an abbreviation thereof), then the name of the corporation with the word or abbreviation which it elects to add for use in Texas is: _____

   B. If the corporate name is not available in Texas, then set forth the name under which the corporation will qualify and transact business in Texas _____
   _____

3.   It is incorporated under the laws of_____

4.   The date of its incorporation is_____ and the period of duration is _____ (State "perpetual" or term of years)

5.   The address of its principal office in the state or country under the laws of which it is incorporated is:_____

6.   The street address of its proposed registered office in Texas is (a P.O. Box is not sufficient)
   _____

   and the name of its proposed registered agent in Texas at such address is _____
   _____

7.   The purpose or purposes of the corporation which it proposes to pursue in the transaction of business in Texas are:

8.   It is authorized to pursue such purpose or purposes in the state or country under the laws of which it is incorporated.
   _____

9.   The names and respective addresses of its directors are:

NAME   ADDRESS

_____   _____

_____   _____

_____   _____

10.   The names and respective addresses of its officers are:

NAME   ADDRESS   OFFICE
                        (city and state)

_____   _____   _____

_____   _____   _____

_____   _____   _____

11.   The aggregate number of shares which it has authority to issue, itemized by classes, par value of shares, shares without par value, and series, if any, within a class, is:

NUMBER OF SHARES	CLASS	SERIES	PAR VALUE PER SHARE OR STATEMENT THAT SHARES ARE WITHOUT PAR VALUE
_____	_____	_____	_____
_____	_____	_____	_____
_____	_____	_____	_____

12.   The aggregate number of its issued shares, itemized by classes, par value of shares, shares without par value, and series, if any, within a class, is:

NUMBER OF SHARES	CLASS	SERIES	PAR VALUE PER SHARE OR STATEMENT THAT SHARES ARE WITHOUT PAR VALUE
_____	_____	_____	_____
_____	_____	_____	_____
_____	_____	_____	_____

13. The amount of its stated capital is $_____ . (See instructions for definition of stated capital.)

14. Consideration of the value of at least One Thousand Dollars ($1,000.00) has been paid for the issuance of its shares.

15. The application is accompanied by a certificate issued by the secretary of state or other authorized officer of the jurisdiction of incorporation evidencing the corporate existence and dated within 90 days of the date of receipt of the application.

_____

Name of Corporation

By:_____

Its_____

Authorized Officer

Form No. 301
Revised 6/96

The Office of the Secretary of State does not discriminate on the basis of race, color, national origin, sex, religion, age or disability in employment or the provision of services.

CERTIFICATE OF ACCEPTANCE OF APPOINTMENT
BY
RESIDENT AGENT

In the matter of _____

(Name of business entity)

I, _____, hereby state that on _____

(name of resident agent in articles)   (date)

I accepted the appointment as resident agent for the above named business entity.

The street address of the resident agent in this state is as follows:

_____   _____

(street address)   (suite number)

_____ , Nevada   _____

(city)   (zip code)

_____   _____

(authorized signature)   (date)

*If the resident agent is an individual, the signature must be of that individual.
*If the resident agent is an entity, the signature must be of a person authorized by the entity to sign.

CORPORATE BYLAWS

Reprinted by permission of the 'Lectric Law Library Legal Website at www.lectlaw.com.

(Note: When necessary these should be modified to comply with the laws of the state of incorporation and the particulars of the specific situation.—staff)

Bylaws

"Company"

Article I—Offices

Section 1. The registered office of the corporation shall be at:

"Address".

The registered agent in charge thereof shall be:

"Name".

Section 2. The corporation may also have offices at such other places as the Board of Directors may from time to time appoint or the business of the corporation may require.

Article II—Seal

Section 1. The corporate seal shall have inscribed thereon the name of the corporation, the year of its organization and the words "Corporate Seal, 'State'".

Article III—Stockholders' Meetings

Section 1. Meetings of stockholders shall be held at the registered office of the corporation in this state or at such place, either within or without this state, as may be selected from time to time by the Board of Directors.

Section 2. Annual Meetings: The annual meeting of the stockholders shall be held on the 3rd Wednesday of February in each year if not a legal holiday, and if a legal holiday, then on the next secular day following at 10:00 o'clock A.M., when they shall elect a Board of Directors and transact such other business as may properly be brought before the meeting. If the annual meeting for election of directors is not held on the date designated therefor, the directors shall cause the meeting to be held as soon thereafter as convenient.

Section 3. Election of Directors: Elections of the directors of the corporation shall be by written ballot.

Section 4. Special Meetings: Special meetings of the stockholders may be called at any time by the Chairman, or the Board of Directors, or stockholders entitled to cast at least one-fifth of the votes which all stockholders are entitled to cast at the particular meeting. At any time, upon written request of any person or persons who have duly called a special meeting, it shall be the duty of the Secretary to fix the date of the meeting, to be held not more than sixty days after receipt of the request, and to give due notice thereof. If the Secretary shall neglect or refuse to fix the date of the meeting and give notice thereof, the person or persons calling the meeting may do so. Business transacted at all special meetings shall be confined to the objects stated in the call and matters germane thereto, unless all stockholders entitled to vote are present and consent. Written notice of a special meeting of stockholders stating the time and place and object thereof, shall be given to each stockholder entitled to vote thereat at least thirty days before such meeting, unless a greater period of notice is required by statute in a particular case.

Section 5. Quorum: A majority of the outstanding shares of the corporation entitled to vote, represented in person or by proxy, shall constitute a quorum at a meeting of stockholders. If less than a majority of the outstanding shares entitled to vote is represented at a meeting, a majority of the shares so represented may adjourn the meeting from time to time without further notice. At such adjourned meeting at which a quorum shall be present or represented, any business may be transacted which might have been transacted at the meeting as originally noticed. The stockholders present at a duly organized meeting may continue to transact business until adjournment, notwithstanding the withdrawal of enough stockholders to leave less than a quorum.

Section 6. Proxies: Each stockholder entitled to vote at a meeting of stockholders or to express consent or dissent to corporate action in writing without a meeting may authorize another person or persons to act for him by proxy, but no such proxy shall be voted or acted upon after three years from its date, unless the proxy provides for a longer period. A duly executed proxy shall be irrevocable if it states that it is irrevocable and if, and only as long as, it is coupled with an interest sufficient in law to support an irrevocable power. A proxy may be made irrevocable regardless of whether the interest with which it is coupled is an interest in the stock itself or an interest in the corporation generally. All proxies shall be filed with the Secretary of the meeting before being voted upon.

Section 7. Notice of Meetings: Whenever stockholders are required or permitted to take any action at a meeting, a written notice of the meeting shall be given which shall state the place, date and hour of the meeting, and, in the case of a special meeting, the purpose or purposes for which the meeting is called. Unless otherwise provided by law, written notice of any meeting shall be given not less than ten nor more than sixty days before the date of the meeting to each stockholder entitled to vote at such meeting.

Section 8. Consent in Lieu of Meetings: Any action required to be taken at any annual or special meeting of stockholders or a corporation, or any action which may be taken at any annual or special meeting of such stockholders, may be taken without a meeting, without prior notice and without a vote, if a consent in writing, setting forth the action so taken, shall be signed by the holders of outstanding stock having not less than the minimum number of votes that would be necessary to authorize or take such action at a meeting at which all shares entitled to vote thereon were present and voted. Prompt notice of the taking of the corporate action without a meeting by less than unanimous written consent shall be given to those stockholders who have not consented in writing.

Section 9. List of Stockholders: The officer who has charge of the stock ledger of the corporation shall prepare and make, at least ten days before every meeting of stockholders, a complete list of the stockholders entitled to vote at the meeting, arranged in alphabetical order, and showing the address of each stockholder and the number of shares registered in the name of each stockholder. No share of stock upon which any installment is due and unpaid shall be voted at any meeting. The list shall be open to the examination of any stockholder, for any purpose germane to the meeting, during ordinary business hours, for a period of at least ten days prior to the meeting, either at a place within the city where the meeting is to be held, which place shall be specified in the notice of the meeting, or, of not so specified, at the place where the meeting is to be held. The list shall also be produced and kept at the time and place of the meeting during the whole time thereof, and may be inspected by any stockholder who is present.

Article IV—Directors

Section 1. The business and affairs of this corporation shall be managed by its Board of Directors, _____ in number. The directors need not be residents of this state or stockholders in the corporation. They shall be elected by the stockholders at the annual meeting of stockholders of the corporation, and each director shall be elected for the term of one year, and shall serve until his successor shall be elected and shall qualify or until his earlier resignation or removal.

Section 2. Regular Meetings: Regular meetings of the Board shall be held without notice, at least quarterly, at the registered office of the corporation, or at such other time and place as shall be determined by the Board.

Section 3. Special Meetings: Special Meetings of the Board may be called by the Chairman on two days' notice to each director, either personally or by mail, fax or by telegram; special meetings shall be called by the President or Secretary in like manner and on like notice on the written request of a majority of the directors in office.

Section 4. Quorum: A majority of the total number of directors shall constitute a quorum for the transaction of business.

Section 5. Consent in Lieu of Meeting: Any action required or permitted to be taken at any meeting of the Board of Directors, or of any committee thereof, may be taken without a meeting if all members of the Board or committee, as the case may be, consent thereto in writing, and the writing or writings are filed with the minutes of proceedings of the Board or committee. The Board of Directors may hold its meetings, and have an office or offices, outside of this state.

Section 6. Conference Telephone: One or more directors may participate in a meeting of the Board, or a committee of the Board or of the stockholders, by means of conference telephone or similar communications equipment by means of which all persons participating in the meeting can hear each other; participation in this manner shall constitute presence in person at such meeting.

Section 7. Compensation: Directors as such, shall not receive any stated salary for their services, but by resolution of the Board, a fixed sum and expenses of attendance at each regular or special meeting of the Board PROVIDED, that nothing herein contained shall be construed to preclude any director from serving the corporation in any other capacity and receiving compensation therefor.

Section 8. Removal: Any director or the entire Board of Directors may be removed, with or without cause, by the holders of a majority of the shares then entitled to vote at an election of directors, except that when cumulative voting is permitted, if less than the entire Board is to be removed, no director may be removed without cause if the votes cast against his removal would be sufficient to elect him if then cumulatively voted at an election of the entire Board of Directors, or, if there be classes of directors, at an election of the class of directors of which he is a part.

Article V—Officers

Section 1. The executive officers of the corporation shall be chosen by the directors and shall be a Chairman, President, Secretary and Chief Financial Officer. The Board of Directors may also choose one or more Vice Presidents and such other officers as it shall deem necessary. Any number of offices may be held by the same person.

Section 2. Salaries: Salaries of all officers and agents of the corporation shall be fixed by the Board of Directors.

Section 3. Term of Office: The officers of the corporation shall hold office for one year and until their successors are chosen and have qualified. Any officer or agent elected or appointed by the Board of Directors may be removed by the Board of Directors whenever in its judgment the best interest of the corporation will be served thereby.

Section 4. Chairman: The Chairman shall preside at all meetings of the stockholders and directors; he shall see that all orders and resolutions of the Board are carried into effect, subject, however, to the right of the directors to delegate any specific powers, except such as may be by statute exclusively conferred on the Chairman, to any other officer or officers of the corporation. He shall execute bonds, mortgages and other contracts requiring a seal, under the seal of the corporation. He shall be ex officio a member of all committees.

Section 5. President: The President shall attend all sessions of the Board. The President shall be the chief executive officer of the corporation; he shall have general and active management of the business of the corporation, subject, however, to the right of the directors to delegate any specific powers, except such as may be by statute exclusively conferred on the President, to any other officer or officers of the corporation. He shall have the general power and duties of supervision and management usually vested in the office of President of a corporation.

Section 6. Secretary: The Secretary shall attend all sessions of the Board and all meetings of the stockholders and act as clerk thereof, and record all the votes of the corporation and the minutes of all its transactions in a book to be kept for that purpose, and shall perform like duties for all committees of the Board of Directors when required. He shall give, or cause to be given, notice of all meetings of the stockholders and of the Board of Directors, and shall perform such other duties as may be prescribed by the Board of Directors or President, and under whose supervision he shall be. He shall keep in safe custody the corporate seal of the corporation, and when authorized by the Board, affix the same to any instrument requiring it.

Section 7. Chief Financial Officer: The Chief Financial Officer shall have custody of the corporate funds and securities and shall keep full and accurate accounts of receipts and disbursements in books belonging to the corporation, and shall keep the moneys of the corporation in separate account to the credit of the corporation. He shall disburse the funds of the corporation as may be ordered by the Board, taking proper vouchers for such disbursements, and shall render to the President and directors, at the regular meetings of the Board, or whenever they may require it, an account of all his transactions as Chief Financial Officer and of the financial condition of the corporation.

Article VI—Vacancies

Section 1. Any vacancy occurring in any office of the corporation by death, resignation, removal or otherwise, shall be filled by the Board of Directors. Vacancies and newly created directorships resulting from any increase in the authorized number of directors may be filled by a majority of the directors then in office, although not less than a quorum, or by a sole remaining director. If at any time, by reason of death or resignation or other cause, the corporation should have no directors in office, than any officer or any stockholder of an executor, administrator, trustee or guardian of a stockholder, or other fiduciary entrusted with like responsibility for the person or estate of stockholder, may call a special meeting of stockholders in accordance with the provisions of these Bylaws.

Section 2. Resignations Effective at Future Date: When one or more directors shall resign from the Board, effective at a future date, a majority of the directors then in office, including those who have so resigned, shall have power to fill such vacancy or vacancies, the vote thereon to take effect when such resignation or resignations shall become effective.

Article VII—Corporate Records

Section 1. Any stockholder of record, in person or by attorney or other agent, shall, upon written demand under oath stating the purpose thereof, have the right during the usual hours for business to inspect for any proper purpose the corporation's stock ledger, a list of its stockholders, and its other books and records, and to make copies or extracts therefrom. A proper purpose shall mean a purpose reasonably related to such person's interest as a stockholder. In every instance where an attorney or other agent shall be the person who seeks the right to inspection, the demand under oath shall be accompanied by a power of attorney or such other writing which authorizes the attorney or other agent to so act on behalf of the stockholder. The demand under oath shall be directed to the corporation as its registered office in this state or at its principal place of business.

Article VIII—Stock Certificates, Dividends

Section 1. The stock certificate of the corporation shall be numbered and registered in the share ledger and transfer books of the corporation as they are issued. They shall bear the corporate seal and shall be signed by the President.

Section 2. Transfers: Transfers of shares shall be made on the books of the corporation upon surrender of the certificates therefor, endorsed by the person named in the certificate or by attorney, lawfully constituted in writing. No transfer shall be made which is inconsistent with law.

Section 3. Lost Certificate: The corporation may issue a new certificate of stock in the place of any certificate theretofore signed by it, alleged to have been lost, stolen or destroyed, and the corporation may require the owner of the lost, stolen or destroyed certificate, or his legal representative to give the corporation a bond sufficient to indemnify it against any claim that may be make against it on account of the alleged loss, theft or destruction of any such certificate or the issuance of such new certificate.

Section 4. Record Date: In order that the corporation may determine the stockholders entitled to notice of or to vote at any meeting of stockholders or any adjournment thereof, or the express consent to corporate action in writing without a meeting, or entitled to receive payment of any dividend or other distribution or allotment of any rights, or entitled to exercise any rights in respect of any change, conversion or exchange of stock or for the purpose of any other lawful action, the Board of Directors may fix, in advance, a record date, which shall not be more than sixty nor less than ten days before the date of such meeting, nor more than sixty days prior to any other action.

If no record date is fixed:

(a) The record date for determining stockholders entitled to notice of or to vote at a meeting of stockholders shall be at the close of business on the day next preceding the day on which notice is given, or if notice is waived, at the close of business on the day next preceding the day on which the meeting is held.

(b) The record date for determining stockholders entitled to express consent to corporate action in writing without a meeting, when no prior action by the Board of Directors is necessary, shall be the day on which the first written consent is expressed.

(c) The record date for determining stockholders for any other purpose shall be at the close of business on the day on which the Board of Directors adopts the resolution relating thereto.

(d) A determination of stockholders of record entitled to notice of or to vote at a meeting of stockholders shall apply to any adjournment of the meeting; provided, however, that the Board of Directors may fix a new record date for the adjourned meeting.

Section 5. Dividends: The Board of Directors may declare and pay dividends upon the outstanding shares of the corporation from time to time and to such extent as they deem advisable, in the manner and upon the terms and conditions provided by the statute and the Certificate of Incorporation.

Section 6. Reserves: Before payment of any dividend there may be set aside out of the net profits of the corporation such sum or sums as the directors, from time to time, in their absolute discretion, think proper as a reserve fund to meet contingencies, or for equalizing dividends, or for repairing or maintaining any property of the corporation, or for such other purpose as the directors shall think conducive to the interests of the corporation, and the directors may abolish any such reserve in the manner in which it was created.

Article IX—Miscellaneous Provisions

Section 1. Checks: All checks or demands for money and notes of the corporation shall be signed by such officer or officers as the Board of Directors may from time to time designate.

Section 2. Fiscal Year: The fiscal year shall begin on the first day of January.

Section 3. Notice: Whenever written notice is required to be given to any person, it may be given to such person, either personally or by sending a copy thereof through the mail, by fax, or by telegram, charges prepaid, to his address appearing on the books of the corporation, or supplied by him to the corporation for the purpose of notice. If the notice is sent by mail, telegraph, or by fax, it shall be deemed to have been given to the person entitled thereto when deposited in the United States mail, with a telegraph office for transmission to such person, or faxed. Such notice shall specify the place, day and hour of the meeting and, in the case of a special meeting of stockholders, the general nature of the business to be transacted.

Section 4. Waiver of Notice: Whenever any written notice is required by statute, or by the Certificate or the Bylaws of this corporation, a waiver thereof in writing, signed by the person or persons entitled to such notice, whether before or after the time stated therein, shall be deemed equivalent to the giving of such notice. Except in the case of a special meeting of stockholders, neither the business to be transacted at nor the purpose of the meeting need be specified in the waiver of notice of such meeting. Attendance of a person, either in person or by proxy, at any meeting shall constitute a waiver of notice of such meeting, except where a person attends a meeting for the express purpose of objecting to the transaction of any business because the meeting was not lawfully called or convened.

Section 5. Disallowed Compensation: Any payments made to an officer or employee of the corporation such as a salary, commission, bonus, interest, rent, travel or entertainment expense incurred by him, which shall be disallowed in whole or in part as a deductible expense by the Internal Revenue Service, shall be reimbursed by such officer or employee to the corporation to the full extent of such disallowance. It shall be the duty of the directors, as a Board, to enforce payment of each such amount disallowed. In lieu of payment by the officer or employee, subject to the determination of the directors, proportionate amounts may be withheld from his future compensation payments until the amount owed to the corporation has been recovered.

Section 6. Resignations: Any director or other officer may resign at any time, such resignation to be in writing, and to take effect from the time of its receipt by the corporation, unless some time be fixed in the resignation, and then from that date. The acceptance of a resignation shall not be required to make it effective.

Article X—Annual Statement

Section 1. The President and Board of Directors shall present at each annual meeting a full and complete statement of the business and affairs of the corporation for the preceding year. Such statement shall be prepared and presented in whatever manner the Board of Directors shall deem advisable and need not be audited by a certified public accountant.

Article XI—Amendments

Section 1. These Bylaws may be amended or repealed by the vote of stockholders entitled to cast at least a majority of the votes which all stockholders are entitled to cast thereon, at any regular or special meeting of the stockholders, duly convened after notice to the stockholders of that purpose.

CORPORATE SHAREHOLDERS'
AGREEMENT

Reprinted by permission of the 'Lectric Law Library Legal Website at www.lectlaw.com.

(Note: When necessary these should be modified to comply with the laws of the state of incorporation and the particulars of the specific situation.)

Corporate Shareholders Agreement

THIS SHAREHOLDERS AGREEMENT is made by and among Shareholder 1 ("Share1"), Shareholder 2 ("Share2"), and Shareholder 3 ("Share3") (Share1, Share2 and Share3 and any subsequent person or entity holding Common Stock of the Company hereinafter sometimes referred to individually as a "Shareholder" and collectively as the "Shareholders") and Company Name, a Delaware corporation (the "Company").

Witnesseth:

WHEREAS, in order to insure the harmonious and successful management and control of the Company, and to provide for an orderly and fair disposition of shares of common stock of the Company now or hereafter owned by any Shareholder;

NOW, THEREFORE, in consideration of the mutual promises of the parties hereto, and intending to be legally bound, the parties hereby agree as follows:

1. Definitions.

   (a) "Offering Shareholder" means any Shareholder, or his personal representatives, heirs, administrators, and executors, as the case may be, who pursuant to this Agreement must or does offer all or any of his Shares to the Company or the Continuing Shareholders.

   (b) "Continuing Shareholders" means all Shareholders other than an Offering Shareholder.

   (c) "Shares" means shares of Common Stock of the Company now or hereafter owned by any Shareholder.

   (d) "Buyer" means the Company of those Continuing Shareholders who purchase an Offering Shareholder's Shares pursuant to this Agreement.

   (e) "Management Shareholder" means Share1, Share2 and Share3.

   (f) "Nonmanagement Shareholder" means any Shareholder other than a Management Shareholder.

2. Purchase for Investment. Each Shareholder represents and warrants that he is acquiring and has acquired his Shares for his own account for investment and not with a view to, or for resale in connection with, any distribution thereof or with any present intent of selling any portion thereof.

3. Transfers of Shares. A Shareholder may not transfer, give, convey, sell, pledge, bequeath, donate, assign, encumber or otherwise dispose of any Shares except pursuant to this Agreement.

   (a) Transfers to the Company. Notwithstanding anything to the contrary contained in this Agreement, a Shareholder may give, sell, transfer or otherwise dispose of all or any of his Shares to the Company at such price and on such terms and conditions as such Shareholder and the Board of Directors of the Company may agree.

   (b) Transfer to Others. Except as provided for in Paragraph 3(a) above, a Shareholder desiring to dispose of some or all of his Shares may do so only pursuant to a bona fide offer to purchase (the "Offer") and after compliance with the following provisions. Such Shareholder shall first give written notice to the Company and the other Shareholders of his intention to dispose of his Shares, identifying the number of Shares he desires to dispose of, the proposed purchase price per Share and the name of the proposed purchaser and attaching an exact copy of the Offer received by such Shareholder.

      (i) The Company's Right to Purchase. The Company shall have the exclusive right to purchase all of the Shares which the Offering Shareholder proposes to sell at the proposed purchase price per Share. The Company shall exercise this right to purchase by giving written notice to the Offering Shareholder (with a copy thereof to each of the Continuing Shareholders) within thirty (30) days after receipt of the notice from the Offering Shareholder (the "30-Day Period") that the Company elects to purchase the Shares subject to the Offer and setting forth a date and time for closing which shall be not later than ninety (90) days after the date of such notice from the Company. At the time of closing, the Offering Shareholder shall deliver to the Company certificates representing the Shares to be sold, together with stock powers duly endorsed in blank. The Shares shall be delivered by the Offering Shareholder free of any and all liens and encumbrances. All transfer taxes and documentary stamps shall be paid by the Offering Shareholder.

      (ii) The Continuing Shareholders Right to Purchase. If the Company fails to exercise its right to purchase pursuant to subparagraph (i) above, the Continuing Shareholders shall have the right for an additional period of thirty (30) days (the "Additional 30-Day Period") commencing at the expiration of the 30-Day Period to purchase the Shares which the Offering Shareholder proposes to sell at the proposed purchase price per Share. The Continuing Shareholders shall exercise this right to purchase by giving written notice to the Offering Shareholder prior to the expiration of the Additional 30-Day Period that they elect to purchase his Shares and setting forth a date and time for closing which shall be not later than ninety (90) days after the expiration of the Additional 30 Day Period. Any purchase of Shares by all or some of the Continuing Shareholders shall be made in such proportion as they might agree among themselves or, in the absence of any such agreement, pro rata in proportion to their ownership of Shares of the Company (excluding the Offering Shareholder's Shares) at the time of such offer, but in any event one or more of the Continuing Shareholders must agree to purchase all the Shares which the Offering Shareholder proposes to sell. At the time of closing, the Offering Shareholder shall deliver to Buyer certificates representing the Shares to be sold, together with stock powers duly endorsed in blank. Said Shares shall be delivered by the Offering Shareholder free and clear of any and all liens and encumbrances. All transfer taxes and documentary stamps shall be paid by the Offering Shareholder.

(iii) Performance of Acceptance. When exercising the rights granted in Paragraphs 3(b)(i) and (ii) hereof, Buyer must elect to purchase all Shares which the Offering Shareholder proposes to sell for the price and upon the same terms for payment of the price as are set forth in the Offer; provided, however, that if said offer received by the Offering Shareholder shall provide for any act or action to be done or performed by the party making such Offer at any time before or within thirty (30) days after the last day for exercise of Buyer's right to purchase pursuant to Paragraphs (3)(b)(i) and (ii) hereof, then the Buyer shall be deemed to have complied with the terms and conditions of such Offer if Buyer does or performs such act or action within thirty (30) days after the last day for exercise of Buyer's right to purchase pursuant to Paragraphs 3(b)(i) and (ii) hereof.

(iv) Sale to Third Party. If either the Company or some or all of the Continuing Shareholders do not elect to purchase all of the Shares which the Offering Shareholder proposes to sell, the Offering Shareholder may accept the Offer which the Offering Shareholder mailed with his notice to the Company pursuant to Paragraph 3(b) hereof and transfer all (but not less than all) of the Shares which he proposes to sell pursuant thereto on the same terms and conditions set forth in such Offer, provided that any transferee of such Shares shall be bound by this Agreement as provided by Paragraph 10 hereof, and further provided that if such sale is not completed within one hundred twenty (120) days after the date notice is received by the Company under Paragraph 3(b) hereof, all such Shares shall again become subject to the restrictions and provisions of this Agreement.

(v) Right of Co-Sale. Notwithstanding any other provision hereof, in the event the Offering Shareholder receives an Offer from an unaffiliated third party (the "Offeror") to purchase from such Shareholder not less than twenty percent (20%) of the Shares owned by such Shareholder and such Shareholder intends to accept such Offer, the Offering Shareholder shall, after complying with the provisions of Paragraph 3(b)(i) and (ii) above and before accepting such Offer, forward a copy of such Offer to the Company and each of the Continuing Shareholders. The Offering Shareholder shall not sell any such Shares to the Offeror unless the terms of the Offer are extended by the Offeror to the Continuing Shareholders pro rata in proportion to their ownership of Shares of the Company (excluding the Offering Shareholder's Shares) at the time of such Offer. The Continuing Shareholders shall have ten (10) days from the date of the foregoing Offer to accept such Offer.

(c) Share1, Share2 and Share3 may each during their lifetimes transfer all, but not less than all, of their Shares to said Shareholder's spouse or a lineal descendant of such Shareholder, so long as prior to such transfer (i) such person, the Company, and all the Shareholders amend this Agreement to the reasonable satisfaction of such person, the Company and all the Shareholders to provide the parties to this Agreement with the rights, remedies and effect provided in this Agreement as if no such transfer had occurred, and (ii) the proposed transferee agrees in a writing satisfactory to the Company and all Shareholders that such person shall vote for Share1, Share2 and Share3 (or their nominees) as directors of the Company in accordance with Paragraph 14 hereof and shall be bound by all the terms and conditions of this Agreement.

4. Right of First Refusal.

(a) Except in the case of Excluded Securities (as defined below), the Company shall not issue, sell or exchange, agree to issue, sell or exchange, or reserve or set aside for issuance, sale or exchange, any (i) shares of Common Stock or any other equity security of the Company which is convertible into Common Stock or any other equity security of the Company, (ii) any debt security of the Company which is convertible into Common Stock or any other equity security of the Company, or (iii) any option, warrant or other right to subscribe for, purchase or otherwise acquire any equity security or any such debt security of the Company, unless in each case the Company shall have first offered to sell to each Shareholder, pro rata in proportion to such Shareholder's then ownership of Shares of the Company, such securities (the "Offered Securities") (and to sell thereto such Offered Securities not subscribed for by the other Shareholders as hereinafter provided), at a price and on such other terms as shall have been specified by the Company in writing delivered to such Shareholder (the "Stock Offer"), which Stock Offer by its terms shall remain open and irrevocable of a period of 10 days (subject to extension pursuant to the last sentence of subsection (b) below) from the date it is delivered by the Company to the Shareholder.

(b) Notice of each Shareholder's intention to accept, in whole or in part, a Stock Offer shall be evidenced by a writing signed by such Shareholder and delivered to the Company prior to the end of the 10-day period of such Stock Offer, setting forth such portion of the Offered Securities as such Shareholder elects to purchase (the "Notice of Acceptance"). If any Shareholder shall subscribe for less than his pro rata share of the Offered Securities to be sold, the other subscribing Shareholders shall be entitled to purchase the balance of that Shareholder's pro rata share in the same proportion in which they were entitled to purchase the Offered Securities in the first instance (excluding for such purposes such Shareholder), provided any such other Shareholder elected by a Notice of Acceptance to purchase all of his pro rata share of the Offered Securities. The Company shall notify each Shareholder within five (5) days following the expiration of the 10-day period described above of the amount of Offered Securities which each Shareholder may purchase pursuant to the foregoing sentence, and each Shareholder shall then have ten (10) days from the delivery of such notice to indicate such additional amount, if any, that such Shareholder wishes to purchase.

(c) In the event that Notices of Acceptance are not given by the Shareholders in respect of all the Offered Securities, the Company shall have one hundred twenty (120) days from the expiration of the foregoing 10-day or 25-day period, whichever is applicable, to sell all or any part of such Offered Securities as to which a Notice of Acceptance has not been given by the Shareholders (the "Refused Securities") to any other person or persons, but only upon terms and conditions in all respects, including, without limitation, unit price and interest rates, which are no more favorable, in the aggregate, to such other person or persons or less favorable to the Company than those set forth in the Stock Offer. Upon the closing, which shall include full payment to the Company, of the sale to such other person or persons of all the Refused Securities, the Shareholders shall purchase from the Company, and the Company shall sell to the Shareholders the Offered Securities in respect of which Notices of Acceptance were delivered to the Company by the Shareholders, at the terms specified in the Stock Offer.

(d) In each case, any Offered Securities not purchased by the Shareholders or other person or persons in accordance with Section 4(c) may not be sold or otherwise disposed of until they are again offered to the Shareholders under the procedures specified in Sections 4(a), (b) and (c).

(e) The rights of the Shareholders under this Section 4 shall not apply to the following securities (the "Excluded Securities"):

(i) Any (A) shares of Common Stock or any other equity security of the Company which is convertible into Common Stock or any other equity security of the Company, (B) debt security of the Company which is convertible into Common Stock or any other equity security of the Company, or (C) option, warrant or other right to subscribe for, purchase or otherwise acquire any equity security or any such debt security of the Company (collectively, an "Equity Security") if the issuance of such Equity Security does not alter the respective proportions of ownership (on a fully diluted basis) by Share1, Share2 and Share3, as among themselves, of Equity Securities immediately prior to the issuance of such Equity Security;

(ii) Common Stock issued as a Stock dividend or upon any stock split or other subdivision or combination of the outstanding shares of Common Stock;

(iii) Securities issued pursuant to the acquisition by the Company of another corporation to the stockholders of such other corporation by merger or purchase of substantially all of the assets whereby the Company owns not less than fifty-one percent (51%) of the voting power of such other corporations; and

(iv) Common Stock issued in connection with a firm underwritten public offering of shares of Common Stock, registered pursuant to the Securities Act.

5. Sale or Redemption Upon Termination of Employment or Upon Disability or Upon Death. Upon the termination of a Management Shareholder's employment or other relationship with the Company (including without limitation, any position as an officer, director, consultant, joint venturer, independent contractor, or promoter to or of the Company) for whatever reason, the disability (as defined below) of a Management Shareholder, or the death of a Management or Nonmanagement Shareholder (any such event hereinafter a "Triggering Event"), such Shareholder (or his heirs, executors, guardian or personal representative) within sixty (60) days after the Triggering Event shall offer to sell all, but no less than all, of the Shares owned by the Shareholder. Each offer shall be made to the Company in writing and shall exist for a period of ninety (90) days after such offer has been received by the Company. If the Company fails to purchase all of the Shares offered, the offer to sell shall be made in writing to all of the Continuing Shareholders in such proportion as the Continuing Shareholders may agree among themselves, or in the absence of agreement, pro rata in proportion to their then ownership of Shares of the Company (excluding the Offering Shareholder's Shares), and shall exist for a period of ninety (90) days after the offer has been received by all of the Continuing Shareholders. For purposes of this Agreement, "disability" of a particular person means the inability, due to a physical or mental condition, of such person to maintain his employment or other relationship with the Company (including without limitation, fulfilling his duties in any position as an officer, director, consultant, joint venturer, independent contractor, or promoter to or of the Company) or to conduct his normal daily activities on behalf of the Corporation for any six (6) consecutive month period.

6. Purchase Price. The purchase price for all Shares purchased pursuant to Paragraph 5 hereof shall be determined as follows:

(a) The Company or the Continuing Shareholders, as the case may be, within thirty (30) days after receipt of any offer referred to in Paragraph 5 above, shall notify the Offering Shareholder of the price at which the Company or the Continuing Shareholders, as the case may be, are willing to purchase the Shares.

(b) In the event the Offering Shareholder objects to the purchase price established in accordance with Paragraph 6(a) above, the Offering Shareholder shall have the right to solicit offers to buy the Shares in accordance with the provisions of Paragraph 3(b) of this Agreement. The right to solicit offers shall be subject to the terms and conditions of Section 3(b) and (c) hereof, including without limitation, the rights of first refusal and co-sale and the period during which any right of first refusal must be exercised but shall not be subject to the one hundred twenty (120)-day period referred to in Paragraph 3(b)(iv) of this Agreement.

7. Payment of Purchase Price. The purchase price for all Shares purchased pursuant to Paragraph 5 hereof shall be paid at the closing of the sale.

8. Put and Call Options.

(a) Put and Call Options. Each Shareholder shall have the right and option upon the written declaration (a "Declaration") by such Shareholder to the other Shareholders and the Company of the occurrence of an "impasse" (as defined below) to sell to the Continuing Shareholders all of his Shares, and the Continuing Shareholders shall have the obligation to either (i) purchase all of such Shares owned by the offering Shareholder in such proportion as the Continuing Shareholders may agree upon, and if they cannot so agree, pro rata in proportion to their then ownership of Shares of the Company (excluding the Offering Shareholder's Shares) or (ii) if the Continuing Shareholders are unable or unwilling to purchase all of the Shares owned by the Offering Shareholder, sell all of their Shares to the Offering Shareholder, and the Offering Shareholder shall have the obligation to buy such Shares.

(b) Impasse. An "impasse" shall be conclusively evidenced by (i) either Share1, Share2 or Share3 or their respective representative, voting opposite the others at a vote at a shareholders meeting or at a vote at a meeting of the Board of Directors of the Company (or failing to attend such meetings upon due notice if such failure results in the lack of a quorum making such vote impossible), which vote is on a material issue, not in the ordinary course of business, and affecting the business, assets or operations of the Company, including, but not limited to, a proposal to merge, liquidate, consolidate or dissolve the Company, or to sell, lease or dispose of all or substantially all of the assets of the Company or to amend the substantive provisions of the Company's bylaws or articles of incorporation, or to issue or redeem stock, or to declare dividends of any kind, and (ii) either Share1, Share2 or Share3 notifying the others and the Company and any other Shareholders within thirty (30) days after such meeting, proposed meeting or vote that an "impasse" has occurred. The put and call rights granted to each Shareholder under this Paragraph 8 are independent of the other rights granted to the Shareholders and the Company under the other terms of this Agreement and such rights are not mutually exclusive or inconsistent.

(c) Exercise of Option. The Continuing Shareholders shall exercise any option provided for in this Paragraph 8 within thirty (30) days after receipt of a Declaration. Any closing of the sale of Shares pursuant to such exercise shall occur within ninety (90) days after receipt of a Declaration.

(d) Purchase Price. Any purchase or sale of Shares sold pursuant to this Paragraph 8 shall be at the price as set forth in the Declaration delivered by the Shareholder exercising his right to sell his shares and shall be paid at the closing of the sale of the Shares.

9. Rights Upon Registration. In the event that the Company shall register or qualify any or all of the common stock of the Company under the Securities Act of 1933, as amended (or any similar statute then in force), on an appropriate registration statement, the Company shall give the Shareholders written notice thereof, and upon written request of a Shareholder, received by the Company not later than fifteen (15) days after receipt by the Shareholder of such notice, the Company will include in the registration statement filed by the Company with the Securities and Exchange Commission all Shares held by such Shareholder with respect to which the Shareholder shall have so requested registration.

10. Agreement Binding on All Persons Interested in Shares. Each person who now or hereafter acquires any legal or equitable interest in any Shares shall be bound by the terms of this Agreement. No issuance or transfer of Shares shall be effective and the Company shall not enter any issue or transfer upon the stock books of the Company or issue a certificate in the name of any person unless the Company is satisfied that such person is, and in a manner satisfactory to the Company has acknowledged being, bound by this Agreement.

11. Closing. Except as otherwise agreed to or expressly provided for herein, closing pursuant to the exercise of a right to purchase or sell Shares pursuant to this Agreement shall be held at the principal executive offices of the Company.

12. Entry of Legend Upon Stock Certificates. The following legend shall be immediately entered on each stock certificate representing Shares owned by the Shareholders:

"The gift, sale, mortgage, pledge, hypothecation or other encumbering or transfer of the shares of the capital stock represented by this certificate is restricted in accordance with the terms and conditions of a Shareholders Agreement dated the (DATE) day of (YEAR), a copy of which is on file at the principal executive offices of the Company. Said Shareholders' Agreement restricts the ability of the Shareholder to sell, give, pledge, bequeath or otherwise transfer or dispose of this stock certificate and the shares of capital stock represented by it."

13. After Acquired Shares—Subsequent Shareholders. The terms and conditions of this Agreement shall specifically apply not only to Shares owned by Shareholders at the time of execution of this Agreement, but also to any Shares acquired by any Shareholder subsequent to such execution.

14. Board of Directors. At each election of the Board of Directors of the Company, the Shareholders shall vote their Shares to elect three directors of the Company, one director being Share1, or his nominee, one director being Share2, or his nominee, and one director being Share3, or his nominee.

15. Community and Marital Property Laws. Notwithstanding anything to the contrary contained herein, the following terms shall control to the extent community property laws or other marital property laws apply to the Shares of any Shareholder.

(a) Lifetime Transfers. The provisions of this Agreement regarding restrictions against the transfer of Shares shall apply to any interest of the spouse of any Shareholder in such Shares (said spouse is hereinafter referred to as a "Spouse").

(b) Transfers Upon Death of Spouse. If the Spouse of a Shareholder predeceases such Shareholder and has failed to bequeath to such Shareholder the deceased Spouse's entire marital property interest, if any, in the Shares held by the Shareholder, or if the Spouse of a Shareholder is adjudicated to be bankrupt or insolvent, or makes an assignment for the benefit of his or her creditors (collectively referred to herein as an "Event"), then to the extent necessary to divest the Spouse of any interest in the Shares of such Stockholder, within three (3) months after the date of the occurrence of the Event, the Shareholder shall have the option to and must purchase such marital property interest of his or her Spouse or the estate of the deceased Spouse, as the case may be, in the Shares held by the Shareholder at a price equal to the lesser of either the value of the Spouse's marital property interest in such Shares or the book value of such Shares.

(c) Marital Dissolution. Any decree of dissolution, separate maintenance agreement or other property settlement between a Shareholder and his or her Spouse shall provide that the entire marital property interest of the Spouse in the Shares of the Shareholder shall be granted to the Shareholder as part of the division of the property of the marriage and the Spouse shall release and the Shareholder shall accept any marital property interest of such Spouse in the Shares. If payment for such Shares is ordered by the Court or demanded by the Spouse, no consideration shall be required, but if the Shareholder volunteers consideration for said release of interest it shall be no greater than the lesser of either the value of the Spouse's marital property interest in such Shares or the book value of the Spouse's martial property interest in such Shares.

(d) Inclusion of Marital Property. Any purchase of the Shares of a Shareholder pursuant to any provision of this Agreement shall include without limitation or condition the entire marital property interest of the Spouse of such Shareholder in the Shares being purchased.

(e) Determination of Value. Book value and the value of a Spouse's interest in the Shares of a Shareholder for purposes of this Paragraph 15 shall be determined by the Shareholder. The Company and the other Shareholders shall not be responsible for the determination of the value of the marital property of any Spouse of a Shareholder, the determination of book value, or the purchase of or payment for such Spouse's marital property interest in the Shares of a Shareholder.

16. Insurance. The Company may, if it so desires, purchase insurance policies on the life of any Management Shareholder for the purpose of payment for stock purchases or as key man insurance. If any Shareholder on whose life the Company owns an insurance policy shall at any time during his lifetime sell all of his Shares, then that Shareholder shall have the right to purchase from the Company the insurance policy or policies on his life at the cash surrender value, if any. The Company shall deliver the policy or policies on the life of such Shareholder upon payment of the cash surrender value, if any, and shall execute any necessary instruments of transfer and change of beneficiary forms.

17. Subchapter S Election. The Company may elect to be taxed as a small business corporation under Subchapter S of the Internal Revenue Code, as amended from time to time (the "Code"), or such other provisions of law as may hereafter be applicable to such an election, and for state income tax purposes, if available (hereinafter, an "Election"). Each Shareholder and the Company agree to execute and file the necessary forms for making and maintaining an Election, and each Shareholder agrees to deliver to the Company the consent of the spouse of such Shareholder if such consent is required for the Election under any community or marital property laws or otherwise. The Shareholders and the Company agree that they will take such other actions as may be deemed necessary or advisable by counsel to the Company to exercise or maintain the Election. The Shareholders shall maintain the Election unless the Management Shareholders unanimously agree otherwise or in the event that the Board of Directors requests that the Shareholders revoke the election, in which case the Shareholders shall promptly execute and deliver to the Company such documents as may be necessary to revoke the Election. None of the Shareholders, without the consent of all of the Management Shareholders, shall take any action or position, or make any transfer or other disposition of his Shares of the Company which may result in the termination or revocation of the Election. In the event of an inadvertent termination of the Election as described in Section 1362(f) of the Code or other applicable law, the Shareholders shall agree to make such adjustments as may be required to continue the Election, as provided in Section 1362 (f)(4) of the Code or other applicable law.

18. Pro Rata Allocations. All items of income and loss of the Company shall be assigned pro rata to each day throughout the year. However, the Shareholders hereby consent to make an election pursuant to Section 1362(c)(3) of the Code or Section 1377(a)(2) of the Code in the event that the Board of Directors determines such elections to be in the best interest of a majority of the Shareholders.

19. Authorization. The Company is authorized to enter into this Agreement by virtue of a resolution passed at a meeting of the Board of Directors.

20. Notices. Notices and declarations under this Agreement shall be in writing and sent by registered or certified mail, return receipt requested, postage paid, to the Company at its principal executive offices and to Shareholders at their last address as shown on the records of the Company or at such other address with respect to any party hereto as such party shall notify the other Shareholders and the Company in writing in the manner specified herein.

21. Termination. The rights and obligations of the Company and the Shareholders under this Agreement shall terminate upon written agreement of all then existing Shareholders or upon the registration or qualification of any or all of the Common Stock of the Company pursuant to Paragraph 9 hereof.

22. Severability. The various provisions of this Agreement are severable from each other and from the other provisions of the Agreement, and in the event that any provision in this Agreement shall be held to be invalid or unenforceable by a court of competent jurisdiction, the remainder of this Agreement shall be fully effective, operative and enforceable.

23. Free and Clear of Encumbrances. All Shares sold pursuant to the terms of this Agreement shall be free of any and all liens and encumbrances and accompanied by stock powers duly endorsed in blank.

24. Binding Effect. This Agreement shall be binding upon and inure to the benefit of the parties hereto and their respective heirs, personal representatives, executors, administrators, successors and assigns.

25. Gender. Pronouns used herein are to be interpreted as referring to both the masculine and feminine gender.

26. Governing Law. This Agreement shall be construed and interpreted in accordance with the laws of the State of California without reference to conflict of laws principles except to the extent that the community or marital property laws of any state would otherwise be applicable to a particular situation, in which event, such community or marital property laws shall apply to the particular situation.

27. Entire Agreement. This instrument contains the entire agreement of the parties and may be changed only by an agreement in writing signed by the Company and all persons then owning Shares.

28. Counterparts. This Agreement may be executed in one or more counterparts each of which shall be deemed an original and all of which together shall be deemed to be one and the same instrument.

IN WITNESS WHEREOF, the parties hereto have duly executed this Agreement on the day and year set forth below.

_____   _____
Shareholder 1   Date

_____   _____
Shareholder 2   Date

_____   _____
Shareholder 3   Date

SPOUSAL CONSENT TO
SHAREHOLDERS AGREEMENT

The undersigned being the spouse of SHAREHOLDER [NUMBER], one of the Shareholders named in the foregoing Shareholders Agreement (the "Agreement"), hereby acknowledges that:

1. I have read the foregoing Agreement in its entirety and understand that:

    (a) Upon the occurrence of certain events as specified in the Agreement, the Company, my spouse, and the other Shareholders will have the right to and may be obligated to purchase Shares owned by another Shareholder at a price and on terms and conditions set forth in the Agreement;

    (b) Any purchase of the Shares of any Shareholder will include his or her entire interest in such Shares and any community property interest and other marital property interest of the spouse of such Shareholder; and

    (c) The Agreement imposes certain restrictions on any attempts by me to transfer any interest I may have in the Company or any Shares of the Company by virtue of my marriage and confers on my spouse the right and obligation to purchase any interest I may have in the Company or any Shares of the Company upon the occurrence of certain events.

2. I hereby approve and agree to be bound to all of the terms of the Agreement and agree that any interest (community property or otherwise) that I may have in the Company or any Shares of the Company shall be subject to the terms of this spousal consent and the Agreement.

3. I agree that my spouse may join in any future amendments of modifications to the Agreement without any notice to me and without any signature, acknowledgment, agreement or consent on my part.

4. I agree that I will transfer or bequeath any interest I may have in the Company or any Shares of the Company by my will, outright and free of trust to my spouse.

5. I acknowledge that I have been advised and have been encouraged to seek independent counsel of my own choosing to represent me in matters regarding the Shareholders Agreement and my execution of this spousal consent.

6. I hereby consent to the Company and my spouse making and maintaining the Subchapters S Election (if applicable) under the Internal Revenue Code, as amended from time to time.

_____   _____

Spouse's Signature   Date

WAIVER OF NOTICE OF
MEETING OF DIRECTORS

Reprinted by permission of the 'Lectric Law Library Legal Website at www.lectlaw.com.

WAIVER OF NOTICE
FIRST MEETING OF THE
BOARD OF DIRECTORS

[COMPANY NAME]

WE, THE UNDERSIGNED, being the directors elected by the incorporators of the above named corporation, DO HEREBY WAIVE NOTICE of the time, place and purpose of the first meeting of the Board of Directors of said corporation.

We designate the _____ th day of _____ , 19 _____ at 9:35 o'clock ____ .M. as the time and [FULL ADDRESS] as the place of said meeting; the purpose of said meeting being to elect officers, authorize the issue of the capital stock, authorize the purchase of property if necessary for the business of the corporation, and the transaction of such other business as may be necessary or advisable to facilitate and complete the organization of said corporation, and to enable it to carry on its contemplated business.

Dated: _____ , 19 _____

_____
[NAME 1]

_____
[NAME 2]

_____
[NAME 3]

MINUTES OF INITIAL MEETING
OF THE BOARD OF DIRECTORS

Reprinted by permission of the 'Lectric Law Library Legal Website at www.lectlaw.com.

MINUTES OF INITIAL MEETING
OF THE BOARD OF DIRECTORS
OF [NAME OF COMPANY]

The first meeting of the Board of Directors was held at [PLACE] on the _____ th day of
_____ , 19 _____ at _____ o'clock _____ .M.

Present:

[Name 1]

[Name 2]

[Name 3]

constituting a quorum of the Board.

[Name 3] acted as Chairman and [Name 3] was appointed temporary Secretary of the meeting.

The Secretary presented and read a waiver of notice of the meeting, signed by all the directors.

The minutes of the organization meeting of incorporators were read and approved.

The following persons were nominated to the offices set opposite their respective names, to serve for one year and until their successors are chosen and qualify:

[Name 2]–Chairman

[Name 3]–Vice-Chairman

[Name 1]–President

[Name 3]–Secretary

[Name 3]–Chief Financial Officer

All the directors present having voted, the Chairman announced that the aforesaid had been unanimously chosen as said officers, respectively.

The Chairman thereupon took the chair and the Secretary thereupon entered upon the discharge of his duties.

Upon motion, duly made, seconded and carried, it was RESOLVED, That the stock certificates of this corporation shall be in the form submitted at this meeting.

Upon motion, duly made, seconded and carried, it was RESOLVED, That the seal, an impression of which is herewith affixed, be adopted as the corporate seal of this corporation.

The Secretary was authorized and directed to procure the proper corporate books.

Upon motion, duly made, seconded and carried, it was RESOLVED, That the officers of this corporation be authorized and directed to open a bank account in the name of the corporation, in accordance with a form of bank resolution attached to the minutes of this meeting.

[Name 3] reported the following balances in the bank accounts of the corporation at [BANK]:

Savings # _____ : $ _____

Checking # _____ : $ _____

Upon motion, duly made, seconded and carried, the following preambles and resolutions were unanimously adopted:

WHEREAS, The following offer has been made to the corporation in consideration of the issuance of full paid and non-assessable shares of the corporation:

Price = $ _____ per share

_____ shares issued to [Name 1]

_____ shares issued to [Name 2]

_____ shares issued to [Name 3]

([Name 1], [Name 2] and [Name 3] hereafter known as "Offerors.")

WHEREAS, In the judgment of this Board of Directors of this corporation, said offer is good and sufficient consideration for the shares demanded therefor and necessary for the business of this corporation, Now, therefore, be it

RESOLVED, That the aforesaid offer be and is hereby accepted and that the President and Secretary of this corporation be and they hereby are authorized and directed to execute in the name and on behalf of this corporation, and under its corporate seal, such agreement or agreements as may be necessary in accordance with said offer.

FURTHER RESOLVED, That the President and Secretary be and they hereby are authorized and directed to issue and deliver in accordance with said offer certificates of full paid and non-assessable shares of this corporation to the said Offerors.

Upon motion, duly made, seconded and carried, the following preambles and resolutions were unanimously adopted:

WHEREAS, The following loans have been offered to the corporation in consideration of the issuance of promissory notes from the corporation:

[LIST]

WHEREAS, In the judgment of this Board of Directors of this corporation, said offer is good and sufficient consideration for the loan offered therefor and necessary for the business of this corporation,

Now, therefore, be it RESOLVED, That the aforesaid offer be and is hereby accepted and that the proper officers of this corporation be and they hereby are authorized and directed to execute in the name and on behalf of this corporation, and under its corporate seal, such agreements, copies of which are attached hereto, as may be necessary in accordance with said offer.

Upon motion, duly made, seconded and carried, it was

RESOLVED, That in compliance with the laws of the State of [State], this corporation have and continuously maintain a registered office within the State of [State] and have an agent at all times in charge thereof, upon which agent process against this corporation may be served, and that the books and records of the corporation shall be available for examination by any stockholder for any proper purpose as provided by law.

Upon motion, duly made, seconded and carried, it was

RESOLVED, That the proper officers of the corporation be and they hereby are authorized and directed on behalf of the corporation, and under its corporate seal, to make and file such certificate, report or other instrument as may be required by law to be filed in any state, territory, or dependency of the United States, or in any foreign country, in which said officers shall find it necessary or expedient to file the same to authorize the corporation to transact business in such state, territory, dependency or foreign country.

Upon motion, duly made, seconded and carried, it was

RESOLVED, That the Chief Financial Officer be and hereby is authorized to pay all fees and expenses incident to and necessary for the organization of the corporation.

There being no further business, the meeting upon motion adjourned.

_____
Secretary

MINUTES OF ORGANIZATIONAL
MEETING OF INCORPORATORS,
WITH WAIVER OF NOTICE

Reprinted by permission of the 'Lectric Law Library Legal Website at www.lectlaw.com.

WAIVER OF NOTICE OF
ORGANIZATION MEETING
OF INCORPORATORS

[NAME OF COMPANY]

WE, THE UNDERSIGNED, being all the incorporators of the corporation above named, organized under the laws of the State of [STATE], DO HEREBY WAIVE NOTICE of the time, place and purpose of the organization meeting of said incorporators, and do fix the _____ th day of _____ , _____ at _____ o'clock ____ .M. as the time, and [PLACE] as the place of said meeting.

And we do hereby waive all the requirements of the statutes of [STATE] as to the notice of this meeting, and do consent to the transaction of such business as may come before the meeting.

Dated: _____

_____
[NAME 1]

_____
[NAME 2]

_____
[NAME 3]

MINUTES OF ORGANIZATION
MEETING OF INCORPORATORS

Reprinted by permission of the 'Lectric Law Library Legal Website at www.lectlaw.com.

MINUTES OF ORGANIZATION
MEETING OF INCORPORATORS

[NAME OF COMPANY]

The organization meeting of the incorporators was held on the _____ th day of _____ , 19 ____ at [TIME] o'clock ____ . M., at [PLACE] pursuant to a written waiver of notice, signed by all the incorporators fixing said time and place.

The following incorporators were present in person:

[Name 1]

[Name 2]

[Name 3]

being all of the incorporators of the corporation.

[Name] acted as Chairman and [Name] was appointed Secretary of the meeting.

The Chairman announced that a Certificate of Incorporation had been issued to this corporation by the Department of State and that a certified copy of the Certificate had been forwarded for recording in the Office of the Recorder of Deeds and instructed the Secretary to cause a copy of the Certificate of Incorporation to be prefixed to the minutes.

Upon motion, duly made, seconded and carried, it was:
RESOLVED, That the Certificate of Incorporation of the corporation be and it hereby is accepted and that this corporation proceed to do business thereunder.
The Secretary presented a form of Bylaws for the regulation of the affairs of the corporation, which were read article by article.

Upon motion, duly made, seconded and carried:

RESOLVED, That the Bylaws presented at this meeting, as amended and attached to the Minutes, were unanimously adopted and the Secretary was instructed to cause the same to be inserted in the minute book immediately following the copy of the Certificate of Incorporation.

The Chairman stated that the next business before the meeting was the election of a Board of Directors.

After discussion, [Name 1], [Name 2] and [Name 3] were nominated for directors of the corporation, to hold office for the ensuing year and until others are chosen and qualified in their stead. No other nominations having been made, the vote was taken and the aforesaid nominees declared duly elected.

Upon motion, duly made, seconded and carried, it was RESOLVED, That the Board of Directors be and they are hereby authorized to issue the capital stock of this corporation to the full amount or number of shares authorized by the Certificate of Incorporation, in such amounts and proportions as from time to time shall be determined by the Board, and to accept in full or in part payment thereof such property as the Board may determine shall be good and sufficient consideration and necessary for the business of the corporation.

Upon motion, duly made, seconded and carried, the meeting thereupon adjourned.

     Secretary

SECTION 1244 CLAUSE

Reprinted by permission of the 'Lectric Law Library Legal Website at www.lectlaw.com.

SECTION 1244 CLAUSE

The Board of Directors has determined that the Corporation shall be organized and managed so that it is a "Small Business Corporation" as defined in IRC Sec. 1244 (c)(1), as amended, and so that the shares issued by the Corporation are "Section 1244 Stock" as defined in IRC Sec. 1244 (c)(1), as amended. Compliance with this section will enable shareholders to treat the loss on the sale or exchange of their shares as an "ordinary loss" on their personal income tax returns.

RESOLVED, that the proper officers of the Corporation are authorized to sell and issue common shares in an aggregate amount of money and other property (as a contribution to capital and as paid in surplus), which together with the aggregate amount of common shares outstanding at the time of issuance, does not exceed $1,000,000, and

RESOLVED, that the sale and issuance of shares shall be conducted in compliance with IRC Sec. 1244, so that the Corporation and its shareholders may obtain the benefits of IRC Sec. 1244, and further

RESOLVED, that the proper officers of the Corporation are directed to maintain such accounting records as are necessary so that any shareholder that experiences a loss on the transfer of common shares of the Corporation may determine whether they qualify for "ordinary loss" deduction treatment on their personal income tax returns.

MINUTES OF ANNUAL STOCKHOLDERS' MEETING

Reprinted by permission of the 'Lectric Law Library Legal Website at www.lectlaw.com.

MINUTES OF ANNUAL MEETING OF STOCKHOLDERS

OF

_____ , INC. was duly held on _____ , 19 ____
at _____ . All of the Directors of the Corporation were present and signed the Waiver of Notice which is on file herewith.

On motion duly made and seconded it was voted:

1. That _____ be elected Director of the Corporation for the coming year; and

2. that _____ be elected for the coming year.

3. [any other significant business]

There being no further business to come before the meeting at this time, it was voted to adjourn.

ATTEST: _____
                    Secretary

Form **1120**		U.S. Corporation Income Tax Return		OMB No. 1545-0123
Department of the Treasury Internal Revenue Service		For calendar year 1998 or tax year beginning .... , 1998, ending .... , 19 ... ▶ Instructions are separate. See page 1 for Paperwork Reduction Act Notice.		**1998**

A	Check if a:	Use IRS label. Other- wise, print or type.	Name		B Employer identification number
1	Consolidated return (attach Form 851) ☐				
2	Personal holding co. (attach Sch. PH) ☐		Number, street, and room or suite no. (If a P.O. box, see page 5 of instructions.)		C Date incorporated
3	Personal service corp. (as defined in Temporary Regs. sec. 1.441-4T— see instructions) ☐		City or town, state, and ZIP code		D Total assets (see page 5 of instructions)

E Check applicable boxes: (1) ☐ Initial return (2) ☐ Final return (3) ☐ Change of address $

Income	1a	Gross receipts or sales	**b** Less returns and allowances	**c** Bal ▶	1c
	2	Cost of goods sold (Schedule A, line 8)			2
	3	Gross profit. Subtract line 2 from line 1c			3
	4	Dividends (Schedule C, line 19)			4
	5	Interest			5
	6	Gross rents			6
	7	Gross royalties			7
	8	Capital gain net income (attach Schedule D (Form 1120))			8
	9	Net gain or (loss) from Form 4797, Part II, line 18 (attach Form 4797) .			9
	10	Other income (see page 6 of instructions—attach schedule)			10
	11	**Total income.** Add lines 3 through 10 . . . . ▶			11

Deductions (See instructions for limitations on deductions.)	12	Compensation of officers (Schedule E, line 4)			12
	13	Salaries and wages (less employment credits)			13
	14	Repairs and maintenance			14
	15	Bad debts			15
	16	Rents			16
	17	Taxes and licenses			17
	18	Interest			18
	19	Charitable contributions (see page 8 of instructions for 10% limitation) .			19
	20	Depreciation (attach Form 4562)	20		
	21	Less depreciation claimed on Schedule A and elsewhere on return . .	21a		21b
	22	Depletion			22
	23	Advertising			23
	24	Pension, profit-sharing, etc., plans			24
	25	Employee benefit programs			25
	26	Other deductions (attach schedule)			26
	27	**Total deductions.** Add lines 12 through 26 . . . . ▶			27
	28	Taxable income before net operating loss deduction and special deductions. Subtract line 27 from line 11			28
	29	**Less:** **a** Net operating loss deduction (see page 9 of instructions) . .	29a		
		b Special deductions (Schedule C, line 20)	29b		29c

Tax and Payments	30	**Taxable income.** Subtract line 29c from line 28				30
	31	**Total tax** (Schedule J, line 12)				31
	32	**Payments: a** 1997 overpayment credited to 1998	32a			
	b	1998 estimated tax payments . .	32b			
	c	Less 1998 refund applied for on Form 4466	32c (	) **d** Bal ▶	32d	
	e	Tax deposited with Form 7004			32e	
	f	Credit for tax paid on undistributed capital gains (attach Form 2439) . . .			32f	
	g	Credit for Federal tax on fuels (attach Form 4136). See instructions . . .			32g	32h
	33	Estimated tax penalty (see page 10 of instructions). Check if Form 2220 is attached . . . ▶ ☐				33
	34	**Tax due.** If line 32h is smaller than the total of lines 31 and 33, enter amount owed				34
	35	**Overpayment.** If line 32h is larger than the total of lines 31 and 33, enter amount overpaid . . .				35
	36	Enter amount of line 35 you want: **Credited to 1999 estimated tax** ▶ Refunded ▶				36

Sign Here	Under penalties of perjury, I declare that I have examined this return, including accompanying schedules and statements, and to the best of my knowledge and belief, it is true, correct, and complete. Declaration of preparer (other than taxpayer) is based on all information of which preparer has any knowledge.
	▶ _____ _____ ▶ _____ Signature of officer Date Title

Paid Preparer's Use Only	Preparer's signature	▶	Date	Check if self-employed ☐	Preparer's social security number
	Firm's name (or yours if self-employed) and address	▶		EIN ▶	
				ZIP code ▶	

Cat. No. 11450Q

182

Form 1120 (1998)   Page **2**

Schedule A   Cost of Goods Sold (See page 10 of instructions.)

1	Inventory at beginning of year	1		
2	Purchases	2		
3	Cost of labor	3		
4	Additional section 263A costs (attach schedule)	4		
5	Other costs (attach schedule)	5		
6	**Total.** Add lines 1 through 5	6		
7	Inventory at end of year	7		
8	**Cost of goods sold.** Subtract line 7 from line 6. Enter here and on page 1, line 2	8		

9a Check all methods used for valuing closing inventory:

   (i) ☐ Cost as described in Regulations section 1.471-3

   (ii) ☐ Lower of cost or market as described in Regulations section 1.471-4

   (iii) ☐ Other (Specify method used and attach explanation.) ▶ --

  b Check if there was a writedown of subnormal goods as described in Regulations section 1.471-2(c) . . . . ▶ ☐

  c Check if the LIFO inventory method was adopted this tax year for any goods (if checked, attach Form 970) . . . . . ▶ ☐

  d If the LIFO inventory method was used for this tax year, enter percentage (or amounts) of closing inventory computed under LIFO . . . . | 9d | |

  e If property is produced or acquired for resale, do the rules of section 263A apply to the corporation? . . . . . ☐ Yes ☐ No

  f Was there any change in determining quantities, cost, or valuations between opening and closing inventory? If "Yes," attach explanation . . . . ☐ Yes ☐ No

Schedule C   Dividends and Special Deductions (See page 11 of instructions.)

		(a) Dividends received	(b) %	(c) Special deductions (a) × (b)
1	Dividends from less-than-20%-owned domestic corporations that are subject to the 70% deduction (other than debt-financed stock)		70	
2	Dividends from 20%-or-more-owned domestic corporations that are subject to the 80% deduction (other than debt-financed stock)		80	
3	Dividends on debt-financed stock of domestic and foreign corporations (section 246A)		see instructions	
4	Dividends on certain preferred stock of less-than-20%-owned public utilities . . .		42	
5	Dividends on certain preferred stock of 20%-or-more-owned public utilities . . .		48	
6	Dividends from less-than-20%-owned foreign corporations and certain FSCs that are subject to the 70% deduction		70	
7	Dividends from 20%-or-more-owned foreign corporations and certain FSCs that are subject to the 80% deduction		80	
8	Dividends from wholly owned foreign subsidiaries subject to the 100% deduction (section 245(b))		100	
9	**Total.** Add lines 1 through 8. See page 12 of instructions for limitation			
10	Dividends from domestic corporations received by a small business investment company operating under the Small Business Investment Act of 1958		100	
11	Dividends from certain FSCs that are subject to the 100% deduction (section 245(c)(1))		100	
12	Dividends from affiliated group members subject to the 100% deduction (section 243(a)(3))		100	
13	Other dividends from foreign corporations not included on lines 3, 6, 7, 8, or 11 .			
14	Income from controlled foreign corporations under subpart F (attach Form(s) 5471) .			
15	Foreign dividend gross-up (section 78)			
16	IC-DISC and former DISC dividends not included on lines 1, 2, or 3 (section 246(d)) .			
17	Other dividends			
18	Deduction for dividends paid on certain preferred stock of public utilities			
19	**Total dividends.** Add lines 1 through 17. Enter here and on line 4, page 1 . . ▶			
20	**Total special deductions.** Add lines 9, 10, 11, 12, and 18. Enter here and on line 29b, page 1 . . . . . . ▶			

Schedule E   Compensation of Officers (See instructions for line 12, page 1.)

Complete Schedule E only if total receipts (line 1a plus lines 4 through 10 on page 1, Form 1120) are $500,000 or more.

(a) Name of officer	(b) Social security number	(c) Percent of time devoted to business	Percent of corporation stock owned		(f) Amount of compensation
			(d) Common	(e) Preferred	
1		%	%	%	
		%	%	%	
		%	%	%	
		%	%	%	
		%	%	%	

2	Total compensation of officers	
3	Compensation of officers claimed on Schedule A and elsewhere on return	
4	Subtract line 3 from line 2. Enter the result here and on line 12, page 1	

Form 1120 (1998)

Schedule J   Tax Computation (See page 13 of instructions.)

1 Check if the corporation is a member of a controlled group (see sections 1561 and 1563) . . . . ▶ ☐
   Important: Members of a controlled group, see instructions on page 13.

2a If the box on line 1 is checked, enter the corporation's share of the $50,000, $25,000, and $9,925,000 taxable income brackets (in that order):

(1) ☐ $ _____ | _____ | (2) ☐ $ _____ | _____ | (3) $ _____ | _____

b Enter the corporation's share of: (1) Additional 5% tax (not more than $11,750) $ _____ | _____
                                       (2) Additional 3% tax (not more than $100,000) $ _____ | _____

3 Income tax. Check if a qualified personal service corporation under section 448(d)(2) (see page 13) . ▶ ☐ | 3 |
4a Foreign tax credit (attach Form 1118) . . . . | 4a |
 b Possessions tax credit (attach Form 5735) . . . . | 4b |
 c Check: ☐ Nonconventional source fuel credit ☐ QEV credit (attach Form 8834) | 4c |
 d General business credit. Enter here and check which forms are attached: ☐ 3800
    ☐ 3468 ☐ 5884 ☐ 6478 ☐ 6765 ☐ 8586 ☐ 8830 ☐ 8826
    ☐ 8835 ☐ 8844 ☐ 8845 ☐ 8846 ☐ 8820 ☐ 8847 ☐ 8861 | 4d |
 e Credit for prior year minimum tax (attach Form 8827) . . . . | 4e |
5 **Total credits.** Add lines 4a through 4e . . . . | 5 |
6 Subtract line 5 from line 3 . . . . | 6 |
7 Personal holding company tax (attach Schedule PH (Form 1120)) . . . . | 7 |
8 Recapture taxes. Check if from: ☐ Form 4255 ☐ Form 8611 . . . . . . | 8 |
9 Alternative minimum tax (attach Form 4626) . . . . | 9 |
10 Add lines 6 through 9 . . . . | 10 |
11 Qualified zone academy bond credit (attach Form 8860) . . . . | 11 |
12 **Total tax.** Subtract line 11 from line 10. Enter here and on line 31, page 1 . . . . | 12 |

Schedule K   Other Information (See page 15 of instructions.)

		Yes	No
1	Check method of accounting: **a** ☐ Cash		
	b ☐ Accrual **c** ☐ Other (specify) ▶		
2	See page 17 of the instructions and state the:		
a	Business activity code no. (**NEW**) ▶		
b	Business activity ▶		
c	Product or service ▶		
3	At the end of the tax year, did the corporation own, directly or indirectly, 50% or more of the voting stock of a domestic corporation? (For rules of attribution, see section 267(c).)		
	If "Yes," attach a schedule showing: **(a)** name and identifying number, **(b)** percentage owned, and **(c)** taxable income or (loss) before NOL and special deductions of such corporation for the tax year ending with or within your tax year.		
4	Is the corporation a subsidiary in an affiliated group or a parent-subsidiary controlled group?		
	If "Yes," enter employer identification number and name of the parent corporation ▶		
5	At the end of the tax year, did any individual, partnership, corporation, estate or trust own, directly or indirectly, 50% or more of the corporation's voting stock? (For rules of attribution, see section 267(c).)		
	If "Yes," attach a schedule showing name and identifying number. (Do not include any information already entered in **4** above.) Enter percentage owned ▶		
6	During this tax year, did the corporation pay dividends (other than stock dividends and distributions in exchange for stock) in excess of the corporation's current and accumulated earnings and profits? (See sections 301 and 316.) . . .		
	If "Yes," file Form 5452. If this is a consolidated return, answer here for the parent corporation and on **Form 851,** Affiliations Schedule, for each subsidiary.		

		Yes	No
7	Was the corporation a U.S. shareholder of any controlled foreign corporation? (See sections 951 and 957.) . . .		
	If "Yes," attach Form 5471 for each such corporation. Enter number of Forms 5471 attached ▶		
8	At any time during the 1998 calendar year, did the corporation have an interest in or a signature or other authority over a financial account (such as a bank account, securities account, or other financial account) in a foreign country?		
	If "Yes," the corporation may have to file Form TD F 90-22.1. If "Yes," enter name of foreign country ▶		
9	During the tax year, did the corporation receive a distribution from, or was it the grantor of, or transferor to, a foreign trust? If "Yes," the corporation may have to file Form 3520 . .		
10	At any time during the tax year, did one foreign person own, directly or indirectly, at least 25% of: **(a)** the total voting power of all classes of stock of the corporation entitled to vote, or **(b)** the total value of all classes of stock of the corporation? If "Yes,"		
a	Enter percentage owned ▶		
b	Enter owner's country ▶		
c	The corporation may have to file Form 5472. Enter number of Forms 5472 attached ▶		
11	Check this box if the corporation issued publicly offered debt instruments with original issue discount . ▶ ☐		
	If so, the corporation may have to file Form 8281.		
12	Enter the amount of tax-exempt interest received or accrued during the tax year ▶ $		
13	If there were 35 or fewer shareholders at the end of the tax year, enter the number ▶		
14	If the corporation has an NOL for the tax year and is electing to forego the carryback period, check here ▶ ☐		
15	Enter the available NOL carryover from prior tax years (Do not reduce it by any deduction on line 29a.) ▶ $		

Form 1120 (1998)

Schedule L	Balance Sheets per Books	Beginning of tax year		End of tax year	
	Assets	(a)	(b)	(c)	(d)
1	Cash				
2a	Trade notes and accounts receivable . . .				
b	Less allowance for bad debts	( )		( )	
3	Inventories				
4	U.S. government obligations				
5	Tax-exempt securities (see instructions) . .				
6	Other current assets (attach schedule) . .				
7	Loans to stockholders				
8	Mortgage and real estate loans				
9	Other investments (attach schedule) . . .				
10a	Buildings and other depreciable assets . .				
b	Less accumulated depreciation	( )		( )	
11a	Depletable assets				
b	Less accumulated depletion	( )		( )	
12	Land (net of any amortization)				
13a	Intangible assets (amortizable only) . . .				
b	Less accumulated amortization	( )		( )	
14	Other assets (attach schedule)				
15	Total assets				
	Liabilities and Stockholders' Equity				
16	Accounts payable				
17	Mortgages, notes, bonds payable in less than 1 year				
18	Other current liabilities (attach schedule) . .				
19	Loans from stockholders				
20	Mortgages, notes, bonds payable in 1 year or more				
21	Other liabilities (attach schedule)				
22	Capital stock: a Preferred stock . . .				
	b Common stock . . .				
23	Additional paid-in capital				
24	Retained earnings—Appropriated (attach schedule)				
25	Retained earnings—Unappropriated . . .				
26	Adjustments to shareholders' equity (attach schedule)				
27	Less cost of treasury stock		( )		( )
28	Total liabilities and stockholders' equity . .				

Note: *You are not required to complete Schedules M-1 and M-2 below if the total assets on line 15, column (d) of Schedule L are less than $25,000.*

Schedule M-1	Reconciliation of Income (Loss) per Books With Income per Return (See page 16 of instructions.)

1	Net income (loss) per books		7	Income recorded on books this year not included on this return (itemize):	
2	Federal income tax			Tax-exempt interest $	
3	Excess of capital losses over capital gains .			....	
4	Income subject to tax not recorded on books this year (itemize):		8	Deductions on this return not charged against book income this year (itemize):	
	....		a	Depreciation . . . . $..........	
5	Expenses recorded on books this year not deducted on this return (itemize):		b	Contributions carryover $	
a	Depreciation . . . . $			....	
b	Contributions carryover $			....	
c	Travel and entertainment $				
	....		9	Add lines 7 and 8	
6	Add lines 1 through 5		10	Income (line 28, page 1)—line 6 less line 9	

Schedule M-2	Analysis of Unappropriated Retained Earnings per Books (Line 25, Schedule L)

1	Balance at beginning of year		5	Distributions: a Cash	
2	Net income (loss) per books			b Stock	
3	Other increases (itemize):			c Property	
	....		6	Other decreases (itemize):	
	....		7	Add lines 5 and 6	
4	Add lines 1, 2, and 3		8	Balance at end of year (line 4 less line 7)	

⊛

Form **1120-A**	**U.S. Corporation Short-Form Income Tax Return**	OMB No. 1545-0890
Department of the Treasury Internal Revenue Service	See separate instructions to make sure the corporation qualifies to file Form 1120-A. For calendar year 1998 or tax year beginning ...., 1998, ending ...., 19.....	**1998**

A Check this box if the corp. is a personal service corp. (as defined in Temporary Regs. section 1.441-4T—see instructions) ▶ ☐	Use IRS label. Other-wise, print or type.	Name	**B** Employer identification number
		Number, street, and room or suite no. (If a P.O. box, see page 5 of instructions.)	**C** Date incorporated
		City or town, state, and ZIP code	**D** Total assets (see page 5 of instructions) $

E Check applicable boxes: (1) ☐ Initial return (2) ☐ Change of address

F Check method of accounting: (1) ☐ Cash (2) ☐ Accrual (3) ☐ Other (specify) . . ▶

Income

1a Gross receipts or sales	**b** Less returns and allowances	**c** Balance ▶	**1c**
2 Cost of goods sold (see page 10 of instructions)			**2**
3 Gross profit. Subtract line 2 from line 1c			**3**
4 Domestic corporation dividends subject to the 70% deduction			**4**
5 Interest			**5**
6 Gross rents .			**6**
7 Gross royalties .			**7**
8 Capital gain net income (attach Schedule D (Form 1120)) . .			**8**
9 Net gain or (loss) from Form 4797, Part II, line 18 (attach Form 4797)			**9**
10 Other income (see page 6 of instructions)			**10**
11 **Total income.** Add lines 3 through 10 . . . . ▶			**11**

Deductions

(See instructions for limitations on deductions.)

12 Compensation of officers (see page 7 of instructions)			**12**
13 Salaries and wages (less employment credits)			**13**
14 Repairs and maintenance			**14**
15 Bad debts			**15**
16 Rents			**16**
17 Taxes and licenses			**17**
18 Interest			**18**
19 Charitable contributions (see page 8 of instructions for 10% limitation)			**19**
20 Depreciation (attach Form 4562)	**20**		
21 Less depreciation claimed elsewhere on return	**21a**		**21b**
22 Other deductions (attach schedule)			**22**
23 **Total deductions.** Add lines 12 through 22 . . . . . . ▶			**23**
24 Taxable income before net operating loss deduction and special deductions. Subtract line 23 from line 11			**24**
25 **Less: a** Net operating loss deduction (see page 9 of instructions). .	**25a**		
b Special deductions (see page 11 of instructions)	**25b**		**25c**

Tax and Payments

26 **Taxable income.** Subtract line 25c from line 24			**26**
27 **Total tax** (from page 2, Part I, line 7)			**27**
28 **Payments:**			
a 1997 overpayment credited to 1998	**28a**		
b 1998 estimated tax payments .	**28b**		
c Less 1998 refund applied for on Form 4466	**28c** ( )	**Bal ▶**	**28d**
e Tax deposited with Form 7004			**28e**
f Credit for tax paid on undistributed capital gains (attach Form 2439).			**28f**
g Credit for Federal tax on fuels (attach Form 4136). See instructions .			**28g**
h Total payments. Add lines 28d through 28g			**28h**
29 Estimated tax penalty (see page 10 of instructions). Check if Form 2220 is attached . . . . ▶ ☐			**29**
30 Tax due. If line 28h is smaller than the total of lines 27 and 29, enter amount owed			**30**
31 Overpayment. If line 28h is larger than the total of lines 27 and 29, enter amount overpaid . . .			**31**
32 Enter amount of line 31 you want: **Credited to 1999 estimated tax ▶**		**Refunded ▶**	**32**

Sign Here

Under penalties of perjury, I declare that I have examined this return, including accompanying schedules and statements, and to the best of my knowledge and belief, it is true, correct, and complete. Declaration of preparer (other than taxpayer) is based on all information of which preparer has any knowledge.

▶ Signature of officer	Date	▶ Title

Paid Preparer's Use Only	Preparer's signature ▶	Date	Check if self-employed ▶ ☐	Preparer's social security number
	Firm's name (or yours if self-employed) and address ▶		EIN ▶	
			ZIP code ▶	

For Paperwork Reduction Act Notice, see page 1 of the instructions.   Cat. No. 11456E   Form **1120-A** (1998)

Form 1120-A (1998) Page **2**

Part I Tax Computation (See page 13 of instructions.)

1 Income tax. If the corporation is a qualified personal service corporation (see page 13), check here ▶ ☐	**1**	
2a General business credit. Check if from Form(s): ☐ 3800 ☐ 3468		
☐ 5884 ☐ 6478 ☐ 6765 ☐ 8586 ☐ 8830 ☐ 8826		
☐ 8835 ☐ 8844 ☐ 8845 ☐ 8846 ☐ 8820 ☐ 8847 ☐ 8861 **2a**		
b Credit for prior year minimum tax (attach Form 8827) **2b**		
3 **Total credits.** Add lines 2a and 2b	**3**	
4 Subtract line 3 from line 1	**4**	
5 Recapture taxes. Check if from: ☐ Form 4255 ☐ Form 8611 . . .	**5**	
6 Alternative minimum tax (attach Form 4626)	**6**	
7 **Total tax.** Add lines 4 through 6. Enter here and on line 27, page 1	**7**	

Part II Other Information (See page 15 of instructions.)

1 See page 17 and state the: **a** Business activity code no. **(NEW)** ▶ ....

 b Business activity ▶ ....

 c Product or service ▶ ....

2 At the end of the tax year, did any individual, partnership, estate, or trust own, directly or indirectly, 50% or more of the corporation's voting stock? (For rules of attribution, see section 267(c).) . . . . ☐ Yes ☐ No

 If "Yes," attach a schedule showing name and identifying number.

3 Enter the amount of tax-exempt interest received or accrued during the tax year . . . . ▶ |$ |

4 Enter amount of cash distributions and the book value of property (other than cash) distributions made in this tax year . . . . ▶ |$ |

5a If an amount is entered on line 2, page 1, enter amounts from worksheet on page 11:

 (1) Purchases . . . .

 (2) Additional sec. 263A costs (attach schedule) . . . .

 (3) Other costs (attach schedule) .

 b If property is produced or acquired for resale, do the rules of section 263A apply to the corporation? . . . . . ☐ Yes ☐ No

6 At any time during the 1998 calendar year, did the corporation have an interest in or a signature or other authority over a financial account (such as a bank account, securities account, or other financial account) in a foreign country? . . . . . ☐ Yes ☐ No
 If "Yes," the corporation may have to file Form TD F 90-22.1
 If "Yes," enter the name of the foreign country ▶ ....

Part III Balance Sheets per Books

		(a) Beginning of tax year		(b) End of tax year	
Assets	1 Cash				
	2a Trade notes and accounts receivable				
	b Less allowance for bad debts	(	)	(	)
	3 Inventories				
	4 U.S. government obligations				
	5 Tax-exempt securities (see instructions)				
	6 Other current assets (attach schedule)				
	7 Loans to stockholders				
	8 Mortgage and real estate loans				
	9a Depreciable, depletable, and intangible assets . . .				
	b Less accumulated depreciation, depletion, and amortization	(	)	(	)
	10 Land (net of any amortization)				
	11 Other assets (attach schedule)				
	12 Total assets				
Liabilities and Stockholders' Equity	13 Accounts payable				
	14 Other current liabilities (attach schedule)				
	15 Loans from stockholders				
	16 Mortgages, notes, bonds payable				
	17 Other liabilities (attach schedule)				
	18 Capital stock (preferred and common stock)				
	19 Additional paid-in capital				
	20 Retained earnings				
	21 Adjustments to shareholders' equity (attach schedule) .				
	22 Less cost of treasury stock	(	)	(	)
	23 Total liabilities and stockholders' equity				

Part IV Reconciliation of Income (Loss) per Books With Income per Return (You are not required to complete Part IV if the total assets on line 12, column (b), Part III are less than $25,000.)

1 Net income (loss) per books		6 Income recorded on books this year not included on this return (itemize)..................	
2 Federal income tax.			
3 Excess of capital losses over capital gains. .		7 Deductions on this return not charged against book income this year (itemize)..................	
4 Income subject to tax not recorded on books this year (itemize)		....	
5 Expenses recorded on books this year not deducted on this return (itemize)		8 Income (line 24, page 1). Enter the sum of lines 1 through 5 less the sum of lines 6 and 7 . . .	

187

SCHEDULE D (Form 1120)	Capital Gains and Losses	OMB No. 1545-0123

Department of the Treasury Internal Revenue Service

To be filed with Forms 1120, 1120-A, 1120-IC-DISC, 1120-F, 1120-FSC, 1120-H, 1120-L, 1120-ND, 1120-PC, 1120-POL, 1120-REIT, 1120-RIC, 1120-SF, 990-C, and certain Forms 990-T

1998

Name _____ Employer identification number _____

Part I Short-Term Capital Gains and Losses—Assets Held One Year or Less

(a) Kind of property and description (Example, 100 shares of Z Co.)	(b) Date acquired (mo., day, yr.)	(c) Date sold (mo., day, yr.)	(d) Sales price (see instructions)	(e) Cost or other basis (see instructions)	(f) Gain or (loss) ((d) less (e))
1					

2 Short-term capital gain from installment sales from Form 6252, line 26 or 37 . . . . **2**
3 Short-term gain or (loss) from like-kind exchanges from Form 8824 . . . . **3**
4 Unused capital loss carryover (attach computation) . . . . **4** ( )
5 Net short-term capital gain or (loss). Combine lines 1 through 4 . . . . **5**

Part II Long-Term Capital Gains and Losses—Assets Held More Than One Year

6					

7 Enter gain from Form 4797, column (g), line 7 or 9 . . . . **7**
8 Long-term capital gain from installment sales from Form 6252, line 26 or 37 . . . . **8**
9 Long-term gain or (loss) from like-kind exchanges from Form 8824 . . . . **9**
10 Net long-term capital gain or (loss). Combine lines 6 through 9 . . . . **10**

Part III Summary of Parts I and II

11 Enter excess of net short-term capital gain (line 5) over net long-term capital loss (line 10). . . **11**
12 Net capital gain. Enter excess of net long-term capital gain (line 10) over net short-term capital loss (line 5) **12**
13 Add lines 11 and 12. Enter here and on Form 1120, page 1, line 8, or the proper line on other returns. **13**
Note: If losses exceed gains, see **Capital losses** in the instructions below.

Instructions

Section references are to the Internal Revenue Code unless otherwise noted.

Purpose of Schedule

Use Schedule D to report sales and exchanges of capital assets and gains on distributions to shareholders of appreciated capital assets.

Report sales, exchanges, and distributions of property other than capital assets on **Form 4797**, Sales of Business Property. Include on Form 4797 a sale, exchange, or distribution of property used in a trade or business; involuntary conversions (from other than casualties or thefts); gain from the disposition of oil, gas, or geothermal property; and the section 291 adjustment to section 1250 gains. See the instructions for Form 4797 for more details.

If property is involuntarily converted because of a casualty or theft, use **Form 4684**, Casualties and Thefts.

Parts I and II

Generally, a corporation must report sales and exchanges even if there is no gain or loss. Use Part I to report the sale, exchange, or distribution of capital assets held one year or less. Use Part II to report the sale, exchange, or distribution of capital assets held more than one year. Use the trade dates for the dates of acquisition and sale of stocks and bonds on an exchange or over-the-counter market.

What is a capital asset? Each item of property the corporation held (whether or not connected with its trade or business) is a capital asset **except:**

1. Assets properly included in inventory or property held mainly for sale to customers.

2. Depreciable or real property used in the trade or business.

3. Certain copyrights; literary, musical, or artistic compositions; letters or memoranda; or similar property.

4. Accounts or notes receivable acquired in the ordinary course of trade or business for services rendered or from the sale of property described in **1** above.

5. U.S. Government publications, including the Congressional Record, that the corporation received from the Government, other than by purchase at the normal sales price, or that the corporation got from another taxpayer who had received it in a similar way, if the corporation's basis is determined by reference to the previous owner's basis.

Capital losses. Capital losses are allowed only to the extent of capital gains. A net capital loss is carried back 3 years and forward 5 years as a short-term capital loss. Carry back a capital loss to the extent it does not increase or produce a net operating loss in the tax year to which it is carried. Foreign expropriation capital losses cannot be carried back, but are carried forward 10 years. A net capital loss for a regulated investment company is carried forward 8 years.

For Paperwork Reduction Act Notice, see page 1 of the Instructions for Forms 1120 and 1120-A. Cat. No. 11460M Schedule D (Form 1120) 1998

Special Rules for the Treatment of Certain Gains and Losses

Note: *For more information, get **Pub. 544**, Sales and Other Dispositions of Assets, and **Pub. 542**, Corporations.*

● **Loss from a sale or exchange between the corporation and a related person.** Except for distributions in complete liquidation of a corporation, no loss is allowed from the sale or exchange of property between the corporation and certain related persons. See section 267 for details.

● **Loss from a wash sale.** The corporation cannot deduct a loss from a wash sale of stock or securities (including contracts or options to acquire or sell stock or securities) unless the corporation is a dealer in stock or securities and the loss was sustained in a transaction made in the ordinary course of the corporation's trade or business. A wash sale occurs if the corporation acquires (by purchase or exchange), or has a contract or option to acquire, substantially identical stock or securities within 30 days before or after the date of the sale or exchange. See section 1091 for more information.

● **Like-kind exchanges.** An exchange of business or investment property for property of a like kind is reported on **Form 8824**, Like-Kind Exchanges.

● **At-risk limitations (section 465).** If the corporation sold or exchanged a capital asset used in an activity to which the at-risk rules apply, combine the gain or loss on the sale or exchange with the profit or loss from the activity. If the result is a net loss, complete **Form 6198**, At-Risk Limitations. Report any gain from the capital asset on Schedule D and on Form 6198.

● **Gains and losses from passive activities.** A closely held or personal service corporation that has a gain or loss that relates to a passive activity (section 469) may be required to complete **Form 8810**, Corporate Passive Activity Loss and Credit Limitations, before completing Schedule D. A Schedule D loss may be limited under the passive activity rules. See Form 8810 for more detailed information.

● **Gain on distributions of appreciated property.** Generally, gain (but not loss) is recognized on a nonliquidating distribution of appreciated property to the extent that the property's fair market value exceeds its adjusted basis. See section 311 for more information.

● **Gain or loss on distribution of property in complete liquidation.** Generally, gain or loss is recognized on property distributed in a complete liquidation. Treat the property as if it had been sold at its fair market value. An exception to this rule applies for liquidations of certain subsidiaries. See sections 336 and 337 for more information and other exceptions to the general rules.

● **Gains and losses on section 1256 contracts and straddles.** Use **Form 6781**, Gains and Losses From Section 1256 Contracts and Straddles, to report these gains and losses.

● **Gain or loss on certain short-term Federal, state, and municipal obligations.** Such obligations are treated as capital assets in determining gain or loss. On any gain realized, a portion is treated as ordinary income and the balance as a short-term capital gain. See section 1271.

● **Gain from installment sales.** If the corporation has a gain this year from the casual sale of real or personal property (other than inventory) and is to receive any payment in a later year, it must use the installment method (unless it elects not to—see below) and file **Form 6252**, Installment Sale Income. Also use Form 6252 if a payment is received this year from a sale made in an earlier year on the installment method.

The corporation may elect out of the installment method by reporting the full amount of the gain on a timely filed return (including extensions).

The installment method may not be used for sales of stock or securities (or certain other property described in the regulations) traded on an established securities market. See section 453(k).

● **Rollover of publicly traded securities gain into specialized small business investment companies (SSBICs).** A corporation that sells publicly traded securities at a gain may elect under section 1044 to postpone all or part of the gain if the seller buys stock or a partnership interest in an SSBIC during the 60-day period that begins on the date the securities are sold.

An SSBIC is any partnership or corporation licensed by the Small Business Administration under section 301(d) of the Small Business Investment Act of 1958. The corporation must recognize gain on the sale to the extent the proceeds from the sale exceed the cost of the SSBIC stock or partnership interest purchased during the 60-day period that began on the date of the sale (and not previously taken into account). The gain a corporation may postpone each tax year is limited to the lesser of **(a)** $250,000 or **(b)** $1 million, reduced by the gain previously excluded under section 1044. The basis of the SSBIC stock or partnership interest is reduced by any postponed gain.

To make the election to postpone gain, complete line 1 or line 6, whichever applies, showing the entire gain realized in column (f). Directly below the line on which the gain is reported, enter "SSBIC Rollover" in column (a). Enter the amount of the postponed gain (in parentheses) in column (f). Also, attach a schedule showing **(a)** how you figured the postponed gain, **(b)** the name of the SSBIC in which you purchased common stock or a partnership interest, **(c)** the date of that purchase, and **(d)** the new basis in that SSBIC stock or partnership interest.

For more details, see section 1044.

● **Gain or loss on an option to buy or sell property.** See sections 1032 and 1234 for the rules that apply to a purchaser or grantor of an option.

● **Gain or loss from a short sale of property.** Report the gain or loss to the extent that the property used to close the short sale is considered a capital asset in the hands of the taxpayer.

● **Constructive sales treatment for certain appreciated financial positions.** Generally, if the corporation holds an appreciated financial position in stock or certain other interests, it may have to recognize gain if it enters into a constructive sale (such as a "short sale against the box"). See **Pub. 550**, Investment Income and Expenses, for more details.

● **Gains and losses of foreign corporations from the disposition of investment in U.S. real property.** Foreign corporations are required to report gains and losses from the disposition of U.S. real property interests. See section 897 for details.

● **Gains on certain insurance property.** Form 1120-L filers with gains on property held on December 31, 1958, and certain substituted property acquired after 1958 should see section 818(c).

● **Loss from the sale or exchange of capital assets of an insurance company taxable under section 831.** Under the provisions of section 834(c)(6), capital losses of a casualty insurance company are deductible to the extent that the assets were sold to meet abnormal insurance losses or to provide for the payment of dividend and similar distributions to policyholders.

● **Loss from securities that are capital assets that become worthless during the year.** Except for securities held by a bank, treat the loss as a capital loss as of the last day of the tax year. (See section 582 for the rules on the treatment of securities held by a bank.)

● **Disposition of market discount bonds.** See section 1276 for rules on the disposition of market discount bonds.

● **Capital gain distributions.** Report capital gain distributions paid by regulated investment companies or real estate investment trusts as long-term capital gains on line 6 regardless of how long the corporation owned stock in the fund.

Specific Instructions

Lines 1 and 6, column (d). Enter either the gross sales price or the net sales price. If the net sales price is entered, do not increase the cost or other basis in column (e) by any expenses reflected in the net sales price.

Lines 1 and 6, column (e). In determining gain or loss, the basis of property will generally be its cost. See section 1012 and the related regulations. Exceptions to the general rule are provided in sections in subchapters C, K, O, and P of the Code. For example, if the corporation acquired the property by dividend, liquidation of a corporation, transfer from a shareholder, reorganization, bequest, contribution or gift, tax-free exchange, involuntary conversion, certain asset acquisitions, or wash sale of stock, see sections 301 (or 1059), 334, 362 (or 358), 1014, 1015, 1031, 1033, 1060, and 1091, respectively. Attach an explanation if the corporation uses a basis other than actual cash cost of the property.

If the gross sales price is reported in column (d), increase the cost or other basis by any expense of sale such as broker's fees, commissions, or option premiums before entering an amount in column (e).

If the corporation is allowed a charitable contribution deduction because it sold property in a bargain sale to a charitable organization, figure the adjusted basis for determining gain from the sale by dividing the amount realized by the fair market value and multiplying that result by the adjusted basis. No loss is allowed in a bargain sale to a charity.

See section 852(f) for the treatment of certain load charges incurred in acquiring stock in a mutual fund with a reinvestment right.

Form **1120-W**
(WORKSHEET)

Department of the Treasury
Internal Revenue Service

Estimated Tax for Corporations

For calendar year 1999, or tax year beginning .... , 1999, and ending .... , ...

(Keep for the corporation's records—Do *not* send to the Internal Revenue Service.)

OMB No. 1545-0975

1999

1	Taxable income expected in the tax year	**1**	
	(Qualified personal service corporations (defined in the instructions), skip lines 2 through 13 and go to line 14.)		
2	Enter the smaller of line 1 or $50,000. (Members of a controlled group, see instructions.) . .	**2**	
3	Subtract line 2 from line 1	**3**	
4	Enter the smaller of line 3 or $25,000. (Members of a controlled group, see instructions.) . .	**4**	
5	Subtract line 4 from line 3	**5**	
6	Enter the smaller of line 5 or $9,925,000. (Members of a controlled group, see instructions.) .	**6**	
7	Subtract line 6 from line 5	**7**	
8	Multiply line 2 by 15%	**8**	
9	Multiply line 4 by 25%	**9**	
10	Multiply line 6 by 34%	**10**	
11	Multiply line 7 by 35%	**11**	
12	If line 1 is greater than $100,000, enter the smaller of 5% of the excess over $100,000 or $11,750. Otherwise, enter -0-. (Members of a controlled group, see instructions.)	**12**	
13	If line 1 is greater than $15 million, enter the smaller of 3% of the excess over $15 million or $100,000. Otherwise, enter -0-. (Members of a controlled group, see instructions.)	**13**	
14	**Total.** Add lines 8 through 13. (Qualified personal service corporations, multiply line 1 by 35%.)	**14**	
15	Estimated tax credits (see instructions)	**15**	
16	Subtract line 15 from line 14	**16**	
17	Recapture taxes	**17**	
18	Alternative minimum tax (see instructions)	**18**	
19	Add lines 16 through 18	**19**	
20	Qualified zone academy bond credit (see instructions)	**20**	
21	**Total.** Subtract line 20 from line 19	**21**	
22	Credit for Federal tax paid on fuels (see instructions)	**22**	
23	Subtract line 22 from line 21. **Note:** *If the result is less than $500, the corporation is not required to make estimated tax payments*	**23**	
24a	Enter the tax shown on the corporation's 1998 tax return. **CAUTION: *See instructions before completing this line***	**24a**	
b	Enter the smaller of line 23 or line 24a. If the corporation is required to skip line 24a, enter the amount from line 23 on line 24b	**24b**	

		(a)	(b)	(c)	(d)
25	**Installment due dates.** (See instructions.) . . . . . ▶	**25**			
26	**Required installments.** Enter 25% of line 24b in columns **(a)** through **(d)** unless the corporation uses the annualized income installment method, the adjusted seasonal installment method, or is a "large corporation." (See instructions.)	**26**			

For Paperwork Reduction Act Notice, see the instructions on page 6.   Cat. No. 11525G   Form **1120-W** (1999)

Schedule A Annualized Income Installment Method and/or Adjusted Seasonal Installment Method. (See pages 5 and 6 of the instructions.)

Part I—Annualized Income Installment Method

			(a)	(b)	(c)	(d)
1	Annualization periods (see instructions).	1	First ___ months	First ___ months	First ___ months	First ___ months
2	Enter taxable income for each annualization period (see instructions).	2				
3	Annualization amounts (see instructions).	3				
4	Annualized taxable income. Multiply line 2 by line 3.	4				
5	Figure the tax on the amount in each column on line 4 by following the same steps used to figure the tax for line 14, page 1 of Form 1120-W.	5				
6	Enter other taxes for each annualization period (see instructions).	6				
7	Total tax. Add lines 5 and 6.	7				
8	For each annualization period, enter the same type of credits as allowed on lines 15, 20, and 22, page 1 of Form 1120-W (see instructions).	8				
9	Total tax after credits. Subtract line 8 from line 7. If zero or less, enter -0-.	9				
10	Applicable percentage.	10	25%	50%	75%	100%
11	Multiply line 9 by line 10.	11				
12	Add the amounts in all preceding columns of line 41 (see instructions).	12	/////			
13	**Annualized income installments.** Subtract line 12 from line 11. If zero or less, enter -0-.	13				

Part II—Adjusted Seasonal Installment Method
(Use this method only if the base period percentage for any 6 consecutive months is at least 70%.)

			(a)	(b)	(c)	(d)
14	Enter taxable income for the following periods:		First 3 months	First 5 months	First 8 months	First 11 months
a	Tax year beginning in 1996	14a				
b	Tax year beginning in 1997	14b				
c	Tax year beginning in 1998	14c				
15	Enter taxable income for each period for the tax year beginning in 1999.	15				
16	Enter taxable income for the following periods:		First 4 months	First 6 months	First 9 months	Entire year
a	Tax year beginning in 1996	16a				
b	Tax year beginning in 1997	16b				
c	Tax year beginning in 1998	16c				
17	Divide the amount in each column on line 14a by the amount in column (d) on line 16a.	17				
18	Divide the amount in each column on line 14b by the amount in column (d) on line 16b.	18				
19	Divide the amount in each column on line 14c by the amount in column (d) on line 16c.	19				

Form 1120-W (WORKSHEET) 1999   Page **3**

			(a) First 4 months	(b) First 6 months	(c) First 9 months	(d) Entire year
20	Add lines 17 through 19.	20				
21	Divide line 20 by 3.	21				
22	Divide line 15 by line 21.	22				
23	Figure the tax on the amount on line 22 by following the same steps used to figure the tax for line 14, page 1 of Form 1120-W.	23				
24	Divide the amount in columns (a) through (c) on line 16a by the amount in column (d) on line 16a.	24				
25	Divide the amount in columns (a) through (c) on line 16b by the amount in column (d) on line 16b.	25				
26	Divide the amount in columns (a) through (c) on line 16c by the amount in column (d) on line 16c.	26				
27	Add lines 24 through 26.	27				
28	Divide line 27 by 3.	28				
29	Multiply the amount in columns (a) through (c) of line 23 by the amount in the corresponding column of line 28. In column (d), enter the amount from line 23, column (d).	29				
30	Enter other taxes for each payment period (see instructions).	30				
31	Total tax. Add lines 29 and 30.	31				
32	For each period, enter the same type of credits as allowed on lines 15, 20, and 22, page 1 of Form 1120-W (see instructions).	32				
33	Total tax after credits. Subtract line 32 from line 31. If zero or less, enter -0-.	33				
34	Add the amounts in all preceding columns of line 41 (see instructions).	34				
35	**Adjusted seasonal installments.** Subtract line 34 from line 33. If zero or less, enter -0-.	35				

Part III—Required Installments

			1st installment	2nd installment	3rd installment	4th installment
36	If only one of the above parts is completed, enter the amount in each column from line 13 or line 35. If both parts are completed, enter the **smaller** of the amounts in each column from line 13 or line 35.	36				
37	Divide line 24b, page 1 of Form 1120-W, by 4, and enter the result in each column. (**Note:** *"Large corporations," see the instructions for line 26 on page 5 for the amount to enter.*)	37				
38	Enter the amount from line 40 for the preceding column.	38				
39	Add lines 37 and 38.	39				
40	If line 39 is more than line 36, subtract line 36 from line 39. Otherwise, enter -0-.	40				
41	**Required installments.** Enter the **smaller** of line 36 or line 39 here and on line 26, page 1 of Form 1120-W.	41				

General Instructions

Section references are to the Internal Revenue Code unless otherwise noted.

A Change To Note

Certain corporations may take the qualified zone academy bond credit into account in figuring the amount of any installment of estimated tax. For more information, see **Form 8860,** Qualified Zone Academy Bond Credit.

Who Must Make Estimated Tax Payments

● Corporations generally must make installment payments of estimated tax if they expect their estimated tax (income tax less credits) to be $500 or more.

● S corporations must also make estimated tax payments for certain taxes. S corporations should see the instructions for **Form 1120S,** U.S. Income Tax Return for an S Corporation, to figure their estimated tax payments.

● Tax-exempt organizations subject to the unrelated business income tax and private foundations use **Form 990-W,** Estimated Tax on Unrelated Business Taxable Income for Tax-Exempt Organizations, to figure the amount of their estimated tax payments.

When To Make Estimated Tax Payments

The installments are due by the 15th day of the **4th, 6th, 9th, and 12th** months of the tax year. If any date falls on a Saturday, Sunday, or legal holiday, the installment is due on the next regular business day.

Underpayment of Estimated Tax

A corporation that does not make estimated tax payments when due may be subject to an underpayment penalty for the period of underpayment (section 6655), using the underpayment rate determined under section 6621(a)(2).

Overpayment of Estimated Tax

A corporation that has overpaid its estimated tax may apply for a quick refund if the overpayment is at least 10% of its expected income tax liability **and** at least $500.

Quick refund. To apply for a quick refund, file **Form 4466,** Corporation Application for Quick Refund of Overpayment of Estimated Tax, before the 16th day of the 3rd month after the end of the tax year, but before the corporation files its income tax return. Do not file Form 4466 before the end of the corporation's tax year.

Depository Method of Tax Payment

Some corporations (described below) are required to electronically deposit all depository taxes, including corporation income tax and estimated tax payments.

Electronic deposit requirement. The corporation must make electronic deposits of all depository tax liabilities that occur after 1998 if:

● It was required to electronically deposit taxes in prior years,

● It deposited more than $50,000 in social security, Medicare, railroad retirement, and withheld income taxes in 1997, or

● It **did not** deposit social security, Medicare, railroad retirement, or withheld income taxes in 1997, but it deposited more than $50,000 in other taxes under section 6302 (such as the corporate income tax) in 1997.

For details, see Regulations section 31.6302-1(h).

The Electronic Federal Tax Payment System (EFTPS) must be used to make electronic deposits. If the corporation is required to make electronic deposits and fails to do so, it may be subject to a 10% penalty.

Corporations that are not required to make electronic deposits may voluntarily participate in EFTPS. To enroll in EFTPS, call 1-800-945-8400 or 1-800-555-4477. For general information about EFTPS, call 1-800-829-1040.

Deposits with Form 8109. If the corporation does not use EFTPS, deposit corporation income tax payments (and estimated tax payments) with **Form 8109,** Federal Tax Deposit Coupon. Do not send deposits directly to an IRS office. Mail or deliver the completed Form 8109 with the payment to a qualified depositary for Federal taxes or to the Federal Reserve bank (FRB) servicing the corporation's geographic area. Make checks or money orders payable to that depositary or FRB. To help ensure proper crediting, write the corporation's EIN, the tax period to which the deposit applies, and "Form 1120" on the check or money order. Be sure to darken the "1120" box on the coupon. Records of these deposits will be sent to the IRS.

A penalty may be imposed if the deposits are mailed or delivered to an IRS office rather than to an authorized depositary or FRB. For more information on deposits, see the instructions in the coupon booklet (Form 8109) and **Pub. 583,** Starting a Business and Keeping Records.

Refiguring Estimated Tax

If after the corporation figures and deposits estimated tax, it finds that its tax liability for the year will be more or less than originally estimated, it may have to refigure its required installments. If earlier installments were underpaid, the corporation may owe a penalty for underpayment of estimated tax.

An immediate catchup payment should be made to reduce the amount of any penalty resulting from the underpayment of any earlier installments, whether caused by a change in estimate, failure to make a deposit, or a mistake.

Specific Instructions

Line 1—Qualified Personal Service Corporations

A qualified personal service corporation is taxed at a flat rate of 35% on taxable income. A corporation is a qualified personal service corporation if it meets **both** of the following tests:

● Substantially all of the corporation's activities involve the performance of services in the fields of health, law, engineering, architecture, accounting, actuarial science, performing arts, or consulting, and

● At least 95% of the corporation's stock, by value, is owned, directly or indirectly, by **(1)** employees performing the services, **(2)** retired employees who had performed the services listed above, **(3)** any estate of an employee or retiree described above, or **(4)** any person who acquired the stock of the corporation as a result of the death of an employee or retiree (but only for the 2-year period beginning on the date of the employee's or retiree's death). See Temporary Regulations section 1.448-1T(e) for details.

Lines 2, 4, and 6

Members of a controlled group. Members of a controlled group enter on line 2 the smaller of the amount on line 1 or their share of the $50,000 amount. On line 4, enter the smaller of the amount on line 3 or their share of the $25,000 amount. On line 6, enter the smaller of the amount on line 5 or their share of the $9,925,000 amount.

Equal apportionment plan. If no apportionment plan is adopted, members of a controlled group must divide the amount in each taxable income bracket equally among themselves. For example, Controlled Group AB consists of Corporation A and Corporation B. They do not elect an apportionment plan. Therefore, each corporation is entitled to:

● $25,000 (one-half of $50,000) on line 2,

● $12,500 (one-half of $25,000) on line 4, and

● $4,962,500 (one-half of $9,925,000) on line 6.

Unequal apportionment plan. Members of a controlled group may elect an unequal apportionment plan and divide the taxable income brackets as they want. There is no need for consistency among taxable income brackets. Any member may be entitled to all, some, or none of the taxable income bracket. However, the total amount for all members cannot be more than the total amount in each taxable income bracket.

Line 12

Additional 5% tax. Members of a controlled group are treated as one group to figure the applicability of the additional 5% tax and the additional 3% tax. If an additional tax applies, each member will pay that tax based on the part of the amount used in each taxable income bracket to reduce that member's tax. See section 1561(a). Each member of the group must enter on line 12 its share of the smaller of 5% of the taxable income in excess of $100,000, or $11,750.

Line 13

Additional 3% tax. If the additional 3% tax applies, each member of the controlled group must enter on line 13 its share of the smaller of 3% of the taxable income in excess of $15 million, or $100,000. See **Line 12** above.

Line 15

For information on **tax credits** the corporation may take, see the discussion of credits in the Instructions for Form 1120, lines 4a through 4e, Schedule J (Form 1120-A, lines 2a and 2b, Part I), or the instructions for the applicable line and schedule of other income tax returns.

Line 18

Alternative minimum tax (AMT) is generally the excess of tentative minimum tax for the tax year over the regular tax for the tax year. See section 55 for definitions of tentative minimum tax and regular tax. A limited amount of the foreign tax credit may be used to offset the minimum tax.

Note: *Skip this line if the corporation meets the qualifications of a "small corporation." See* **Form 4626,** *Alternative Minimum Tax—Corporations, and section 55(e) for details.*

Line 20

Complete **Form 8860,** Qualified Zone Academy Bond Credit, if the corporation qualifies to take this credit.

Line 22

Complete **Form 4136,** Credit for Federal Tax Paid on Fuels, if the corporation qualifies to take this credit. Include on line 22 any credit the corporation is claiming under section 4682(g)(2) for tax on ozone-depleting chemicals.

Line 24a

Figure the corporation's 1998 tax in the same way that line 23 of this worksheet was figured, using the taxes and credits from the 1998 income tax return.

If a return was not filed for the 1998 tax year showing a liability for at least some amount of tax, **or** if the 1998 tax year was for less than 12 months, do not complete line 24a. Instead, skip line 24a and enter the amount from line 23 on line 24b. Large corporations, see the instructions for line 26 below.

Line 25

Calendar year taxpayers: Enter 4-15-99, 6-15-99, 9-15-99, and 12-15-99, respectively, in columns (a) through (d).

Fiscal year taxpayers: Enter the 15th day of the 4th, 6th, 9th, and 12th months of your tax year in columns (a) through (d).

If the regular due date falls on a Saturday, Sunday, or legal holiday, enter the next business day.

Line 26

Payments of estimated tax should reflect any 1998 overpayment that the corporation chose to credit against its 1999 tax. The overpayment is credited against unpaid required installments in the order in which the installments are required to be paid.

Annualized income installment method and/or adjusted seasonal installment method. If the corporation's income is expected to vary during the year because, for example, it operates its business on a seasonal basis, it may be able to lower the amount of one or more

required installments by using the annualized income installment method and/or the adjusted seasonal installment method. For example, a ski shop, which receives most of its income during the winter months, may be able to benefit from using one or both of these methods in figuring one or more of its required installments.

To use one or both of these methods to figure one or more required installments, use Schedule A on pages 2 and 3. If Schedule A is used for any payment date, it must be used for all payment due dates. To arrive at the amount of each required installment, Schedule A automatically selects the smallest of **(a)** the annualized income installment, **(b)** the adjusted seasonal installment (if applicable), or **(c)** the regular installment under section 6655(d)(1) (increased by any recapture of a reduction in a required installment under section 6655(e)(1)(B)).

Large corporations. A large corporation is a corporation that had, or its predecessor had, taxable income of $1 million or more for any of the 3 tax years immediately preceding the 1999 tax year. For this purpose, taxable income is modified to exclude net operating loss or capital loss carrybacks or carryovers. Members of a controlled group, as defined in section 1563, must divide the $1 million amount among themselves according to rules similar to those in section 1561.

If the annualized income installment method or adjusted seasonal installment method is not used, follow the instructions below to figure the amounts to enter on line 26. (If the annualized income installment method and/or the adjusted seasonal installment method are used, these instructions apply to line 37 of Schedule A.)

● **If line 23 is smaller than line 24a:** Enter 25% of line 23 in columns (a) through (d) of line 26.

● **If line 24a is smaller than line 23:** Enter 25% of line 24a in column (a) of line 26. In column (b), determine the amount to enter as follows:

1. Subtract line 24a from line 23,

2. Add the result to the amount on line 23, and

3. Multiply the result in **2** above by 25% and enter the result in column (b).

Enter 25% of line 23 in columns (c) and (d).

Schedule A

If only the annualized income installment method (Part I) is used, complete Parts I and III of Schedule A. If only the adjusted seasonal installment method (Part II) is used, complete Parts II and III. If both methods are used, complete all three parts. Enter in each column on line 26, page 1, the amounts from the corresponding column of line 41.

Caution: *Do not figure any required installment until after the end of the month preceding the due date for that installment.*

Part I—Annualized Income Installment Method

Line 1

Annualization periods. Enter in the space on line 1, columns (a) through (d), respectively, the annualization periods that the corporation is using, based on the options listed below. For example, if the corporation elects Option 1, enter on line 1 the annualization periods 2, 4, 7, and 10, in columns (a) through (d), respectively.

Caution: *Use Option 1 or Option 2 only if the corporation elected to use one of these options by filing* **Form 8842,** *Election To Use Different Annualization Periods for Corporate Estimated Tax, on or before the due date of the first required installment payment. Once made, the election is irrevocable for the particular tax year.*

	1st Installment	2nd Installment	3rd Installment	4th Installment
Standard option	3	3	6	9
Option 1 . . .	2	4	7	10
Option 2 . . .	3	5	8	11

Line 2

If a corporation has income includible under section 936(h) (Puerto Rico and possessions tax credits) or section 951(a) (controlled foreign corporation income), special rules apply.

Amounts includible in income under section 936(h) or 951(a) (and allocable credits) generally must be taken into account in figuring the amount of any annualized income installment as the income is earned. The amounts are figured in a manner similar to the way in which partnership income inclusions (and allocable credits) are taken into account in figuring a partner's annualized income installments as provided in Regulations section 1.6654-2(d)(2).

Safe harbor election. Corporations may be able to elect a prior year safe harbor election. Under the election, an eligible corporation is treated as having received ratably during the tax year items of income under sections 936(h) and 951(a) (and allocable credits) equal to a specified percentage of the amounts shown on the corporation's return for the first preceding tax year (the second preceding tax year for the first and second required installments).

For more information, see section 6655(e)(4) and Rev. Proc. 95-23, 1995-1 C.B. 693.

Line 3

Annualization amounts. Enter the annualization amounts for the option used on line 1. For example, if the corporation elects Option 1, enter on line 3 the annualization amounts 6, 3, 1.71429, and 1.2, in columns (a) through (d), respectively.

	1st Installment	2nd Installment	3rd Installment	4th Installment
Standard option	4	4	2	1.33333
Option 1 . . .	6	3	1.71429	1.2
Option 2 . . .	4	2.4	1.5	1.09091

Line 6

Enter any **other taxes** the corporation owed for the months shown in the headings used to figure annualized taxable income. Include the same taxes used to figure lines 17 and 18 of Form 1120-W.

Alternative minimum tax. Compute the AMT by figuring alternative minimum taxable income under section 55. Alternative minimum taxable income is based on the corporation's income and deductions for the annualization period entered in each column on line 1. Multiply alternative minimum taxable income by the annualization amounts (line 3) used to figure annualized taxable income. Subtract the exemption amount under section 55(d)(2).

Note: *Skip this line if the corporation meets the qualifications of a "small corporation." See Form 4626 and section 55(e) for details.*

Line 8

Enter the credits to which the corporation is entitled for the months shown in each column on line 1. Do not annualize any credit. However, when figuring the credits, annualize any item of income or deduction used to figure the credit. For more details, see Rev. Rul. 79-179, 1979-1 C.B. 436.

Line 12

Before completing line 12 in columns (b) through (d), complete the following items in each of the preceding columns: line 13; Part II (if applicable); and Part III. For example, complete line 13, Part II (if using the adjusted seasonal installment method), and Part III, in column (a) before completing line 12 in column (b).

Part II—Adjusted Seasonal Installment Method

Complete this part only if the corporation's base period percentage for any 6 consecutive months of the tax year equals or exceeds 70%. The base period percentage for any period of 6 consecutive months is the average of the three percentages figured by dividing the taxable income for the corresponding 6-consecutive-month period in each of the 3 preceding tax years by the taxable income for each of their respective tax years.

Example. An amusement park with a calendar year tax year receives the largest part of its taxable income during a 6-month period, May through October. To compute its base period percentage for this 6-month period, the amusement park figures its taxable income for each May–October period in 1996, 1997, and 1998. It then divides the taxable income for each May–October period by the total taxable income for that particular tax year. The resulting percentages are 69% (.69) for May–October 1996, 74% (.74) for May–October 1997, and 67% (.67) for May–October 1998. Because the average of 69%, 74%, and 67% is 70%, the base period percentage for May through October 1999 is 70%. Therefore, the amusement park qualifies for the adjusted seasonal installment method.

Line 30

Enter any **other taxes** the corporation owed for the months shown in the column headings above line 14 of Part II. Include the same taxes used to figure lines 17 and 18 of Form 1120-W.

Alternative minimum tax. Compute the AMT by figuring alternative minimum taxable income under section 55. Alternative minimum taxable income is based on the corporation's income and deductions for the months shown in the column headings above line 14 of Part II. Divide the alternative minimum taxable income by the amounts shown on line 21. Subtract the exemption amount under section 55(d)(2). For columns (a) through (c) only, multiply the alternative minimum tax by the amounts shown on line 28.

Note: *Skip this line if the corporation meets the qualifications of a "small corporation." See Form 4626 and section 55(e) for details.*

Line 32

Enter the credits to which the corporation is entitled for the months shown in the column headings above line 14 of Part II.

Line 34

Before completing line 34 in columns (b) through (d), complete lines 35 through 41 in each of the preceding columns. For example, complete lines 35 through 41 in column (a) before completing line 34 in column (b).

Paperwork Reduction Act Notice. Your use of this form is optional. It is provided to aid the corporation in determining its tax liability.

You are not required to provide the information requested on a form that is subject to the Paperwork Reduction Act unless the form displays a valid OMB control number. Books or records relating to a form or its instructions must be retained as long as their contents may become material in the administration of any Internal Revenue law. Generally, tax returns and return information are confidential, as required by section 6103.

The time needed to complete this form will vary depending on individual circumstances. The estimated average time is:

Form	Recordkeeping	Learning about the law or the form	Preparing the form
1120-W	7 hr., 25 min.	1 hr., 53 min.	2 hr., 5 min.
1120-W, Sch. A (Pt. I)	11 hr., 14 min.	12 min.	23 min.
1120-W, Sch. A (Pt. II)	23 hr., 26 min.	. . . .	23 min.
1120-W, Sch. A (Pt. III)	5 hr., 16 min.	. . . .	5 min.

If you have comments concerning the accuracy of these time estimates or suggestions for making this form simpler, we would be happy to hear from you. You can write to the Tax Forms Committee, Western Area Distribution Center, Rancho Cordova, CA 95743-0001. **DO NOT** send the tax form to this office. Instead, keep the form for your records.

Form **7004**
(Rev. July 1998)
Department of the Treasury
Internal Revenue Service

Application for Automatic Extension of Time To File Corporation Income Tax Return

OMB No. 1545-0233

Name of corporation

Employer identification number

Number, street, and room or suite no. (If a P.O. box or outside the United States, see instructions.)

City or town, state, and ZIP code

Check type of return to be filed:

☐ Form 1120   ☐ Form 1120-FSC   ☐ Form 1120-ND   ☐ Form 1120-REIT   ☐ Form 1120-SF
☐ Form 1120-A   ☐ Form 1120-H   ☐ Form 1120-PC   ☐ Form 1120-RIC
☐ Form 1120-F   ☐ Form 1120-L   ☐ Form 1120-POL   ☐ Form 1120S

☐ Form 990-C   ▶   **Note:** *Other 990 filers (i.e., Form 990, 990-EZ, 990-BL, 990-PF, and certain filers of Form 990-T (see*
☐ Form 990-T   *instructions))* **must** *use Form 2758 to request an extension of time to file.*

Form 1120-F filers: Check here if you do not have an office or place of business in the United States . . . . ▶ ☐

1a I request an automatic 6-month (or, for certain corporations, 3-month) extension of time
until ...., ... , to file the income tax return of the corporation named above for ▶ ☐ calendar
year .... or ▶ ☐ tax year beginning.............................., ... , and ending .... , ...

b If this tax year is for less than 12 months, check reason:
☐ Initial return   ☐ Final return   ☐ Change in accounting period   ☐ Consolidated return to be filed

2 If this application also covers subsidiaries to be included in a consolidated return, complete the following:

Name and address of each member of the affiliated group	Employer identification number	Tax period

3 Tentative tax (see instructions)	**3**	
4 **Credits:**		
a Overpayment credited from prior year. **4a**		
b Estimated tax payments for the tax year **4b**		
c Less refund for the tax year applied for on Form 4466 . . . . . **4c** ( ) Bal ▶ **4d**		
e Credit for tax paid on undistributed capital gains (Form 2439) . . **4e**		
f Credit for Federal tax on fuels (Form 4136) **4f**		
5 Total. Add lines 4d through 4f	**5**	
6 **Balance due.** Subtract line 5 from line 3. **Deposit this amount electronically or with a Federal Tax Deposit (FTD) Coupon** (see instructions)	**6**	

Signature.—Under penalties of perjury, I declare that I have been authorized by the above-named corporation to make this application, and to the best of my knowledge and belief, the statements made are true, correct, and complete.

_____   _____   _____
(Signature of officer or agent)   (Title)   (Date)

For Paperwork Reduction Act Notice, see instructions.   Cat. No. 13804A   Form **7004** (Rev. 7-98)

General Instructions

Section references are to the Internal Revenue Code unless otherwise noted.

A Change To Note

Form 990-T and Form 990-C filers must now send Form 7004 to the following address: Internal Revenue Service Center, Ogden, UT 84201-0012.

Purpose of form. Form **7004,** Application for Automatic Extension of Time To File Corporation Income Tax Return, is used by a corporation to request a 6-month extension of time to file its income tax return.

The extension will be granted if you properly complete this form, file it, and pay any balance due on line 6 by the due date for the return for which the extension applies. Foreign corporations that use the automatic 3-month extension of time to file under Regulations section 1.6081-5 (see below) must pay the balance due by the 15th day of the 6th month following the close of the tax year.

Do not file Form 7004 if you want a 3-month extension of time to file and pay under Regulations section 1.6081-5. Instead, attach a statement to the corporation's tax return stating that the corporation qualifies for the extension to file and pay under Regulations section 1.6081-5 because it is one of the following:

● A foreign corporation that maintains an office or place of business in the United States.

● A domestic corporation that transacts its business and keeps its books and records of account outside the United States and Puerto Rico.

● A domestic corporation whose principal income is from sources within the possessions of the United States.

If the corporation is unable to file its return within the 3-month period extended under Regulations section 1.6081-5, file Form 7004 to request an additional 3-month extension. Foreign corporations that maintain an office or place of business in the United States are not considered taxpayers abroad and therefore may not obtain an extension of time to file beyond 6 months from the original due date of the tax return. See Rev. Rul. 93-85, 1993-2 C.B. 297.

Note: *Certain filers of Form 990-T (section 401(a), 408(a), and other trusts) or Form 1120-ND (section 4951 taxes) should use Form 2758, Application for Extension of Time To File Certain Excise, Income, Information, and Other Returns, to request an extension. Form 2758 must also be used by all filers of Forms 990, 990-EZ, 990-PF, and 990-BL.*

When and where to file. Generally, Form 7004 must be filed by the due date of the return with the Internal Revenue Service Center where the corporation will file the return. However, Form 990-T and Form 990-C filers must send Form 7004 to Ogden, UT 84201-0012. **DO NOT** attach Form 7004 to the corporation's tax return.

A foreign corporation that does not have an office or place of business in the United States should file Form 7004 by the 15th day of the 6th month following the close of the tax year.

Payment of tax. Form 7004 does not extend the time for payment of tax.

Foreign corporations that do not have an office or place of business in the United States may pay the tax by check or money order, made payable to the "Internal Revenue Service."

Foreign corporations with an office or place of business in the United States and domestic corporations must deposit all income tax payments with a **Form 8109,** Federal Tax Deposit Coupon, or use the Electronic Federal Tax Payment System (EFTPS), if applicable.

Note: *On all checks or money orders, write the corporation's employer identification number, the type of tax, and the tax year to which the payment applies.*

Penalty for not paying tax. The penalty for late payment of taxes is usually ½ of 1% of the unpaid tax for each month or part of a month the tax is unpaid. The penalty cannot exceed 25% of the amount due. The penalty will not be imposed if the corporation can show that the failure to pay on time was due to reasonable cause.

If you are allowed an extension of time to file, you will not be charged a late payment penalty if **(a)** the tax shown on line 3 (or the amount of tax paid by the regular due date of the return) is at least 90% of the tax shown on line 31 of Form 1120, or the comparable line on other returns, and **(b)** you pay the balance due shown on the return by the extended due date.

Termination of extension. The IRS may terminate the automatic extension at any time by mailing a notice of termination to the corporation or to the person who requested the extension. The notice will be mailed at least 10 days before the termination date given in the notice.

Specific Instructions

Address. Include the suite, room, or other unit number after the street address. If the Post Office does not deliver mail to the street address and the corporation has a P.O. box, show the box number instead of the street address.

If your address is outside the United States or its possessions or territories, in the space for "city or town, state, and ZIP code," enter the information in the following order: city, province or state, and country. Follow the country's practice for entering the postal code. Do not abbreviate the country name.

Line 1a—Extension date. A foreign corporation with an office or place of business in the United States that uses the automatic extension of time to file provided in Regulations section 1.6081-5 can use Form 7004 to obtain an additional 3-month extension. See **Purpose of form** above.

Note: *For all filers, the date that is entered on line 1a cannot be later than 6 months from the original due date of the return.*

Line 1b—Short tax year. If you checked the box for change in accounting period, you must have applied for approval to change your tax year unless certain conditions have been met. See **Form 1128,** Application To Adopt, Change, or Retain a Tax Year, and **Pub. 538,** Accounting Periods and Methods, for details.

Line 2—Affiliated group members. Enter the name and address, employer identification number, and tax period for each member of the affiliated group. Generally, all members of an affiliated group must have the same tax period. However, if a group member is required to file a separate return for a short period, and an extension of time to file is being requested, a separate Form 7004 must be filed for that period. See Regulations section 1.1502-76 for details.

Note: *Failure to list members of the affiliated group on line 2 may result in the group's inability to elect to file a consolidated return. For details, see Regulations section 301.9100-1 through 3.*

Line 3—Tentative tax. Enter the tentative amount of total tax for the year, reduced by any nonrefundable credits against the tax. This will usually be the tax shown on Form 1120, line 31, or the comparable line of other returns.

Line 4—Credits. Enter the credits described on lines 4a through 4f. On line 4b, include special estimated tax payments for certain life insurance companies and beneficiaries of trusts. On line 4f, include any credit for tax on ozone-depleting chemicals under section 4682(g)(2). Include any

backup withholding in the total for line 5. Describe a "write-in" amount on the dotted line next to the entry space (e.g., for backup withholding, show the amount on the dotted line next to line 5 and write "backup withholding" next to it). For more information about "write-in" credits, see the Instructions for Forms 1120 and 1120-A, lines 32b through 32h.

Line 6—Balance due. This is the amount of tax you are required to deposit.

Note: *Except for certain foreign corporations described under Payment of tax, make all deposits with a Federal depository bank or use the Electronic Federal Tax Payment System (EFTPS), if applicable. DO NOT include your payment with Form 7004.*

If the corporation expects to have a net operating loss carryback, the corporation may reduce the amount to be deposited to the extent of the overpayment resulting from the carryback, providing all other prior year tax liabilities have been fully paid and a **Form 1138,** Extension of Time for Payment of Taxes by a Corporation Expecting a Net Operating Loss Carryback, accompanies Form 7004.

Interest will be charged on any part of the final tax due not shown on line 6. The interest is figured from the original due date of the return to the date of payment.

For certain domestic and foreign corporations that use the automatic extension of time to file under Regulations section 1.6081-5, interest is figured from the 15th day of the 3rd month following the end of the tax year to the date of payment.

Signature. The person authorized by the corporation should sign the Form 7004. This person may be: **(1)** An officer of the corporation; **(2)** A duly authorized agent holding a power of attorney; **(3)** A person currently enrolled to practice before the IRS; or **(4)** An attorney or certified public accountant qualified to practice before the IRS.

Paperwork Reduction Act Notice. We ask for the information on this form to carry out the Internal Revenue laws of the United States. You are required to give us the information. We need it to ensure that you are complying with these laws and to allow us to figure and collect the right amount of tax.

You are not required to provide the information requested on a form that is subject to the Paperwork Reduction Act unless the form displays a valid OMB control number. Books or records relating to a form or its instructions must be retained as long as their contents may become material in the administration of any Internal Revenue law. Generally, tax returns and return information are confidential, as required by section 6103.

The time needed to complete and file this form will vary depending on individual circumstances. The estimated average time is:

Recordkeeping	. . 5 hr., 30 min.
Learning about the law or the form	. . . . 58 min.
Preparing the form	. 2 hr., 1 min.
Copying, assembling, and sending the form to the IRS	. . . 16 min.

If you have comments concerning the accuracy of these time estimates or suggestions for making this form simpler, we would be happy to hear from you. You can write to the Tax Forms Committee, Western Area Distribution Center, Rancho Cordova, CA 95743-0001. **DO NOT** send the tax form to this address. Instead, see **When and where to file** above.

RESOLUTION BY BOARD
OF DIRECTORS ELECTING
S CORPORATION STATUS

WHEREAS the directors have considered the alternatives as to the taxable status of the corporation and, (with tax counsel,)* determined that S corporation status would be the most beneficial to the corporation and the stockholders, and

WHEREAS all of the stockholders have consented to this election,

RESOLVED that the President is directed to prepare and submit to the Internal Revenue Service an Internal Revenue Service Form 2556, Election by a Small Business Corporation, complete with a consent statement signed by all stockholders. This form is to be submitted within thirty (30) days from the date hereof.

* If applicable.

Form **2553**
(Rev. September 1997)
Department of the Treasury
Internal Revenue Service

Election by a Small Business Corporation
(Under section 1362 of the Internal Revenue Code)
► For Paperwork Reduction Act Notice, see page 2 of instructions.
► See separate instructions.

OMB No. 1545-0146

Notes: 1. *This election to be an S corporation can be accepted only if all the tests are met under **Who May Elect** on page 1 of the instructions; all signatures in Parts I and III are originals (no photocopies); and the exact name and address of the corporation and other required form information are provided.*

2. *Do not file **Form 1120S**, U.S. Income Tax Return for an S Corporation, for any tax year before the year the election takes effect.*

3. *If the corporation was in existence before the effective date of this election, see **Taxes an S Corporation May Owe** on page 1 of the instructions.*

Part I   Election Information

Please Type or Print

Name of corporation (see instructions)	A Employer identification number
Number, street, and room or suite no. (If a P.O. box, see instructions.)	B Date incorporated
City or town, state, and ZIP code	C State of incorporation

D Election is to be effective for tax year beginning (month, day, year) . . . . ► / /

E Name and title of officer or legal representative who the IRS may call for more information   F Telephone number of officer or legal representative
(   )

G If the corporation changed its name or address after applying for the EIN shown in **A** above, check this box . . . . ► ☐

H If this election takes effect for the first tax year the corporation exists, enter month, day, and year of the **earliest** of the following: (1) date the corporation first had shareholders, (2) date the corporation first had assets, or (3) date the corporation began doing business . . . . ► / /

I Selected tax year: Annual return will be filed for tax year ending (month and day) ► . . . .

If the tax year ends on any date other than December 31, except for an automatic 52-53-week tax year ending with reference to the month of December, you **must** complete Part II on the back. If the date you enter is the ending date of an automatic 52-53-week tax year, write "52-53-week year" to the right of the date. See Temporary Regulations section 1.441-2T(e)(3).

J Name and address of each shareholder; shareholder's spouse having a community property interest in the corporation's stock; and each tenant in common, joint tenant, and tenant by the entirety. (A husband and wife (and their estates) are counted as one shareholder in determining the number of shareholders without regard to the manner in which the stock is owned.)	K Shareholders' Consent Statement. Under penalties of perjury, we declare that we consent to the election of the above-named corporation to be an S corporation under section 1362(a) and that we have examined this consent statement, including accompanying schedules and statements, and to the best of our knowledge and belief, it is true, correct, and complete. We understand our consent is binding and may not be withdrawn after the corporation has made a valid election. (Shareholders sign and date below.)		L Stock owned		M Social security number or employer identification number (see instructions)	N Share-holder's tax year ends (month and day)
	Signature	Date	Number of shares	Dates acquired		

Under penalties of perjury, I declare that I have examined this election, including accompanying schedules and statements, and to the best of my knowledge and belief, it is true, correct, and complete.

Signature of officer ►   Title ►   Date ►

See Parts II and III on back.   Cat. No. 18629R   Form **2553** (Rev. 9-97)

Form 2553 (Rev. 9-97)   Page **2**

Part II Selection of Fiscal Tax Year (All corporations using this part must complete item O and item P, Q, or R.)

O Check the applicable box to indicate whether the corporation is:

   1. ☐ A new corporation adopting the tax year entered in item I, Part I.

   2. ☐ An existing corporation retaining the tax year entered in item I, Part I.

   3. ☐ An existing corporation changing to the tax year entered in item I, Part I.

P Complete item P if the corporation is using the expeditious approval provisions of Rev. Proc. 87-32, 1987-2 C.B. 396, to request **(1)** a natural business year (as defined in section 4.01(1) of Rev. Proc. 87-32) or **(2)** a year that satisfies the ownership tax year test in section 4.01(2) of Rev. Proc. 87-32. Check the applicable box below to indicate the representation statement the corporation is making as required under section 4 of Rev. Proc. 87-32.

   1. Natural Business Year ▶ ☐ I represent that the corporation is retaining or changing to a tax year that coincides with its natural business year as defined in section 4.01(1) of Rev. Proc. 87-32 and as verified by its satisfaction of the requirements of section 4.02(1) of Rev. Proc. 87-32. In addition, if the corporation is changing to a natural business year as defined in section 4.01(1), I further represent that such tax year results in less deferral of income to the owners than the corporation's present tax year. I also represent that the corporation is not described in section 3.01(2) of Rev. Proc. 87-32. (See instructions for additional information that must be attached.)

   2. Ownership Tax Year ▶ ☐ I represent that shareholders holding more than half of the shares of the stock (as of the first day of the tax year to which the request relates) of the corporation have the same tax year or are concurrently changing to the tax year that the corporation adopts, retains, or changes to per item I, Part I. I also represent that the corporation is not described in section 3.01(2) of Rev. Proc. 87-32.

Note: *If you do not use item P and the corporation wants a fiscal tax year, complete either item Q or R below. Item Q is used to request a fiscal tax year based on a business purpose and to make a back-up section 444 election. Item R is used to make a regular section 444 election.*

Q Business Purpose—To request a fiscal tax year based on a business purpose, you must check box Q1 and pay a user fee. See instructions for details. You may also check box Q2 and/or box Q3.

   1. Check here ▶ ☐ if the fiscal year entered in item I, Part I, is requested under the provisions of section 6.03 of Rev. Proc. 87-32. Attach to Form 2553 a statement showing the business purpose for the requested fiscal year. See instructions for additional information that must be attached.

   2. Check here ▶ ☐ to show that the corporation intends to make a back-up section 444 election in the event the corporation's business purpose request is not approved by the IRS. (See instructions for more information.)

   3. Check here ▶ ☐ to show that the corporation agrees to adopt or change to a tax year ending December 31 if necessary for the IRS to accept this election for S corporation status in the event (1) the corporation's business purpose request is not approved and the corporation makes a back-up section 444 election, but is ultimately not qualified to make a section 444 election, or (2) the corporation's business purpose request is not approved and the corporation did not make a back-up section 444 election.

R Section 444 Election—To make a section 444 election, you must check box R1 and you may also check box R2.

   1. Check here ▶ ☐ to show the corporation will make, if qualified, a section 444 election to have the fiscal tax year shown in item I, Part I. To make the election, you must complete **Form 8716**, Election To Have a Tax Year Other Than a Required Tax Year, and either attach it to Form 2553 or file it separately.

   2. Check here ▶ ☐ to show that the corporation agrees to adopt or change to a tax year ending December 31 if necessary for the IRS to accept this election for S corporation status in the event the corporation is ultimately not qualified to make a section 444 election.

Part III Qualified Subchapter S Trust (QSST) Election Under Section 1361(d)(2)*

Income beneficiary's name and address	Social security number
Trust's name and address	Employer identification number

Date on which stock of the corporation was transferred to the trust (month, day, year) . . . . ▶   /   /

In order for the trust named above to be a QSST and thus a qualifying shareholder of the S corporation for which this Form 2553 is filed, I hereby make the election under section 1361(d)(2). Under penalties of perjury, I certify that the trust meets the definitional requirements of section 1361(d)(3) and that all other information provided in Part III is true, correct, and complete.

_____   _____
Signature of income beneficiary or signature and title of legal representative or other qualified person making the election   Date

*Use Part III to make the QSST election only if stock of the corporation has been transferred to the trust on or before the date on which the corporation makes its election to be an S corporation. The QSST election must be made and filed separately if stock of the corporation is transferred to the trust after the date on which the corporation makes the S election.

Instructions for Form 2553

(Revised September 1997)

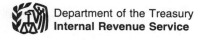

Department of the Treasury
Internal Revenue Service

Election by a Small Business Corporation

Section references are to the Internal Revenue Code unless otherwise noted.

General Instructions

Purpose.— To elect to be an S corporation, a corporation must file Form 2553. The election permits the income of the S corporation to be taxed to the shareholders of the corporation rather than to the corporation itself, except as noted below under **Taxes an S Corporation May Owe.**

Who May Elect.— A corporation may elect to be an S corporation only if it meets all of the following tests:

1. It is a domestic corporation.

2. It has no more than 75 shareholders. A husband and wife (and their estates) are treated as one shareholder for this requirement. All other persons are treated as separate shareholders.

3. Its only shareholders are individuals, estates, certain trusts described in section 1361(c)(2)(A), or, for tax years beginning after 1997, exempt organizations described in section 401(a) or 501(c)(3). Trustees of trusts that want to make the election under section 1361(e)(3) to be an electing small business trust should see Notice 97-12, 1997-3 I.R.B. 11.

Note: *See the instructions for Part III regarding qualified subchapter S trusts.*

4. It has no nonresident alien shareholders.

5. It has only one class of stock (disregarding differences in voting rights). Generally, a corporation is treated as having only one class of stock if all outstanding shares of the corporation's stock confer identical rights to distribution and liquidation proceeds. See Regulations section 1.1361-1(1) for more details.

6. It is not one of the following ineligible corporations:

   a. A bank or thrift institution that uses the reserve method of accounting for bad debts under section 585;

   b. An insurance company subject to tax under the rules of subchapter L of the Code;

   c. A corporation that has elected to be treated as a possessions corporation under section 936; or

   d. A domestic international sales corporation (DISC) or former DISC.

7. It has a permitted tax year as required by section 1378 or makes a section 444 election to have a tax year other than a permitted tax year. Section 1378 defines a permitted tax year as a tax year ending December 31, or any other tax year for which the corporation establishes a business purpose to the satisfaction of the IRS. See Part II for details on requesting a fiscal tax year based on a business purpose or on making a section 444 election.

8. Each shareholder consents as explained in the instructions for column K.

See sections 1361, 1362, and 1378 for additional information on the above tests.

An election can be made by a parent S corporation to treat the assets, liabilities, and items of income, deduction, and credit of an eligible wholly-owned subsidiary as those of the parent. For details, see Notice 97-4, 1997-2 I.R.B. 24.

Taxes an S Corporation May Owe.— An S corporation may owe income tax in the following instances:

1. If, at the end of any tax year, the corporation had accumulated earnings and profits, and its passive investment income under section 1362(d)(3) is more than 25% of its gross receipts, the corporation may owe tax on its excess net passive income.

2. A corporation with net recognized built-in gain (as defined in section 1374(d)(2)) may owe tax on its built-in gains.

3. A corporation that claimed investment credit before its first year as an S corporation will be liable for any investment credit recapture tax.

4. A corporation that used the LIFO inventory method for the year immediately preceding its first year as an S corporation may owe an additional tax due to LIFO recapture.

For more details on these taxes, see the Instructions for Form 1120S.

Where To File.— File this election with the Internal Revenue Service Center listed below.

If the corporation's principal business, office, or agency is located in	Use the following Internal Revenue Service Center address
New Jersey, New York (New York City and counties of Nassau, Rockland, Suffolk, and Westchester)	Holtsville, NY 00501
New York (all other counties), Connecticut, Maine, Massachusetts, New Hampshire, Rhode Island, Vermont	Andover, MA 05501
Florida, Georgia, South Carolina	Atlanta, GA 39901
Indiana, Kentucky, Michigan, Ohio, West Virginia	Cincinnati, OH 45999
Kansas, New Mexico, Oklahoma, Texas	Austin, TX 73301
Alaska, Arizona, California (counties of Alpine, Amador, Butte, Calaveras, Colusa, Contra Costa, Del Norte, El Dorado, Glenn, Humboldt, Lake, Lassen, Marin, Mendocino, Modoc, Napa, Nevada, Placer, Plumas, Sacramento, San Joaquin, Shasta, Sierra, Siskiyou, Solano, Sonoma, Sutter, Tehama, Trinity, Yolo, and Yuba), Colorado, Idaho, Montana, Nebraska, Nevada, North Dakota, Oregon, South Dakota, Utah, Washington, Wyoming	Ogden, UT 84201
California (all other counties), Hawaii	Fresno, CA 93888
Illinois, Iowa, Minnesota, Missouri, Wisconsin	Kansas City, MO 64999
Alabama, Arkansas, Louisiana, Mississippi, North Carolina, Tennessee	Memphis, TN 37501
Delaware, District of Columbia, Maryland, Pennsylvania, Virginia	Philadelphia, PA 19255

When To Make the Election.— Complete and file Form 2553 **(a)** at any time before the 16th day of the 3rd month of the tax year, if filed during the tax year the election is to take effect, or **(b)** at any time during the preceding tax year. An election made no later than 2 months and 15 days after the beginning of a tax year that is less than 2½ months long is treated as timely made for that tax year. An election made after the 15th day of the 3rd month but before the end of the tax year is effective for the next year. For example, if a calendar tax year

corporation makes the election in April 1998, it is effective for the corporation's 1999 calendar tax year.

However, an election made after the due date will be accepted as timely filed if the corporation can show that the failure to file on time was due to reasonable cause. To request relief for a late election, the corporation generally must request a private letter ruling and pay a user fee in accordance with Rev. Proc. 97-1, 1997-1 I.R.B. 11 (or its successor). But if the election is filed within 6 months of its due date and the original due date for filing the corporation's initial Form 1120S has not passed, the ruling and user fee requirements do not apply. To request relief in this case, write "FILED PURSUANT TO REV. PROC. 97-40" at the top of page 1 of Form 2553, attach a statement explaining the reason for failing to file the election on time, and file Form 2553 as otherwise instructed. See Rev. Proc. 97-40, 1997-33 I.R.B. 50, for more details.

See Regulations section 1.1362-6(b)(3)(iii) for how to obtain relief for an inadvertent invalid election if the corporation filed a timely election, but one or more shareholders did not file a timely consent.

Acceptance or Nonacceptance of Election.— The service center will notify the corporation if its election is accepted and when it will take effect. The corporation will also be notified if its election is not accepted. The corporation should generally receive a determination on its election within 60 days after it has filed Form 2553. If box Q1 in Part II is checked on page 2, the corporation will receive a ruling letter from the IRS in Washington, DC, that either approves or denies the selected tax year. When box Q1 is checked, it will generally take an additional 90 days for the Form 2553 to be accepted.

Do not file Form 1120S for any tax year before the year the election takes effect. If the corporation is now required to file **Form 1120,** U.S. Corporation Income Tax Return, or any other applicable tax return, continue filing it until the election takes effect.

Care should be exercised to ensure that the IRS receives the election. If the corporation is not notified of acceptance or nonacceptance of its election within 3 months of date of filing (date mailed), or within 6 months if box Q1 is checked, take follow-up action by corresponding with the service center where the corporation filed the election. If the IRS questions whether Form 2553 was filed, an acceptable proof of filing is **(a)** certified or registered mail receipt (timely filed) from the U.S. Postal Service or its equivalent from a designated private delivery service (see Notice 97-26, 1997-17 I.R.B. 6); **(b)** Form 2553 with accepted stamp; **(c)** Form 2553 with stamped IRS received date; or **(d)** IRS letter stating that Form 2553 has been accepted.

End of Election.— Once the election is made, it stays in effect until it is terminated. If the election is terminated in a tax year beginning after 1996, the corporation (or a successor corporation) can make another election on Form 2553 only with IRS consent for any tax year before the 5th tax year after the first tax year in which the termination took effect. See Regulations section 1.1362-5 for more details.

Cat. No. 49978N

Specific Instructions

Part I

Note: *All corporations must complete Part I.*

Name and Address of Corporation.— Enter the true corporate name as stated in the corporate charter or other legal document creating it. If the corporation's mailing address is the same as someone else's, such as a shareholder's, enter "c/o" and this person's name following the name of the corporation. Include the suite, room, or other unit number after the street address. If the Post Office does not deliver to the street address and the corporation has a P.O. box, show the box number instead of the street address. If the corporation changed its name or address after applying for its employer identification number, be sure to check the box in item G of Part I.

Item A. Employer Identification Number (EIN).— If the corporation has applied for an EIN but has not received it, enter "applied for." If the corporation does not have an EIN, it should apply for one on **Form SS-4,** Application for Employer Identification Number. You can order Form SS-4 by calling 1-800-TAX-FORM (1-800-829-3676).

Item D. Effective Date of Election.— Enter the beginning effective date (month, day, year) of the tax year requested for the S corporation. Generally, this will be the beginning date of the tax year for which the ending effective date is required to be shown in item I, Part I. For a new corporation (first year the corporation exists) it will generally be the date required to be shown in item H, Part I. The tax year of a new corporation starts on the date that it has shareholders, acquires assets, or begins doing business, whichever happens first. If the effective date for item D for a newly formed corporation is later than the date in item H, the corporation should file Form 1120 or Form 1120-A for the tax period between these dates.

Column K. Shareholders' Consent Statement.— Each shareholder who owns (or is deemed to own) stock at the time the election is made must consent to the election. If the election is made during the corporation's tax year for which it first takes effect, any person who held stock at any time during the part of that year that occurs before the election is made, must consent to the election, even though the person may have sold or transferred his or her stock before the election is made.

An election made during the first 2½ months of the tax year is effective for the following tax year if any person who held stock in the corporation during the part of the tax year before the election was made, and who did not hold stock at the time the election was made, did not consent to the election.

Each shareholder consents by signing and dating in column K or signing and dating a separate consent statement described below. The following special rules apply in determining who must sign the consent statement.

- If a husband and wife have a community interest in the stock or in the income from it, both must consent.
- Each tenant in common, joint tenant, and tenant by the entirety must consent.
- A minor's consent is made by the minor, legal representative of the minor, or a natural or adoptive parent of the minor if no legal representative has been appointed.
- The consent of an estate is made by the executor or administrator.

- The consent of an electing small business trust is made by the trustee.
- If the stock is owned by a trust (other than an electing small business trust), the deemed owner of the trust must consent. See section 1361(c)(2) for details regarding trusts that are permitted to be shareholders and rules for determining who is the deemed owner.

Continuation sheet or separate consent statement.—If you need a continuation sheet or use a separate consent statement, attach it to Form 2553. The separate consent statement must contain the name, address, and EIN of the corporation and the shareholder information requested in columns J through N of Part I. If you want, you may combine all the shareholders' consents in one statement.

Column L.— Enter the number of shares of stock each shareholder owns and the dates the stock was acquired. If the election is made during the corporation's tax year for which it first takes effect, do not list the shares of stock for those shareholders who sold or transferred all of their stock before the election was made. However, these shareholders must still consent to the election for it to be effective for the tax year.

Column M.— Enter the social security number of each shareholder who is an individual. Enter the EIN of each shareholder that is an estate, a qualified trust, or an exempt organization.

Column N.— Enter the month and day that each shareholder's tax year ends. If a shareholder is changing his or her tax year, enter the tax year the shareholder is changing to, and attach an explanation indicating the present tax year and the basis for the change (e.g., automatic revenue procedure or letter ruling request).

Signature.— Form 2553 must be signed by the president, treasurer, assistant treasurer, chief accounting officer, or other corporate officer (such as tax officer) authorized to sign.

Part II

Complete Part II if you selected a tax year ending on any date other than December 31 (other than a 52-53-week tax year ending with reference to the month of December).

Box P1.— Attach a statement showing separately for each month the amount of gross receipts for the most recent 47 months as required by section 4.03(3) of Rev. Proc. 87-32, 1987-2 C.B. 396. A corporation that does not have a 47-month period of gross receipts cannot establish a natural business year under section 4.01(1).

Box Q1.— For examples of an acceptable business purpose for requesting a fiscal tax year, see Rev. Rul. 87-57, 1987-2 C.B. 117.

In addition to a statement showing the business purpose for the requested fiscal year, you must attach the other information necessary to meet the ruling request requirements of Rev. Proc. 97-1 (or its successor). Also attach a statement that shows separately the amount of gross receipts from sales or services (and inventory costs, if applicable) for each of the 36 months preceding the effective date of the election to be an S corporation. If the corporation has been in existence for fewer than 36 months, submit figures for the period of existence.

If you check box Q1, you will be charged a $250 user fee (subject to change). Do not pay the fee when filing Form 2553. The service center will send Form 2553 to the IRS in

Washington, DC, who, in turn, will notify the corporation that the fee is due.

Box Q2.— If the corporation makes a back-up section 444 election for which it is qualified, then the election will take effect in the event the business purpose request is not approved. In some cases, the tax year requested under the back-up section 444 election may be different than the tax year requested under business purpose. See **Form 8716,** Election To Have a Tax Year Other Than a Required Tax Year, for details on making a back-up section 444 election.

Boxes Q2 and R2.— If the corporation is not qualified to make the section 444 election after making the item Q2 back-up section 444 election or indicating its intention to make the election in item R1, and therefore it later files a calendar year return, it should write "Section 444 Election Not Made" in the top left corner of the first calendar year Form 1120S it files.

Part III

Certain qualified subchapter S trusts (QSSTs) may make the QSST election required by section 1361(d)(2) in Part III. Part III may be used to make the QSST election only if corporate stock has been transferred to the trust on or before the date on which the corporation makes its election to be an S corporation. However, a statement can be used instead of Part III to make the election.

Note: *Use Part III only if you make the election in Part I (i.e., Form 2553 cannot be filed with only Part III completed).*

The deemed owner of the QSST must also consent to the S corporation election in column K, page 1, of Form 2553. See section 1361 (c)(2).

Paperwork Reduction Act Notice.— We ask for the information on this form to carry out the Internal Revenue laws of the United States. You are required to give us the information. We need it to ensure that you are complying with these laws and to allow us to figure and collect the right amount of tax.

You are not required to provide the information requested on a form that is subject to the Paperwork Reduction Act unless the form displays a valid OMB control number. Books or records relating to a form or its instructions must be retained as long as their contents may become material in the administration of any Internal Revenue law. Generally, tax returns and return information are confidential, as required by section 6103.

The time needed to complete and file this form will depend on individual circumstances. The estimated average time is:

Recordkeeping .... 6 hr., 28 min.

Learning about the
law or the form.................................. 3 hr., 41 min.

Preparing, copying,
assembling, and sending
the form to the IRS.......................... 3 hr., 56 min.

If you have comments concerning the accuracy of these time estimates or suggestions for making this form simpler, we would be happy to hear from you. You can write to the Tax Forms Committee, Western Area Distribution Center, Rancho Cordova, CA 95743-0001. **DO NOT** send the form to this address. Instead, see **Where To File** on page 1.

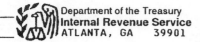 Department of the Treasury
Internal Revenue Service
ATLANTA, GA   39901

Date of this notice: JUNE 30, 1997
Taxpayer Identifying Number
Form: Tax Period:

For assistance you may
call us at:

Or you may write to us at
the address shown at the
left. If you write, be
sure to attach the bottom
part of this notice.

NOTICE OF ACCEPTANCE AS AN S-CORPORATION

YOUR ELECTION TO BE TREATED AS AN S-CORPORATION WITH AN ACCOUNTING PERIOD OF DECEMBER IS ACCEPTED. THE ELECTION IS EFFECTIVE BEGINNING MAR. 27, 1997, SUBJECT TO VERIFICATION IF WE EXAMINE YOUR RETURN.

IF YOUR EFFECTIVE DATE IS NOT AS REQUESTED, IT WILL HAVE BEEN CHANGED FOR ONE OF TWO REASONS. EITHER YOUR ELECTION WAS MADE AFTER THE 15TH DAY OF THE THIRD MONTH OF THE TAX YEAR TO WHICH IT APPLIES, BUT BEFORE THE END OF THAT TAX YEAR, OR THE ELECTION WHEN SUBMITTED WAS INCOMPLETE, AND REQUESTED INFORMATION WAS RECEIVED AFTER THE FILING PERIOD. IN EITHER CASE, YOUR ELECTION IS INVALID FOR THE TAX YEAR REQUESTED AND HAS THEREFORE, BEEN TREATED AS THOUGH IT WERE MADE FOR THE NEXT TAX YEAR.

PLEASE KEEP THIS NOTICE IN YOUR PERMANENT RECORDS AS VERIFICATION OF YOUR ACCEPTANCE AS AN S-CORPORATION.

IF YOU HAVE ANY QUESTIONS ABOUT THIS NOTICE OR THE ACTIONS WE HAVE TAKEN, PLEASE WRITE TO US AT THE ADDRESS SHOWN ABOVE. IF YOU PREFER, YOU MAY CALL US AT THE IRS TELEPHONE NUMBER LISTED IN YOUR LOCAL DIRECTORY. AN EMPLOYEE THERE MAY BE ABLE TO HELP YOU; HOWEVER, THE OFFICE AT THE ADDRESS SHOWN ON THIS NOTICE IS MOST FAMILIAR WITH YOUR CASE.

IF YOU WRITE TO US, PLEASE PROVIDE YOUR TELEPHONE NUMBER AND THE MOST CONVENIENT TIME FOR US TO CALL SO WE CAN CONTACT YOU TO RESOLVE YOUR INQUIRY. PLEASE RETURN THE BOTTOM PART OF THIS NOTICE TO HELP US IDENTIFY YOUR CASE.

THANK YOU FOR YOUR COOPERATION.

CASH DISTRIBUTIONS
REQUIRED TO MEET
INCOME TAX OBLIGATION

Cash Distributions. If the Company is operated under an S Corporation election in the previous year, the Company will disburse cash distributions to the Shareholders annually, on or before April 10, which will be in a sufficient amount for the Shareholders to pay their incremental federal and state income tax liability that is caused by the distributable "ordinary income (loss) from trade or business activities" as stated on the Company's federal and state income tax returns for the previous year.

(This clause should be modified to reflect the state's taxation of S corporations.)

Form 1120S

Department of the Treasury
Internal Revenue Service

U.S. Income Tax Return for an S Corporation

▶ Do not file this form unless the corporation has timely filed
Form 2553 to elect to be an S corporation.
▶ See separate instructions.

OMB No. 1545-0130

19**98**

For calendar year 1998, or tax year beginning _____ , 1998, and ending _____ , 19 ___

A Effective date of election as an S corporation	Use IRS label. Otherwise, please print or type.	Name	C Employer identification number
		Number, street, and room or suite no. (If a P.O. box, see page 10 of the instructions.)	D Date incorporated
B NEW bus. code no. (see pages 26–28)		City or town, state, and ZIP code	E Total assets (see page 10) $

F Check applicable boxes: (1) ☐ Initial return   (2) ☐ Final return   (3) ☐ Change in address   (4) ☐ Amended return
G Enter number of shareholders in the corporation at end of the tax year ▶

Caution: *Include only trade or business income and expenses on lines 1a through 21. See the instructions for more information.*

Income

1a	Gross receipts or sales |_____| **b** Less returns and allowances |_____| **c** Bal ▶	1c	
2	Cost of goods sold (Schedule A, line 8)	2	
3	Gross profit. Subtract line 2 from line 1c	3	
4	Net gain (loss) from Form 4797, Part II, line 18 *(attach Form 4797)*	4	
5	Other income (loss) *(attach schedule)*	5	
6	**Total income (loss).** Combine lines 3 through 5 . . . . ▶	6	

Deductions (see page 11 of the instructions for limitations)

7	Compensation of officers.	7	
8	Salaries and wages (less employment credits)	8	
9	Repairs and maintenance.	9	
10	Bad debts	10	
11	Rents	11	
12	Taxes and licenses.	12	
13	Interest	13	
14a	Depreciation *(if required, attach Form 4562)* 14a		
b	Depreciation claimed on Schedule A and elsewhere on return . . 14b		
c	Subtract line 14b from line 14a	14c	
15	Depletion **(Do not deduct oil and gas depletion.)**	15	
16	Advertising	16	
17	Pension, profit-sharing, etc., plans	17	
18	Employee benefit programs	18	
19	Other deductions *(attach schedule)*	19	
20	**Total deductions.** Add the amounts shown in the far right column for lines 7 through 19 . ▶	20	
21	Ordinary income (loss) from trade or business activities. Subtract line 20 from line 6	21	

Tax and Payments

22	**Tax: a** Excess net passive income tax *(attach schedule).* . . . 22a		
b	Tax from Schedule D (Form 1120S) 22b		
c	Add lines 22a and 22b (see page 14 of the instructions for additional taxes)	22c	
23	**Payments: a** 1998 estimated tax payments and amount applied from 1997 return 23a		
b	Tax deposited with Form 7004 . . . . 23b		
c	Credit for Federal tax paid on fuels *(attach Form 4136)* . . . 23c		
d	Add lines 23a through 23c	23d	
24	Estimated tax penalty. Check if Form 2220 is attached . . . . . . ▶☐	24	
25	**Tax due.** If the total of lines 22c and 24 is larger than line 23d, enter amount owed. See page 4 of the instructions for depository method of payment . . . . . ▶	25	
26	**Overpayment.** If line 23d is larger than the total of lines 22c and 24, enter amount overpaid ▶	26	
27	Enter amount of line 26 you want: **Credited to 1999 estimated tax** ▶ |_____ **Refunded** ▶	27	

Please Sign Here

Under penalties of perjury, I declare that I have examined this return, including accompanying schedules and statements, and to the best of my knowledge and belief, it is true, correct, and complete. Declaration of preparer (other than taxpayer) is based on all information of which preparer has any knowledge.

▶ _____   _____   ▶ _____
Signature of officer   Date   Title

Paid Preparer's Use Only

Preparer's signature	▶	Date	Check if self-employed ▶ ☐	Preparer's social security number
Firm's name (or yours if self-employed) and address	▶		EIN ▶	
			ZIP code ▶	

For Paperwork Reduction Act Notice, see the separate instructions.   Cat. No. 11510H   Form **1120S** (1998)

Form 1120S (1998)   Page **2**

Schedule A — Cost of Goods Sold (see page 15 of the instructions)

1	Inventory at beginning of year	1
2	Purchases	2
3	Cost of labor	3
4	Additional section 263A costs (attach schedule)	4
5	Other costs (attach schedule)	5
6	**Total.** Add lines 1 through 5	6
7	Inventory at end of year	7
8	**Cost of goods sold.** Subtract line 7 from line 6. Enter here and on page 1, line 2	8

9a Check all methods used for valuing closing inventory:

    (i) ☐ Cost as described in Regulations section 1.471-3

    (ii) ☐ Lower of cost or market as described in Regulations section 1.471-4

    (iii) ☐ Other (specify method used and attach explanation) ▶ ....

  b Check if there was a writedown of "subnormal" goods as described in Regulations section 1.471-2(c) . . . . . . ▶ ☐

  c Check if the LIFO inventory method was adopted this tax year for any goods (if checked, attach Form 970). . . . . . ▶ ☐

  d If the LIFO inventory method was used for this tax year, enter percentage (or amounts) of closing inventory computed under LIFO . . . . 9d |

  e Do the rules of section 263A (for property produced or acquired for resale) apply to the corporation?. . . . . ☐ Yes ☐ No

  f Was there any change in determining quantities, cost, or valuations between opening and closing inventory? . . ☐ Yes ☐ No
    If "Yes," attach explanation.

Schedule B — Other Information

		Yes	No
1	Check method of accounting: **(a)** ☐ Cash **(b)** ☐ Accrual **(c)** ☐ Other (specify) ▶		
2	Refer to the list on pages 26 through 28 of the instructions and state the corporation's principal:		
	(a) Business activity ▶ .... **(b)** Product or service ▶		
3	Did the corporation at the end of the tax year own, directly or indirectly, 50% or more of the voting stock of a domestic corporation? (For rules of attribution, see section 267(c).) If "Yes," attach a schedule showing: **(a)** name, address, and employer identification number and **(b)** percentage owned.		
4	Was the corporation a member of a controlled group subject to the provisions of section 1561?		
5	At any time during calendar year 1998, did the corporation have an interest in or a signature or other authority over a financial account in a foreign country (such as a bank account, securities account, or other financial account)? (See page 15 of the instructions for exceptions and filing requirements for Form TD F 90-22.1.) . . . . If "Yes," enter the name of the foreign country ▶		
6	During the tax year, did the corporation receive a distribution from, or was it the grantor of, or transferor to, a foreign trust? If "Yes," the corporation may have to file Form 3520. See page 15 of the instructions.		
7	Check this box if the corporation has filed or is required to file **Form 8264,** Application for Registration of a Tax Shelter . . . . ▶ ☐		
8	Check this box if the corporation issued publicly offered debt instruments with original issue discount . . ▶ ☐		
	If so, the corporation may have to file **Form 8281,** Information Return for Publicly Offered Original Issue Discount Instruments.		
9	If the corporation: **(a)** filed its election to be an S corporation after 1986, **(b)** was a C corporation before it elected to be an S corporation **or** the corporation acquired an asset with a basis determined by reference to its basis (or the basis of any other property) in the hands of a C corporation, and **(c)** has net unrealized built-in gain (defined in section 1374(d)(1)) in excess of the net recognized built-in gain from prior years, enter the net unrealized built-in gain reduced by net recognized built-in gain from prior years (see page 16 of the instructions) . . . . . ▶ $		
10	Check this box if the corporation had accumulated earnings and profits at the close of the tax year (see page 16 of the instructions) . . . . ▶ ☐		

CORPORATIONS

Schedule K	Shareholders' Shares of Income, Credits, Deductions, etc.		
	(a) Pro rata share items		(b) Total amount

Income (Loss)	1 Ordinary income (loss) from trade or business activities (page 1, line 21)	1	
	2 Net income (loss) from rental real estate activities *(attach Form 8825)*	2	
	3a Gross income from other rental activities **3a**		
	b Expenses from other rental activities *(attach schedule)* **3b**		
	c Net income (loss) from other rental activities. Subtract line 3b from line 3a	3c	
	4 Portfolio income (loss):		
	a Interest income	4a	
	b Ordinary dividends	4b	
	c Royalty income	4c	
	d Net short-term capital gain (loss) *(attach Schedule D (Form 1120S))*	4d	
	e Net long-term capital gain (loss) *(attach Schedule D (Form 1120S))*:		
	(1) 28% rate gain (loss) ▶ .... (2) Total for year ▶	4e(2)	
	f Other portfolio income (loss) *(attach schedule)*	4f	
	5 Net section 1231 gain (loss) (other than due to casualty or theft) *(attach Form 4797)*	5	
	6 Other income (loss) *(attach schedule)*	6	
Deductions	7 Charitable contributions *(attach schedule)*	7	
	8 Section 179 expense deduction *(attach Form 4562)*	8	
	9 Deductions related to portfolio income (loss) (itemize)	9	
	10 Other deductions *(attach schedule)*	10	
Investment Interest	11a Interest expense on investment debts	11a	
	b (1) Investment income included on lines 4a, 4b, 4c, and 4f above	11b(1)	
	(2) Investment expenses included on line 9 above	11b(2)	
Credits	12a Credit for alcohol used as a fuel *(attach Form 6478)*	12a	
	b Low-income housing credit:		
	(1) From partnerships to which section 42(j)(5) applies for property placed in service before 1990	12b(1)	
	(2) Other than on line 12b(1) for property placed in service before 1990	12b(2)	
	(3) From partnerships to which section 42(j)(5) applies for property placed in service after 1989	12b(3)	
	(4) Other than on line 12b(3) for property placed in service after 1989	12b(4)	
	c Qualified rehabilitation expenditures related to rental real estate activities *(attach Form 3468)*	12c	
	d Credits (other than credits shown on lines 12b and 12c) related to rental real estate activities	12d	
	e Credits related to other rental activities	12e	
	13 Other credits	13	
Adjustments and Tax Preference Items	14a Depreciation adjustment on property placed in service after 1986	14a	
	b Adjusted gain or loss	14b	
	c Depletion (other than oil and gas)	14c	
	d (1) Gross income from oil, gas, or geothermal properties	14d(1)	
	(2) Deductions allocable to oil, gas, or geothermal properties	14d(2)	
	e Other adjustments and tax preference items *(attach schedule)*	14e	
Foreign Taxes	15a Type of income ▶		
	b Name of foreign country or U.S. possession		
	c Total gross income from sources outside the United States *(attach schedule)*	15c	
	d Total applicable deductions and losses *(attach schedule)*	15d	
	e Total foreign taxes (check one): ▶ ☐ Paid ☐ Accrued	15e	
	f Reduction in taxes available for credit *(attach schedule)*	15f	
	g Other foreign tax information *(attach schedule)*	15g	
Other	16 Section 59(e)(2) expenditures: a Type ▶ .... b Amount ▶	16b	
	17 Tax-exempt interest income	17	
	18 Other tax-exempt income	18	
	19 Nondeductible expenses	19	
	20 Total property distributions (including cash) other than dividends reported on line 22 below	20	
	21 Other items and amounts required to be reported separately to shareholders *(attach schedule)*		
	22 Total dividend distributions paid from accumulated earnings and profits	22	
	23 **Income (loss).** (Required only if Schedule M-1 must be completed.) Combine lines 1 through 6 in column (b). From the result, subtract the sum of lines 7 through 11a, 15e, and 16b	23	

Form 1120S (1998)

Page **4**

Schedule L	Balance Sheets per Books	Beginning of tax year		End of tax year	
	Assets	(a)	(b)	(c)	(d)
1	Cash				
2a	Trade notes and accounts receivable				
b	Less allowance for bad debts				
3	Inventories				
4	U.S. Government obligations				
5	Tax-exempt securities				
6	Other current assets (attach schedule)				
7	Loans to shareholders				
8	Mortgage and real estate loans				
9	Other investments (attach schedule)				
10a	Buildings and other depreciable assets				
b	Less accumulated depreciation				
11a	Depletable assets				
b	Less accumulated depletion				
12	Land (net of any amortization)				
13a	Intangible assets (amortizable only)				
b	Less accumulated amortization				
14	Other assets (attach schedule)				
15	Total assets				
	Liabilities and Shareholders' Equity				
16	Accounts payable				
17	Mortgages, notes, bonds payable in less than 1 year				
18	Other current liabilities (attach schedule)				
19	Loans from shareholders				
20	Mortgages, notes, bonds payable in 1 year or more				
21	Other liabilities (attach schedule)				
22	Capital stock				
23	Additional paid-in capital				
24	Retained earnings				
25	Adjustments to shareholders' equity (attach schedule)				
26	Less cost of treasury stock		( )		( )
27	Total liabilities and shareholders' equity				

Schedule M-1 Reconciliation of Income (Loss) per Books With Income (Loss) per Return (You are not required to complete this schedule if the total assets on line 15, column (d), of Schedule L are less than $25,000.)

1 Net income (loss) per books

2 Income included on Schedule K, lines 1 through 6, not recorded on books this year (itemize): ....

3 Expenses recorded on books this year not included on Schedule K, lines 1 through 11a, 15e, and 16b (itemize):
a Depreciation $ ....
b Travel and entertainment $ ....

4 Add lines 1 through 3

5 Income recorded on books this year not included on Schedule K, lines 1 through 6 (itemize):
a Tax-exempt interest $ ....

6 Deductions included on Schedule K, lines 1 through 11a, 15e, and 16b, not charged against book income this year (itemize):
a Depreciation $ ....

7 Add lines 5 and 6

8 Income (loss) (Schedule K, line 23). Line 4 less line 7

Schedule M-2 Analysis of Accumulated Adjustments Account, Other Adjustments Account, and Shareholders' Undistributed Taxable Income Previously Taxed (see page 24 of the instructions)

		(a) Accumulated adjustments account	(b) Other adjustments account	(c) Shareholders' undistributed taxable income previously taxed
1	Balance at beginning of tax year			
2	Ordinary income from page 1, line 21			
3	Other additions			
4	Loss from page 1, line 21	( )		
5	Other reductions	( )	( )	
6	Combine lines 1 through 5			
7	Distributions other than dividend distributions			
8	Balance at end of tax year. Subtract line 7 from line 6			

SCHEDULE D
(Form 1120S)

Department of the Treasury
Internal Revenue Service

Capital Gains and Losses and Built-In Gains

▶ Attach to Form 1120S.

▶ See separate instructions.

OMB No. 1545-0130

19**98**

Name

Employer identification number

Part I Short-Term Capital Gains and Losses—Assets Held One Year or Less

(a) Description of property (Example, 100 shares of "Z" Co.)	(b) Date acquired (mo., day, yr.)	(c) Date sold (mo., day, yr.)	(d) Sales price	(e) Cost or other basis (see instructions)	(f) Gain or (loss) ((d) minus (e))	
1						

2	Short-term capital gain from installment sales from Form 6252, line 26 or 37 . .	2	
3	Short-term capital gain or (loss) from like-kind exchanges from Form 8824 . . .	3	
4	Combine lines 1 through 3 in column (f) and enter here	4	
5	Tax on short-term capital gain included on line 32 below	5	( )
6	**Net short-term capital gain or (loss).** Combine lines 4 and 5. Enter here and on Form 1120S, Schedule K, line 4d or 6	6	

Part II Long-Term Capital Gains and Losses—Assets Held More Than One Year

(a) Description of property (Example, 100 shares of "Z" Co.)	(b) Date acquired (mo., day, yr.)	(c) Date sold (mo., day, yr.)	(d) Sales price	(e) Cost or other basis (see instructions)	(f) Gain or (loss) ((d) minus (e))	(g) 28% rate gain or (loss) * (see instr. below)
7						

8	Long-term capital gain from installment sales from Form 6252, line 26 or 37 . .	8	
9	Long-term capital gain or (loss) from like-kind exchanges from Form 8824 . . .	9	
10	Combine lines 7 through 9 in column (f) and enter here	10	
11	Tax on long-term capital gain included on lines 24 and 32 below	11	( )( )
12	Combine lines 7 through 11 in column (g). Enter here and on Form 1120S, Schedule K, line 4e(1) or 6	12	
13	**Net long-term capital gain or (loss).** Combine lines 10 and 11 in column (f). Enter here and on Form 1120S, Schedule K, line 4e(2) or 6	13	

* 28% rate gain or (loss) includes ALL "collectibles gains and losses" (as defined in the instructions).

Part III Capital Gains Tax (See instructions **before** completing this part.)

14	Enter section 1231 gain from Form 4797, line 9, column (g)	14	
15	Net long-term capital gain or (loss). Combine lines 10 and 14	15	
	Note: If the corporation is liable for the excess net passive income tax (Form 1120S, page 1, line 22a) or the built-in gains tax (Part IV below), see the line 16 instructions before completing line 16.		
16	Net capital gain. Enter excess of net long-term capital gain (line 15) over net short-term capital loss (line 4)	16	
17	Statutory minimum	17	$25,000
18	Subtract line 17 from line 16	18	
19	Enter 34% of line 18	19	
20	Taxable income (attach computation schedule)	20	
21	Enter tax on line 20 amount (attach computation schedule).	21	
22	Net capital gain from substituted basis property (attach computation schedule)	22	
23	Enter 35% of line 22	23	
24	**Tax.** Enter the smallest of line 19, 21, or 23 here and on Form 1120S, page 1, line 22b	24	

Part IV Built-In Gains Tax (See instructions **before** completing this part.)

25	Excess of recognized built-in gains over recognized built-in losses (attach computation schedule) . .	25	
26	Taxable income (attach computation schedule)	26	
27	Net recognized built-in gain. Enter the smallest of line 25, line 26, or line 9 of Schedule B	27	
28	Section 1374(b)(2) deduction	28	
29	Subtract line 28 from line 27. If zero or less, enter -0- here and on line 32	29	
30	Enter 35% of line 29	30	
31	Business credit and minimum tax credit carryforwards under section 1374(b)(3) from C corporation years	31	
32	**Tax.** Subtract line 31 from line 30 (if zero or less, enter -0-). Enter here and on Form 1120S, page 1, line 22b	32	

For Paperwork Reduction Act Notice, see the Instructions for Form 1120S.   Cat. No. 11516V   Schedule D (Form 1120S) 1998

SCHEDULE K-1	**Shareholder's Share of Income, Credits, Deductions, etc.**	OMB No. 1545-0130
(Form 1120S)	▶ See separate instructions.	**1998**
Department of the Treasury Internal Revenue Service	For calendar year 1998 or tax year beginning _____ , 1998, and ending _____ , 19 ___	

Shareholder's identifying number ▶ _____ | **Corporation's identifying number** ▶ _____

Shareholder's name, address, and ZIP code | Corporation's name, address, and ZIP code

A Shareholder's percentage of stock ownership for tax year (see instructions for Schedule K-1) . . . . . . ▶ _____ %

B Internal Revenue Service Center where corporation filed its return ▶ _____

C Tax shelter registration number (see instructions for Schedule K-1) . . . . . . ▶ _____

D Check applicable boxes: **(1)** ☐ Final K-1 **(2)** ☐ Amended K-1

	(a) Pro rata share items		(b) Amount	(c) Form 1040 filers enter the amount in column (b) on:
Income (Loss)	**1** Ordinary income (loss) from trade or business activities . . .	1		See pages 4 and 5 of the Shareholder's Instructions for Schedule K-1 (Form 1120S).
	2 Net income (loss) from rental real estate activities	2		
	3 Net income (loss) from other rental activities	3		
	4 Portfolio income (loss):			
	a Interest	4a		Sch. B, Part I, line 1
	b Ordinary dividends	4b		Sch. B, Part II, line 5
	c Royalties	4c		Sch. E, Part I, line 4
	d Net short-term capital gain (loss)	4d		Sch. D, line 5, col. (f)
	e Net long-term capital gain (loss):			
	(1) 28% rate gain (loss)	e(1)		Sch. D, line 12, col. (g)
	(2) Total for year	e(2)		Sch. D, line 12, col. (f)
	f Other portfolio income (loss) *(attach schedule)*	4f		(Enter on applicable line of your return.)
	5 Net section 1231 gain (loss) (other than due to casualty or theft)	5		See Shareholder's Instructions for Schedule K-1 (Form 1120S).
	6 Other income (loss) *(attach schedule)*	6		(Enter on applicable line of your return.)
Deductions	**7** Charitable contributions *(attach schedule)*	7		Sch. A, line 15 or 16
	8 Section 179 expense deduction	8		See page 6 of the Shareholder's Instructions for Schedule K-1 (Form 1120S).
	9 Deductions related to portfolio income (loss) *(attach schedule)* .	9		
	10 Other deductions *(attach schedule)*	10		
Investment Interest	**11a** Interest expense on investment debts	11a		Form 4952, line 1
	b (1) Investment income included on lines 4a, 4b, 4c, and 4f above	b(1)		See Shareholder's Instructions for Schedule K-1 (Form 1120S).
	(2) Investment expenses included on line 9 above	b(2)		
Credits	**12a** Credit for alcohol used as fuel	12a		Form 6478, line 10
	b Low-income housing credit:			
	(1) From section 42(j)(5) partnerships for property placed in service before 1990	b(1)		
	(2) Other than on line 12b(1) for property placed in service before 1990	b(2)		Form 8586, line 5
	(3) From section 42(j)(5) partnerships for property placed in service after 1989	b(3)		
	(4) Other than on line 12b(3) for property placed in service after 1989	b(4)		
	c Qualified rehabilitation expenditures related to rental real estate activities	12c		
	d Credits (other than credits shown on lines 12b and 12c) related to rental real estate activities	12d		See page 7 of the Shareholder's Instructions for Schedule K-1 (Form 1120S).
	e Credits related to other rental activities	12e		
	13 Other credits	13		

For Paperwork Reduction Act Notice, see the Instructions for Form 1120S. Cat. No. 11520D **Schedule K-1 (Form 1120S) 1998**

	(a) Pro rata share items		(b) Amount	(c) Form 1040 filers enter the amount in column (b) on:
Adjustments and Tax Preference Items	**14a** Depreciation adjustment on property placed in service after 1986	14a		See page 7 of the Shareholder's Instructions for Schedule K-1 (Form 1120S) and Instructions for Form 6251
	b Adjusted gain or loss	14b		
	c Depletion (other than oil and gas)	14c		
	d (1) Gross income from oil, gas, or geothermal properties . . .	d(1)		
	(2) Deductions allocable to oil, gas, or geothermal properties .	d(2)		
	e Other adjustments and tax preference items *(attach schedule)* .	14e		
Foreign Taxes	**15a** Type of income ▶			Form 1116, Check boxes
	b Name of foreign country or U.S. possession ▶			
	c Total gross income from sources outside the United States *(attach schedule)*	15c		Form 1116, Part I
	d Total applicable deductions and losses *(attach schedule)* . . .	15d		
	e Total foreign taxes (check one): ▶ ☐ Paid ☐ Accrued .	15e		Form 1116, Part II
	f Reduction in taxes available for credit *(attach schedule)* . . .	15f		Form 1116, Part III
	g Other foreign tax information *(attach schedule)*	15g		See Instructions for Form 1116
Other	**16** Section 59(e)(2) expenditures: **a** Type ▶			See Shareholder's Instructions for Schedule K-1 (Form 1120S).
	b Amount	16b		
	17 Tax-exempt interest income	17		Form 1040, line 8b
	18 Other tax-exempt income	18		See pages 7 and 8 of the Shareholder's Instructions for Schedule K-1 (Form 1120S).
	19 Nondeductible expenses	19		
	20 Property distributions (including cash) other than dividend distributions reported to you on Form 1099-DIV	20		
	21 Amount of loan repayments for "Loans From Shareholders" . .	21		
	22 Recapture of low-income housing credit:			
	a From section 42(j)(5) partnerships	22a		Form 8611, line 8
	b Other than on line 22a	22b		

Supplemental Information	**23** Supplemental information required to be reported separately to each shareholder *(attach additional schedules if more space is needed):*

211

10 | LIMITED LIABILITY COMPANIES (LLCS)

In many respects, this business form is the best of all worlds. It combines the flexibility of a partnership with the limited liability of a corporation. Yet, it is taxed at only one level—that of the individual member of the LLC.

The process of forming an LLC is more like that of starting a partnership than of starting a corporation. In fact, if you think of an LLC as a partnership with limited liability of all of the partners, you won't be too far from the actual facts. Here are the steps to getting started, with emphasis on the differences between starting an LLC and starting a partnership or corporation.

Caution: The concept of Limited Liability Companies is relatively new. Although the first LLC laws appeared in the early 1980s (in Florida), they did not appear in the statutes of most states until the mid-1990s, and not all states recognized LLCs until 1997. Therefore, unlike the areas of partnerships and corporations, where most state statutes fairly closely follow the same rules, state laws about LLCs vary considerably and are still being updated. Check your state law before proceeding with setting up an LLC.

INITIAL FORMS THAT START YOUR LIMITED LIABILITY COMPANY

During the life of your LLC, you will, like all businesses, have myriads of government forms to file and records to keep. However, only two or three forms are all it takes to officially set up your business as an LLC in your state.

Reservation of an LLC Name

As for a corporation, your state may allow you to reserve the name you have chosen for 30 to 90 days (depending on which state you're in) while you work out the details of your LLC.

Articles of Organization

Most states have a standard fill-in-the-blanks form you can use, and some, such as California (pp. 218–221), require that form be used. Some states require that two people act as organizers, while in others there only needs to be one. As you can see in these examples, there is little information required in these forms.

Like corporations, the LLC is usually not considered to exist until the articles have been accepted by the secretary of state or whatever state department handles LLC registration.

Annual Reports

States generally require LLCs to file some type of annual report that updates various information on file with the secretary of state or similar state authority. The requirements vary by state, but find out when they are due. California, for instance, requires the first statement of information within 90 days after the acceptance of the articles of organization.

OPERATING AGREEMENT OF AN LLC

Just as a partnership should have a partnership agreement and a corporation must have bylaws, an LLC needs an "operating agreement." Like its counterparts, this document lays out rules that cover questions such as:

- What will be the life span of the LLC, or will it exist for an indefinite period?
- Who will be the manager(s) of the LLC?
- What is the procedure for replacing managers?
- How will managers' compensation be determined?
- What decisions require a vote of the LLC membership? When will a super-majority or unanimous vote be necessary?
- Can a member transfer his or her interest to another person or entity? If so, does that new member have the same voting privileges as the original member?
- What happens upon the death of a member? Transfer of interest, sale back to the LLC by the member's estate, or some other provision?
- How will profits and losses be allocated to the members?

- How will cash distributions be determined and distributed?
- Are members prohibited from engaging in competing or related businesses?

Because the area of LLC law is so new and varies greatly from state to state, operating agreements are still being developed by the legal profession. The example that appears on pages 222–232 (the Form for Georgia) can help you determine what should be in your LLC's operating agreement, but this is definitely an area in which one size does not fit all. Engage a corporate attorney to help you, after you and your LLC members have decided what decisions should be reflected in the agreement. Spend your professional-fees budget to find out if your plan is legal in the state(s) in which you plan to operate.

LLCs AND THE SECURITIES LAWS

The comments for limited partnerships apply equally to limited liability companies.

INCOME TAX STATUS AND FORMS, LLC

Before 1997, determining the tax status of an LLC was a game of semantics with the IRS. The reason was some arcane rules about whether the LLC had more attributes of a corporation than attributes of a noncorporation. That is, the LLC could be taxed as a corporation or as a partnership, depending on several factors. Who won the game was never certain until the statute of limitations had run out or the IRS examined the LLC's return and both sides pursued appeals through the federal courts.

Amazingly, the IRS did away with those rules (effective January 1, 1997) and, in their place, promulgated rules that amount to checking the box to answer the question, "How would you like to be taxed?" Of course, the rules really can't be that simple. There are 24 pages of regulations about how you check the box! How they affect a new LLC boils down to this:

- An LLC with more two or more members will be taxed as a partnership unless it "checks the box" to be taxed as a corporation.
- A single-member LLC will be taxed as a sole proprietorship, unless it "checks the box" to elect to be taxed as a corporation. In other words, it cannot be taxed as a partnership. That doesn't obviate the advisability of forming a single-member LLC and filing a Schedule C as a sole proprietorship (in those states that allow a single-owner LLC) in order to gain limited liability.
- If a corporation is the member of a single-member LLC, the LLC would be treated as a branch of the corporation. In this situation, if you want

the new business to be taxed separately, form a corporation rather than an LLC.

Multimember LLCs

Until these check-the-box rules became effective, LLCs which filed partnership income tax returns were always in danger of the IRS reclassifying them as corporations, which would give the LLC the "privilege" of paying the double taxation of a C corporation. (By the time the IRS made this change of classification, it would be too late to elect S corporation status.) Now, however, LLCs can proceed without this tax cloud hanging overhead.

Single-Member LLCs

Suppose a sole proprietor wants the limited liability of an LLC and taxation as a C corporation. (This could be a goal if the sole proprietor did not want to draw any cash out of the business for several years.) He or she could:

1. Form an LLC and check the box for classification as "an association taxable as a corporation."
2. Form a C corporation of which he or she is the sole stockholder.

Because these rules are new and LLCs are relatively new, exactly how the IRS examiners and the courts will interpret them is not certain. Therefore, for the present, it would probably be wiser to elect the C corporation route. For instance, at some future date, the individual might want to sell the business. Selling the stock is relatively simple. Just how an LLC that is taxed as a corporation would be taxed when it sells ownership is not yet clear. Also, because some states do not permit single-member LLCs, the individual owner might not enjoy limited liability when the business expanded its operations to such a state.

The Check-the-Box Form

The check-the-box election is made on IRS Form 8832, Entity Classification Election (pp. 233–236). A new LLC with one or more members that wants to be taxed as a corporation would check boxes 1a and 2a.

A new single-member LLC wanting to be taxed as a sole proprietorship would not file this form. An LLC of two or more members wanting to be taxed as a partnership would not file this form. See the "Domestic default rule" and the "Eligible entity" definition in the instructions to the form.

IMPORTANT: If you do not accept the default classification (partnership, for your multimember LLC), you must file this form within 75 days of the start of the LLC for the election to be effective for your first year.

States vary as to exactly when the articles of organization become effective (either when filed, when accepted, or when approved), so file early.

OTHER FORMS AN LLC SHOULD FILE

The IRS wants to hear from an LLC just as it wants forms filed by other types of business entities. There are no special income tax forms for LLCs. They use whatever form applies to the type of entity classification they have chosen. Specifically:

- If an LLC of two or more members accepts the default classification of partnership, it files Form 1065, U.S. Partnership Return of Income.
- If an LLC of two or more members checks the box to elect taxation as a corporation, it files Form 1120, U.S. Corporation Income Tax Return. (In theory, it probably could elect S corporation status and file Form 1120S, but that scenario seems pointless, because it would then be saddled with the disadvantages of both business forms.)
- If a single-member LLC accepts the default classification of sole proprietor, it files a Schedule C, Profit or Loss from Business (Sole Proprietorship).
- If a single-member LLC elects tax classification as a corporation, it files Form 1120, U.S. Corporation Income Tax Return.

The above forms are reproduced as follows:

- Schedule C of Form 1040: In Chapter 7, pages 61–69
- Form 1065, Partnership Return: In Chapter 8, pages 85–121
- Form 1120, Corporation Return: In Chapter 9, pages 182–189

RECORDS AN LLC SHOULD KEEP

LLCs have been legal, in only some states, for less than 20 years, and they have become popular only in the last five years. Corporations, on the other hand, have been around for centuries. For corporations, time has allowed the development of laws, court decisions, and various regulations that determine how corporations should be operated. Hence, we have the formalities of stockholders' meetings, board of directors' meetings, election of officers, and all the other procedures covered in our discussion of corporations.

For LLCs, there are no centuries of precedent in the regulation and formalities of LLCs in the United States. How formal should the records be? For starters, look at the law in your state. For example, Florida law states the minimum records to be maintained by an LLC (see page 237).

It would be wise to go beyond the minimum that your state's statutes require. Certainly, you should keep minutes of all meetings of the LLC's members. If your articles of organization or the operating agreement delegates the management to managers, you should also keep minutes of their meetings about significant matters. Follow the general format of corporate minutes, but substitute "members" for stockholders and "managers" for board of directors and officers.

The important thing is to keep a clear record of major decisions. Don't worry if you don't throw around "whereas," "hereinabove," and "resolved" as does a lawyer.

LIMITED LIABILITY PARTNERSHIP (LLP)

You may often find this term in connection with LLCs, where "partnership" replaces "company" in the name of the type of entity. (There are also variations in the LLP term in several states.) The significance is this:

While most businesses can protect their owners from nearly all types of liability by operating as a corporation or LLC, that protection is not available for various professionals. While professionals can protect themselves from the liability that arises from events such as a client slipping on a banana peel, they are not always protected from *professional* negligence. If you fall in your accountant's waiting room, you may not be able to collect damages beyond the assets of his or her LLP. However, if he or she files the wrong tax return and it costs you $3,000,000 in IRS penalties, you should be able to collect from his or her personal assets. (Good luck, most accountants don't have $3,000,000 lying about.)

In other words, professionals cannot protect themselves from liability from professional negligence, so states do not allow them to use the LLC type of business form. Instead, states allow them to organize as an LLP, which offers limited liability *except* for professional liability. (In an LLP, however, a professional is protected from liability arising from the act of another professional who is a member of the same LLP.) To which professions does this apply? The states vary widely. In some, the LLP rules apply only to lawyers and accountants. In others, they apply to several professions.

The forms that an LLP files with a secretary of state are specialized for LLPs. The IRS and state tax forms that it files are identical to those for an LLC.

State of California
Bill Jones
Secretary of State

LLC-1

LIMITED LIABILITY COMPANY
ARTICLES OF ORGANIZATION

IMPORTANT - Read the instructions before completing the form.
This document is presented for filing pursuant to Section 17050 of the California Corporations Code.

1. Limited liability company name:
   (End the name with LLC, L.L.C., Limited Liability Company or Ltd. Liability Co.)

2. Latest date (month/day/year) on which the limited liability company is to dissolve.

3. The purpose of the limited liability company is to engage in any lawful act or activity for which a limited liability company may be organized under the Beverly-Killea Limited Liability Company Act.

4. Enter the name of initial agent for service of process and check the appropriate provision below:

   _____ , which is

   [ ] an individual residing in California.

   [ ] a corporation which has filed a certificate pursuant to Section 1505 of the California Corporations Code. Skip Item 5 and proceed to Item 6.

5. If the initial agent for service of process is an individual, enter a business or residential address in California:

   Address:

   City: State: California   Zip Code:

6. The limited liability company will be managed by: **(check one)**

   [ ] one manager   [ ] more than one manager   [ ] limited liability company members

7. If other matters are to be included in the Articles of Organization attach one or more separate pages.
   Number of pages attached, if any: [   ]

Describe type of business of the Limited Liability Company.

	For Secretary of State Use
Declaration: It is hereby declared that I am the person who executed this instrument, which execution is my act and deed.	
	File No. _____
_____ Signature of organizer	
_____ Type or print name of organizer	
Date: _____ , 19 _____	

SEC/STATE (REV. 10/98)   FORM LLC-1 – FILING FEE: $70
Approved By Secretary Of State

INSTRUCTIONS FOR COMPLETING THE ARTICLES OF ORGANIZATION (LLC-1)

All references are to the California Corporations Code unless otherwise indicated.
Type or legibly print in black ink.

DO NOT ALTER THIS FORM

Item 1. Enter the name of the limited liability company which must end with the words "LLC", "L.L.C." or "Limited Liability Company". The words "Limited" and "Company" may be abbreviated to "Ltd." and "Co." Section 17051(a)(1). The name of the limited liability company may not contain the words "bank", "insurance company", "insurer", "trust", "trustee", "incorporated", "inc.", "corporation", or "corp." Section 17052(d).

Professional limited liability companies are prohibited from forming or registering in California.

Item 2. Enter the latest date (month/day/year) on which the limited liability company is to dissolve. Section 17051(a)(2).

Item 3. The articles of organization must contain the following statement of purpose which is preprinted on the form and may not be altered: "The purpose of the limited liability company is to engage in any lawful act or activity for which a limited liability company may be organized under the Beverly-Killea Limited Liability Company Act". Section 17051(a)(3). If the provisions limiting or restricting the business of the limited liability company are desired refer to Item 7 for instructions on attaching additional pages.

Item 4. Enter the name and address of the initial agent for service of process. Check the appropriate provision indicating whether the initial agent is an individual residing in California or a corporation which has filed a certificate pursuant to Section 1505 of the California Corporations Code. Section 17051(a)(5).

Item 5. Enter a business or residential address in California, "in care of" (c/o) is not acceptable.

Item 6. Check the appropriate provision indicating whether the limited liability company is to be managed by one manager, more than one manager, or the limited liability company members. Section 17051(a)(6).

Item 7. The articles of organization may contain additional provisions including, but not limited to, provisions limiting or restricting the business in which the limited liability company may engage, powers that the limited liability company may exercise, admission of members, events that will cause a dissolution, or limitations on the authority of managers or members to bind the limited liability company. Such matters must be submitted on single-sided, standard white paper. Number and identify each page as an attachment to the articles of organization. Enter the number of pages attached to the form, if any, in Item 7. Section 17051(c).

Briefly describe the general type of business that constitutes the principal business activity of the limited liability company. Note restrictions in the rendering of professional services by Limited Liability Companies. Professional services are defined in California Corporations Code 13401(a) as: "any type of professional services that may be lawfully rendered only pursuant to a license, certification, or registration authorized by the Business and Professions Code or the Chiropractic Act."

Declaration: The articles of organization must be executed with an original signature. Facsimiles and photocopies of the articles of organization are not acceptable for the purpose of filing with the Secretary of State. The person executing the articles of organization need not be a member or manager of the limited liability company. Section 17051(a).

- The fee for filing the articles of organization with the Secretary of State is seventy dollars ($70). Section 17701(b).

- Send the executed document and filing fee to:

- Return the acknowledgment of filing to:

Office of the Secretary of State
Limited Liability Company Unit
P.O. Box 944228
Sacramento, CA 94244-2280

Name: _____
Firm/Company: _____
Address: _____
City: _____
State: _____ Zip Code: _____

State of California
Secretary of State
Bill Jones

LIMITED LIABILITY COMPANY – STATEMENT OF INFORMATION

A $10.00 FILING FEE MUST ACCOMPANY THIS FORM.

IMPORTANT – Read Instructions On Back Before Completing This Form.

1. LIMITED LIABILITY COMPANY NAME

THIS SPACE FOR FILING USE ONLY

2. SECRETARY OF STATE FILE NUMBER

3. JURISDICTION OF FORMATION

4. STREET ADDRESS OF PRINCIPAL EXECUTIVE OFFICE   CITY AND STATE   ZIP CODE

5. STREET ADDRESS IN CALIFORNIA OF OFFICE WHERE RECORDS ARE MAINTAINED (FOR DOMESTIC ONLY)   CITY   ZIP CODE

CA

LIST THE NAME AND COMPLETE ADDRESS OF ANY MANAGER OR MANAGERS, AND CHIEF EXECUTIVE OFFICER, IF ANY, OR IF NONE HAVE BEEN APPOINTED OR ELECTED, PROVIDE THE NAME AND ADDRESS OF EACH MEMBER. (CHECK THE APPROPRIATE DESIGNATION). ATTACH ADDITIONAL PAGES IF NECESSARY.

6. NAME   [ ] MANAGER

ADDRESS   [ ] CHIEF EXECUTIVE OFFICER

CITY   STATE   ZIP CODE   [ ] MEMBER

7. NAME   [ ] MANAGER

ADDRESS   [ ] CHIEF EXECUTIVE OFFICER

CITY   STATE   ZIP CODE   [ ] MEMBER

8. NAME THE AGENT FOR SERVICE OF PROCESS AND CHECK THE APPROPRIATE PROVISION BELOW:

_____, WHICH IS

[ ] AN INDIVIDUAL RESIDING IN CALIFORNIA. PROCEED TO ITEM 9.

[ ] A CORPORATION WHICH HAS FILED A CERTIFICATE PURSUANT TO SECTION 1505. PROCEED TO ITEM 10.

9. STREET ADDRESS OF THE AGENT FOR SERVICE OF PROCESS IN CALIFORNIA.   CITY   ZIP CODE

CA

10. DESCRIBE TYPE OF BUSINESS OF THE LIMITED LIABILITY COMPANY.

11. NUMBER OF PAGES ATTACHED, IF ANY.

12. I DECLARE THAT THIS STATEMENT IS TRUE, CORRECT AND COMPLETE.

_____   _____
SIGNATURE OF INDIVIDUAL AUTHORIZED TO SIGN   DATE

_____
TYPE OR PRINT NAME AND TITLE OF PERSON SIGNING

DUE DATE:

SEC/STATE FORM LPS/LLC-12 (Rev. 6/97)

INSTRUCTIONS FOR COMPLETING THE STATEMENT OF INFORMATION (LLC-E012)

IF NOT FILLED OUT CORRECTLY, THIS FORM WILL BE RETURNED.

DO NOT ALTER THIS FORM

Type or legibly print in black ink.

- Attach the ten dollar ($10.00) fee for filing the Statement of Information (LLC-E012) and send the executed document and filing fee to:

  Secretary of State
  Limited Liability Company Unit
  P.O. Box 944228
  Sacramento, CA 94244-2280

- If a plain copy of the filed document is requested, please submit an additional five dollars ($5.00). If a certified copy of the filed document is requested, please submit an additional ten dollars ($10.00).

- Fill in the items as follows:

Item 1. Enter the name of the limited liability company.

Item 2. Enter the file number issued by the California Secretary of State.

Item 3. Enter the jurisdiction (state or country) of formation of the limited liability company.

Item 4. Enter the complete street address, city, state and zip code, of the principal executive office. **DO NOT** show a P.O. Box or abbreviate the name of the city.

Item 5. Enter the street address, city and zip code of the office required to be maintained, pursuant to subdivision (a) of Section 17057 if the limited liability company was formed under the laws of the State of California. **DO NOT** enter a P.O. Box or abbreviate the name of the city.

Item 6-7. Enter the name and complete business or residence addresses of any manager or managers and the chief executive officer, if any, appointed or elected in accordance with the articles of organization or operating agreement or, if no manager has been so elected or appointed, the name and business or residence address of each member. Attach additional pages if necessary. **DO NOT** abbreviate the name of the city. Check the appropriate box to designate the status of the individual named.

Item 8. Enter the name of the agent for service of process in California. The agent for service of process must be an individual residing in California or a corporation which has filed a certificate pursuant to Section 1505 (CCC). Check the appropriate provision.

Item 9. If an individual is designated as the agent for service of process, enter a business or residential street address in California. **DO NOT** enter a P.O. Box, "in care of" (c/o), or abbreviate the name of the city. **DO NOT** enter an address if a corporation is designated as the agent for service of process.

Item 10. Briefly describe the general type of business that constitutes the principal business activity of the limited liability company.

Item 11. Enter the number of pages attached, if any.

Item 12. The Statement of Information (LLC-E012) must be executed with an original signature of an individual authorized to sign as provided in Section 17056 or 17451 (CCC). Enter date signed.

- All references, unless otherwise indicated, are to Section 17060 of the California Corporations Code (CCC).

- For further information contact the Limited Liability Company Unit at (916) 653-3795.

SOS-BP-LLC-E012 (Rev. 8/1997)

LIMITED LIABILITY COMPANY
OPERATING AGREEMENT

Reprinted by permission of Scott Withrow, Esquire, Atlanta, Georgia

LIMITED LIABILITY
COMPANY OPERATING
AGREEMENT OF
XXXX, LLC

THIS LIMITED LIABILITY COMPANY OPERATING AGREEMENT ("Agreement"), dated as of the _____ day of _____ , 19 _____ by and between the undersigned members (collectively, "Members").

WITNESSETH

In consideration of the covenants and mutual agreements hereinafter set forth, the parties hereto (hereinafter collectively referred to as the "Members") agree as follows:

1. FORMATION OF LIMITED LIABILITY COMPANY. The Members hereby form a limited liability company (hereinafter referred to as the "Company") pursuant to the provisions of the Georgia Limited Liability Company Act ("Act"). Articles of Organization have been filed with the Georgia Secretary of State in accordance with the Act.

2. GENERAL PROVISIONS.

   a. Name. The name of the Company shall be XXXX, LLC. The Company may also conduct business under such trade name(s) as the Managers may determine.

THE LIMITED LIABILITY COMPANY INTERESTS IN XXXX, LLC HAVE NOT BEEN REGISTERED UNDER EITHER THE SECURITIES ACT OF 1933, AS AMENDED (THE "FEDERAL ACT"), IN RELIANCE UPON THE EXEMPTION FROM REGISTRATION CONTAINED IN SECTIONS 3(a)(11), 3(b) OR 4(2) THEREOF OR REGULATION D PROMULGATED THEREUNDER, OR THE GEORGIA SECURITIES ACT OR 1973, AS AMENDED (THE "GEORGIA ACT"), IN RELIANCE UPON THE EXEMPTION PROVIDED BY O.C.G.A. 10-5-9(13) THEREOF, OR OTHER STATE SECURITIES LAWS. SUCH INTERESTS MUST BE ACQUIRED BY THE MEMBERS FOR INVESTMENT AND NOT WITH A VIEW TO, OR FOR RESALE IN CONNECTION WITH, A

DISTRIBUTION OF SUCH INTERESTS, AND SUCH INTERESTS MAY NOT BE OFFERED FOR SALE, SOLD, TRANSFERRED, ASSIGNED, OR HYPOTHECATED IN THE ABSENCE OF COMPLIANCE WITH THE TERMS OF THIS AGREEMENT AND (i) AN EFFECTIVE REGISTRATION STATEMENT WITH RESPECT TO THE INTEREST UNDER THE FEDERAL ACT, THE GEORGIA ACT OR OTHER APPLICABLE STATE SECURITIES LAWS OF (ii) AN OPINION OF COUNSEL SATISFACTORY TO THE COMPANY THAT SUCH INTERESTS WILL BE OFFERED FOR SALE, SOLD, TRANSFERRED, ASSIGNED, OR HYPOTHECATED ONLY IN A TRANSACTION WHICH IS EXEMPT UNDER THE FEDERAL ACT, THE GEORGIA ACT OR OTHER APPLICABLE STATE SECURITIES LAWS, OR WHICH IS OTHERWISE IN COMPLIANCE WITH SUCH ACTS.

b. <u>Purpose.</u> The general purpose of the Company is to engage in any lawful activities permitted under the Act.

c. <u>Principal Office.</u> The principal office and place of business of the Company shall be _____ , or such place as the Managers may from time to time determine.

d. <u>Term.</u> The period of duration of the limited liability company shall be perpetual subject only to dissolution and termination of the Company in accordance with the provisions of Section 10 of this Agreement.

3. MEMBERS.

a. <u>Membership Units.</u> The interests in the Company of each Member, including the right to vote on, consent to, or otherwise participate in any decision or action of or by the Members pursuant to this Agreement or the Act, shall initially be divided into units (the "Units"). The Members and their respective Units in the Company shall be as set forth on the Schedule of Members, Capital and Units attached hereto as <u>Schedule A.</u> The Managers may issue certificates of interest to the holders of the Units in such form as they may consider appropriate.

b. <u>Authority of Members.</u> No Member acting alone shall have any power or authority to bind the Company unless the Member has been authorized by the Managers to act as an agent of the Company.

c. <u>Limitation on Liability.</u> No Member shall have any personal liability for any debts or losses of the Company beyond his respective capital contributions, except as provided by law.

d. <u>Actions by Managers with Respect to Sales of Units.</u> The Managers shall, with respect to any sale of Units, (i) make a notation in the appropriate records of the Company with respect to such sale, and (ii) obtain a written representation from each purchaser of Units as to his or her investment intent.

4. ASSIGNMENT OF INTERESTS IN COMPANY. The Units, and any interest in the Units, may not be sold, conveyed, transferred, pledged or assigned, voluntarily or involuntarily (including by operation of law or otherwise), except in accordance with the provisions of this section. Any attempt to sell, convey, transfer, pledge or assign any interest in the Units in violation of this Agreement or any applicable state or federal law shall be void and of no effect.

   a. Units are Restricted Securities. Units have not been registered under the Securities Act of 1933 as amended ("Securities Act") or under the securities laws of any state, and may not be offered, sold, pledged, hypothecated or otherwise transferred unless and until registered under the Securities Act or, in the opinion of counsel in form and substance satisfactory to the Company, such offer, sale, pledge, hypothecation or transfer is in compliance therewith.

   b. Right of First Refusal on Sale of Units. Any Member desiring to sell all or less than all of his or her Units to a person or entity other than one of the other Members for any reason shall first notify the Company in writing of his or her intention to sell, stating the name and address of the proposed purchaser, the number of Units proposed to be sold, the consideration proposed to be received therefore, and the proposed terms of sale. The Company shall have the exclusive right and privilege to purchase the Units proposed to be sold for the consideration and upon the terms stated in such written notice at any time within 30 days of the later of (i) receipt of such written notice, or (ii) appointment of Managers to act on the Company's behalf. If the Company does not purchase the Units so offered, during the next succeeding 60-day period the Member desiring to sell Units may then sell such Units to the person and at the price and terms stated in the offer. If the Units are not so sold, they shall not be subsequently sold without first again offering them to the Company as herein above provided. This Section 4.b. shall not be construed as limiting in any way the authority and discretion of the Members either to give or withhold their consent to any proposed assignment of Units by a Member under Section 4.c., even though the Company shall not have exercised its rights and privilege to purchase such Units.

   c. Consent Required for Substitution of New Member. Subject to Sections 4.a. and 4.b., an assignee of any Units may become a Member only upon (i) execution and delivery by the assignee of a written acceptance and adoption of this Agreement, as the same may be amended, together with such other documents, if any, as the Managers may require; (ii) the payment to the Company by the Member selling his or her Units of all reasonable expenses incurred by the Company in connection with such assignment; and (iii) with the unanimous written consent of the Members, which consent may, in each case, be given or denied in the absolute discretion of each Member. Upon such execution and consent, when applicable, but not otherwise, the assignee shall, with respect to the Units assigned, be admitted to the Company and become a substituted Member therein. This Section 4 shall not apply to initial admission of Members pursuant to Section 3 of this Agreement or to transfers of Unit between existing Members of the Company.

5. CAPTIAL.

    a. <u>Capital Contributions of Members.</u> In exchange for his or her Units in the Company, each Member agrees to contribute to the Company an initial capital contribution in the amount set forth opposite his or her name on <u>Schedule A</u> attached to this Agreement and incorporated herein by this reference.

    b. <u>No Right to Withdraw Capital.</u> No interest shall accrue on any contribution to the capital of the Company, and no Member shall have the right to withdraw from the Company or be repaid any contribution of capital except as otherwise specifically provided herein.

    c. <u>Capital Accounts.</u> A separate capital account shall be maintained for each Member. There shall be credited to each Member's capital account: 1) the amount of cash and the fair market value of any property contributed by the Member, and 2) the Member's share of the profits of the Company; and there shall be charged against each Member's capital account: 1) the amount of all distributions to the Member, and 2) the Member's share of losses of the Company. No Member shall be liable for any deficit or negative balance in his or her capital account.

6. DISTRIBUTIONS.

    a. <u>Distributions of Cash Flow.</u> The "cash flow" of the Company may be distributed among the Members pro rata based on the number of all Units. Such distributions shall occur at least annually within ninety (90) days after the end of each calendar year and with such greater frequency as the Managers shall determine is consistent with the orderly administration of the business of the Company. No distribution shall be made to any Member is such distribution is prohibited by Section 14-11-407 of the Act. The "cash flow" of the Company shall be equal to the taxable income of the Company, increased by the amount allowable as depreciation on the Company's assets, the amount of any amortization deduction and the amount of any other items deductible for federal income tax purposes in excess of actual cash payments with respect thereto, and decreased by the amount of any repayment of the principal portion of any debt of the Company, all cash expenditures not deductible for federal income tax purposes or the amount thereof in excess of the amount deductible for federal income tax purposes, and the amount of all other expenses and all reserves set aside by the Managers as they shall determine are necessary or desirable to provide for actual or contingent liabilities, working capital requirements of the Company, and for other purposes necessary or incidental to the proper management function of the business of the Company.

    b. <u>No Liability for Distributions.</u> Upon any such distribution made in good faith, the Managers shall incur no liability even though such distribution results in the Company retaining insufficient funds for the operation of its business, which insufficiency results in loss to the Company or necessitates requesting any additional capital contributions from the Members or the borrowing of funds by the Company.

7. PROFITS AND LOSSES. Except as otherwise provided in this Agreement, taxable income, gain, loss, deduction or credit shall be allocated among the Members in the same manner as distributions are made or, if no distributions are made during the period, pro rata based on the number of all Units. If any Units have been transferred or assigned during any taxable year, allocation of the interest represented thereby shall be prorated between the transferor and the transferee based upon the time the transferor and transferee held the Units during the year.

8. MANAGEMENT.

   a. <u>Appointment of Managers.</u> _____ and _____ are appointed Managers of the Company, and shall serve until his or her resignation, removal or until his or her successor has been appointed and has undertaken his or her duties.

   b. <u>Authority of the Managers.</u> Except as otherwise expressly provided herein, all decisions respecting any matter set forth in this Agreement or otherwise affecting or arising out of conduct of the business of the Company shall be made by the Managers. The Managers shall have the exclusive right and full authority to manage, conduct and operate the Company business and to make all decisions regarding the operation of the Company business and to perform any and all other acts or activities customary or incident to the management of the Company business. Specifically, but not by way of limitation, the Managers shall be authorized to: (i) employ such agents, employees, managers, accountants, attorneys, consultants and other persons necessary or appropriate to carry out the business and affairs of the Company and to pay as an expense of the Company such reasonable fees, expenses, salaries, wages and other compensation to such persons as the Managers shall determine; (ii) cause to be paid all amounts due and payable by the Company to any person or entity; (iii) pay, expend, renew, modify, adjust, submit to arbitration, prosecute, defend or compromise upon such terms as the Managers may determine and upon such evidence as it may deem sufficient any obligation, suit, liability, cause of action or claim, including taxes, either in favor of or against the Company; (iv) make any and all expenditures or investments of excess funds in obligations which the Managers, in their sole discretion, deem necessary or appropriate in connection with the management of the affairs of the Company and the carrying out of its obligations and responsibilities under this Agreement; (v) lease Company property on such terms and conditions a the Managers shall determine to be in the interest of the Company; (vi) incur such indebtedness on behalf of the Company as the Managers deem necessary to carry out business and affairs of the Company; (vii) purchase insurance insuring the Managers and/or employees of the Company from personal liability for actions taken in good faith on behalf of the Company; (viii) execute on behalf of the Company all instruments and documents; (ix) hold and own any Company real and/or personal properties in the name of the Company; (x) enter into other agreements on behalf of the Company; and (xi) all other acts as may be necessary or appropriate to the conduct of the Company business. With respect to all of their obligations, powers and responsibilities under this Agreement, the Managers are authorized to execute and deliver for and on behalf of the Company such deeds, leases, notes, contracts, agreements, assignments, bills of sale, security agreements, deeds to secure debt and other documents in such form and such terms and conditions as they shall deem proper.

c. <u>Liability of Managers.</u> The Managers shall not be liable, responsible or accountable in damages or otherwise to the Company or any Member for, and the Company shall indemnify and save harmless the Managers from as set forth below, any loss or damage incurred by reason of breach of duty of care or other duty as Managers, provided that the Managers were not guilty of intentional misconduct or a knowing violation of the law or receipt of a personal benefit in violation or breach of any provision of this Agreement. The satisfaction of any indemnification and any saving harmless shall be from and limited to Company assets, no Managers or employee or representative of Managers having any personal liability on account thereof. The Managers, their agents and employees shall be entitled to rely on information, opinions, reports or statements, including without limitation financial statements or other financial data prepared or presented in accordance with O.C.G.A. 14-11-305.

d. <u>Limitations on Authority of Managers.</u> Notwithstanding any provisions of this Agreement to the contrary, unless having first obtained the consent of Members representing a majority of the total Units in the Company, the Managers shall not authorize the substitution of a new Manager, or incur any indebtedness on behalf of the Company for which the Members (other than the Managers) would be personally liable. The Members agree that any other approval or dissenters' rights of the Members provided in the Act, including without limitation Sections 14-11-308 and 14-11-1002 of the Act, shall not apply unless specifically provided in this Agreement.

e. <u>Removal of Managers.</u> The Members may from time to time remove any Manager only for "cause" (as defined herein), and only upon the affirmative vote of Members holding a majority of the total Units in the Company. For purposes of this Agreement, the term "cause" is defined as: (i) fraud, defalcation, misappropriation, criminal activity, or (ii) the failure of any Manager to cure any material breach of this Agreement by such Manager within thirty (30) days of written notice from the other Members specifying the nature of such breach.

f. <u>Action by Managers.</u> The Managers shall act jointly on all matters, except that either Manager may separately authorize Company expenditures of indebtedness not to exceed $10,000.00 per transaction.

g. <u>Appointment and Substitution of New Manager.</u> Within ninety (90) days of any event resulting in the withdrawal of all Managers, the Members holding a majority of the total Units in the Company shall appoint a new Manager, and the person so elected shall become a substitute Manager upon the execution and delivery of a written acceptance and adoption of this Agreement, as the same may have been amended, together with such other documents, if any, as counsel for the Company may require. Failure of the Members to appoint a new Manager within the time period specified in this Section 8.g. shall result in the dissolution of the Company.

9. BOOKS, RECORDS AND MEETINGS.

   a. <u>Books and Records.</u> The Managers shall keep, or cause to be kept, at the principal office of the Company, full and true books and records of account for the Company, which shall be available for reasonable inspection and examination by the Members or their duly authorized representatives during normal business hours upon prior written request to the Managers. The Managers shall not be required to deliver or mail copies of the Articles of Organization, or any amendment or cancellation thereof to the Members.

   b. <u>Accounting Period, Annual Financial Statements.</u> The accounting period of the Company shall be the calendar year ending December 31. The Managers shall provide each Member with a financial statement of the Company within a reasonable time after the end of the calendar year.

   c. <u>Federal Income Taxes.</u> The Managers shall cause the preparation and timely filing of all tax returns required to be filed by the Company pursuant to the Code and all other tax returns deemed necessary and required in each jurisdiction in which the Company does business. Within a reasonable time after the close of each Company year, the Managers shall furnish a report to each Member of the net profits or losses of the Company together with a statement indicating the Member's share in profits or losses for such year. In addition, each Member shall be provided with such additional information as may be reasonably required in preparing his or her own state and federal income tax returns.

   d. <u>Meetings.</u> The Managers shall hold regular annual meetings at times and places to be selected by the Managers. In addition, the Members holding a total of twenty-five percent (25%) of the Units in the Company may call a special meeting to be held at the principal place of business of the Company at any time after the giving of ten (10) business days' prior notice to all of the Members. Any Member may waive notice of or attendance at any meeting of the Members, and may attend by proxy, telephone or any other electronic communication device or may execute a signed written consent. At such meeting, the Members shall transact such business as may properly be brought before the meeting. The Managers shall keep minutes of all meetings of the Members. The minutes shall be placed in the company records of the Company.

   e. <u>Action Without Meeting.</u> Any action required by the Act or by this Agreement to be taken by the Members may be taken without a meeting if written consents setting forth the action so taken shall be signed by Members holding a majority of all Units entitled to vote and such consents shall have the same force and effect as a vote of the Members. Any such signed consents shall be placed in the minute book of the Company and forwarded to any Members who did not consent to the particular action in accordance with Section 14-11-309 of the Act.

10. DISSOLUTION AND TERMINATION.

    a. <u>Events of Dissolution.</u> The Company is dissolved and its affairs shall be wound up upon the first to occur of the following: (i) the written consent of all Members to dissolve; or (ii) ninety (90) days after any event of dissociation (as defined in Section 14-11-601(a) of the Act) with respect to any Member, unless within such ninety (90)-day period the Company is continued by the written consent of all other Members.

    b. <u>No Right to Withdraw.</u> No Member may withdraw from the Company by voluntary action without the prior written consent of all remaining Members, which consent may be given or denied in the absolute discretion of each Member.

    c. <u>Liquidation.</u> The dissolution of the Company shall be effective as of the date on which the event occurs giving rise to such dissolution, but the Company shall continue in existence to wind up and liquidate its business and distribute any remaining assets as provided herein. Notwithstanding the dissolution of the Company prior to the winding-up of the Company, the business of Company and the rights of the members shall continue to be governed by this Agreement. Upon dissolution of the company, the Managers, or (in the absence of Managers) a liquidator appointed with the consent of Members holding a majority of the total Units, shall liquidate the assets of the Company, apply and distribute the proceeds thereof as contemplated by this Agreement and file the certificate of termination. The liquidation of the assets of the Company and the discharge of the Liabilities of the Company shall be completed within a reasonable time, as determined by the Managers.

    d. <u>Distributions in Liquidation.</u> Upon the dissolution of the Company and incident to the winding-up of the Company's business and affairs, the Managers (or liquidator, as applicable) shall pay or make provision for the payment of all liabilities and obligations of the Company, actual or contingent, and all expenses of liquidation. Any amounts deemed necessary be the Managers (or liquidator) to provide a reserve for any unforeseen liabilities and obligations may, in the Managers' (or liquidator's) discretion, be deposited in a bank or trust company upon such terms and for such period of time as the Managers (or liquidator) may determine. Following the payment of, or provision for, the liabilities of the Company as aforesaid, the remaining assets of the Company shall be distributed to the Members proportionately in accordance with the remaining positive balances in their capital accounts. Such dissolution distributions may be in cash, in kind or evidences of indebtedness or in any other form of property, or in any combination thereof, as determined in the sole discretion of the Managers. Should evidences of indebtedness be included in any such distribution, however, the Managers may, in their sole discretion, hold such evidences of indebtedness in trust on behalf of the Members to collect the payments made thereon and to distribute same to the Members in the proper proportions when payments are collected, it being agreed that such an arrangement will facilitate payments to the Members on any such evidences of indebtedness.

e. <u>No Recourse.</u> Upon dissolution, each Member shall look solely to the assets of the Company for the return of his or her investment, and if the property remaining after payment or discharge of the debts and liabilities of the Company is insufficient to return the capital contributions of any Member, such Member shall have no recourse against any other Member or any Managers.

11. AMENDMENTS.

a. <u>Amendments.</u> Amendments to this Agreement may be proposed by any Member. A proposed amendment shall be adopted and be effective as an amendment hereto if it receives the affirmative vote of the holders of the majority of the total Units.

b. <u>Restrictions on Amendments.</u> Notwithstanding Section 11.a. hereof, this Agreement shall not be amended without the consent of each Member adversely affected if such amendment would (i) modify the limited liability of such Member; or (ii) alter the interest of such Member in the profits, losses, or distributions of the Company.

12. MISCELLANEOUS.

a. <u>Notices.</u> Any and all notices, elections, consent or demands permitted or required to be made under this Agreement shall be made in accordance with Section 14-11-311 of the Act.

b. <u>Successors and Assigns.</u> Subject to the restrictions on transfers set forth herein, this Agreement and each and every provision hereof shall be binding upon and shall inure to the benefit of the Members, their respective successors, successors in title, heirs and assigns, and each and every successor in interest to any Member, whether such successor acquires such an interest by way of gift, purchase, foreclosure or by any other method, shall hold interest subject to all the terms and provisions of this Agreement.

c. <u>Applicable Law.</u> This Agreement and the rights of the parties hereunder shall be governed by the laws of the State of Georgia.

d. <u>Counterparts.</u> This Agreement may be executed in any number of counterparts, all of which taken together shall be deemed one original instrument notwithstanding that all parties are not signatory to the same counterpart.

e. <u>Entire Agreement.</u> This Agreement contains the entire agreement among the Members with respect to the subject matter hereof.

f. <u>Captions and Pronouns.</u> The captions in this Agreement and the particular pronouns used herein, whether masculine, feminine, or neuter, are inserted for convenience and identification only and are in no way intended to describe, interpret, define or limit the scope, extent or intent of this Agreement or any provision hereof. Where the content demand, the singular shall include the plural and the plural shall mean the singular.

g. <u>Investment Representation and Indemnity Agreement.</u> Each of the Members (and its assignees and transferees) by execution of an agreement to be bound by the terms of this Agreement represents to each of the other Members, to the Managers and to the Company that it is acquiring the interest in the Company for the purpose of investment and not with a view to, or for resale in connection with, any distribution of said interest. Furthermore, each of the Members (and its assignees and transferees) agrees to indemnify the other Members, the Managers, the Company and any agent, affiliate or legal counsel of such parties, from any and all loss, damage, liability, claims and expenses incurred, suffered or sustained by any of them in any manner because of the falsity of any representation contained in this paragraph, including, without limitation, liability for violation of the securities laws of the United States or of any state which violation would not have occurred had such representation been true.

h. <u>Other Ventures.</u> Any of the Members may engage in or possess an interest in other business ventures of every nature and description, independently or with others, including, but not limited to, the ownership, financing, leasing, operation, management, syndication, brokerage, and development of real property; and neither the Company nor the Members shall have any right by virtue of this Agreement in and to such independent ventures or to the income or profits derived therefrom.

i. <u>Income Tax Elections.</u> All elections required or permitted to be made by the Company under the Code shall be made by the Managers as determined in their sole discretion.

j. <u>Severability.</u> If any provision of this Operating Agreement or the application thereof to any person or circumstance shall be invalid, illegal or unenforceable to any extent, the remainder of this Operating Agreement and the application thereof shall not be affected and shall be enforceable to the fullest extent permitted by law.

IN WITNESS WHEREOF, this Agreement has been executed by each of the Members as of the day and year first above written.

MEMBERS:

_____

_____

_____

SCHEDULE A

SCHEDULE OF MEMBERS,
CAPITAL AND UNITS

Name and Address	Capital	Number of Units
_____	_____	_____
_____	_____	_____
_____	_____	_____
_____	_____	_____
_____	_____	_____
_____	_____	_____

These forms are made available for example purposes only. The forms must be tailored to the particular circumstances of each limited liability company. Consultation with competent corporate counsel is strongly recommended. Parties using these forms do so entirely at their own risk.

Form **8832**
(December 1996)

Department of the Treasury
Internal Revenue Service

Entity Classification Election

OMB No. 1545-1516

Please Type or Print

| Name of entity | Employer identification number (EIN) |

Number, street, and room or suite no. If a P.O. box, see instructions.

City or town, state, and ZIP code. If a foreign address, enter city, province or state, postal code and country.

1 **Type of election** (see instructions):

a ☐ Initial classification by a newly-formed entity (or change in current classification of an existing entity to take effect on January 1, 1997)

b ☐ Change in current classification (to take effect later than January 1, 1997)

2 **Form of entity** (see instructions):

a ☐ A domestic eligible entity electing to be classified as an association taxable as a corporation.

b ☐ A domestic eligible entity electing to be classified as a partnership.

c ☐ A domestic eligible entity with a single owner electing to be disregarded as a separate entity.

d ☐ A foreign eligible entity electing to be classified as an association taxable as a corporation.

e ☐ A foreign eligible entity electing to be classified as a partnership.

f ☐ A foreign eligible entity with a single owner electing to be disregarded as a separate entity.

3 Election is to be effective beginning (month, day, year) (see instructions) . . . . ▶ ___ / ___ / ___

4 Name and title of person whom the IRS may call for more information | **5** That person's telephone number

Consent Statement and Signature(s) (see instructions)

Under penalties of perjury, I (we) declare that I (we) consent to the election of the above-named entity to be classified as indicated above, and that I (we) have examined this consent statement, and to the best of my (our) knowledge and belief, it is true, correct, and complete. If I am an officer, manager, or member signing for all members of the entity, I further declare that I am authorized to execute this consent statement on their behalf.

Signature(s)	Date	Title

For Paperwork Reduction Act Notice, see page 2.   Cat. No. 22598R   Form **8832** (12-96)

General Instructions

Section references are to the Internal Revenue Code unless otherwise noted.

Paperwork Reduction Act Notice

We ask for the information on this form to carry out the Internal Revenue laws of the United States. You are required to give us the information. We need it to ensure that you are complying with these laws and to allow us to figure and collect the right amount of tax.

You are not required to provide the information requested on a form that is subject to the Paperwork Reduction Act unless the form displays a valid OMB control number. Books or records relating to a form or its instructions must be retained as long as their contents may become material in the administration of any Internal Revenue law. Generally, tax returns and return information are confidential, as required by section 6103.

The time needed to complete and file this form will vary depending on individual circumstances. The estimated average time is:

Recordkeeping . . .1 hr., 20 min.
**Learning about the
law or the form** . . .1 hr., 41 min.
**Preparing and sending
the form to the IRS** . . . .17 min.

If you have comments concerning the accuracy of these time estimates or suggestions for making this form simpler, we would be happy to hear from you. You can write to the Tax Forms Committee, Western Area Distribution Center, Rancho Cordova, CA 95743-0001. **DO NOT** send the form to this address. Instead, see **Where To File** on page 3.

Purpose of Form

For Federal tax purposes, certain business entities automatically are classified as corporations. See items **1** and **3** through **8** under the definition of corporation on this page. Other business entities may choose how they are classified for Federal tax purposes. Except for a business entity automatically classified as a corporation, a business entity with at least two members can choose to be classified as either an association taxable as a corporation or a partnership, and a business entity with a single member can choose to be classified as either an association taxable as a corporation or disregarded as an entity separate from its owner.

Generally, an eligible entity that does not file this form will be classified under the default rules described below. An eligible entity that chooses not to be classified under the default rules or that wishes to change its current classification must file Form 8832 to elect a classification. The IRS will use the information entered on this form to establish the entity's filing and reporting requirements for Federal tax purposes.

Default Rules

Existing entity default rule.— Certain domestic and foreign entities that are already in existence before January 1, 1997, and have an established Federal tax classification, generally do not need to make an election to continue that classification. However, for an eligible entity with a single owner that claimed to be a partnership under the law in effect before January 1, 1997, that entity will now be disregarded as an entity separate from its owner. If an existing entity decides to change its classification, it may do so subject to the rules in Regulations section 301.7701-3(c)(1)(iv). A foreign eligible entity is treated as being in existence prior to the effective date of this section only if the entity's classification is relevant at any time during the 60 months prior to January 1, 1997.

Domestic default rule.— Unless an election is made on Form 8832, a domestic eligible entity is:

1. A partnership if it has two or more members.

2. Disregarded as an entity separate from its owner if it has a single owner.

Foreign default rule.— Unless an election is made on Form 8832, a foreign eligible entity is:

1. A partnership if it has two or more members and at least one member does not have limited liability.

2. An association if all members have limited liability.

3. Disregarded as an entity separate from its owner if it has a single owner that does not have limited liability.

Definitions

Business entity.— A business entity is any entity recognized for Federal tax purposes that is not properly classified as a trust under Regulations section 301.7701-4 or otherwise subject to special treatment under the Code. See Regulations section 301.7701-2(a).

Corporation.— For Federal tax purposes, a corporation is any of the following:

1. A business entity organized under a Federal or state statute, or under a statute of a federally recognized Indian tribe, if the statute describes or refers to the entity as incorporated or as a corporation, body corporate, or body politic.

2. An association (as determined under Regulations section 301.7701-3).

3. A business entity organized under a state statute, if the statute describes or refers to the entity as a joint-stock company or joint-stock association.

4. An insurance company.

5. A state-chartered business entity conducting banking activities, if any of its deposits are insured under the Federal Deposit Insurance Act, as amended, 12 U.S.C. 1811 et seq., or a similar Federal statute.

6. A business entity wholly owned by a state or any political subdivision thereof.

7. A business entity that is taxable as a corporation under a provision of the Code other than section 7701(a)(3).

8. A foreign business entity listed in Regulations section 301.7701-2(b)(8). However, a foreign business entity listed in those regulations generally will not be treated as a corporation if all of the following apply:

a. The entity was in existence on May 8, 1996.

b. The entity's classification was relevant (as defined below) on May 8, 1996.

c. No person (including the entity) for whom the entity's classification was relevant on May 8, 1996, treats the entity as a corporation for purposes of filing that person's Federal income tax returns, information returns, and withholding documents for the tax year including May 8, 1996.

d. Any change in the entity's claimed classification within the 60 months prior to May 8, 1996, was a result of a change in the organizational documents of the entity, and the entity and all members of the entity recognized the Federal tax consequences of any change in the entity's classification within the 60 months prior to May 8, 1996.

e. The entity had a reasonable basis (within the meaning of section 6662) for treating the entity as other than a corporation on May 8, 1996.

f. Neither the entity nor any member was notified in writing on or before May 8, 1996, that the classification of the entity was under examination (in which case the entity's classification will be determined in the examination).

Binding contract rule.—If a foreign business entity described in Regulations section 301.7701-2(b)(8)(i) is formed after May 8, 1996, under a written binding contract (including an accepted bid to develop a project) in effect on May 8, 1996, and all times thereafter, in which the parties agreed to engage (directly or indirectly) in an active and substantial business operation in the jurisdiction in which the entity is formed, **8** on page 2 is applied by substituting the date of the entity's formation for May 8, 1996.

Eligible entity.—An eligible entity is a business entity that is not included in items **1** or **3** through **8** under the definition of corporation on page 2.

Limited liability.—A member of a foreign eligible entity has limited liability if the member has no personal liability for any debts of or claims against the entity by reason of being a member. This determination is based solely on the statute or law under which the entity is organized (and, if relevant, the entity's organizational documents). A member has personal liability if the creditors of the entity may seek satisfaction of all or any part of the debts or claims against the entity from the member as such. A member has personal liability even if the member makes an agreement under which another person (whether or not a member of the entity) assumes that liability or agrees to indemnify that member for that liability.

Partnership.—A partnership is a business entity that has **at least** two members and is not a corporation as defined on page 2.

Relevant.—A foreign eligible entity's classification is relevant when its classification affects the liability of any person for Federal tax or information purposes. The date the classification of a foreign eligible entity is relevant is the date an event occurs that creates an obligation to file a Federal tax return, information return, or statement for which the classification of the entity must be determined.

Effect of Election

The resulting tax consequences of a change in classification remain the same no matter how a change in entity classification is achieved. For example, if an organization classified as an association elects to be classified as a partnership, the organization and its owners must recognize gain, if any, under the rules applicable to liquidations of corporations.

Who Must File

File this form for an **eligible entity** that is one of the following:

• A domestic entity electing to be classified as an association taxable as a corporation.

• A domestic entity electing to change its current classification (even if it is currently classified under the default rule).

• A foreign entity that has more than one owner, all owners have limited liability, and it elects to be classified as a partnership.

• A foreign entity that has at least one owner without limited liability, and it elects to be classified as an association taxable as a corporation.

• A foreign entity with a single owner having limited liability, and it elects to have the entity disregarded as an entity separate from its owner.

• A foreign entity electing to change its current classification (even if it is currently classified under the default rule).

Do not file this form for an eligible entity that is:

• Tax-exempt under section 501(a), or

• A real estate investment trust (REIT), as defined in section 856.

When To File

See the instructions for line 3.

Where To File

File Form 8832 with the Internal Revenue Service Center, Philadelphia, PA 19255. Also attach a copy of Form 8832 to the entity's Federal income tax or information return for the tax year of the election. If the entity is not required to file a return for that year, a copy of its Form 8832 must be attached to the Federal income tax or information returns of all direct or indirect owners of the entity for the tax year of the owner that includes the date on which the election took effect. Although failure to attach a copy will not invalidate an otherwise valid election, each member of the entity is required to file returns that are consistent with the entity's election. In addition, penalties may be assessed against persons who are required to, but who do not, attach Form 8832 to their returns. Other penalties may apply for filing Federal income tax or information returns inconsistent with the entity's election.

Specific Instructions

Employer Identification Number (EIN)

Show the correct EIN on Form 8832. If the entity does not have an EIN, it generally must apply for one on **Form SS-4,** Application for Employer Identification Number. If the filing of Form 8832 is the only reason the entity is applying for an EIN, check the "Other" box on line 9 of Form SS-4 and write "Form 8832" to the right of that box. If the entity has not received an EIN by the time Form 8832 is due, write "Applied for" in the space for the EIN. **Do not** apply for a new EIN for an existing entity that is changing its classification. If you are electing to disregard an entity as separate from its owner, enter the owner's EIN.

Address

Include the suite, room, or other unit number after the street address. If the Post Office does not deliver mail to the street address and the entity has a P.O. box, show the box number instead of the street address.

Line 1

Check box 1a if the entity is choosing a classification for the first time **and** the entity does not want to be classified under the applicable default classification. **Do not** file this form if the entity wants to be classified under the default rules.

Check box 1b if the entity is changing its current classification to take effect later than January 1, 1997, whether or not the entity's current classification is the default classification. However, once an eligible entity makes an election to change its classification (other than an election made by an existing entity to change its classification as of January 1, 1997), the entity cannot change its classification by election again during the 60 months after the effective date of the election. However, the IRS may permit (by private letter ruling) the entity to change its classification by election within the 60-month period if more than 50% of the ownership interests in the entity as of the effective date of the election are owned by persons that did not own any interests in the entity on the effective date of the entity's prior election.

Line 2

Check the appropriate box if you are changing a current classification (no matter how achieved), or are electing out of a default classification. **Do not** file this form if you fall within a default classification that is the desired classification for the new entity.

Line 3

Generally, the election will take effect on the date you enter on line 3 of this form or on the date filed if no date is entered on line 3. However, an election specifying an entity's classification for Federal tax purposes can take effect no more than 75 days prior to the date the election is filed, nor can it take effect later than 12 months after the date on which the election is filed. If line 3 shows a date more than 75 days prior to the date on which the election is filed, the election will take effect 75 days before the date it is filed. If line 3 shows an effective date more than 12 months from the filing date, the election will take effect 12 months after the date the election was filed.

Regardless of the date filed, an election will in no event take effect before January 1, 1997.

Consent Statement and Signatures

Form 8832 must be signed by:

1. Each member of the electing entity who is an owner at the time the election is filed; or

2. Any officer, manager, or member of the electing entity who is authorized (under local law or the organizational documents) to make the election and who represents to having such authorization under penalties of perjury.

If an election is to be effective for any period prior to the time it is filed, each person who was an owner between the date the election is to be effective and the date the election is filed, and who is not an owner at the time the election is filed, must also sign.

If you need a continuation sheet or use a separate consent statement, attach it to Form 8832. The separate consent statement must contain the same information as shown on Form 8832.

FLORIDA STATUTES
608.4101

FLORIDA STATUTES
608.4101

1. Each limited liability company shall keep at its registered office the following records:

   (a) A current list of the full manes and last known business addresses of all members.

   (b) A copy of the articles of organization and all certificates of amendments thereto, together with executed copies of any powers of attorney pursuant to which any certificate was executed.

   (c) Copies of the limited liability company's federal, state, and local income tax returns and reports, if any, for the 3 most recent years.

   (d) Copies of any then-effective regulations and any financial statements of the limited liability company for the 3 most recent years.

   (e) Unless contained in the articles of organization or the regulations, a writing setting out:

      1. The amount of cash and a description and statement of the agreed value of the other property or services contributed by each member and which each member has agreed to contribute.

      2. The times at which or events on the happening of which any additional contributions agreed to be made by each member are to be made.

      3. Any events upon the happening of which limited liability company is to be dissolved and its affairs wound up.

2. Records kept under this section are subject to inspection and copying during ordinary business hours at the reasonable request, and at the expense, of any member.

APPENDIX

SECURITIES AND EXCHANGE COMMISSION (SEC), CONTACT INFORMATION

Small Business Ombudsman
U.S. Securities and Exchange Commission
450 Fifth Street, N.W.
Mail Stop 3-4
Washington, DC 20549
800-SEC-0330
www.sec.gov/smbus

ADDRESSES OF SECRETARIES OF STATE BUSINESS SECTIONS

Most states have internet sites which provide forms and other information about business registration in that state. However, internet addresses do change. If an internet address below does not work, try the National Association of Secretaries of State at:

http://www.nass.org/members/members.htm

This site provides links to business registration offices of most states.

Secretary of State of Alabama
Corporation Section
Montgomery, AL 36103-5616
334-242-5324
http://www.alalinc.net/alsecst

State of Alaska
Department of Commerce and Economic Development
Division of Banking, Securities, and Corporations
P.O. Box 110807
Juneau, AK 99811-0807
907-465-2521
http://www.commerce.state.ak.us/bsc/bsc.htm

Arizona Corporation Commission
1300 West Washington
Phoenix, AZ 85007-2996
602-542-3135
http://www.cc.state.az.us/corp/contact.html

Secretary of State
Corporation Division
Aegon Building
501 Woodlane, Suite 210
Little Rock, AR 72201
501-682-3409
http://www.sosweb.state.ar.us/business.html

California Secretary of State
1500 11th Street
Sacramento, CA 95814
916-653-6814
http://www.ss.ca.gov/cgi-bin/contacts.cgi

Secretary of State of Colorado
Corporations Office
1560 Broadway, Suite 200
Denver, CO 80202
303-894-2200 or 303-894-2203
http://www.state.co.us/gov_dir/sos/contact.html

Office of Secretary of State
State of Connecticut
30 Trinity Street
Hartford, CT 06106
860-509-6001
http://www.state.ct.us/sots/dirstf.htm

Office of Secretary of State
Department of State
Division of Corporations
P.O. Box 898
Dover, DE 19903
302-739-3073
http://www.state.de.us/corp/phone.htm

Florida Department of State
Secretary of State
Division of Corporations
P.O. Box 6327
Tallahassee, FL 32314
850-487-6866
http://www.dos.state.fl.us/doc/corp_dir.html

State of Georgia
Secretary of State
Corporations Division
Suite 315 West Tower
2 Martin Luther King, Jr. Drive
Atlanta, GA 30334
404-656-2817
http://www.sos.state.ga.us/corporations

State of Hawaii
Department of Commerce and Consumer Affairs
Business Registration Division
1010 Richards Street
Honolulu, HI 96810
808-586-2727
http://www.hawaii.gov/dbedt/start/starting.html

Secretary of State of Idaho
700 W. Jefferson, Room 203
Boise, ID 83720-0080
208-334-2300
http://www.idsos.state.id.us

Secretary of State of Illinois
Department of Business Services
Room 328 Howlett Building
Springfield, IL 62756
217-782-2201 or 800-252-8980
http://www.sos.state.il.us/depts/bus_serv
    /bus_home.html

Secretary of State's Office, Corporations Division
302 West Washington Street, Room E-018
Indianapolis, IN 46204
317-232-6576
http://www.state.in.us/sos/bus_service
    /corps/guide.html

Secretary of State of Iowa
Hoover State Office Building, 2nd floor
Des Moines, IA 50319
515-281-5204
http://www.sos.state.ia.us

Kansas Secretary of State
Corporation Division
State Capitol, 2nd Floor
300 S.W. 10th Avenue
Topeka, KS 66612-1594
785-296-7456
http://www.ink.org/public/sos/corpwelc.html

Business Filings
Office of the Secretary of State
700 Capitol Avenue
Suite 152, State Capitol
Frankfort, KY 40601
502-564-3490
http://www.sos.state.ky.us

Secretary of State of Louisiana
Commercial Division
P.O. Box 94125
Baton Rouge, LA 70804-9125
504-922-2675 or 800-259-0001
http://www.sec.state.la.us/first-1.htm

Secretary of State of Maine
Bureau of Corporations, Elections and Commissions
Division of Corporations
101 State House Station
Augusta, ME 04333-0101
207-287-4190
http://www.state.me.us/sos/cec/corp/corp.htm

State of Maryland
State Department of Assessments and Taxation
301 W. Preston Street
Baltimore, MD 21201
410-767-1350

Massachusetts Secretary of the Commonwealth
Corporations Division
One Ashburton Place, Room 1717
Boston, MA 02108
617-727-9640
http://www.state.ma.us/sec/cor/corbarc
    /barcidx.htm

Michigan State Government
Department of Consumer & Industry Services
Corporation, Securities, and Land Development
    Bureau
Corporation Division
Corporations and Securities Bureau
P.O. Box 30054
Lansing, MI 489097554
517-334-6323
http://www.cis.state.mi.us/corp/contact.htm

Business Services Division
Office of the Secretary of State
180 State Office Building
100 Constitution Avenue
St. Paul, MN 55155-1299
612-296-2803

Secretary of State of Mississippi
P.O. Box 136
Jackson, MS 39205-0136
601-359-1350
800-256-3494

Secretary of State of Missouri
State Capitol, Room 209
P.O. Box 778
Jefferson City, MO 65102
573-751-4153
http://mosl.sos.state.mo.us/bus-ser/soscor.html

Business Services Bureau
Secretary of State of Montana
Montana State Capitol, Room 225
P.O. Box 202801
Helena, MT 59620-2801
406-444-3665
http://www.state.mt.us/sos/direct.htm

Secretary of State of Nebraska
Corporate Division
State Capitol, Suite 1301
P.O. Box 94608
Lincoln, NE 68509-4608
402-471-4079

State of Nevada
Secretary of State
101 N. Carson Street, Suite 3
Carson City, NV 89701-4786
775-684-5708

Secretary of State of New Hampshire
Office of the Secretary of State
State House, Room 204
Concord, NH 03301-4989
603-225-4033

State of New Jersey
Department of Treasury
Division of Revenue/Commercial Recording
P.O. Box 308
Trenton, NJ 08625-0308
609-530-6400
http://www.state.nj.us/state/dcr/dcrpg1.html

State of New Mexico
Public Regulation Commission
P.O. Drawer 1269
Santa Fe, NM 87504-1269
505-827-4500
http://www.state.nm.us/scc

New York State Department of State
Division of Corporations, State Records and Uniform
    Commercial Code
41 State Street
Albany, NY 12231-0001
518-473-2492
http://www.dos.state.ny.us/corp/corpwww.html

Secretary of State of North Carolina
The Corporations Division
300 N. Salisbury Street
Raleigh, NC 27603-5909
919-733-4201

Secretary of State of North Dakota
Capitol Building
600 East Boulevard Avenue
Bismarck, ND 58505-0500
701-328-4284

Ohio Secretary of State, Business Services Division
30 East Broad Street, 14th Floor
Columbus, OH 43266-0418
614-466-3910
http://www.state.oh.us/sos/info.html

Secretary of State of Oklahoma
Office of the Secretary of State
191 State Capitol
Oklahoma City, OK 73105
405-521-3911

Oregon Secretary of State
Corporation Division, Business Registry
Public Service Building
225 Capitol Street NE, Suite 151
Salem, OR 97310-1327
503-986-2222
http://www.sos.state.or.us/corporation/corphp.htm

Commonwealth of Pennsylvania
Department of State, Corporation Bureau
P.O. Box 8722
Harrisburg, PA 17105-8722
717-787-1057
http://www.dos.state.pa.us/corp.htm

Secretary of State of Rhode Island
First Stop Business Center
100 North Main Street
Providence, RI 02903
401-222-2185
http://www.state.ri.us/bus/frststp.htm

Secretary of State of South Carolina
Office of the Secretary of State
Edgar Brown Building, Suite 525
P.O. Box 11350
Columbia, SC 29211
803-734-2170
http://www.leginfo.state.sc.us/man98
    /StateOfficers98.html#sec_state

Secretary of State of South Dakota
State Capitol, Suite 204
500 East Capitol
Pierre, SD 57501-5070
605-773-4845
http://www.state.sd.us/state/executive/sos/sos.htm

Secretary of State of Tennessee
Corporations Section
James K. Polk Building, Suite 1800
Nashville, TN 37243-0306
615-741-0537
http://www.state.tn.us/sos/service.htm

Secretary of State of Texas
Statutory Filings Division
Corporations Section
P.O. Box 13697
Austin, TX 78711-3697
512-463-5580
http://www.sos.state.tx.us/function/forms
    /aboutcorp.html

State of Utah
Department of Commerce
Division of Corporations
160 East 300 South
P.O. Box 146705
Salt Lake City, UT 84145-6705
801-530-4849
http://www.commerce.state.ut.us

Secretary of State of Vermont
Office of the Secretary of State
Business Registry Division
109 State Street
Montpelier, VT 05609-1101
802-828-2386
http://www.sec.state.vt.us/where/redstone
    .htm

Commonwealth of Virginia
State Corporation Commission
Division of Information Resources
P.O. Box 1197
Richmond, VA 23218
804-371-9967 or 800-552-7945
http://www.state.va.us/scc/contact.htm

Secretary of State of Washington
Office of the Secretary of State
Corporations Division
505 East Union, 2nd Floor
P.O. Box 40234
Olympia, WA 98504-0234
360-753-7115
http://www.wa.gov/sec/corps.htm

Secretary of State of West Virginia
Building 1, Suite 157-K
1900 Kanawha Boulevard East
Charleston, WV 25305-0770
304-558-6000
http://www.state.wv.us/sos

Secretary of State of Wisconsin
Corporations Division
P.O. Box 7846
Madison, WI 53707-7848
608-266-3590
http://www.wdfi.org

Secretary of State of Wyoming
Capitol Building
Cheyenne, WY 82002
307-777-6217
http://soswy.state.wy.us

INDEX

243